PROGRAMMING JAVABEANS 1.1

Programming JavaBeans 1.1

Reaz Hoque

McGraw-Hill
New York • San Francisco • Washington, D.C. • Auckland
Bogotá • Caracas • Lisbon • London • Madrid • Mexico City
Milan • Montreal • New Delhi • San Juan • Singapore
Sydney • Tokyo • Toronto

Library of Congress Cataloging-in-Publication Data

Hoque, Reaz.
    Programming JavaBeans 1.1 / Reaz Hoque.
        p.   cm.
    Includes index.
    ISBN 0-07-913704-0
    1. JavaBeans. 2. Java (Computer program language) I. Title.
QA76.73.J38H672 1998
005.13'3—dc21   98-17833
                                              CIP

McGraw-Hill

A Division of The McGraw·Hill Companies

1 2 3 4 5 6 7 8 9 0 DOC/DOC 9 0 3 2 1 0 9 8

P/N 029237-X
PART OF ISBN 0-07-913704-0

The sponsoring editor for this book was Michael Sprague and the production supervisor was Sherri Souffrance. It was set in Century Schoolbook by Douglas & Gayle, Limited.

Printed and bound by R. R. Donnelley & Sons Company.

McGraw-Hill books are available at special quantity discounts to use as premiums and sales promotions, or for use in corporate training programs. For more information, please write to Director of Special Sales, McGraw-Hill, 11 West 19th Street, New York, NY 10011. Or contact your local bookstore.

This book is printed on recycled, acid-free paper containing a minimum of 50% recycled de-inked fiber.

DEDICATION

First I want to dedicate this book to my father who has worked so hard for so many years and has cared about me. He still thinks that he needs to provide for me (!).

Secondly I would like to dedicate this book to one of my closest friends, Tarun Sharma. Initially I was going to write this book with Tarun, but his job made it difficult to do so. I wish him all the best.

CONTENTS

Contents

Contents

ACKNOWLEDGMENTS

I wouldn't have thought about writing this book if it weren't for the former McGraw-Hill editor John Wyzalek. As I was finishing my *Programming Web Components* book, John asked me to do this book—and here we are.

Next I want to thank Tarun Sharma, who actually wrote the proposal for the book with me. Tarun has helped me in many ways over the years and I appreciate his support and friendship.

The editor for this book at McGraw-Hill, Michael Sprague, can be tough at times—but he is very professional in what he does. With his years of experience, I think he has done a great job with the book and I appreciate his help.

The book is a success because of all the people who were involved with it. Contributing authors such as Ashutosh Bijoor, Trevor Harmon, Darren Gibbons, Dave Jarvis, Gabriel Minton and John Small have invested many hours working on this book and I can't emphasize enough how grateful I am to each of them for their hard work and contribution.

I would like to extend my thanks to those who gave me permission to include software for the CD. IBM's Sheila Richardson, Bill Reichle, and Terry McElroy were a great help. Thanks to Jonathan Berent from Sun for the BDK software. Special thanks goes to all my friends at EcCubed Inc. such as Adel Khan, Pieter R. Humphrey, Erica Tabor, Shatish Reddy, Terrance Curley, Harsha Kumar, Ephrem Bartolomeos, Naushad Kapasi, and many others for helping me throughout the process and for supporting me.

Many thanks to Stephen from Sun-Canada for reviewing some of the chapters. He was a contributing author for the *Programming Web Components* book.

Last but not least, thanks to the Almighty for giving me the opportunity and the power to work on such big projects. I know I would be nobody if it weren't for God's will. Also thanks to my brother Faisal Hoque and his wife Christine for being there for me all these years and for supporting me all the way.

Component Software Development and JavaBeans

Before we jump to JavaBeans, we need to familiarize ourselves with component software development. This chapter provides details of what CSD (Component Software Development) is, how it came into being, and where JavaBeans plays a role in CSD. To begin, we give meaning to terms such as "component," "component architecture," "component-object programming," and "CSD." Then we compare components and objects. Continuing on, we describe component-related technology versus object-related technology.

Along the way, you will read about the technologies that are available, where they fit in as far as components are concerned, and a bit of history behind them. By the end of this chapter, you should have a good understanding of the differences between components and objects. You should also be aware of what component-related technologies are available to you to date. We suggest that this chapter will set the scene for this book. More information on JavaBeans is discussed in the following chapters.

This Chapter Covers

- What is component software development?
- What are component architectures?
- Current trends versus history.
- Component-object programming.
- How do JavaBeans fit the component-object programming model?
- How does component architecture differ from object architecture?
- Shortcomings of component families.

What Is Component Software Development (CSD)?

In short, CSD is about joining pieces of software together. A component, then, is a software entity that, by itself, performs a single task. More concretely, a component is a formal way of implementing user-interface controls such that application development tools and runtime environments can work with them.

As an analogy, almost everything that is within a home can be thought of as a component. The shower curtains, wallpaper, bathtub, carpeting, lighting fixtures, and so forth are components that make up the interior (one hopes) of a home. The idea is that someone else builds components needed for the creation (be it a home or a software application), and they are put together to form that creation. The components have been tested, are safely constructed, and their usage is clearly defined. In the case of a home, books (or manuals) that you either buy or that come with the item define that item's use. In the case of a component, its interface should come with documentation describing its particulars. The messages the component understands, what the messages do to it, how to change its properties, and its expected behavior.

Going back to the home example, shower curtains, regardless of the curtain rod used, have an expected behavior to catch water. If, for some reason, the shower curtain does not live up to expectations, a new one from another supplier is easily obtained. The ability to swap a component with another (that does the same or similar task) is one of the promises of CSD (provided the components conform to the same interface specification.).

CSD Example

Like most home accessories, components are typically small and don't do anything by themselves. A bathtub, for example, needs water to be useful; a spell-check component needs text. This is not to say that components should not be configurable. A spell-checker component might also allow changing the dictionary's language, allow for spelling variations (British versus American), and ignore words in a separate "user programmed" dictionary.

How the component is used is described by well-defined interfaces. In the case of a spell checker, the interface may dictate that it is first given the name of a text file to check (see Figure 1-1). Then each subsequent check of the text within the file might then return a structure. This structure would indicate the location in the file where it found the mistake and a list of words that closely match the mistake. It is then up to the application that uses the spell checker to present the list of possible substitutions.

Assume that the component is created in such a way that its definition does not depend on the underlying system. There should then be no reason why a great spell checker (in the future) should be restricted to run-

Figure 1-1
Spell-check component usage diagram.

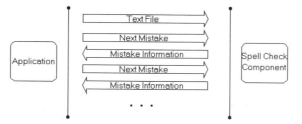

ning only on Macintosh word processors. Word processors should be able to use a user-defined component for any major task. This gets to the issue of favorite components or, in other words, favorite features.

Advantages of CSD

The greatest advantage of CSD is that it shortens the time required to develop full-sized applications. Imagine how long it would take home-builders to construct a house from ground up if they had to create all their components from scratch. Instead of buying bathtubs, carpets, and wall-paper, each item would have to be constructed on-site for every house to build. Because the people working on the components would like to be paid for their time, it becomes obvious that building all the components that are needed on-site is not the way to go. Thus, components are bought to build a home. The same is true with software development. If someone has created certain components that do certain job, a software developer can just drop and drag those components into an application.

When a component is bought, instead of building it as the need arises, much more than the component is purchased. As mentioned, the time it would take to design, build, and test the component comes from buying it. On top of that, resources are saved: the people who would have otherwise spent their time building the component purchased it instead. There is also some assurance that the component being bought has been developed and constructed by people who are experts in that particular field. The last point leads to additional savings in resources. Becoming an expert in a field requires learning what makes a good component (or a bad one). People who have developed the desired component have already done the research and know how to create a well-designed component.

Without detailing the complexities involved with creating components that are needed in order to build an application, the complexity of the entire project is reduced. Instead of determining the details involved in building a door (and its hinges, handles, and locks) that matches the other accessories in a particular home, the door is purchased separately.

From the point of view of the people using the software, components are just features. Given that any word processor will be able to use any spell-check component, people are free to familiarize themselves with one spell checker. This reduces the learning curve as people shift from computer to computer and word processor to word processor. With the advent of the Internet, they can leave their spell checker online somewhere and never be without it—regardless of what computer they are using. This assumes the basic premise that components are built with the capability of running on many different systems. (Currently, this is only possible with JavaBeans.)

Imagine for a moment that all applications running on a given computer (word processors, spreadsheets, personal information managers, notepads, etc.) use the same spell-checker component. If that is true, a person using the spell checker will have a shorter learning curve on applications. The spell-checker component is learned once and then used within all applications and, ideally, on all systems as well.

With CSD, you can make sure which feature your application will have and change the features as often as you want. Considering that developers can select which features (components) make up their applications, it is easy to see that training costs for end users are lower. That is, if applications are trimmed down to what a person will actually use (and what is required by the application to perform its task[s]), the result is customized software that is easiy to master and that saves storage space.

What Are Component Architectures?

Component architectures are software entities that provide the facilities to develop components. To date, there are several different component architectures available. Some of the popular architectures include ActiveX (also known as OLE), DCOM, JavaBeans, and OpenDoc. We will talk more about these later in the chapter.

One goal of the mentioned component architectures is to make components distributed. That is, any given component can be running on any given networked machine at any given time. It is then up to the main controller component to seek out and use the other components available on the network. The classic example portrays this scenario in a client-server environment. However, this need not always be the case. In a peer-to-peer environment, you can think of two clients communicating. One does not necessarily have to be a centralized server. Figure 1-2 illustrates this concept.

From the figure, notice that Client A is running an application that relies on a few components. The components that the application uses may be located on any computer on the network. In this example, some of the components may be on Client B, the Server, or even Client A. To Client A, all distributed components are on a peer's computer. Distinguishing between a client and a server in distributed environments does not matter.

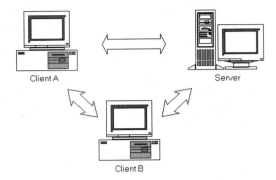

Figure 1-2
Distributed
component
architecture.

Client A

Server

Client B

How the application obtains a handle on a remote component can be done in a myriad of ways. The simplest would be to have a central repository. An application in need of a component searches the repository to obtain the location of the component. Simple, right? However, the disadvantage is that one machine must know about the location of all components.

Ideally, an application should send a request for a component out on the network. The query would be passed along to every computer on the network until the requested component is found and then returned. The disadvantage here is the potential time it would take to obtain the response from the requested component. The protocol for getting the component's response is also heavier. In a distributed environment, you now need to worry about eliminating duplicate queries, timing out on a computer, and so forth.

Current Trends Versus History in CSD

The software development paradigms leading up to CSD follow an interesting migration path. With the advent of microcomputers and mainframes, problems were analyzed in the following manner (known as the waterfall methodology):

1. Describe the problem.

2. Define structures that represent the domain's information.

3. Design high-level algorithms that manipulate the structures in accordance to the problem's specifications.

4. Detail all the inputs and all the expected outputs for every function used in the program (or programs).

5. Write, test, and debug psuedocode by hand on a per module basis.

6. Translate the psuedocode into source.

The only reuse of that methodology came from textbook algorithms within specific problem domains. Actual source code was seldom—if ever—reused. This is the classic "reinventing the wheel" concept that everybody speaks about. Similar solutions to similar problems are arrived at, but each is proprietary in some way by virtue of the hardware, implementation language, or other factors.

The major problem with designing a system's architecture with the waterfall methodology is that it is too rigid. If something as minor as a change to the user interface must be made, it could cause not-so minor portions of code to be rewritten. The ability to test different ways of displaying information (to the user) is almost non-existent. Again, this is due to how rigid (tightly coupled) the system's display is to its model. It is not difficult to see that maintaining the system would be an undesirable job. Modifying code in one place may produce severe problems in another. This is due to the lack of encapsulation in procedural code. Another problem is that it leaves no thought for the people who must punch in the source code, themselves. They became thoughtless animals, merely following the orders of the system's architects. Not a happy place to be for any programmer with half a mind.

The waterfall methodology was desirable, though, because all aspects of development are tested for validity (verification that given inputs produce desired outputs) before they are placed together to form an application. It was also a highly controlled means of software development. The project could easily be divided into distinct tasks, which were then done sequentially, but sometimes in parallel. Nonetheless, each application developed was a hearty task because it had to be written from the ground up each time. That is until source code libraries became popular.

Software Reuse Begins

In the late 1950s, IBM designed the IBM Mathematical FORmula TRANslator. As with most de facto standards, FORTAN was quickly split into different flavors by other companies. The split was so vast that 40 different compilers were produced by 1963. A standard language specification for FORTRAN 66 was introduced by 1972. In the middle of the 1970s, a FORTRAN 66 compiler/interpreter was packaged with most minicomputers and mainframes. This allowed an application to be ported from system to system with great ease and efficiency. ANSI took over from there, documenting a new standard for FORTRAN at the end of 1977 (FORTRAN 77).

During this time, many collections of mathematical libraries were developed for FORTRAN. Some became popular enough to warrant inclusion in FORTRAN 77, where other collections (being slow, cumbersome, or just unpopular) fluttered away in the wind. The libraries for FORTRAN were the first truly comprehensive set of libraries available to programmers. This was why FORTRAN became "King of the Hill" for developing applications.

When computers began to get smaller and more popular in the workplace, commercial applications grew in popularity as well. The C language helped dethrone FORTRAN. By the end of 1989, ANSI cast in stone the standard C language. ISO (International Standards Organization) quickly adopted this standard by 1990. Since then, numerous libraries have been added to the language, and a few different flavors. It was nothing so serious as the FORTRAN language split but significant enough to rip out C's capability of being compiled cross-platform for most major applications. Despite that setback, C gained popularity for other reasons: it gives programmers both high-level and low-level control over the computer, standard libraries facilitate displaying information to and obtaining information from people, the brief (yet cryptic) syntax, and its standard libraries.

With the advent of standard libraries (in general), application development time was reduced. Yet code libraries did not (and do not) address all problems. Most code libraries do not meet at least one of the following criteria:

- Portable (without code modification) across most major hardware platforms
- Operating system independent
- Direct interlanguage communications (COBOL to C, Pascal to FORTRAN, etc.)
- Easy to implement networking functionality over heterogeneous networks

Additionally, code libraries did nothing to change how problems were solved; they merely facilitated development. The waterfall method was still the tried and true means of doing software development for most companies.

Object-Orientation Arrives

It was in the late 1940s and early 1950s that work in the field of artificial intelligence (AI) had concepts of attributes associated with objects: blue blocks, red spheres, etc. By the early 1970s, Alan Kay (who had the idea that computers should be usable by non-experts) aided the development of the Dynabook system. Dynabook's software portion became the Smalltalk language in 1972.

Little more than a whisper, the 1970s coined the term "Object-Oriented" (OO)—accredited to Alan Kay for using the term in describing his thoughts about Smalltalk. If the 1970s whispered OO, the 1980s shouted it. C++, Objective-C, Eiffel and a myriad of other OO languages sprang out of the ether. All of them are based on, or around, objects. In addition, each language has its own advantages and disadvantages.

The idea that the world is made up of objects is nothing new. AI scientists thought about them, and we use them every single day. A desk is an object. A telephone is an object. A stereo is an object. Even an idea is an object. In the old days, people described structures in accordance with the problem and then wrote functions that manipulated the structures (data). No information within the structures was secure. Any function could tinker with data arbitrarily. This in itself is the cause of many software errors: inadvertently changing (or retrieving) data that should not be changed (or retrieved).

OO (idealistically) enforces hiding of information. In other words, no object may alter, or view, the contents of another object without asking it first. The way Object A requests information from Object B is defined by Object B's interface. An interface is a set of messages that an object can understand. The messages for any given object are known, or at least obtainable, by other objects (including itself, if need be). Having a well-defined interface to an object allows its internal workings to be concealed from other objects. This is known as the "black-box" idea. More than that though, software architects can use the interface to describe the problem at the object level, without worrying about the (gory) implementation details. Thus, the description of objects and their interactions in effect solves the problem. What computer language the objects are ultimately coded in is irrelevant, as far as the design is concerned.

Current Software Design Process

The software design process has changed with the advent of objects:

1. Describe the problem.
2. Depict how users interact with the system (known as Use Cases).
3. From the Use Cases, document the system's objects.
4. Determine each object's class, responsibilities, and collaborators.
5. Specify the interface for the classes and objects.
6. Implement the specified interfaces.
7. Test, verify, and go back to any step that has a problem.

The advantage to this approach in software design is that it greatly reduces the ripple effect caused by small changes anywhere in the system, as opposed to previous methodologies, where a small change anywhere in the system can cause large ripple effects throughout the entire system. Because the steps leading toward the solution of the problem aren't tightly coupled, a change in any step (if designed properly) results in a subdued ripple effect into the steps below. One slight change in the first few steps does not cause entire (or major) code rewrites. Usually only a few objects and/or classes need be changed. This is known as iterative development.

Another advantage to developing software iteratively is the ability to safely change how an object functions internally. In the real world, where applications have to be delivered on deadlines, this has significant strategic advantages. The first cut of the application may use objects that go about their business in a brute-force way. For example, a search engine may have an object whose sole responsibility is to return a list of files whose contents have a given keyword. The keyword might reside in any file on the computer. Brute force would dictate that this object searches through every single file on the computer for such a keyword. Depending on the number of files on the computer in question, such a solution would be extremely time-consuming. Yet, if it meant the difference between getting the application delivered on time or not, it may be a viable option. Assuming disk space was not an issue, the object may use a large file that already has all possible keywords indexed to their corresponding files. It would then merely search that one file (possibly via a binary search tree) and quickly return a list of files that match the search criteria.

When the object is modified to use the second means of searching, its interface should not need to change. Because the interface remains the same (that is, the expected inputs and outputs do not change), no other objects that rely on it must change. (This assumes that no other object relies on how long the search object takes to complete its task. Yet in this particular scenario, it would seem more a design flaw than an implementation flaw if such a coupling occurred.) A system in which most objects can have their internal behavior altered, yet still perform to interface specifications, is well designed.

Object-Oriented Libraries

The standard template library (STL) for C++ defines a useful set of well designed classes. By virtue of being a library, one can immediately expect some reuse. Because the library consists of objects, the reuse is increased substantially. With C, there are basic types (arrays, integers, characters, user-defined structures, and real numbers). C++ has the same basic types as C, plus many fundamental building blocks that are used in creating OO applications.

Fundamental to most OO libraries is the concept of a "container" (also called a "bag"). Containers may have objects added to them or removed from them completely arbitrarily. Containers automatically increase or decrease in size (unlike static arrays) depending on the number of objects within. Of course, a container would be virtually useless if there was no way to get at all the objects inside it. In C++ and Smalltalk, there are iterators. In Java, one finds enumerations. All three are functionally equivalent. What they do is start at the "first" object in the container, and on each successive query to the iterator, they return the "next" object in the container, until all objects have been returned once (and once only).

The idea of having a library of classes and objects (such as containers, iterators, text manipulators, etc.) to construct applications is really nothing new. Moreover, for all the libraries out there, the OO technology is still being used in the same fashion as non-OO technology. Design, implement, test, and debug applications without regard to what other people in the industry are doing (or have done). This, fortunately, is quickly changing. People are making known what they have developed and giving other people the opportunity to download and use the developments. The STL is an example of this. Through the Internet, its possible to search for sets of class libraries (for a given language) that can be used to help solve a particular problem—or even solve it entirely.

Smalltalk may have the most comprehensive library available. Some development environments for it have, literally, tens of thousands of objects, all of which are used within a "pure object-oriented development environment." By this, it is meant that *everything* in Smalltalk is an object. In languages such as C++ and Java, basic types are not objects. An integer, for example, can have its behavior modified in Smalltalk (although changing how integers behave is not highly recommended). The behavior of integers in C++ and Java may not be altered by a subclass. (To confuse the issue, Java has both an Integer class and integer basic type. The Integer class, when instantiated, becomes a wrapper for the basic type of integer. This brings Java close to being a pure OO language.)

Most people understand that the reason for not implementing basic types as true objects is for optimization purposes. The classic response to software being too slow is to "wait 18 more months for faster computers to come out." Sometimes though, such a response is not good enough. Improving the algorithms, altering the design, and using compiler- and/or machine-architecture-specific optimization tricks are all viable means of speeding up an application (if need be). Another means by which an application can be sped up is via parallel computing.

Distributed Objects

A rapidly emerging trend is to use many machines networked together in order to help solve problems. Underlying this solution is another problem: the transport layer. How software can communicate (and coordinate efforts) across a network is not a simple task. In an object-based system, the problem is simplified slightly to how messages are sent from an object on one machine to an object on another. In most cases when Object A on Computer A wants to use Object B on Computer B, the application running on Computer A must know the name (IP address) of Computer B. Assuming this is the case, all Computer B needs, then, is a piece of software that listens for incoming requests from other computers, as shown in Figure 1-3 (known as an object request broker (ORB)).

You can think of the ORB as an intermediary between Object A and Object B. In most implementations, though, you'll find that the ORB is well

Figure 1-3
Distributed objects using an ORB.

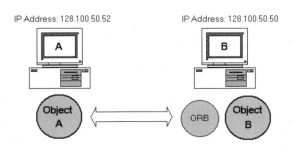

IP Address: 128.100.50.52   IP Address: 128.100.50.50

hidden from the objects involved. Typically, there are two steps in making Object B known to the world. The first step is instantiating Object B. The second is binding that instance of Object B to the ORB. Most ORB implementations enable you to give a name to a particular instance of an object. In this case, we'll assign the name of Object B to *ObjectB*.

Once Object B has been bound to the ORB, Object A may then obtain a handle to it. Getting the handle is usually done in one step. The full name of Object B, in this example, would be `128.100.50.50/ObjectB`. The first portion is the numerical name of the computer where Object B can be found. The second portion (after the slash) is the name of Object B that was registered with the ORB. What happens next is that Computer B's ORB waits for Computer A's Object A (can be any computer on the network) to send a message to Object B. Although hidden, in actuality, Object A's message is sent via the ORB to Object B. The ORB then, depending on its implementation would handle the situation in one of two ways.

The first way is to send Object B over the network to Computer A, and have the application then use Object B as though it were a local object on Computer A (instead of being on Computer B). This process is known as "marshalling an object." The second way to complete the task is to have sent from Object A to Object B the information necessary to carry out the message's instructions successfully. Object B remains on Computer B and the request is executed on Computer B. The results from the operation are sent back to Computer A, where Object A carries on processing as though the message had been sent to an object local to the application.

Both scenarios are advantageous in particular circumstances. The second scenario is useful if Computer B is a powerful high-end server, and Computer A needs a good deal of calculating done. Object B on Computer B would receive a few 1,000 bytes of information to be used in the calculation. The server would quickly compute the result (or results) and have them sent back to Object A on Computer A. This scenario follows the classic client-server model. The client becomes a dumb information display terminal, and the server is used for its compute power.

Now assume Object A must send several terabytes of information to Object B, which is responsible for doing some simple data manipulation on the information and then returning it to Object A. In this situation, it would be far less time-consuming to marshal Object B over to Computer A and have Object A use Object B locally—as depicted in the first scenario. This way the terabytes of information need not be transmitted across the network. It is easy to see that this would be applied when dealing with large databases.

Legacy Systems and Interlanguage Communications

Large databases and legacy systems tend to hang around each other like fruit flies and bananas. Unfortunately, not all systems in the industry today were written with C++, Java, or recent releases of Smalltalk. There are large (and complex) systems coded in languages that date back over two decades (such as COBOL and FORTRAN). A good deal of work must go into applying modern interfaces to applications written in those "ancient" tongues. Mostly this is due to the lack of means to have functions in older computer languages accessed (at runtime) by functions in other languages. (Again, this is something that is changing with newer releases of the older languages.)

Some newer languages have provisions in them that allow for talking with other languages. In Java, the JNI (or Microsoft's RNI) allows a program to access C++ (or C) code and vice-versa. If all that is required is to have a Java program operate with a C/C++ program, the JNI (or RNI, if the application only has to run on one operating system) is probably all that is needed. Alternatively, the open management group (OMG) has developed what is known as the common object request broker architecture (CORBA). It defines a platform-independent and language-independent means to hook together two pieces of software. Any language that is capable of socket (read *network*) communications can have a CORBA implementation written for it. Because CORBA is language-independent, any application written in a computer language for which there is a CORBA implementation has the capability of using any other code with the same constraints.

Thus far, at least the following languages have CORBA implementations available: C++, Java, Smalltalk, CommonLisp, Eiffel, Python, Modula-3, Tcl, Ada, and Ada95. CORBA allows the previously mentioned languages not only to interoperate on an object level but also to operate through the ORB in a distributed environment. Inevitably, CORBA allows a fast integration of software, at a cost. Currently CORBA implementations are not as quick as they should be. The overhead of data transfer across the network is a bottleneck. When gigabit-networking hardware becomes commonplace, speed will no longer be an issue.

The Power of Rapid Application Design

The final speed of code execution, though, is only one small portion of developing applications. The methodology behind bringing applications to realization is an important part. The waterfall methodology to software design was adequate in its day. However, as computers have evolved (more powerful, more flexible, and much more complex), a new way of dealing with ever changing software problems needed to come about. This way of solving problems must meet the ever changing needs of the people who use the applications.

People no longer wish to wait two years (or more) for software. The time-to-market for software applications has been reduced to less than 18 months (known as "Internet time"). With the waterfall methodology, the software's potential users specified the system's architecture at the beginning of the project. Thereafter, they were essentially spoken to no further. By the time the application was complete, potential users might have thought of new things to add or were not completely satisfied with how things looked. Therefore, developers and architects had to go back to the original designs, update them, and possibly start all over again.

With rapid application design (RAD), the people who will be using the application are constantly queried about what does not meet their expectations or what could be improved. This allows the user interface to be updated as need be and even change the design specifications (and hence implementation) iteratively. One of the problems with this methodology is that tools are needed to simplify tasks such as redesigning the user interface.

Early RAD tools (such as Visual Basic) offered developers a way to "paint" the way their application will look and then demonstrate mock functionality to end-users. This is done without the developer having to produce a single line of source code. (At the very least, without having to code any of the complexities to the application without first knowing what the end result should look like.) When the end-users are satisfied, the developers are free to implement the real functionality of the application.

Since 1990, RAD tools have become more powerful, easier to use, and better in the resulting code they produce. Some Smalltalk implementations, for example, have powerful graphical user interface (GUI) builders and wonderfully simple generated code. The downfall is the resulting speed of the code. There are companies that prototype the GUI of their applications in RAD languages like Smalltalk, Visual Basic, or Delphi but do their actual application development entirely in C++. Two main factors guide this principle. The first is that there was a shortage of good RAD tools for C++ (Borland's C++ Builder was one). The second is that the resulting code in Visual Basic, Smalltalk, or Delphi was typically slower than what could be produced in C++. (There are always exceptions to the rule, however.)

The use of Visual Basic, Smalltalk, and Delphi may face a decline as more RAD tools are developed for Java. IBM is guessing that Java will play a major role in the future of software development. As such, they have created VisualAge, A RAD tool for Java that parallels their Visual-Works, a RAD tool for Smalltalk.

The next wave of RAD tools has already begun to offer more than placing widgets (buttons, text fields, scroll regions, etc.) in a window. Currently, with most RAD tools, the interface is constructed, yet the underlying code (the functionality of the interface that was just constructed) remains to be implemented. Components have the capability to change this.

One Component for One Job

Components, being OO in nature, follow a simple rule: one component for one job. That is to say that a spell-check component should only know how to perform spell checking. It should encapsulate the minimum knowledge it needs to completely perform its task and not much else. A spell-check component, for example, should have no understanding of grammar. However, it may have many different spell-check options for the user to select, so long as the options are directly related to spell checking.

Companies (such as Netscape Communications) have already developed several components that follow this idea. Breaking components down into their essentials allows the modular development of larger applications. If components did more than one task, applications being developed might have internal functionality overlap. Imagine a text search component that also asked the user for a filename, instead of having one handed to it from an application (or another component). The way in which it obtained the filename might follow a totally different paradigm than a component whose sole task is to return a filename. Because the developer already has a means by which a filename can be obtained, the search component interferes with the application's functionality, as opposed to enhancing it.

Component-Object Programming (COP)

OOP is about describing how objects interact with one another, which creates a system of objects. Imagine a system that details the relationship

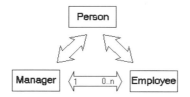

Figure 1-4
Object-oriented
manager-employee
relationship.

between managers and employees. Figure 1-4 shows how the inheritance hierarchy might look in such a system.

The first thing to realize is that a manager is a person, and an employee is a person. They both have information such as a Social Security number, name, date of birth, physical description, and salary. Depending on what is being modeled, it might be necessary to subclass Person into WorkingPerson and remove the salary from Person and add it to WorkingPerson. For the purposes of this system, it can safely be assumed that any Person is indeed working, thus has financial income.

Through inheritance, both manager and employee get the attributes defined in Person. One difference between a manager and an employee is their relationship. A manager is responsible for the actions of zero or more employees. Some might argue that a manager is an employee and hence the inheritance hierarchy should be a straight line without branching. Person subclasses Employee, and Employee subclasses Manager. If the problem domain was set up in such a way that describing the solution in that scenario made things easier, it would be a viable solution. In this example, however, a manager has none of the behavior that an employee does.

An employee, though, always has one manager. If the problem had situations in which an employee could have more than one manager, that can be easily changed. For now, we assume the former, as noted by the 1 and o..n in Figure 1-4. Regardless of how the classes interact with one another, the fundamental principle of object orientation still applies.

Everything is a black box. There is a defined interface for how any object in the application may interact with an Employee object. There is also a defined interface for interacting with a Manager object. The application, then, uses instances of Managers and Employees for whatever purpose it was designed. This is where the major difference between COP and OOP comes into play. COP hides details above the object-interaction level. When using a component, the inner workings (the relationships between the objects used within the component) of that component are oblivious to the application using the component. Let's go back to the text search example.

In the previous example, the text-searching component required a filename and some text to search for within the file. A slight redesign will improve the component's flexibility greatly. Instead of taking in a file-name and text, it will take in an open input stream and ask the user for the text. This simplifies things because the component will no longer have to worry about opening the file (and hence closing it). This means all the error checking that must be done in case something goes wrong when the file is opened (it doesn't exist, it can't be read, or it is out of file handles, etc.) is now someone else's problem. Figure 1-5 shows the internal workings of one possible text searching implementation.

The user-interface portion of the component obtains information about the search parameters, information such as matching case, finding whole words, using wildcards, phonetic comparisons, and so on. It is also responsible for obtaining the text for which to search from the user. It then updates the search options accordingly. When the search engine is asked for the next segment of matching text, it looks at the search options that have been set, and finds the next match within the input stream in respect to them. Each successive match is then returned to the application as an instance of a match object.

As more features are implemented on the search component, its interface (the component interface, not the necessarily the user interface) remains the same. Thus, any application using the component need not worry about those details. From a COP perspective, Figure 1-5 would look the same as Figure 1-6.

The application using the component does not care how it works internally and even less how it is implemented. Although the search com-

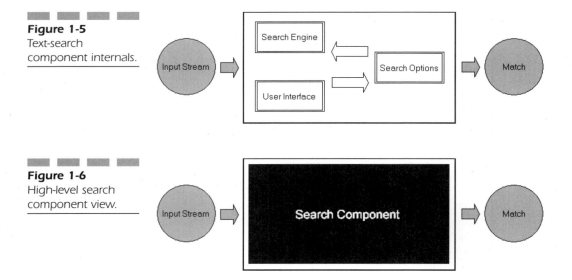

Figure 1-5
Text-search
component internals.

Figure 1-6
High-level search
component view.

ponent keeps returning the next successful match, the application will be quite happy. Inside the match object would be information such as the offset into the input stream where the given match was found. It might also contain the number of characters that were matched. As long as the interface remains the same, information can be added to the match object without having detrimental consequences to the application using any version of the search component.

The search component in Figure 1-6 should give the impression that the internals of the component may not be altered by the application using it. This is an important difference between OOP and COP. Components, when in action, have their internals wholly hidden from the application. All data and state information is inaccessible from the outside world. The only thing that can alter a component's internals directly is the component itself. In a typical OO program, most objects can be used by any other object. (Java can use what are called "inner classes" to hide this. These classes are declared within another class and are therefore hidden from any other class.) A component hides all the objects it uses behind a single interface. The objects a component uses are invisible to the world.

Another item to note about components is that their behavior cannot be inherited. This follows from the inability to alter (directly) a component's internals. A component, when in use, is a complete entity onto itself. A finished component should not need any extra behavior implemented by a subclass. Doing so would lead to a break in encapsulation. It would also increase the probability of errors entering the application. Furthermore, it would add to the amount of testing to ensure errors have not entered the application. Note that objects external to the component may inherit from the objects used within the component, which does not detract from encapsulation, nor does it mean the component itself may be inherited.

Advantages of COP

The first advantage is an additional level of modularity on top of what OOP already offers. Instead of thinking about how any one given object interacts with another, the focus is more on how entire sets of functionality (features) interact. OO does not encapsulate groups of classes and objects. COP hides the information at the class level. That is, it hides how groups of classes and objects communicate with one another when forming a single component. Figures 1-5 and 1-6 demonstrated this idea. In

Java, this would be akin to saying that a given package implements a given interface. Unfortunately, Java has no such facility, yet. (However, it does have JavaBeans.)

OOP languages (such as Java, C++, and Smalltalk) were supposed to be the Holy Grail of software reuse. Although there is a lot more reuse in OO technologies than straight modular code, OO is not the Holy Grail. Some contributing factors include the necessity to distribute the objects in source-code form, which is not conducive to being able to sell software at a reasonable price, "reasonable" being something that not only companies but the public can afford. Having to distribute objects in binary form is also a problem. If C++ was the implementation language, developing a binary for Windows machines, all flavors of UNIX, and the Macintosh would not be an easy undertaking for a major application.

COP, on the other hand, is designed to produce reusable units of software. As mentioned, a software component is completely useless by itself. A component needs other software to use it before any benefit can be sought from it. Figure 1-5 and Figure 1-6 lead into two more benefits to COP. The first is the scalability of the resulting application. Newer, better, functionally richer, and faster versions of the search component can be produced independent of the application. The new component slips over the old version without having to modify any other source code (so long as the interface remains the same across versions). Coupling that idea with the concept of dynamic binding at runtime, the new component can overwrite the old component while the application is still running! Now if that isn't keen, what is?

A second advantage of COP stems from the reduction in complexity. OOP reduces problem complexity by breaking the problem down into its real-world objects. COP breaks it down even further by grouping those real-world objects into individual scenarios. Components, in this light, can be thought of as a unit of work. The work that needs to be completed may be given some information as input. In all cases, though, the component must produce measurable output.

Unit testing, then, can be done on a component-by-component basis. This divides project work quite nicely. People are free to form groups to work on specific components, test them, and at the end, join them together to form high-quality applications. At a project's end, component-based applications are extensible enough that adding another component does not mean the entire system needs to be verified. You can think of an operating system as a software entity that benefits from componentization. Each application that runs under the operating system is akin to a component. Installing a new program extends the entire system's functionality. Without the operating system, the program is useless. Moreover, adding a new game should not interfere with how your word processor works.

With all these advantages, the result is applications that are developed faster, cheaper, and much more reliably than what OO alone has delivered. It should be noted that OO is not required to develop a component. However, a natural synergy exists between COP and OOP that makes developing components using object orientation a reasonable choice.

Component-Object Technologies

The following subsections cover several common buzzwords of the component industry.

OBJECT LINKING AND EMBEDDING (OLE)   OLE is Microsoft's Object Linking and Embedding technology. At the start, OLE was used for writing applications that allowed the existence of compound documents (documents stored within documents). The term OLE has expanded to describe an arsenal of technologies:

- OLE is a foundation for implementing reusable, integrated software components.
- OLE provides a set of object-oriented interfaces and services.
- OLE allows for the management of custom services.
- OLE gives a platform-independent, binary standard for object sharing.

According to Kraig Brockschmidt, "OLE is a unified environment of object-based services with the ability to both customize those services and arbitrarily extend the architecture through custom services, with the overall purpose of enabling rich integration between components." No matter how it is viewed, OLE compromises a fair bit of functionality. It defines an environment whose behavior can be extended via Microsoft's four major integration protocols: COM, OLE Automation, OLE Documents, and OLE Controls. Because COM is described a bit later, we'll tackle the other three protocols.

OLE Automation is categorized under getting and setting single class-specific properties. It defines ways to expose the methods and properties of classes to automation controllers. A controller, then, is anything that controls an OLE automation server. It can be thought of as the way components can make their interface known to the world.

OLE documents are compound documents. They are conceptually nested files. In OLE, this nesting is the main reason behind structured storage. These documents contain components that are either "storages" or streams. Storages are akin to directories; streams are like files. Thus, storages can contain either storages or streams. Streams are then used for reading and writing.

Lastly, OLE controls dictate the way for independently developed applications to become OLE-enabled. The controls are objects that support persistence, embedding, automation, outgoing interfaces, and more.

MICROSOFT'S ACTIVEX   ActiveX controls are software components typically developed by other vendors (that is, not necessarily Microsoft's products). They are used in applications, Web pages, and software development tools. The language support for writing an ActiveX control includes C, C++, Visual Basic, and Microsoft's Java development environment: Visual J++. The downside to ActiveX controls is that they are tied (almost explicitly) to Microsoft's operating systems and web browser. There is work being done on giving them the capability of running on other operating systems.

Many news articles have touted ActiveX as being a competitor to Java and/or JavaBeans. Although portions of ActiveX overlap in functionality with Java/JavaBeans, ActiveX is the next step in data sharing and interoperability between applications. There is, undoubtedly, some competition between ActiveX and Java. Both may be downloaded from Web pages, and both have component technologies. Finally, ActiveX, OLE, and OCX are virtually one in the same. Without OLE, there would be no ActiveX. In addition, OCX is merely the name given to an ActiveX control. The name is derived from the file extension (.ocx) used for ActiveX Controls.

MICROSOFT'S VBX   VBX controls were the starting point for Microsoft's OLE technology. Functionally, OLE was designed to be similar. A VBX control is more constrained than an OLE control:

- Only Visual Basic allows creation of VBX controls.
- VBX controls are 16-bit and tied to the Intel (x86) architecture.
- The VBX architecture was not openly documented by Microsoft (making it difficult for other vendors to provide VBX support in their tools).

A developer might choose to use a VBX control when becoming familiar with COM and OLE would be too time-consuming. That is, to create an OLE control, you must have some knowledge of COM and OLE. VBXs, being a completely separate entity, are less complex and thus should not take as long to learn.

MICROSOFT'S COM, COM+, AND DCOM   Microsoft's Component Object Model (COM) is an interface specification to allow components to communicate with one another. It defines an application programming interface (API) that allows components to be created and then used in integrating custom applications. It also allows a myriad of components to interact. In order to interact, though, the components must adhere to Microsoft's binary standard.

The COM technology permits multiple components to interact on the same machine. DCOM is the next logical step, enabling components to interact over a network. Both COM and DCOM should be thought of as the low-level technology that gives components the capability of interacting. OLE and ActiveX are a higher-level technology, built off COM/DCOM foundations.

With COM/DCOM, the implementation language is irrelevant. As long as the compiler is able to break the language structures into the binary standard, any given component can interact with any other component(s). Another aspect to COM/DCOM is the support for multiple interfaces. Unlike Java, interface names must be unique, as they use a flat naming scheme. Furthermore, once an interface is defined, it should hold to that definition. That is, new methods should not be added nor existing methods modified. Although not enforced, creating immutable interfaces is a suggested COM/DCOM programming practice.

There are a couple of downsides to COM and DCOM. The first is that being based on a native binary format, components written using COM and DCOM specifications are not platform-independent. A recompile is necessary in order to have a COM-DCOM component run on a different platform. The second is a security issue. Nothing prevents malicious code (written either with intent or by accident) from running. Authenticode forces the identification of the creator of the component. However, it still does not prevent malicious code from executing. Lastly, COM+ is the newest addition to Microsoft's component family. According to Microsoft, COM+ is an extension to COM that will make developing components easier. It will allow components to be written in any computer language, using any tool. Additionally, COM+ will be backwardly compatible with COM. That is, applications that use COM will work within the COM+ environment.

BORLAND INTERNATIONAL'S DELPHI ENVIRONMENT   Borland International touts Delphi as being a set of comprehensive, high-performance, visual client/server development tools. Delphi allows easy creation of ActiveX components and OLE automation controllers and has native COM support. It is an object-oriented take on the Pascal language, bundled in an integrated developer's environment (IDE). With Delphi 3, Borland has incorporated DCOM and ActiveX support.

SUN MICROSYSTEMS' JAVABEANS JavaBeans is a component architecture for the Java language. It allows the development of network-aware components. It does what other component architectures fail to do: provide components that work in practical heterogeneous environments. Furthermore, JavaBeans interoperates with COM and ActiveX.

The Holy Grail

Several third-party developers have created components that mirror each other in at least three different languages. That is, they have developed a VBX component that has the exact same functionality as one they've developed in Delphi. Then they mirrored the functionality of the components again, using JavaBeans.

Obviously, this is not aiming towards the Holy Grail of software reuse that CSD is supposed to shoot for. CSD should remain language-, operating system-, and hardware-independent. Keeping components uncoupled from as many factors as possible benefits the people who will be using the component-based applications. This frees the end users from having to purchase a particular piece of hardware and a particular operating system so that they may use a given software package, so people can choose the computer system that suits them, rather than the system (meaning both hardware and software) they purchase having to be everything for everybody.

It should be obvious that one system cannot be everything to everybody. The skill of computer users varies widely from person to person. Some people have never used one, and others can recall flipping switches on a PDP/11. The rest are somewhere in between. Thus, by having components that may be used from system to system, what the end-user buys become irrelevant. Not only do end users benefit from platform-independent components, but so do the developers of the components.

There should be no need for a software vendor to write a VBX component, Delphi component, and an ActiveX component that mirror each other in functionality. A vendor, in theory, should be able to write the component once and have it used in any application. The hardware platform, operating system, language, and developer's toolkit should all be irrelevant. The languages C++, Delphi, and Visual Basic generate platform-specific machine code. Smalltalk and Java generate byte code. Said byte code is then interpreted by a piece of software. Said software—known as a virtual machine (VM)—is tied to a specific environment.

The VM abstracts programmers away from the operating system, hardware platform, and even different versions of those that their software will work. Programmers merely compile their source code into byte code (that the target VMs understand) and walk away knowing that (in theory) their application will run on all operating systems for which there is a virtual machine available. In the future, if a new type of computer system is developed (which is inevitable), a VM can be written for it, too. Therefore, VMs assure software developers that their applications will work on not only all modern computers of today but also the computers of tomorrow.

Another advantage to byte code is that any computer language can have a compiler built for it that generates byte code. Thus, two of the major problems of component development are solved. The first is platform-specific components. The second is development language requirements. There are drawbacks to byte code, though. One of them is efficiency. Interpreted software will be slower, generally, than software that is compiled to a specific hardware and operating system. As computers become faster, though, the noticeable gap between speeds (as far as humans are concerned) will ultimately decline.

The "least common denominator" problem is another drawback to byte code. For a VM to allow all byte code to run, the features the VM offers must be features of all operating systems and hardware platforms. A common user-interface feature in Microsoft Windows is tabbed panels. Assume for the moment that they don't exist on Macintosh platforms. Because the VM must provide only those aspects that every platform has, tabbed panels would not be available. This is unacceptable for any real-world applications.

A work-around to this problem is to find the features programmers use the most that are only available on certain hardware-software platforms. From there, the VM (or the VM's standard libraries) can simply emulate those features. Realizing that unpopular features are not used as often as popular ones, the least-common-denominator problem becomes moot. That is, if a given platform P has a given feature F, and only platform P supports feature F, placing that feature into the JVM may not be necessary.

How Do JavaBeans Fit the COP Model?

JavaBeans are Sun Microsystems' response to the software industry's growing desire for CSD. A JavaBean (usually shortened to "bean") fits into the component-based programming model by virtue of being a component. JavaBeans, as previously stated, is a cross-platform component architecture, written for the Java language. More information on how to use JavaBeans can be found in the next chapter.

JavaBeans and COP

JavaBeans are self-describing software entities. That is, other pieces of software that use JavaBeans can explicitly query the Bean's interface. The interface information that is returned describes the Bean's properties, events, and methods. This information leaves the internal functionality of the Bean completely hidden from the outside world and also leaves the functionality open enough for other components to use it.

Figure 1-7 shows the conceptual model of a component. Other components may register themselves via the Add listener method. When an event is triggered, all listeners are informed of an Action event. The progress bar may send out a 100 percent complete event to all its listeners when its final state is reached. The color of the progress bar may be changed, its orientation modified, and so forth.

Other components are free to plug into the exposed public interface. This implies there may be unnoticed events, unset properties, and methods that are never called. The component is responsible for providing de-

Figure 1-7
How a progress-bar component looks to the world.

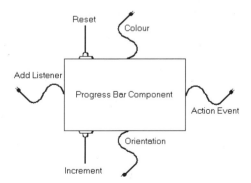

fault behavior in every situation. By doing so, the component becomes contractless. Its state may be changed at any given time by any part of the application, and the component should still perform its task according to its specification. This is unlike the behavior of an object.

An object's state usually has other objects that depend on its state. Other times, an object's events are tightly coupled with other objects. Components move the coupling of objects to a higher level. JavaBeans provides the means to get at component information. Using the Bean Development Kit (BDK) provided free from Sun Microsystems, developers can implement their own components. The BDK allows programmers to describe the interface specifications to their own components. It enables people to define event mechanisms, dictate properties, and register public methods.

Like components, beans flatten out the object hierarchy in a program by encapsulating behavior into units of work. This allows beans to plug into a component-based program with minor changes in the program. It also creates a new market in the computer industry: off-the-shelf components.

JavaBeans in the Industry

Being contractless in nature, all beans (in theory) should interoperate with one another. That is, any given bean should be able to plug in and use any other bean, without modification to either bean. This is what integrated development environments (IDE) are trying to do. Some vendors that currently provide interoperable component-based IDEs include Symantec's Visual Café, Borland's JBuilder, and IBM's VisualAge. Each has specific advantages and disadvantages, detailed in the following subsections.

SYMANTEC'S VISUAL CAFÉ The component library that comes with this product can be extended with components created by software developers using the tool or brought in from a third party. An Interaction Wizard is available to help you. It guides you through hooking-up the components you drag and drop onto their visual Form Designer.

Unfortunately, all components developed with Visual Café require the `SymantecBeanDescriptor` class to be added to the `BeanInfo.java` file of the bean. In other words, Visual Café, although it supports third-party components, requires a proprietary extension.

BORLAND'S JBUILDER Over 100 JavaBeans, with source code, come with JBuilder. In addition, Borland claims commitment to Sun Microsystems'

100 percent pure Java goal. This indicates that software (component based or not) developed using Borland's JBuilder IDE has no proprietary extensions.

IBM'S VISUALAGE This product is an extremely comprehensive development environment. It includes versioning, class browsing, and method browsing in an environment familiar to users of VisualWorks (a Smalltalk development environment). The biggest disadvantage is the system resources required to reasonably use the tool. If you have anything less than a Pentium-133 class machines using less than 64 megabytes of memory, it might be best to look elsewhere.

The computer industry is digging into components, leveraging off the component technologies mentioned previously in this chapter. Most of the component technologies, however, suffer in different ways. Some do not interact (easily or at all) with other components. Some components only run on particular hardware-software platforms. JavaBeans, as we will show in the next chapter, provides a platform-neutral means to develop component-based software.

How Do Component Architectures Differ from Object Architectures?

COP and OOP share many similarities. They use information-hiding strategies: both break down problems into essential building blocks, and both are about reusing portions of the resulting application in other projects. However, components and objects differ in several ways that must be made clear.

An object is built around the following ideas:

- Inheritance.
- Needs other objects to be (re)used properly.
- The interface defines only methods.
- Has only properties (state) and behavior.

A component differs in the following ways:

- No inheritance (although the objects that make up the component may inherit behavior from other objects, possibly in other components).

- The component always appears as a single interface.
- The interface formalizes properties, events, and behavior.
- Easily reused due to its well-defined interface.
- Flat hierarchy: no direct dependencies on other external objects.
- Guaranteed to function in any configuration.
- Typically defines a GUI.
- Has the ability to describe its own interface at runtime.

With the differences between components and objects fresh in your mind, we'll go one step higher and see how the architectures using these two techniques differ.

Object Architectures

With this type of architecture, the programmer is responsible for building everything from the ground up. Typically, a collection of prewritten classes are at the programmer's disposal. C++, for example, has the Standard Template Library. Java has its core libraries. Several Smalltalk implementations come with thousands of classes. This wealth of functionality becomes a valuable tool to a programmer. Yet, the classes in the object libraries don't really perform any specific task. They are the building blocks upon which applications are created.

For many applications, an object library is sufficient for development. A software developer can design the application, define the most appropriate object interactions, and follow the implementation through to its end. This way of developing applications gives more reuse than previous methodologies. However, it is still time-consuming.

Component Architectures

People have come to realize there are units of work that can be modeled. Certain tasks have been written (from the ground up) repeatedly. An example of this would be obtaining the name of a file from the operating system. There are many objects involved in this relatively simple task: input fields, scrolling list boxes, the filenames, OK and Cancel buttons, and so on. As a whole, however, how the filename is retrieved is incidental to the application itself. As such, it follows that this conglomeration of objects can be made into a component. All the application needs to know is how to use the component (i.e., the component's interface specification). The internal workings of the component and the user interface of the component no longer concern the application.

How Is Component Architecture Beneficial?

Software quality is a term broad in its scope. It entails issues such as source code maintainability, the reliability of the software, and the software's efficiency. ISO 9126 gives an overview of these issues, plus three more issues pertaining to the quality of software.

SOURCE CODE MAINTAINABILITY   Components, being modular in nature, may easily be replaced on a per-component basis. Because components are designed to do one task, to replace a component all you need to do is find a component that does that task (or one very similar). From there, it is just a matter of coding to the new interface specification.

RELIABILITY OF THE SOFTWARE   A complete and formal specification of any given component's interface should come with the component. The component can be said to be reliable if its implementation provides a complete, and correct, implementation of its interface specification. The entire application's reliability is, therefore, augmented when constructed from reliable components.

SOFTWARE EFFICIENCY   If a component is too slow, its internal workings can be modified without damaging any other part of the application. Because components completely hide their internal workings, changing how a component implements its task internally assures us of this fact.

SOFTWARE FUNCTIONALITY   As hinted about with the analogy to a house, an application's functionality can be achieved faster than using an object-based architecture. Because off-the-shelf components can be seamlessly integrated, all you need to do is find the component that does the task you're looking for and plug it into your application. With the advent of component repositories, searching for the right component for the task at hand becomes less time-consuming than actually designing, implementing, and testing the component on your own.

COMMON LOOK AND FEEL   Standard components provide the user with a familiar GUI. Depending on the task (searching a document for a word, for example), how the presentation of that task is displayed to the user can be the same across all applications. This provides a single view of heterogeneous information.

PORTABLE COMPONENTS   A component's specification is just that: a description of the interface (events, behavior, and methods) that the component must understand. Words, as we're certain everyone will agree, are completely cross-platform. Thus, porting a component to another platform is a matter of implementing the specification on a different platform. In some cases, no modifications to the internal design are needed, merely a recompilation onto another platform.

Shortcomings of Component Families

Although components sound like a utopian software development, they still face many problems. Two significant problems include integration of different component architectures and cost of adoption.

Integration of Different Component Architectures

Component architecture integration is a problem with a few hurdles in itself:

- How components interoperate with each other.
- How distributed components find each other across a heterogeneous network.
- The development environment/tools used in creating components.

Developer environments for building component-based software applications produce components that can readily integrate into other development environments. We should be able to take a component developed using any given component architecture and have it integrate seamlessly within our component-based software package. If you've written a wonderful search component using OpenDoc, any application should be able to use it. Currently, this isn't as easy as it ought to be. Component distribution mechanisms, platform-dependent binary code, and proprietary protocols all hinder the progress of component development, in general.

COM, as previously mentioned, suffers from being tied to specific platforms, as do DCOM, SOM, and DSOM. ActiveX and OpenDoc, likewise, are platform-dependent. Additionally, the transport layer that provides component connectivity is proprietary. To this point, the only component architecture that is truly platform-independent is JavaBeans. However, it is currently under the rule of Sun Microsystems and as such is proprietary information. However, they have made their specifications open (as Microsoft has with COM) and accept feedback from the public.

Allowing distributed components to roam free about a network and to be used by any application at any given time, is another ideal goal that has not been reached. There are many solutions to this problem, but until all companies developing component architectures agree on a standard solution, that goal will never be reached.

Cost of Adoption

As with most new technologies, component technology will take time before it settles into the mainstream. Already we're seeing advances in the component field from Sun Microsystems, Microsoft, Netscape, Borland International, Oracle, and many other popular software vendors. However, a single methodology and/or technology that solves every problem may never exist.

Components are another way of solving problems. As with every means to solve a problem, a cost is associated with components. For example, commercial-off-the-shelf (COTS) components will need to have their licenses managed. Otherwise, a component license may expire during a project, possibly causing loss of project progression until the license is renewed. Other costs include adapting components to legacy information. To have older components interoperate with new components, a software application may need to rely on some software patterns to ensure successful operation, patterns such as bridging, mediating, or wrapping. It follows that the architecture will gain in complexity and thus requires an increased understanding of the application's architecture. Some aspects to consider before adopting any technology, like components, include

■ What resources are needed in order to adopt the technology?

■ How long might it take to incorporate and/or implement the technology?

■ What barriers exist before the technology can be adopted?

■ Why should this technology be used?

■ Why should this technology not be used?

Some of these aspects should involve thought into the training, consultation costs, software packages, and hardware upgrades that may be needed. Barriers might include company politics, limited in-house expertise, and need.

CONCLUSION

Instead of coding what the widget (like a button, scroll bar, image, input box, etc.) does, RAD tools will allow developers to place their widgets on a canvas and couple them to the functionality of full-blown components. In less than a minute, developers will be able to add a search feature to their application, tie it to their favorite search component, and have it work seamlessly. This scenario is quite idealistic, of course. If application development becomes that simple, the question that begs to be asked is, "What do we need software developers for?" The answer is simple: to develop components.

What goes on behind the scenes to allow such ease of component use will, undoubtedly, be complex. It boils down to giving components the capability of being probed. An application needs to know how to interoperate with the components that are added to it. Where the knowledge of what the component does should be encapsulated is another problem that may need to be addressed. Obviously, an easy solution would have documentation telling the developer what the component is meant to do and how to use it. Yet such a solution, although simple, would mean more work for the developer.

This chapter has touched lightly on a wide range of component-related topics. A brief history leading up to COP has been presented. We've discussed the differences between component architectures and object architectures. Lastly, the industry's main leaders in component technology have been looked at and compared. The following chapters will expand on several of the topics we have covered here, with its focus being geared towards JavaBeans.

A Closer Look at JavaBeans

This chapter provides a more in-depth look into Java-Beans. Many different JavaBeans-related topics are covered in this chapter. First, we'll examine what JavaBeans is and what it has to offer developers. From there, we detail topics such as how to make use of the processing capabilities of multiple computers with JavaBeans (known as distributed computing). We also look at the multi-threading capabilities of JavaBeans. By the end of this chapter, how JavaBeans started, where JavaBeans is useful, what current JavaBeans exist, and the direction Java-Beans is taking should be well understood.

It is very important that while you read, you keep in mind how rapidly technology changes. For example, since we began working on this second chapter, the specification for Glasgow has been altered (aggregation and delegation were eliminated). These days it almost seems as though when a book has gone to print, it has already become outdated. To help you stay in step with what JavaBeans-related technologies have to offer, at the end of this chapter we list a few sites on the World Wide Web you should keep an eye on.

This Chapter Covers

- What is JavaBeans?
- The goal of the JavaBeans API.
- Differences between class libraries and beans.
- Design-rime versus runtime.
- Distributed processing with beans.
- Inter-bean communications.
- Multithreaded beans.
- Internationalization.
- Visibility.
- Security issues.
- Various JavaBeans versions.
- AWT 1.1 versus AWT 1.2.
- Limitations of JavaBeans.

What Is JavaBeans?

The future of computing looks as though it may lie in the arms of components. The Java programming language offers a robust, platform-independent, object-oriented software development environment. When first made publicly available, Java was missing a component architecture. Given that developers want to use components, Sun Microsystems was quick to add one. The result is what they call JavaBeans, the component architecture for Java.

A JavaBean, or "bean," can be an entire application or a component. An application bean can be used alone or embedded within other applications. Component beans, on the other hand, must be used within an application. A calculator bean is an example of an application bean. It is easy to see that many different applications (spreadsheets, financial reports, and word processors) could make use of an embedded calculator. A formatted display bean, however, would be a building block used by an application component. It may allow the application to show precision numbers to a user, in a certain font, using a particular color, and so forth. By itself, the formatted display bean does little.

As described in the first chapter, a component is a software entity that defines a public interface, has behavior and properties, and issues events. Beans encompass these three items. Additionally, beans, with help from the standard Java APIs, can be persistent. These aspects are defined in the following subsections.

Public Interface

The public interface is defined by the methods that are visible to other components and objects. This is conceptually no different from an object's public and private methods. The public methods are the hooks other components use to manipulate, signal, and query a bean with. The difference between a bean's visible methods and an object's visible methods is that you don't know which object (internal to the bean) is having the method invoked upon it.

Behavior and Properties

Obviously, a bean that doesn't contain information (its properties) or cannot perform a measurable unit of work (its behavior) usually makes for a useless component. Through the methods exposed by a bean's public interface, other components may dynamically change the behavior and properties of that bean. By virtue of being a component, the bean must perform its task to specification, regardless of the current state of its properties or its current behavior.

A typical switch, for example, has two positions. Most switches can be moved in two directions: either up and down or left and right. The graphical user interface (GUI) portion of a Switch bean might present itself to the user as shown in Figure 2-1.

Moving the switch to the left, when in position 1, does nothing, as there are no more positions for the switch. Pushing the switch to the right, when in position 1, causes the Switch bean to enter position 2. There is no magic

Figure 2-1
Switch bean with two positions.

Figure 2-2
Switch bean with three positions.

here; the bean exactly models a real-world electronic switch. What gets interesting is that during runtime the number of switch positions may change. Figure 2-2 shows what the Switch bean might look like after another position is added.

Now the behavior of the Switch bean has changed, in accordance with its properties. The addition of another position means that pushing the switch to the right while in position 2 causes the switch to move into position 3. In Figure 2-1, this third position was not possible. It should be clear that beans should have well-defined behavior for any given state. Additionally, the easier it is to predict the behavior of a bean in a given state the more robust the bean.

Event Notification

When the internal state of a bean changes, other components may wish to be informed of the fact. In the Switch bean example, when the switch has moved to a different position, other components may wish to perform an action. The other components don't need to know how the Switch bean changed state. Its state may have changed from a mouse click, a keyboard press, or any other event. The notification process involves software entities that generate events and software entities known as event listeners. Event listeners add themselves to event generators' object notification list. When an event generator has had a state change, it sends a message to all objects on its notification list.

Persistence

An object's capability of storing and retrieving its state across sessions is another fundamental aspect of programming. Java, and thus JavaBeans, provides a simple means to do persistence. Typically, a component will write to disk the information it needs to reconstruct itself sometime in the future. The Java specification (as of version 1.1) defines a way for an application to put objects, and hence components, from memory to disk and vice-versa.

A bean, as mentioned, consists of the previous four features. A bean can be thought of as an autonomous software entity. The JavaBeans architecture is the supporting foundation that allows for the creation of beans. To support beans, the JavaBeans architecture has two aspects that make up its core. These include the layout control service and application builder support.

Layout Control

JavaBeans provides layout control services to help build the visual details of a component. For example, the placement of an input text field, an OK button, and a Cancel button within a component may have been arranged by a programmer in a particular fashion. Furthermore, the position and size of the component may have been set to a certain specification. The layout control services can recreate the graphical details of a component at any given time.

Application Builder Support

A builder tool does nothing more than help developers combine code. It is an abstraction layer above the source code level. Typically, you would see a representation of your code, in some form. These forms can vary from an icon to a name (possibly the name of a method). The tool allows you to connect the various code representations to one another. Within visual tools, this is usually done via drag-and-drop or point-and-click mechanisms. An example of such an application comes free with the Bean Development Kit.

Components make their properties and behavior known to these types of development tools. Using application builder support interfaces, development tools can provide editors, inspectors, and debuggers to help embed components into applications. These interfaces also allow developers to modify state, appearance, and the relationships of components. The modifications are all accomplished without changing any source code.

The Goal of the JavaBeans API

The primary goal of the JavaBeans API is to define a component architecture for Java. This definition allows the creation of third-party components. These components are capable of communicating and working with one another to form applications. It is then up to the end user to fit the components together to obtain the desired application. With the primary goal of JavaBeans in mind, the following subgoals can be thought of as the building blocks by which the primary goal is achieved.

- Keep it simple: creating a difficult-to-understand, complex, poorly documented architecture is a relatively easy endeavor. JavaBeans has been designed from the ground up with simplicity in mind. That is, creating a small component with minimal functionality should not be a chore. Making beans rich in functionality and producing a compact result, should also be possible. That is, the infrastructure supporting the creation and deployment of beans should add a minimal amount of code to the beans themselves.

- Coupled with Java: when considering the other goals of JavaBeans, it's only natural that JavaBeans make use of the infrastructure available from Java. For example, JavaBeans uses reflection. Reflection is the portion of Java that allows an object to query other classes for their public methods, constructors, and member variables. JavaBeans also makes use of Java's object serialization mechanism. Object serialization sets the stage for a bean's persistence, as well as distributed computing. Lastly, the components in the AWT hierarchy are beans by default. This implies that as the AWT matures (desktop integration capabilities, for example), these visible parts of a bean will mature in step.

- Platform independence: one of Java's main goals is to provide developers with a way to create applications (and applets) that can perform their task on any operating system using any hardware. Being based on Java, JavaBeans inherently has that same goal. However, as a component architecture, JavaBeans is also designed to interoperate with other component architectures. These other architectures include Microsoft's COM and ActiveX technologies and Apple's OpenDoc architecture.

- Distributed computing: another trend in the computing industry is the ability to use multiple computers to facilitate a task's completion. JavaBeans does not directly have a means to perform distributed computing. Instead, it sets up the infrastructure to provide freedom to the programmer to pick whatever distributed computing facility is deemed the best solution. To date, this includes CORBA, RMI, COM, proprietary socket communications, and other distributed programming environments.

CORBA is a powerful object-oriented distributed technology. It has the capability to perform interlanguage communications over a network. However, the power behind it comes at the cost of product size. Remote Method Invocation (Java's RMI technology) is slimmer but has disadvantages as well. One disadvantage is that RMI is not well supported in all major Web browsers. Another disadvantage is that it supports only Java-to-Java communications. Proprietary distributed solutions are another viable alternative. The drawbacks there are development time and no interoperability with other software solutions.

Differences between Class Libraries and Beans

Because JavaBeans is tightly coupled to the Java class libraries, the distinction between the two can be easily blurred. Beans make use of class libraries, but class libraries do not make use of beans (at least, not yet). In the paragraphs that follow, we explain how to think of them separately, as well as pointing out their similarities and differences.

Class libraries and beans are akin to models and views, respectively. Typically, beans are associated with visual items. Bar charts, percentage-full gauges, spreadsheet-cell grids, buttons, and such make for good beans, whereas mathematical functions, collections of objects, string parsers, and input/output streams do not make good beans. Tasks where widgets can be altered visually, and possibly programmatically, lend themselves to beans. Another difference is how beans are put together versus how class libraries are used. With beans, you can connect them with a visual tool, and eventually end up with a fully functional application. With class libraries, you usually have no choice but to delve down into the application's source code before you can make any use out of them. Furthermore, class libraries are not self-documenting. They cannot expose themselves, what they do, and even how they function at runtime. Indeed, the programmer must research the APIs, if any, given with the class library to find out how to use the objects and/or functions.

In either case, class libraries and beans provide a measurable unit of work. Moreover, the work they provide is reusable. The `sin()` method in Java's `Math` class can be applied to many applications in many different fields, from processing sound waves to rendering three-dimensional video game graphics. Likewise, a percentage-full gauge is useful for a variety of purposes; from showing how far along an installation has gone to displaying oxygen levels.

Beans use, and at times rely on, Java's class libraries. However, Java's class libraries do not know about beans (except for the JavaBeans API, of course). This one-way usage scheme enables programmers to continue designing, implementing, and testing non-JavaBeans, object-oriented software. At the same time, it enables programmers to look at component software development in an environment they have become familiar using. An important item to note is that sometimes there is no reason to write a bean when a new class library is all you need. Before choosing between a bean and class library, you should ask yourself the following questions:

- Is information being displayed?
- Can the format of the information be changed by the end user?
- Can the user interact with the information?
- Are events triggered by the status of the information?
- Is information being modeled?
- Must the information be obtained programmatically?

If you answered "yes" to the first four, then you probably should look into creating a bean. Positive responses for the last two questions indicate that you might be better off placing the information in a class library. Remember that these are just rules of thumb, and every situation must be examined carefully. There are times that you will find, for whatever reasons, using a bean for modeling invisible components is the correct solution.

Design-Time Versus Runtime

The list of where beans can run is incredibly long. For example, a bean could be running within a particular browser, through a command line Java Virtual Machine, on top of the JavaOS or even on top of a hardware-based Java Virtual Machine. For now, it is sufficient to realize there are two major points of interest. The first is called "design-time" and the second "runtime." In brief, design-time means using an application builder to glue the beans together to form a program. This includes laying the beans on a canvas, customizing their properties, and describing their interactions. Also, a bean must be complete, or at least capable of running, before the application builder can use it. That is, if the bean cannot execute within the application builder, it cannot be run anywhere else. In addition to the developer customizing the beans and their interactions, the bean should give design information to the application builder so that the end-user may also customize the behavior and appearance of the beans.

The main difference between runtime and design-time is the amount of information present for customization of the beans. When designing, there is a great deal of overhead associated with developing a component-based application. Allowing the appearance and behavior of an application to be changed at runtime is counter-productive. That is, when an application is being run, the color and layout of the user interface normally does not need to be changed. Thus, sending all the customization information that an application builder needs along with the final application is a waste of time, bandwidth, memory, and possibly disk space. JavaBeans dictates that customization code is kept separately within its own class. A bean can check to see which environment it currently is running in by using the **isDesignTime()** instance method of the **java.Beans** class. This class defines another instance method called **setDesignTime()** that helps the bean and other programs dictate the environment (runtime versus design-time).

Design-time and runtime are two important stages of the bean development cycle. Design-time is synonymous with customization time. That is, positioning, connecting, and laying out components on a canvas to form an application. Runtime is putting the final application to use. The application could be running in a browser, inside a command line Java Virtual Machine, or remotely on a server. Due to the variety of environments, the bean should be programmed in such a way as not to make any assumptions about its security restrictions. In other words, assume the bean cannot read or write from the local fixed disk and also assume it may not connect to arbitrary hosts on the network.

Distributed Processing with Beans

As we have briefly mentioned, JavaBeans is being developed with distributed computing in mind. In essence, distributed computing is the means by which a bean on a given computer can perform tasks with the help of a bean (or many beans) located on a different computer (or computers). Or perhaps the beans are running on the same computer but at some time in the future may be segregated. The actual transport layer is open, leaving the developer to choose how it should be done. That being said, choosing between local and remote processing should be well thought out.

A solution that involves only local processing is optimal. One computer can communicate with itself much more rapidly than it can with a computer across a network. Furthermore, using a remote computer to help process a task introduces susceptibility to network failures. Therefore, the people who design distributed computing mechanisms are careful in their attempts to minimize the amount of information that must be transferred across the network. There are several different ways to do this, such as data caching. Instead of sending out a single byte of information, the sender buffers the information until a reasonable amount of data has accumulated before sending it to the remote computer. The definition of "reasonable amount" depends on the task at hand. In some cases, each byte of information must be sent out immediately. In other cases, the receiver is able to process megabytes at a time. Real-time communication is an example of the former. Database manipulation is an example of the latter.

The people implementing the distributed system should be aware of what the system is going to need and then write robust beans that perform the necessary peer-to-peer communications. For example, if the system is going to need fast processing on large quantities of data, it might be best to leave all the heavy processing on the server. If the system is highly interactive (as is a video game), you will want most of the classes to be sent from the server to the client. Imagine how slow a game would be if each collision detection had to be transmitted back and forth across the network! Within "The Goal of the JavaBeans API" section earlier in this chapter, we included a brief paragraph describing some of the distribution mechanisms for JavaBeans available to developers. Thus far, all Java platforms should support these remote access technologies:

1. Java RMI

2. Java IDL

3. JDBC

In practice, however, some software vendors have not included all forms of remote access within their Java Virtual Machines. Two possible reasons are behind the deviation. The first is that, due to time constraints, they simply have not released a fully compliant Java Virtual Machine. The second is that they have opted to use their own distributed technology instead. If you do not wish to have a cross-platform, bean-based application, the Java Virtual Machines that lack the remote distribution technologies may provide you with the solution you desire.

Java RMI

Remote Method Invocation (RMI) enables easy development of distributed Java applications. Because RMI is meant explicitly for Java on both the client and server sides, the developer need not learn any new language syntax. Instead, Sun Microsystems provides a simple "Hello World" tutorial that shows the steps involved in creating a distributed application. Scaling their example up to larger applications does not involve much more work than merely defining different remote interfaces. When the interface specifications are coded, the clients and servers implement those interfaces. RMI calls are sent from the client to the server. The underlying structure of how the calls are sent is hidden. Neither the client nor the server needs to know how the information is being sent across the network. Thus, RMI defines a way that developers can create distributed Java-to-Java applications. The methods of a Java object can be invoked from other Java Virtual Machines, including a Java Virtual Machine on a remote machine. Sun Microsystems expects RMI to be one of the more common ways to write networked JavaBeans.

The classic example of RMI proving useful is within a real-time communications application. As previously mentioned, both the client and the server must be written in Java. More than that, however, once RMI is chosen to be the remote-access layer, the implementation language for the client and the server is virtually cast in stone. Client applets then connect to the server, obtain handles on the server objects, and register their existence. Any information the server receives gets sent out to all registered clients. The effect is not only real-time communications but also multiparty, simultaneous, real-time communications. In other words, lots of people are all interacting with one another at the same moment in time.

The simplicity of RMI is another factor that you should consider when deciding on the remote distribution layer for your project. Disregarding the overhead for stub and skeleton code, doing the actual connection between client and server is done in less than five lines of Java source. By a connection, we mean the process by which the client gets a handle to an object on the server. Once the handle is given, consider the connection established. Because that object is just that—an object—the client is free to use it, syntactically, just as it would any other object. The difference, however, is that every call to the remote object must catch the remote exceptions that might be thrown. The reason behind the remote exceptions is simple. At any point in time, the connection between client and server may be closed. When this happens, the client needs a way to gracefully inform the user that the server is no longer available.

Through experience, we have learned that RMI does not hide the details of the server-side objects from the client, as its name implies. This means that when the client requests a handle on an object that resides on the server, the object itself is sent over to the client. More than that, though, any objects contained within the first object also get pushed over to the client. As such, if you have a server application written in Java that talks with non-Java objects (such as those used by COM, DCOM, SOM, ActiveX, and most other platform-dependent object models), most Java Virtual Machines will generate an exception. So although it is called "Remote Method Invocation", be sure to remember that the remote method is sent from the server with the full object to the client before the method gets invoked.

A common word that makes an appearance when people talk about accessing remote objects is "marshaling." Marshaling is the process of sending an object (or method request) from one computer to another. Behind your back, a lot is actually happening. An object is just a bunch of ones and zeros that just happen to mean something to the computer. The memory that represents that object, from start to finish, is not so different from the ones and zeros that make up a file on disk. In Java, objects can be treated as a stream, through a process called "serialization." These object streams conform to the same interface as file input and output streams. These streams, in turn, are just like input and output streams for sockets. Thus, the object is actually written out across the network as a stream. The receiving end reads that stream and reassembles the object into memory. The object, then, is said to have been "marshaled" across (the network).

Java IDL

The interface definition language (IDL) allows Java-based clients to interact with servers written in other computer languages. Moreover, the IDL specification lets many different computer languages interact with one another. The Java IDL is an implementation of the Open Management Group's (OMG) distributed object model, known as the Common Ob-

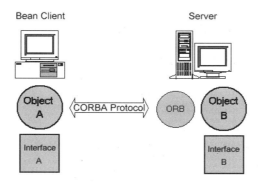

Figure 2-3
Interface definitions and CORBA.

ject Request Broker Architecture (CORBA). All objects that must be used remotely have their interface specified using IDL. Bean clients can invoke the methods of IDL objects running on servers and conversely, the server objects can invoke a bean's methods. The interactions between the client and the server are done using Java stubs that are generated from the IDL interfaces. Figure 2-3 illustrates these relationships.

Before Object A can communicate with Object B, both objects must define their public interfaces. This is done through the IDL. The IDL for each object is then compiled. Consequently, stubs (Interface A) and skeletons (Interface B) are generated on a per-class basis. The stub is the class responsible for forwarding method calls from the client to the server. This forwarded information is passed from client to server via the CORBA protocol. The skeleton on the server receives the information (through two layers of indirection). The method call requested by the client is then invoked on the server, by the corresponding server-side object. The effect, of course, is that the client has just used what it perceives to be a local object but in reality is an object residing on the server. Any return values from the remote method call are sent back to the client as well.

One place CORBA comes in useful is when legacy information systems must be interfaced. Imagine you have a beautiful database with accessing routines written in C. In this case, assume the C code is messy, highly unstructured, but incredibly bullet-proof as long as you don't try to modify the code. Given the solid (albeit nightmarish) C code, a C++ object could be used to wrap up and possibly extend the functionality. However, your boss has just asked you to make the information in the database available from the World Wide Web. Enter the "magic" of CORBA. Using the IDL, you can describe the interface of the C++ object. That interface description is then exposed to Java. In turn, Java can use the C++ object, via its interface definition, as though it were an ordinary Java object.

Once you have the C++ object accessible from Java, which has hooks in the clumsy C code, it is not difficult to see how you can integrate the legacy database with the World Wide Web.

Of course, CORBA solves problems other than interacting with old databases. Because CORBA allows many different computer languages to interoperate, it opens doors for clean, relatively quick, and extensible multilanguage solutions. Using CORBA as a lever to talk between results allows you to pick an optimal language for solving a particular piece of a problem, without having to worry about using that language in places where other computer languages excel. C++ is undisputed and unrivaled for its native computing speed. Smalltalk is well-known for its capability of handling complex object interactions. Finally, Java is most useful when platform-independent GUIs are desired. Using CORBA, it's possible to combine the strengths of all three languages, leaving their weaknesses outside the problem domain.

Java Database Connectivity

The structured query language (SQL) is a standard way of abstracting how information is obtained from relational databases. The Java Database Connectivity (JDBC) API shields component development from the complex infrastructure behind accessing objects within a database. The database being used can be on the client machine or on a remote database server. Open Database Connectivity (ODBC) is a subset of API calls that JDBC builds on. In essence, ODBC allows a program to be abstracted from the database it uses. With ODBC, the program need only interact with the ODBC language. It is then up to an ODBC Manager to determine how best to contend with the database you want to use. The Manager does this via an ODBC driver tailored to that specific database. These details, however, are hidden from the bean as depicted in Figure 2-4.

Beans that rely on JDBC can also connect to ODBC data sources using the bridge for JDBC-to-ODBC. Until more pure JDBC drivers are

Figure 2-4
JDBC details.

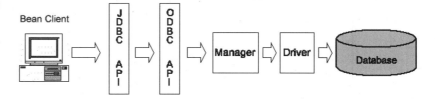

written by database vendors, the bridge should be regarded as an interim solution. JDBC suffers from the same disadvantage as most architectures that have many layers of abstraction: it is slow. However, as we have already hinted, there are different types of JDBC solutions available.

JDBC-TO-ODBC BRIDGE   This is the slowest type of database connectivity you can have in Java. It consists mainly of a translation interface. The interface sits between JDBC and ODBC, translating the JDBC method calls into ODBC calls. As you can probably imagine, having a translator built on top of a language that (in most cases) must already be translated does not make for fast execution times. What follows are a few ways database vendors have worked around the speed deficiencies.

JAVA AND NATIVE   It is a given fact that in almost every circumstance, code compiled to a specific chip architecture (Intel, Motorola, etc.) will run faster than code that must be interpreted before it executes on a specific architecture. So to speed up database access, some vendors have written database drivers that combine Java and native code. The native code talks to the database using the required protocol, for a given relational database. You can see how this is not a good thing if one of your project mandates is to have Java applets that can do remote database access, plus run on multiple chip architectures.

VENDOR-NEUTRAL   Keeping in stride with 100 percent pure Java, a vendor-neutral solution has two steps. The first is an open DBMS protocol is used to relay SQL messages to the machine that stores the database information. A module on the server listens for the messages and then uses a DBMS-specific calling convention to pass the SQL message on to the database manager. These layers of abstraction hide any platform-specific code that may be required on the server-side instead of the client-side. Once again, the extra layer of abstraction, in using the open DBMS protocol, causes a speed deficiency.

VENDOR-SPECIFIC   Also being 100-percent pure Java, this version of database access in Java is almost exactly the same as the previous. The difference is how the DBMS protocol is used. In vendor-specific implementations for Java database connectivity, the SQL messages are relayed to the machine housing the database by a proprietary protocol. The advantage here is that because a proprietary protocol is used to send the request off to the database computer, no interpretation is needed, and hence one layer of abstraction that was in the previous section is removed.

Where Do RMI, IDL, and JDBC Fit?

RMI is a viable solution to problems when you know the client and server applications are going to be implemented using the Java language. It is simpler and usually less expensive than CORBA (although there are freely available CORBA implementations for Java). One of the biggest drawbacks to using RMI is that it ties you to a Java-based solution. IDL should be examined when either the client or the server may change their implementation language. For example, you may want to use Java initially on the server for its rapid prototyping. If you recognize ahead of time that even though the server-side is faster to implement in Java but slower to execute, and you may re-implement the code in C++ on the server, CORBA may be the way to go. The downside to the flexibility CORBA offers is its bulk.

Finally, the JDBC API enables easier access to SQL databases from JavaBeans. Easier, that is, than having to write source code to talk with a SQL database yourself. It abstracts both the location and the type of database from the bean. One disadvantage is that it is not fully supported, in pure Java, by all database vendors. Depending on your situation, however, this disadvantage may prove itself moot.

Inter-Bean Communications

Connecting beans together is a task that comes up often. To allow a bean to make arbitrary data available for other beans to examine (and possibly use) is a task that, as you will see, can be extremely useful. InfoBus is a mechanism enables software developers to build dynamic applications that have a twist. The twist is that the exchange of information between components is based on the content of the information. BeanConnect is Netscape's architecture that is similar to InfoBus but differs in that it allows the communication of applets across a single instance of its Java Virtual Machine, which means the beans could be on totally separate Web pages. In the sections that follow, we examine InfoBus and BeanConnect in turn, showing you how they are meant to be used and how they relate to JavaBeans.

InfoBus

This section examines the InfoBus technology. As with so many other technologies available for beans to communicate (e.g., RMI, IDL, events,

51

and proprietary socket communications) it is important that the role of InfoBus is clearly defined. InfoBus transcends the bounds of JavaBeans, meaning that it can be used by ordinary Java programs as it can be by JavaBeans.

INFOBUS DEFINED The idea of writing an application that can exchange data between components based on that data's content is not super-easy to swallow. Take for example an audio stream whereby each instrument's part can be extracted by name. The audio stream, that is, the information in question, is dynamically tagged by its content. The tags, in this case, might be "Vocals," "Guitar," "Percussion," and "Triangle." Data consumers may then request portions of the data stream that are marked by individual tag names. A tool for teaching music would then be able to extract only the sounds of the "Guitar." The "Guitar" portion of the audio stream might then be played back, plotted visually, or perhaps displayed as sheet music. The founding reason behind InfoBus is the exchange of information between components in a structured way. Strings and numbers are passed over the InfoBus just as easily as their more complex counterparts: lists and arrays. An example of the interaction between components with InfoBus is depicted in Figure 2-5.

As shown in Figure 2-5, the scenario begins when a user interface component publishes an account number acquired from the user. The account number is sent to all interested parties on the InfoBus. In this case, a database query component is listening for the account number. It then talks with the database, using the account number that was posted. When finished, the database query component publishes a table of results, with

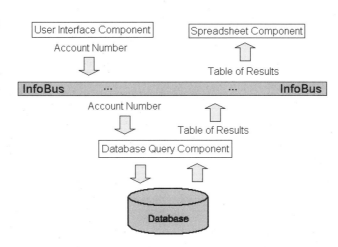

Figure 2-5
InfoBus and component interactions.

respect to the given account, on the InfoBus. Lastly, a spreadsheet component may be interested in giving a visual depiction of any tables that are posted on the InfoBus.

In an event-response model, the interactions are based on an understanding of applet-specific events that have applet-specific responses. InfoBus differs from this way of asynchronous information transfer by using "data flows." The data that flows through the InfoBus must be interpreted at the information-content level. This is in contrast to evaluating specific parameters from event-driven architectures. Three types of components are found within an application that uses InfoBus. These are data consumers, data producers, and data controllers. The role of each will be examined in the following numbered list:

1. Data consumers: True to its name, the data consumers component obtains information from other resources. The information is interpreted, and a unit of work is performed. A data consumer does not necessarily have to place information back on the InfoBus. Indeed, that is the job of data producers. Similarly, nothing prevents a data consumer from being a data producer. Examples of data consumers include spreadsheets, word processors, audio players, and such. Any component that requires information may be a data consumer.

2. Data producers: Data consumers listen on the InfoBus for particular pieces of information. It is up to the data producers to place information on the InfoBus. The producers are responsible for placing data on the InfoBus. They do so in response to requests by data consumers. Examples of data producers include user input dialog components, database query components, and audio streams.

3. Data controllers: The data controllers are optional components. Their main responsibility lies in regulating and directing data flow between producers and consumers. The data controller is an intermediary. Data producers and data consumers do not speak directly, when there is a data controller present. Instead, the producers send information to and consumers retrieve information from the data controller.

INFOBUS DESIGN ELEMENTS   The protocol that is used behind the scenes with InfoBus has three major elements. These include InfoBus participation, data to be exchanged, and data encoding. It is these three elements that give data consumers the capability of examining the information provided by producers.

1. InfoBus participation: all Java components (and Java objects) can access the InfoBus. This is accomplished by the following general steps:

   a. The component requests to join the InfoBus.

   b. A context identifier is associated with the component.

   c. The context identifier is returned to the component.

   d. Once the component is an established part of the InfoBus, it receives information via Java's standard event notification mechanisms.

2. Data to be exchanged: the exchange of information on the InfoBus is asynchronous. When data has been produced, the data producers merely announce the availability of new information. Some examples include the user typing an URL, information from a newly created input stream, or perhaps the results of a database query. Data consumers request information, as such information is required, from the data producers. Consumers may ask for the information at any point in time. For example, a consumer may ask for information when an applet is initialized, when it should display a person's picture, or upon repainting.

3. Data encoding: it should be apparent that different types of data are managed by different types of data producers. The consumers of the data, however, may wish to get the data in simple or complex ways. A simple way, for example, may be a series of several integers. A more complex way would be as an array of those same integer values. To ensure that both consumers and producers can understand each other, InfoBus limits the number of interfaces used for data transmission.

An example of such an interface is the **KeyedAccess** interface. It represents a set of name and value pairs. Because it is a subclass of **CollectionAccess**, components are free to iterate over the set. This has two benefits to the consumer. The first is that it allows the consumer to ask for data dynamically by name. The second is the consumer's capability of getting the list of keys. The producer chooses the most appropriate description type for its data. However, the consumer may interpret the data in two ways. The first is to interpret the information the way that it was packaged by the producer. The second is to interpret the data using a superclass of the package chosen by the producer. For example, a spreadsheet producer may make known its information in the form of an **ArrayAccess** item. One consumer may use it as an

ArrayAccess item because that is the best representation for its needs. Another may use the superclass **CollectionAccess**, because it has no need for the extra behavior provided by the **ArrayAccess** interface.

DATA ACCESS INTERFACES   Each interface used to access information has its own special capabilities. The following sections detail the different interfaces that are available. We also describe how the interfaces are to be used. Please keep in mind that these interface specifications are not cast in stone. As such they can, and undoubtedly will, change as needs arise.

- **DataItem** interface: the keystone of the InfoBus infrastructure. It defines the features for adding and removing changed listeners. That is, consumers wanting to know when the data item has changed. The change indicates that data is waiting to be consumed.

- **ImmediateAccess** interface: purpose of this interface is to allow data values to be retrieved directly from calls to its interface. The data obtained by the consumer can take two major forms, depending on the invoked method. The first is a string representation of the data. The second is the data in the form of an object. Again, how the consumer interprets the information is highly specific to its task.

- **CollectionAccess** interface: Navigating the information present on the InfoBus is a basic feature of the specification. The **CollectionAccess** interface defines ways to add to and remove **DataItems** from the InfoBus. Additionally, it supports access to what is called the **DataCursor**. The **DataCursor** has a dual purpose. It points to the current item of data. It also allows a component to iterate over the collection of **DataItems** through its **getNextItem** and **getPreviousItem** methods.

- **ArrayAccess** interface: a subclass of **CollectionAccess**. It organizes the **DataItems** into an n-dimensional array. The exact dimensions of an **ArrayAccess** object can be obtained at any time. Thus, this interface defines methods to determine dimensions, get specific elements from the collection of data, iterate over all the elements, and subdivide an **ArrayAccess** object into another. Take a simple example, for the last interface definition, of an array that has two columns and five rows. Using the subdivide interface it is possible to create an **ArrayAccess** object that has only one column and five rows. This is useful for eliminating irrelevant information.

- **KeyedAccess** interface: similar to a hash table. Like the **ArrayAccess** interface, it too extends the **CollectionAccess** interface. It differs from an **ArrayAccess** interface in that the elements are indexed by named keys instead of by a numerical value. There is nothing to stop a consumer component from using numerical keys. However, there are cases where it is more natural to obtain information within an array not by its position in the collection, but by the information's name. For example, **KeyedAccess** would be useful for finding the IP address of a machine from a long list of known machine names.

- **RowsetAccess** interface: relational databases conform well to the **RowsetAccess** interface. **DataItems** of this subtype consist of collections of rows, from a data source. This interface has methods that perform many different operations. These operations are as follows:

  Returns the number of columns for a particular instance

  Returns the names and the data types associated with each column

  Points to the next row of data

  Gets column values and row values

  Inserts, updates, and deletes rows

- **DbAccess** interface: databases, legacy systems, information retrieval, and such play an important role in enterprise computing. The **DbAccess** interface provides the bare minimum for database access. The minimum functionality entails retrieval and nonretrieval queries. Any result may optionally be returned as a **DataItem**, subsequently posted on the InfoBus.

INFOBUS BEHAVIOR   The **InfoBus** class is declared final. It defines how new members may join the InfoBus, how data controllers are used, and some security restrictions. However, the default behavior is inadequate in some circumstances. A new interface definition called **InfoBusDefaultPolicy** (or possibly named **InfoBusDefaultPolicies**, as the specification has not been fully fleshed out) is being designed. The previously mentioned behaviors will be moved out of the **InfoBus** class and into this new interface. The new interface specification will enable you to override **InfoBusDefaultPolicy** with your own behaviors in order to change how an instance of InfoBus functions.

UNDER THE HOOD   InfoBus members have a few important aspects. We cover them here to provide a firmer understanding of how InfoBus works. The first aspect is how members access an InfoBus. The second deals with receiving events. The next details the announcement of, and searching for, **DataItems**. Finally, we explain how departures are made from an InfoBus.

ACCESSING AN INFOBUS   When a prospective member of an InfoBus wishes to join the InfoBus, it merely has to set its **InfoBus** property to point to a valid InfoBus instance. A count on the InfoBus is then incremented to represent the number of members connected to that particular InfoBus. To leave, a member calls the **leave** method on its private **InfoBus** property. The InfoBus then checks the number of listeners and members it has. If it does not have any of either, the InfoBus removes itself from its controlling entity. This act allows the InfoBus to be garbage collected.

RECEIVING EVENTS   Having a component on an InfoBus is a moot point if the component cannot send or receive data via the InfoBus! After joining an InfoBus, a component is then free to give an event listener to the InfoBus in order to receive event notifications from the InfoBus. Notice that an event, at this point, is either a "please send data" event (sent from a consumer), or a "data is ready" event (sent from a producer).

A data producer, then, may implement the **InfoBusDataProducer** interface. It may then attach itself to the InfoBus by invoking the InfoBus' **addDataProducer** method. Likewise, a data consumer may implement the **InfoBusDataConsumer** interface. After doing so, it is free to add itself to the InfoBus via the InfoBus **addDataConsumer** method. Note that nothing prevents a component from implementing both interfaces and calling both InfoBus methods. In effect, that component would be notified of both data-ready and data-required events.

DATAITEMS ON THE INFOBUS   There are three main InfoBus events: Data available, data revoked, and data requested. It is up to the data producers to provide data by announcing its availability, via the data available event. Similarly, data producers are responsible for telling via the data revoked event data consumers when data is no longer available. Lastly, data consumers have the capability of requesting data—at any time—by either of two means.

Data consumers may retrieve data by the **InfoBusItemAvailableEvent.requestDataItem** method. It assumes data has already been made available by a producer. If not, it immediately returns null. The second way is by the InfoBus' findDataItem method. When a consumer calls the findDataItem method, a request data event is fired onto the InfoBus. If no data producer can satisfy the request, null is returned. It is important to note that these events, and only these events, are defined in the InfoBus specification. Event propagation of this sort is thought to be relatively expensive.

DEPARTING THE INFOBUS In the web browser environment, an InfoBus member typically stays a member throughout the duration of the applet's life. However, InfoBus members are typically beans. This adds two more environments that need to be considered: the design-time environment and the runtime environment. During design-time, the bean's builder may wish to impose a specific InfoBus onto the bean for development purposes. During initialization, a bean will typically join a specific InfoBus. The builder can force a different instance of an InfoBus on the bean by changing the bean's **InfoBus** property. This ensures that the builder has full control over when the InfoBus gets garbage collected. During runtime, the default behavior should be adequate for the application's purposes.

As mentioned, the InfoBus needs to know when members have left. This allows it to decrement the count of how many members remain so that it can be garbage collected when no members remain. A member leaving the InfoBus occurs outside of the InfoBus' leave method. To keep the architecture clean, an InfoBus implements the **PropertyChangeListener** interface and then adds itself as a listener to each of its members. Thus, when the **InfoBus** property of a member changes, the member informs its list of **PropertyChangeListeners**. This mechanism mimics the behavior of Java's standard Observable and Observer definitions.

INFOBUS AND RMI InfoBus differs from RMI in that RMI deals with the communication of objects across multiple Java Virtual Machines. For doing inter-applet (and hence, inter-bean) communication within a single Java Virtual Machine, InfoBus is a viable solution. This doesn't preclude using both RMI and InfoBus within your solution. It could be that you want information sent from a Java-based server to be posted on the client's InfoBus.

Take an example of a real-time chat server. A chat server, in this case, is a piece of software that enables many people to communicate over the Internet through textual messages sent in real-time. The server receives information coming from a myriad of sources scattered about the Internet. It then sends off the information it receives to all interested clients. The clients in this example are bean-based applications or perhaps trusted-applets. An RMI bean sits snugly on the client machine, waiting to get text from the server. Once received, the RMI bean posts that information on the InfoBus.

From there, any beans listening on the InfoBus are free to do as they choose with the text. One bean may display the stream of text to the console. Another bean in the same application may be programmed to store the text on disk. Still another bean may send the data to a print device! The RMI bean, you can gather, knows absolutely nothing about the meaning of the text it obtains from the server. Building on this idea, it becomes clear that this particular RMI bean can get a lot of reuse.

In essence, the RMI bean does the following:

1. Gets an input stream object via RMI from a given server

2. Reads any information from the input stream

3. Posts that information on the InfoBus

Of course, "RMI bean" is neither an adequate nor fully accurate name for the bean. This is because it does more than just connect to a server using RMI. A better name for this bean might be `RemoteInputStreamProducer`, because it posts the information it obtains from a remote input stream on the InfoBus. The fact that it uses RMI as its connection protocol to the server should be completely hidden from the other beans listening on the InfoBus.

INFOBUS AND INTERNET PROTOCOLS Although InfoBus is intended for communicating within the same Java Virtual Machine, we have already hinted (within the previous section) that other components are free to communicate elsewhere. In addition to RMI, other protocols that may be involved in an application include IIOP, LDAP, and others. the internet inter-object-request-broker protocol (IIOP) is one of the core layers of CORBA. With it, objects written in different computer languages can communicate across a network. Nothing prevents a component from posting the results it gets back from a CORBA request on its InfoBus. Similarly, another useful component wrapper would be around the lightweight directory access protocol (LDAP). LDAP provides a standard means to get directory information from remote sources, information such as the names of employees, telephone numbers, and company addresses. Again, posting such information on an InfoBus could be useful in many applications. Telemarketing is at once a beautiful and horrific example of the power you can leverage from LDAP.

WHY IS INFOBUS NECESSARY? With the other ways to perform communication across objects, this question appears quite often. It should be made clear that the purpose behind InfoBus is to provide dynamic data interchange at runtime. For the other communication models, the type of the data must be known at compile-time. Furthermore, there can be cases where the communication event is driven by the content of the data. This is the asynchronous behavior of InfoBus.

TIP: *An InfoBus Advantage Can Be a Disadvantage. An advantage with InfoBus is that the data arrives from an unknown source. Within the realm of object-oriented programming, unknown sources is an advantage because they create an additional layer of abstraction between components. From a practical point of view, however, the extra layer equates to overhead. For critical real-time applications, the increased overhead may prove to be too costly. If that is the case, a proprietary solution for communications between objects living within the same Java Virtual Machine must be used.*

BENEFITS OF INFOBUS Because the InfoBus infrastructure is a standard, you can rely on it being there for you to use at any time. This means that your development time is cut, because you don't have to develop a proprietary solution for inter-bean communication within the same Java Virtual Machine. Not having to develop code means not having to test and debug it, as well. This, in turn, saves you even more time. However, if you do find an error within the InfoBus implementation, you are then dependent on another company's time schedule to remedy the error. (Given the turn-around time Sun Microsystems has shown to date, this point is almost rendered moot). It is a simple architecture. InfoBus is designed to be as simple and efficient as possible, yet still be generic in its scope. This directly implies that, being simple, it is easy to learn; furthermore, it is easy to add the InfoBus technology to your own software.

BeanConnect

Netscape, seeing a need for inter-Java Virtual Machine communication between objects, developed BeanConnect. The main difference between BeanConnect and InfoBus is that InfoBus does not take into consideration beans existing on separate web pages. In other words, the single applet model, according to Netscape, "does not provide a shared execution context for multiple objects." Additionally, Netscape sees five advantages to their BeanConnect model.

1. Shared execution space: similar to one of the reasons behind InfoBus, a single Java Virtual Machine should allow all

components within it to communicate. Because a Java-enabled web browser uses a single instance of a Java Virtual Machine, there should be no reason why components created on one page should not be able to interact with components created on a different page. Keep in mind that security restrictions are imposed in this sort of inter-component communications.

2. HTML forms, and forms parsing: without going to the server to parse a submitted form, BeanConnect allows forms to first go through a piece of Java code for validation. This means that the client machine (on which the applet is executing) is responsible for ensuring the information submitted is in the correct format, prior to submission. One advantage to this means of form parsing is that the server-side CGI script becomes easier to write.

3. Use of Java and JavaScript: simple BeanConnect programs are composed of embedded objects with interactions controlled via JavaScript and LiveConnect, all within the context of the HTML pages that declared the embedded objects. This follows from knowing that all BeanConnect programs are developed by placing Java objects inside one or more HTML pages. In other words, the objects used across web pages in a BeanConnect program talk with one another through JavaScript. In a more complex scenario, it is possible to use a single object to control the program logic. The very same program logic, in the simpler cases, is controlled by JavaScript. Alternatively, there is nothing preventing the use of both Java and JavaScript to form the program logic.

4. Control over the lifetime of program objects: BeanConnect programs have a special "embedded owner." The embedded owner object, written in Java, manages the start-up and lifetime of the BeanConnect program and its Java components. The program is active so long as any HTML page that contains a reference to the embedded owner is still open. When the last HTML page that holds a reference to the embedded owner is closed, the BeanConnect program is asked whether a shutdown of the program may proceed. The program is free to answer no and wait for the termination of the Java Virtual Machine (that is, the user exits the Web browser). Until the Java Virtual Machine actually terminates, the program is free to continue executing.

5. Multipage and multiframe operation: a Java program object can be embedded as many HTML pages as required. Furthermore, it can be placed within many different frames within those pages. To

minimize resources (such as memory and CPU), only the first instance of the Java program object is instantiated. Any other references to the Java program object get a handle back to the first instantiation.

MultiThreaded Beans

Today's operating systems make the creation of multithreaded applications a breeze, that is, the ability to create applications that have two (or more) things going on simultaneously. As such, the Java language has a way to help guard against some of the problems that rise in multithreaded environments. Because JavaBeans is based on the Java language, and the Java language has built-in multithreading, you might guess that Java-Beans has multithreaded capabilities; and you would be right.

Simultaneous Access

Multiple beans can be used simultaneously by different applications as resources. This implies that a bean's properties and methods may be called on at any time from any number of sources. As well, the bean can fire off any event at any time to any object that is listening for the event. These facts, in turn, mean that race conditions, deadlocks, and all problems found in multithreaded environments can occur in beans.

The "Synchronized" Keyword

To a certain extent, the multithreading problems can be eliminated using the **synchronized** keyword. It ensures that when a method is called, no other object can invoke that method until the first call has finished. Keep in mind that in some cases, race conditions, deadlocks, and such can still happen through design defects. The bean's design, however, should be thought out enough to eliminate all possible erroneous conditions.

BAD SYNCHRONIZED EXAMPLE The **synchronized** keyword, at the time of writing, can be used in two ways. First, entire methods can be declared **synchronized**. Second, blocks of code can be declared **synchronized**. Examine the source code in Listing 2-1.

▬ ▬ ▬ ▬ ▬

Listing 2-1
Incorrect
multithreaded code
example.

```
 1: public class BadExample {
 2:    private int result = 0;
 3:
 4:    public BadExample() { }
 5:
 6:    public void showResult() {
 7:       result++;
 8:
 9:       if( result == 1 )
10:          System.out.println( result );
11:    }
12: }
```

▬ ▬ ▬ ▬ ▬

Listing 2-2
Good synchronized
example.

```
 1: public class GoodExample {
 2:    private int result = 0;
 3:
 4:    public GoodExample() { }
 5:
 6:    public void showResult() {
 7:       if( (result > 42) && (result < 84) )
 8:          return;
 9:
10:       synchronized( this ) {
11:          result++;
12:
13:          if( result == 1 )
14:             System.out.println( result );
15:       }
16:    }
17: }
```

At first glance, it appears as though line 10 always writes **1** to standard output on the first call to **showResult()**. However, in a multithreaded environment, this is not necessarily the case. Assume two threads invoke the **showResult()** method of the same instance of **BadExample**, at almost the same time. The first thread executes line 7, making **result** equal to 1. The first thread stops execution, giving the second thread some time to run. The second thread calls **showResult()** and then stops at line 9 to allow the first thread to carry on. The value of **result** is now 2. When the first thread continues, the condition at line 9 fails. Consequently, line 10 never executes.

To ensure the code behaves as it would in a single-threaded environment, line 6 should be rewritten as follows:

```
public synchronized void showResult() {
```

GOOD SYNCHRONIZED EXAMPLE   In the above scenario, the second thread is forced to wait until the first thread exits the method. Similarly, you could make the critical section of the **showResult()** method synchronized. In the source code in Listing 2-2, lines 10 through 15 may be executed only by one thread at one time.

Line 10 refers to "this" because locks, in Java, can only be obtained at the class or object level. Every object has a monitor that is acquired whenever a thread enters one of its synchronized methods. If another thread already holds the monitor, the second caller will block until the monitor is released. Static methods make use of class monitors.

WHY HAVE TWO DIFFERENT WAYS TO SYNCHRONIZE?   One reason for the difference is efficiency. Calls to synchronized methods are slower than calls to regular methods. This is because of the overhead to ensure all other threads are locked out. There are cases where a test can be made before entering a critical section of code. The result of the test decides whether the critical code (lines 10 through 15) must execute. Lines 7 and 8, above, over-simplify this idea. When **result** has values more than 42 and less than 84, the method simply exits. This avoids the overhead of evaluating the critical section. If it happened that **result** was within the aforementioned range for a high percentage of calls to **showResult()**, the increase in efficiency would be dramatic (assuming, of course, that **showResult()** is part of the program that gets called a lot).

WARNING: *One item to remember is that, generally put, beans will be run as applets. As an application, a bean is free to change thread execution priority, as well as create priority-level threads. As an applet, within some Java-enabled Web browsers, the bean may be restricted from setting its execution priority, as well as creating priority-level threads. Be cautious when changing thread priorities lest the browser throw an unsuspecting SecurityException on you. Proper thread synchronization is an important part to creating JavaBeans. Because components are usually autonomous software entities, it is easy to forget that under the hood they are simply a tight collection of objects. Being objects subjects them to the pitfalls of multithreaded environments. The* **synchronized** *keyword helps to avoid the pitfalls. However, be ware that synchronization is not the end-all, be-all solution to dead-locks, race-conditions, and other problems created with multithreaded environments. The problems can still occur, just not as easily.*

Internationalization of JavaBeans

The Internet has brought the world closer together. It is now possible for you to give in a matter of minutes a program to somebody who lives halfway across the globe. That person's native tongue, however, may be quite different from your own. The language barrier, therefore, is a problem that internationalization solves. Ideally, programs should have the capability of displaying information to users in their native language. Additionally, there are cultural differences in the meaning behind different icons. A closed fist with the thumb sticking up, for example, means one of two things in North America. The first is that the person is looking for a free car ride (hitchhiking). The second means everything, within context, is okay.

To an Australian, however, such an image is quite insulting. Thus, the conventions you use in a program should either be universal in meaning (a task that is difficult to do), or they should be selected according to the locale of the program. Instead of using the "thumb's up" symbol in Australia, your program may choose to use the abbreviation "OK", instead. Other details of internationalization include text formatting (accented characters, punctuation, numerical representations, etc.), the appearance of dates (mm/dd/yy, dd-mm-yy, etc.), currency (dollars, yen, marks, etc.), and user-defined objects. To understand how internationalization works in Java, we look at six aspects Sun Microsystems took into consideration throughout its design.

Default to Internationalization

Instead of internationalization being a feature that can be added to a program some time during the program's development, Java code should be international by default. This makes internationalization a part of the code from the start of development. The hope is that it will make writing international code easier than writing noninternational code.

Object-Oriented

An OO design enables locale-sensitive classes to encapsulate the language-dependent information they need. This is opposed to querying a central state object, as depicted in Figure 2-6. The traditional global

Figure 2-6
Traditional global
locale state
information.

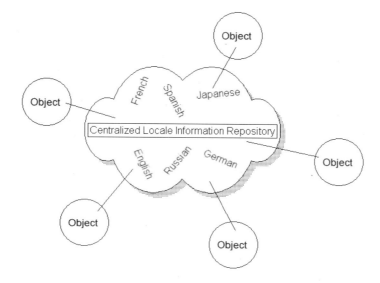

state for displaying locale dependent information is neither highly dynamic nor an extensible OO design. Figure 2-6 shows the architecture behind a traditional means for gathering locale-dependent information.

One object is responsible for maintaining all information about all locales and has the capability of retrieving that information at the request of other objects. This is inherently bad because the global state object must be shared by several objects, thereby creating interdependencies between objects. The dependencies can be reduced, ideally eliminated, by using a more flexible approach. In Java, classes that are sensitive to locale (such as those that display textual messages) store the information they need internally. This alleviates the need to get the same information from a centralized state object. The result is that indirect coupling between classes is removed. That is, the objects are more autonomous in nature.

Multilingual

Support for many individual languages is a big bonus but still has a limit. There will be situations when communication across multiple languages becomes a problem. As such, one of the goals behind Java's internationalization is the support for multilingual contexts. As a simple example, when a native German speaker visits France, she may desire banking machine messages to be displayed in German instead of French.

Platform Independent

Keeping in stride with one of Java's most important features is another requirement for internationalization. There should be no restrictions on the platform that internationalized code can execute on. Currently, Java cannot leverage off a system's language install base, because not all languages might be supported from the initial install. Typically, only the language of locale would be installed. So the internationalization scheme must be independent of the underlying hardware and operating system used.

Unicode Support

Unicode is a built-in character type for Java. Traditional ASCII character encoding easily supports all English letters (upper- and lowercase), punctuation, numbers, yet leaves enough room for over 130 additional characters. Chinese characters, because they represent words, easily number over 5,000 for daily usage. Recognizing that a program should be worldwide in scope, Unicode addresses this issue by using 16 bits to represent characters instead of the eight bits used by ASCII. As such, Unicode can represent more than 65,000 characters. This is compared to 256 characters in ASCII. The result is the ability to display characters in Chinese, Japanese, Korean, Russian, and many other languages.

Backward Compatible

Programs written to previous Java specifications, namely those that did not fully support internationalization, should still compile and run without modification to current internationalization specifications. This is akin to the idea that bytecode generated in accordance to the 1.0.2 Java specification should still run in browsers that support the 1.1 (or better) Java specification.

Programming for the Future

Internationalization tends to be an afterthought in most projects. In the near future, providing support for multiple languages in your programs will be a necessity. Multiple-language support will be necessary to keep in step with competition and necessary because the expanse distances of the world are quickly diminishing. With a smaller world in mind, recognize that, in general, a program's target audience becomes broader in scope. People prefer to work with software that interacts with them using their native tongue. By using internationalization you free yourself from being tied to a specific language.

Visibility of Beans

There are times when a bean may not have a visible user interface. Server software, for example, when active, typically does not have a GUI. A bean may choose to use the **java.beans.Visibility** interface. This interface allows the application builder or runtime environment to ascertain whether the bean needs a GUI.

Four Visibility Methods

There are four methods to the **visibility** interface. One answers True or False if the bean absolutely needs to use a GUI. Another instructs the bean not to use a GUI. Similarly, the third method answers if the bean has been told not to use a GUI. Lastly, there is a method to instruct the bean that it is okay to use a GUI.

Visibility Usage

Because these methods are abstract (that is, defined in an interface), it is up to the underlying bean to control the behavior in each case. For example, if the bean is instructed not to use a GUI, it may choose to hide all its visible parts. On the other hand, there is nothing preventing the bean from simply ignoring the request if a GUI is a critical part of its functionality.

Developer Control

The **Visibility** interface is designed for developers to give them more control over how, when, and even if a GUI is necessary. For most situations, the default visibility scheme provided by the environment will be suitable for a bean. Additionally, because end-users may wind up seeing the names of the methods, they have been given names that do not follow the getXYZ and setXYZ convention.

JavaBeans Security Issues

With the advent of applets and Web browsers, pieces of software (the applets) can run without the user being aware of their presence. In a perfect world, this would not pose a problem. However, at least four factors mandate a security guard be imposed on applet.

1. Software is prone to errors.
2. Software should not have the capability of doing something a user does not want it to do.
3. People write software to damage computer systems, for various reasons.
4. People write software to illegally obtain confidential information, for various reasons.

Applets fall into two categories: trusted and untrusted. By default, most Web browsers consider applets untrusted. As such, untrusted applets may not read or write arbitrary files. Additionally, untrusted applets can only open a connection to the host from where they came. Trusted applets, like regular applications, have no security restrictions imposed by the browser. The details behind creating a trusted applet are beyond the scope of this chapter. Here are some things to keep in mind while writing a bean:

■ Good bean design: given that beans are run, typically, as applets and given the aforementioned restrictions on untrusted applets, you should develop your bean such that it can be run as an untrusted applet. In other words, try to design the bean such that you eliminate its dependency on disk access and/or communicating with different servers on a network. There are a few more security-related aspects to designing your JavaBeans. These include design-time versus runtime security restrictions, serialization, and GUI merging. We examine each in the following sections.

■ Design-time versus runtime security restrictions: At design-time, beans run in trusted mode. Application builder tools are free to examine the internal structure of a bean. This process is called "introspection." The tool is then able to see the interfaces, methods, and member variables that compose a given bean. Reflection is also used to determine a bean's functionality and public facilities.

While designing, both the designer and the builder tool have full access to all portions of the bean. The portions of the bean that are declared public are the only parts that can be used by other objects at run-time. Therefore, trying to access a private method, or member, at run-time will result in a security violation. Remember that it is possible to dynamically invoke a method by its name, and that it is possible to obtain handles to private methods through reflection.

■ Serialization: You can expect your beans to undergo serialization at both design-time and runtime. Serialization enables objects, and hence beans, to be treated as streams. This is how the persistent storage and retrieval of beans occurs. It also means they can be readily transported across the network from one computer to another. While in the runtime environment, the bean should expect its parent application to handle where the streams are read from and written to. Attempting to access random files from within an untrusted bean applet will result in a security exception, if run from a secure browser.

■ GUI merging: the ability for a bean to merge its GUI features with that of the parent application is dependent on whether or not the bean is trusted. As an example, an untrusted applet bean will be unable to merge its menu choices with the menu choices present on the Web browser. Instead, the browser will ensure that the two menus are kept separate and distinct.

■ Protecting the end-user: All the security features that we have described are in place to protect the end-user. Be aware that the security restrictions do not apply to trusted applets and applications. Inherently, beans face other security guards due to being so tightly coupled with Java. Another security mechanism indirectly imposed on beans, for example, is bytecode verification.

Various JavaBeans Versions

Since JavaSoft announced and released the JavaBeans 1.0 specification, JavaSoft has been getting a lot of feedback from the industry. This feedback has given JavaSoft a good reason to enhance JavaBeans. Thus Java-

Soft is gradually enhancing JavaBeans with various versions. For example, JavaBeans 1.0 only has event notification, public method exposing, properties, and persistence. JavaBeans 1.1 has added drag-and-drop capabilities, runtime environment services, and a data typing and object registry framework. Then there is a new type of JavaBeans called Enterprise JavaBeans that is taking the industry by storm. It is more focused on developing server-side beans, and applications, that don't tend to have a GUI associated with them.

JavaBeans Version 1.0

In February of 1997, Sun Microsystems released the Java Development Kit, version 1.1. At the same time, the first cut at JavaBeans was released. This leads to an important item of interest: JavaBeans will not work if used with any version of Java prior to the 1.1 specification. In practice, this means widespread use of the JDK 1.0.2 specification. As an initial cut, the first version of JavaBeans fills in Java's missing component software development gap. However, like most first cuts at new technology, there is room for refinement. Just as the Abstract Window Toolkit (AWT) gives developers a rudimentary library for building graphical output layouts, JavaBeans version 1.0 gives developers a rudimentary means to develop components. With the essentials for component development in place, Sun Microsystems is continuing its efforts to bring a robust component development to developers. While doing so, the company is also keeping in mind compatibility for components already in the marketplace.

The release of a component software model for Java let people know that Sun Microsystems is taking Java into the future. Microsoft has had component software development for their operating system for a few years now. Equally so, component architectures have started to enter mainstream programming. This is easily seen when you enumerate through all the different vendors that provide component architecture solutions. Not to mention the number of component software vendors. Sun Microsystems stepped into the component arena with JavaBeans for at least three very good reasons.

The first is to let developers (and managers) know that Sun Microsystems is staying in touch with current events. The second is to provide a standard component architecture before any other company could step in and pull the rug out from under them. The third, but most important and most obvious is for the programmers. They wanted a way to do component software development in a platform-independent way, so Sun Microsystems gave them one. As you've read, as an initial cut it covered those three bases just fine. However, from a practical point of view, JavaBeans 1.0 has flaws.

JavaBeans Version 1.1

Code-named Glasgow, this is the second release of the JavaBeans component model specification. Its goal is to address the known limitations of the previous version of JavaBeans. In doing so, it tackles one major drawback to JavaBeans and knocks down a few others. This major drawback is JavaBeans' incapability of easily creating complex components. Moreover, to create them so that they merge with their runtime environment in a seamless fashion. To do this, Glasgow adds four new features to the JavaBeans component model:

- Runtime environment services
- Object delegation and aggregation model
- Data typing and object registry framework
- Drag-and-drop capabilities

RUNTIME ENVIRONMENT SERVICES   Also known as the Runtime Containment and Services Protocol, this feature allows a bean to acquire more information about its environment during runtime. Within Java-Beans 1.0, the only software entity the bean has access to is the core Java APIs. Being so constrained, it isn't unfathomable that beans might be duplicating functionality already on the system. The services protocol is designed to provide a standard means for beans to discover attributes and services that are within their runtime environment. On the same note, this mechanism allows the environment and containing bean to make its capabilities known to a particular bean. Figure 2-7 depicts this proposal.

As you can see, this addition greatly extends the power of beans. They are no longer limited to using only their own resources. By adding a Bean context, beans are now distributed along a hierarchy that can be traversed. That is, a bean can ask for the other beans within their own context, within the parent's context, or within a child's context. From there, it is just a matter of asking the bean what it can do! How you discover a bean's capabilities will be covered in later chapters.

OBJECT DELEGATION AND AGGREGATION MODEL   Glasgow's draft specification had an interesting solution to work around Java's lack of multiple inheritance. In essence, multiple inheritance allows an object

Figure 2-7
Bean containment
model.

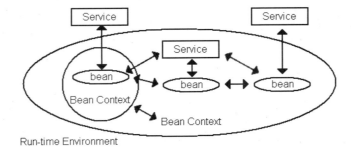

Figure 2-8
Object delegation
and aggregation
model.

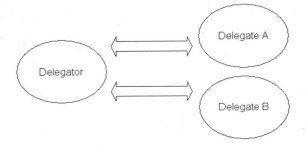

to behave similar to multiple objects, instead of just its superclass. Without adding the complexities to Java (in order to support true multiple inheritance), Glasgow defined a delegation and aggregation model.

The **Delegator** object in Figure 2-8 simulates multiple inheritance by redirecting calls it receives and does not implement, over to the appropriate delegate. Objects wanting to use the **Delegator** object can verify that it is an instance of either Delegate A or Delegate B. This is done using the public method **boolean isInstanceOf** (Class **delegateInterface**). If the method returns True, the objects can safely assume the **Delegator** object behaves like a regular subclass of the given **delegateInterface**. In the case of Figure 2-8, this method would return true for either class **Delegate A** or class **Delegate B**. However, since its proposal, the implementation of this model has been deferred until a future release of JavaBeans. The reason behind the deferral stems from the term "aggregation". The term implies that the proposed model solves many problems that it does not address nor should it. As such, Glasgow will not have a multiple inheritance mechanism.

DATA TYPING AND OBJECT REGISTRY FRAMEWORK   One factor missing from JavaBeans, as it is from Java, is the ability to give data a standard type identifier. For example, files on DOS-based machines have a three-character file name extension. If the filename ends with .EXE, the operating system knows that it is an executable file. One reason why the filename extension metaphor cannot be used in this scenario is that filename extensions are not supported across all operating systems. Audio streams, video streams, pictures, and other types of data need a mechanism by which they can be identified. The bean can query the data's type, via a registry of known types, and then perform the appropriate action if it knows how to handle the data.

DRAG-AND-DROP CAPABILITIES Clearly, being able to drag an item from one bean to another is an essential proponent of user interfaces. Glasgow taps into the platform-dependent facilities for doing drag-and-drop, exposing a common interface to all JavaBeans (thus maintaining cross-platform compatibility). To transfer information from bean to bean, the existing "java.awt.datatransfer" package is used. This then, shows another example of the coupling that exists between JavaBeans and Java.

Java strives to be 100-percent platform independent. At the same time, Sun Microsystems wants to make Java an integral part of existing operating system platforms. To get closer to a seamless integration between the Java Virtual Machine and the operating system itself, drag-and-drop capabilities must interoperate with native software applications. There are a few problems that remain to be tackled. One problem is how to transfer data in a standard way from Java to a native application. The native drag-and-drop capabilities use their own proprietary-information exchange techniques, which poses a relatively large stumbling block. A smaller problem is conforming to the native drag-and-drop gestures: that is, how the mouse cursor looks when a drag is initiated, when over a non-drop target, and over a valid drop target.

JavaBeans Version 1.2

At the time of writing, Sun Microsystems was supposed to release the specification for the next version of JavaBeans. However, the public release of the specification has been postponed to the first quarter of 1998. It will be code-named Edinburgh.

Enterprise JavaBeans

The purpose behind Enterprise JavaBeans is to ease the creation of scaleable business applications using Java-based technologies. By

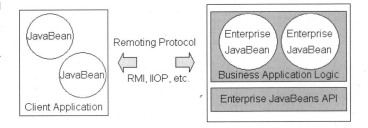

Figure 2-9
Enterprise JavaBeans
model.

scaleable it is meant that the application should easily grow, and change (as different needs arise). JavaBeans, by itself, is intended to focus on client-side GUI-driven applications. These include spreadsheets, word processors, e-mail packages, and such. JavaBeans Enterprise, however, is geared towards business logic on the server.

In Figure 2-9, the roles of the different types of beans are clearly defined. Regular JavaBeans reside on the client machine. They provide the view into the information model built by the Enterprise JavaBeans. The protocol used for connecting the two types of beans is undefined. Different factors will play a role in deciding which protocol performs the best with respect to a given application's functionality. As you can see, Enterprise JavaBeans adds another distinct entity to the different portions of an application. One advantage to Enterprise JavaBeans is that now software developers can focus their time in specific areas of development, as shown in Figure 2-9. With this extra layer of data abstraction, reuse is also augmented. Different application views (shown on the left side of the figure) can use the technologies present on the Business Application Logic side.

Enterprise JavaBeans is most useful for building financial, payroll, and inventory management applications. In essence, applications that must communicate with databases make good subjects for Enterprise Java-Beans. They shield the client applications from the complex details of database transactions. Other examples that fit the Enterprise JavaBeans application model include generic server-side software. A HyperText Transport Protocol (HTTP) server fits the role of Enterprise JavaBeans. Similarly, a high-score server for games also fits this role.

AWT 1.1 Versus AWT 1.2

It should be clear to you that JavaBeans was initially designed with the idea that most beans would have a GUI attached. Immediately, this created a need for a mechanism by which beans could display themselves to users.

The mechanism used came about in the form of the Abstract Window Toolkit (AWT). In other words, Java programs that have a GUI use the standard AWT APIs. As an initial cut at the specification, AWT 1.0 allows developers to write simple applets with quick and dirty user-interface features. However, the AWT 1.0 used the lowest common denominator widgets. For example, if the text area input field did not exist on one of the major operating system platforms (X-Windows, Windows, Solaris, OS/2, MacOS, etc.), it was not included as part of the standard API.

For building increasingly complex programs, a larger suite of widgets is required. To ensure that all widgets perform the same on all operating systems, emulation may be required. AWT version 1.1 expanded on version AWT 1.0. An improved event model to trap widget events was added. Consequently, more events were added to the AWT API. The shift from AWT 1.0 to AWT 1.1 allowed the creation of more robust user interfaces. It also augmented the functionality that a bean could encompass. This was due, in part, to the event models of beans and the AWT being similar. However, like most new technologies, there is always room for improvement.

AWT 1.2 has been coined the Java Foundation Classes (JFC). "Exciting changes" is the phrase used by Sun Microsystems to describe their plans for this next revision of the AWT. Also in their plans are major architectural enhancements. Judging from past history, this may mean that any applications that use JFC may not work on browsers that only support AWT 1.1 features. What remains to be seen is whether AWT 1.1 compliant applications will run (without modification) under JFC-compliant Web browsers, just as AWT 1.0 compliant applications can still run under AWT 1.1 compliant Web browsers—for the time being. The following sections show some of the plans Sun Microsystems has for the future.

- Look-and-feel: a person that has worked with a Macintosh for years may become uncomfortable when asked to use a computer running Microsoft Windows. AWT 1.0 was developed so that it used the native look-and-feel to match the executing operating system. However, according to Sun Microsystems, there are plenty of developers that would like to have the same look-and-feel to their programs across all platforms. Thus, a person familiar with how a Macintosh operates can use the same Java application on a Microsoft Windows-based computer—with a minimal learning curve.

- Drag and drop: transferring arbitrary data between two components via the drag-and-drop metaphor is not only an expected feature but is quickly becoming an essential feature. Essential in that, when used properly, it can greatly improve a person's work efficiency. As such, a data transfer mechanism has been designed. The mechanism will allow the transfer of arbitrary data between components as well as between components and the system's clipboard.

■ Two-dimensional rendering: AWT 1.2 has added support for arbitrary transformations. Some transformations supplied by this package include rotating an object, scaling it, and translations. The package is designed to ensure that renderings are done in a resolution-independent manner. This leads to the support of different presentation devices (such as printers and video displays).

In addition to extending the graphical portions of the AWT, the textual portions will also receive a facelift. Included in the enhancements for text are

■ Advanced text layout

■ Antialiased text rendering

■ Extended font support

The advanced text layout covers the more common types of strings that would normally be displayed, strings where font changes occur, with different languages (and hence character sets), and even aligned in multiple directions (horizontally, vertically, etc.). Antialiasing is a technique used to smooth the edges of something. When used against text, antialiasing produces a softer, more professional look—text that looks printed, as opposed to computerized. Extended font support adds many new controls for displaying text. The new controls include rotating text, writing multicolored characters, and more.

■ Other AWT 1.2 Enhancements: the additions to the AWT 1.2 are substantial and mostly useful. The two-dimensional rendering adds a lot of weight to the new AWT. That weight is distributed mostly over the new graphics rendering capabilities (Bezier paths, arbitrary fill styles, transparency, etc.). The remainder of the two-dimensional rendering package defines the superior text controls, improved image handling, and better color management.

Limitations of Beans Today

As you can see, JavaBeans helps ease component software development a great deal. However, there are some limitations that JavaBeans still needs to overcome. Creating medium-and large-sized applications using Java-Beans 1.0 is not entirely feasible. JavaBeans provides a simple, uniform way to develop and integrate components. Currently, it is more suited for making small GUI components. This section describes some of the problems with JavaBeans 1.0, as well as problems with JavaBeans 1.1.

The Java Virtual Machine

Beans execute within a Java Virtual Machine. As such, they only know of the VM. Any other system services not explicitly defined by the VM are hidden from the bean. This creates two problems. The first is duplication, the second is resource inefficiency. Although closely related, they do have a subtle difference. You can think of duplication as one of the reasons for the resource inefficiency.

DUPLICATION Previously, we mentioned in the 1.0 specification of JavaBeans that beans have no way of knowing what resources are available to them. A bean may require a certain service that the operating system has available. However, because the bean can only see what the VM shows it, that service will go unnoticed and hence unused by the bean. This means, in turn that the bean must duplicate that service's functionality within itself.

RESOURCE INEFFICIENCY Having two pieces of code on the same computer performing the same task is a waste. The resources that are available to the bean are underused. Furthermore, a native operating system service typically, completes its task much faster than would the same service constructed in Java. For example, every robust operating system comes with a print spooler. As such, if a spooler exists on the system, there should be no need to use a Java-based print spooler. If we know that a spooler does not exist, an applet may then download a print spooler component to use, which is obviously the less efficient way to go.

Single Inheritance

Only single inheritance is supported in JavaBeans and Java. This limits the complexity that can be achieved in designing an object-oriented application. This tends to be a battle in the world of computer science akin to some religious disagreements. Some people believe that multiple inheritance is an essential feature to object-oriented languages. Others believe that multiple inheritance is seldom used properly, thus adding confusion to the source code.

An upside to multiple inheritance is that it allows the real world to be modeled more accurately. The Australian platypus, for example, is a mammal and an animal that lays eggs. It should be apparent that mammals exhibit certain behavior and animals that lay eggs have particular behavior. In Java, you would have to subclass from mammal (getting all the behavior associated with mammals) and then implement the egg-laying interface. This is bad because you do not get to reuse any of the code that egg-laying animals use. A downside to multiple inheritance is that hierarchies can quickly become difficult to understand. If done improperly, multiple inheritance hierarchies become a nightmare to maintain. Human family trees are simple to follow because the hierarchy, typically, increases in factors of two. Nothing stops programmers from developing objects whose roots are founded by many different parents. Another reason is that it increases the complexity of compilers for the language.

Sun Microsystems decided it was easiest not to deal with multiple inheritance. The result is that Java language does not support multiple inheritance. Consequently, there is no way to directly insert multiple inheritance behavior into JavaBeans. Glasgow had a means to do multiple inheritance via aggregation and delegation, but Sun Microsystems has since removed that aspect from the JavaBeans 1.1 specification.

Data-Type Associations

JavaBeans has no way to associate a particular type of data with a specific bean. A video bean, for example, may have the capability of taking an incoming video stream and previewing it. However, when the browser happens on a video stream, it has no way of finding the video stream bean. Ideally, the beans should be able to describe their behavior in a standard fashion.

Dynamic Data Exchange

Dynamic exchange of information between beans is severely limited. For example, dynamically exchanging the information a person typed within a text field over to a search engine bean is not possible in the 1.0 specification of JavaBeans. Using two objects, the task is trivial. You merely pass the text string as a parameter to a method on the receiving object. Using two arbitrary beans, however, the task becomes more difficult. Because the beans may not know about each other, a uniform way is needed to pass information back and forth, without knowing particular interface specifications.

JavaBeans Evolution

Although these limitations can be detrimental to a project, it is important to remember that the JavaBeans specification is evolving. Throughout its evolution, the limitations JavaBeans faces will eventually disappear. This should be apparent by the new features listed in Glasgow. However, as promised, we will describe some of the limitations present in Glasgow. Once again, Sun Microsystems already has plans for the future Edinburgh, as it is code named, version of JavaBeans. As Glasgow solved some of the problems present in JavaBeans 1.0, Edinburgh should solve some of the problems that Glasgow faces.

Limitations of JavaBeans 1.1

You, no doubt, are well aware that there are software (and hardware) limitations imposed on any new computer-related item that shows up in the industry. Glasgow is not an exception. The next few sections cover a couple of the direct limitations of Glasgow, as well as delving into some of the universal challenges that Glasgow must meet. The universal problems can be thought of as implicitly imposed limitations of Glasgow simply because it is a software entity.

Software Evolution

One aspect of dealing with new technology that is simultaneously frustrating and invigorating is the fact that it is always changing. Frustrating because we are limited to, even dependent on, the schedules of other people. For many projects this is not only bad but can be detrimental to a project's success. For example, if a solution to your JavaBeans-based project uses multiple inheritance, waiting for multiple inheritance to become part of the JavaBeans specification may kill your project. Alternatively, implementing your own proprietary workaround may consume too much time and hence kill your project. It is these sort of "waiting games" that aren't inherent limits of the technology but wind up limiting your project's scope. It is invigorating because we strive to keep on top of the latest and greatest technologies that become available. And we do so to stay in step with the other companies who also thrive on pushing the threshold of technology.

Multiple Inheritance

A concrete limitation to JavaBeans 1.1 is the lack of multiple inheritance. There are many cases where the behavior of an object depends on the behavior, or is related to the behavior, of two other classes. The platypus example showed how this can be the case when you try to model reality. However, as we have mentioned, Sun Microsystems does have plans to include some form of multiple inheritance in a future version of JavaBeans. As discussed, the evolutionary limits are imposed; we will just have to wait.

End-User Support

Although JavaBeans is designed to let end-users have much more control over their application, the means by which they can do so is still slightly convoluted. What the end-user typically sees is a list of method names for components that adhere to a quasi-standard naming scheme. Along with the method names comes a description of what the methods actually do. Although it will let some end-users alter application behavior, it is still very close to actual programming for general end-users to follow. This is not a dig on the intelligence of end-users, but rather an understanding of how much time they want to spend learning and modifying an application as opposed to actually using it.

Commercial Beans

Before an explosion of easy-to-use software packages can hit the market, there must be many easy-to-use components available to programmers. At the time of writing, only a few companies have produced commercially available beans. This in turn implies a shortage of varied functionality. For general, mundane, everyday tasks, you could look and find yourself a bean that can do the job. For the more specifically tailored applications, the diversification of beans has not happened. As such, JavaBeans has the promise of being a fast emerging technology. At the same time, this is both a problem and an opportunity. The problem, obviously, is that there aren't enough beans to perform many of the necessary tasks for custom applications. The opportunity is the niche markets that will abound. Plenty of beans need to be built, which means plenty of sales will, inevitably, be made.

JavaBeans 1.1 Adoption and Support

If the project you are working on is going to take a lot of time, the rest of this section probably does not apply to you. Anything over a year in the Internet-related software industry fits the term "a lot of time." The install base of Java Virtual Machines that must be able to execute code written to the JavaBeans (or Java) 1.1 specification must be significant before you can expect a large return on software developed to that specification. This can be anything from Web browsers to Java development kits to operating system ports of Sun's Java Virtual Machine.

This is a limitation that applies equally to Java applets as it does to beans contained within applets. As new versions of Java (and JavaBeans) make an appearance, target customers fall further behind what is currently available. This happens for a number of reasons, one of the more likely is the adage, "If it ain't broke, don't fix it." The saying means that if something is working, and it does what you want it to, why fiddle with something on the off chance that it might be better? There are companies that have neither the time nor the resources to keep everybody's desktop computer up to the status quo. It boils down to this: when you write your beans, be sure you know what your target market is going to be. Obviously if you write beans using the older technology, you reach the greatest target audience. However, if your beans will take a while to design, implement, and test, by all means write toward the future.

CONCLUSION

In this chapter, we have shown how the JavaBeans component architecture is tightly integrated with development tools. Also, we have described the means by which the GUI can persist across sessions, thanks to the layout control services. Lastly, it should be made clear that there is a split between what a bean's role is and what functionality the JavaBeans component architecture provides. Keeping the provisions of the JavaBeans architecture in mind, all beans have the following abilities:

- Can be an application
- Can be a component used by an application
- Has a public interface (methods)
- Has behavior and properties (behavior)
- Can notify others of internal changes via events (event notification)
- Internal state can be saved across sessions (persistence)

There are a few more aspects of JavaBeans we'd like to stress here: how simple JavaBeans is meant to be for end-users, the coupling Java and JavaBeans share, and where distributed computing will play a part. The simplicity of JavaBeans is the first aspect to keep in mind. It is hoped that by building a simple software development framework, the doors of application construction will open to a much larger audience. The idea of having end-users being able to "program" their own applications is, in some ways, a utopian goal. Whether this goal is reached only time will tell.

Having a tight coupling between the Java language and JavaBeans is not so much as a goal as an unavoidable convenience. Platform independence should be thought of more concretely as component architecture interoperability. This is another logical extension to Java's founding goals. We can only hope that the pair are well matched, for if the Java language gets split (as have FORTRAN, Smalltalk, Pascal, and so forth) into different flavors, the effects will be quite detrimental to JavaBeans.

Distributed computing will play a crucial role in the future of components. Distribution of components will be used for the purposes of computing power, combined with convenience. It should be noted that the lack of a standard distribution mechanism for JavaBeans might prove to be a more of a setback than liberation. If JavaBeans is to be simple enough so that it appeals to a large audience, there is a need for a plug-and-play distribution technology.

Finally, JavaBeans is a rapidly emerging technology. New features, architectural improvements, and the changing needs of software developers will define the shape of JavaBeans in the future. The best way to stay on top of the swift changes is to frequent several essential Java-related homepages. These include:

- JavaSoft at `http://www.javasoft.com`
- JavaWorld at `http://www.javaworld.com`
- Netscape at `http://www.netscape.com`
- Cup O' Joe at `http://www.cupojoe.com/`
- Net News Central at `http://www.javaworld.com/javaworld/netnews/netnews.index.html`

Your First JavaBean 1.0 Component

Now that you've learned about the features of JavaBeans, it's time to start applying them. This chapter will go over the features of the Beans Development Kit and how to develop your own beans. Note that this chapter will touch on some JavaBeans features that you will learn more about in Chapters 4, 5, and 6.

If you haven't already downloaded the Java Development Kit (JDK) and the Beans Development Kit, now is the time to do so. These are both available from the Java-Soft web site at **http://www.javasoft.com/** and on the CD-ROM included with this book.

This Chapter Covers

- Using the Beans Development Kit.
- Manipulating beans and creating applets.
- Creating and packaging a simple bean that performs marquee-like scrolling.
- Properties and events.
- Customizing beans.
- Serialization.

The Beans Development Kit (BDK)

It is not actually necessary to download the BDK to start developing Java-Beans, because the classes and tools necessary for beans development are included with JDK1.1. The BDK is a just a collection of sample code, documentation, and software that makes beans development easier. The primary feature of the BDK is the testbed for your beans, the BeanBox.

The BeanBox

The BeanBox is a simple Java application that will enable you to test your beans in their native environment. With the BeanBox you can:

- Drag and drop beans onto the customization window
- Edit and customize beans
- Connect beans through event handlers
- Connect bound properties on different beans
- Save and restore sets of beans
- Get an introspection report on a bean
- Add new beans from JAR files

Although it is possible to create applets using the BeanBox, it is not meant to be an application development tool. It is only a testing environment—like a playground where your beans will take their first steps.

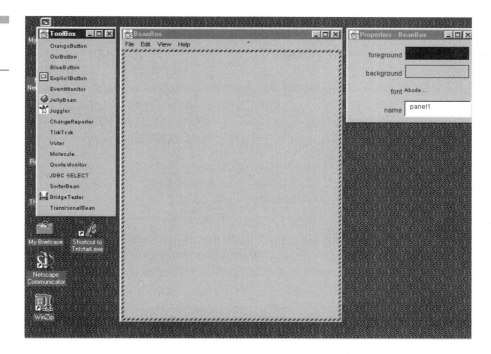

Figure 3-1
The BeanBox in action.

Using the BeanBox

Launch the BeanBox using the batch script provided in the BDK. These examples are for the Windows platform; however their UNIX counterparts are very similar.

```
C:\> cd BDK\beanbox
C:\BDK\beanbox> run
```

The BeanBox starts, loading the example beans as it does. You should now be looking at the three windows that make up the BeanBox: The BeanBox, the ToolBox, and the PropertySheet windows. (Figure 3-1)

The ToolBox window contains all the beans currently configured for use with the BDK. The main BeanBox window is the area where we place these beans and set up their interactions. You can choose a bean from the ToolBox and click in the BeanBox to place it for use. Beans can be moved around, and some can be resized once they have been dropped in the BeanBox.

As beans are selected, the PropertySheet window updates itself to show the properties of the currently selected bean. If you have ever had experience using Visual development environments, such as Delphi or Visual Café, you will be familiar with the property sheets.

Manipulating Beans

To get a better understanding of how developing software with the Bean-Box works, we will create a small applet.

1. The first step is to restart the BDK so that we are dealing with a fresh window. Alternatively, File->Clear can be used to remove any components.

2. Select Juggler from the toolbox and place it on the main window.

3. Select a button from the Toolbox and place it on the window, below and to the left of the Juggler. Repeat this last step with another button, but place it to the lower right of the Juggler.

4. Select one of the buttons and change the label to Stop, using the properties window. Repeat this step with the other button, changing the label to Start. The BeanBox should now look like Figure 3-2.

Figure 3-2
The BeanBox with Juggler and two buttons.

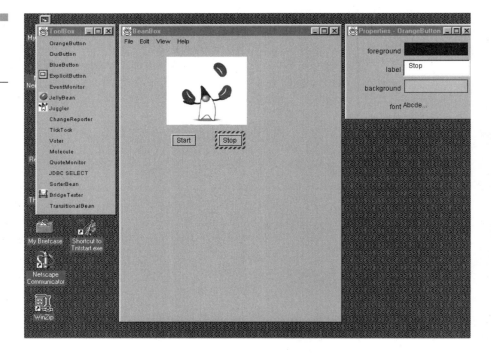

5. This step links these buttons and enables our buttons. Click the button labeled Stop and choose Edit->Events->button push->actionPerformed. There will now be a red line that is "stuck" to the mouse pointer. Point this line to the Juggler and click it. The EventTargetDialog window should pop up with a list of methods the Juggler supports. Choose stopJuggling and click OK. The **button pushed** event of the stop button is now linked to the **stopJuggling** method of the Juggler. If the Stop button is clicked, the juggler should stop juggling. Repeat this step for the Start button, except link the **button pushed** event to the **startJuggling** method.

We have now created a simple application without writing any code. We can even automatically convert these beans into an applet if we desire.

Creating an Applet from the BeanBox

The BeanBox has built-in support for creating applets. The applet it creates will be the same size as the BeanBox window; by resizing the BeanBox window the applet won't be as big. To create an applet, choose File->MakeApplet... A dialog box appears, asking where to save the applet. Choose OK to accept the default settings. The BeanBox now compiles and creates the support files necessary for the applet.

Testing the Applet

Let's open another command-line window and change to the directory of the newly created applet.

```
C:\BDK\beanbox> cd tmp\myApplet
```

The BeanBox will also have created a readme file, called **myApplet_readme**, which contains useful information about the applet we have just created. To view the applet, either Internet Explorer 4.0 or Netscape 4.0 (you will need the JDK 1.1 update for Netscape, available at **http://developer.netscape.com/**) can be used. For most situations, the appletviewer that ships with the JDK is sufficient (see Figure 3-3). To view the applet using the JDK1.1 appletviewer, type

```
C;\BDK\beanbox\tmp\myApplet> appletviewer myApplet.html
```

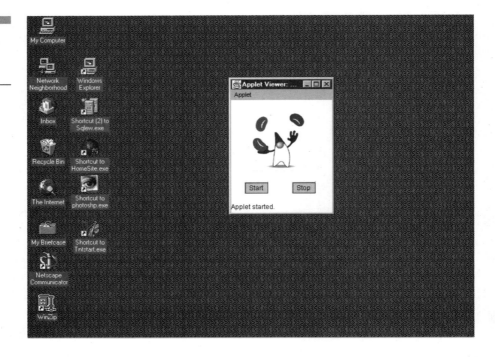

Loading JARs into the BeanBox

In the directory created by the BeanBox (**tmp/myApplet/**), the majority of the files saved have the suffix of .jar. This is short for Java ARchive, and these files are a compressed collection of files, similar to ZIP files. We will go over JAR files later, but it is important to know that beans are typically packaged inside JAR files.

When the BeanBox created the applet, it packaged it in a JAR file. Interestingly, it not only created it as an applet but also as a bean. If we go back to the BeanBox, there is an item under the File menu called Load-Jar... Choose this menu and when the file selector appears, find the JAR file corresponding to the applet we created earlier (myApplet.jar). The BeanBox loads the JAR file and adds it to the toolbox. We can now select our myApplet bean from the toolbox and add it to the BeanBox.

This is an example of how powerful component development can be. We can build larger beans out of smaller ones and save them in a software library for future use. Component development can save a large amount of development time by leveraging existing code for use in new projects.

We are now ready to dive in and start creating our own beans.

Tutorial: Creating a Bean

Our first bean will be a simple one, meant to demonstrate the steps involved in creating JavaBeans. This section will go over the steps in creating a simple bean that enables us to add marquee-like scrolling to our applications.

Let's take a look at the code in Listing 3-1.

Listing 3-1
Say hello to JavaBean.

```
import java.awt.event.*;
import java.awt.Graphics;
import java.awt.*;

public class TextScrollBean extends Panel implements
    Runnable {

    String text = null;            // Our scrolling string
    Thread kicker = null;          // The thread that keeps
                                      things moving
    int speed=10;                  // The speed of the
                                      marquee
    int x = 0;                     // The initial x
                                      position of the
                                      text
    int y = 30;                    // The y position of
                                      the text
    int stringwidth;               // The width of our
                                      string
    int width = 250;               // The width of our
                                      panel
    int height = 50;               // The height of our
                                      panel
    FontMetrics fm;                // Used to calculate the
                                      string length

    public TextScrollBean() {
        // Define our string and set the font.
        text = "Beans make components easy";
        setFont(new Font("TimesRoman",Font.BOLD,36));
        // Start the thread animating
        start();
    }

    public Dimension getPreferredSize() {
        return (new Dimension(width, height));
    }
```

Continues

Listing 3-1
Concluded.

```java
    public void start() {
        // Start our thread
        if (kicker == null) {
                    kicker = new Thread(this);
                    kicker.start();
        }
    }

    public void stop() {
        //Stop our thread
        kicker = null;
    }

    public void run() {
        // This method orchestrates the scrolling text
        // While the thread runs, it repaints the
        // string in a new
        // position each time
        while (kicker != null) {
                try {
                        Thread.sleep(speed);
                } catch (InterruptedException e) {
                        e.printStackTrace();
                }
                repaint();
        }
        kicker = null;
    }

    public void paint(Graphics g) {
        // Calculate the width of our string
        fm = g.getFontMetrics();
        stringwidth = fm.stringWidth(text);

        // Draw the string in the correct position
        g.drawString(text, x, y);
        // Calculate the next position of the string
        if (x <= (-stringwidth)) {
                x=width;
        } else {
                x-;
        }
    }

}
```

Create and save this into a file called **TextScrollBean.java** and compile it using javac.

```
C:\beans\TextScroll> javac TextScrollBean.java
```

At this stage, the question may arise, "How is this different from any other Java program?" Beans development isn't any different from normal Java development; the only requirement is that we include a set of methods that allows beans-enabled environments to access the features of our code. This code doesn't look very unusual; the only unconventional method is `getPreferredSize()`.

```
public Dimension getPreferredSize() {
        return (new Dimension(width, height));
}
```

This method tells the BeanBox what size to display our bean after we have placed it in the BeanBox. We go over specialized bean methods shortly.

Converting Code into a Bean

Although this code has the necessary functionality, it is not yet a bean. Beans must be packaged into JAR files, using the jar utility. This utility is similar to the **tar** command on UNIX systems.

MANIFEST FILES Manifest files store information about the classes stored within the bean. If we were developing a bean with several support classes, we would define the primary bean within the manifest file. For our example, the manifest file is quite simple. Create a file called **manifest.txt** and type the following information:

```
Manifest-Version: 1.0

Name: TextScrollBean.class
Java-Bean: True
```

The first line indicates which version of the manifest specification we are following. If more information is required about this specification, it is available online at **http://java.sun.com/products/jdk/1.1/docs/guide/jar/manifest.html**. The next line gives the name of our class, and the last line tells any software that is interested that it is indeed a bean.

Now we are ready to create our JAR file. Invoke the **jar** command in the following manner:

```
C:\beans\TextScroll> jar cfm TextScrollBean.jar
        manifest.txt TextScrollBean.class
```

This will create a jar file with the name **TextScrollBean.jar**, a manifest file called **manifest.txt**, containing one class, **TextScrollBean.class**. Note

Figure 3-4
TextScrollBean
inside the BeanBox.

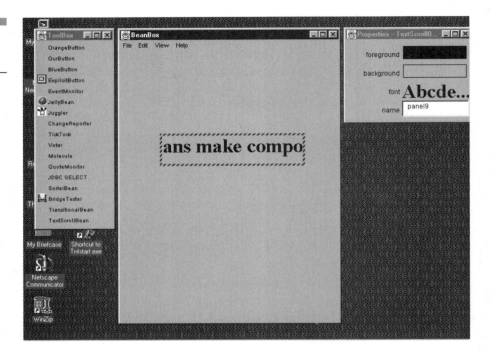

that we could name the manifest file anything we like; the JAR file will store it internally using its own name.

We have now packaged our code in a JAR file, making it into a full-fledged bean. To test it out, fire up the BeanBox, and load the JAR file using File->LoadJar... The bean should now show up on the ToolBox; if it doesn't, check for errors at the command-line window where we launched the BeanBox.

If the bean loaded correctly, choose it from the ToolBox and place it on the BeanBox. The screen should now look similar to Figure 3-4.

Try selecting the bean and adjusting some of its properties. We can change the background and text color, size, and font by manipulating the properties. The BeanBox has used reflection to find out our applets capabilities.

Properties

Properties are characteristics, or attributes, of our beans that are publicly available. There are four main types of properties: simple, indexed, bound, and constrained. Some properties can be combined, for example, constrained properties should also be bound properties. Properties can be read-only, write-only, or read/write.

Simple Properties

Simple properties typically refer to public variables within an object, but they are not restricted to this. Simple properties represent a single value and are defined and retrieved with the combination of **get** and **set** methods. For example, if we wanted to add the capability of changing the string in our **TextScrollBean**, we could create a **getTextString** method that would return the current value of the string, and a **setTextString** method to change the value. If the property we were accessing was boolean, we would use **isPropertyName** in place of **getPropertyName**. When the BeanBox introspects the **TextScrollBean**, it will find these two methods and know that **string** is a property that can be changed.

Add the following two methods after the **getPreferredSize** method to the code for **TextScrollBean.java**:

```
public String getTextString() {
      return text;
}

public String setTextString(String newtext) {
      text = newtext;
}
```

Compile, JAR, and load the bean into the BeanBox. There should now be an new property on the PropertySheet, called **textString** (Figure 3-5). Try changing this string to see how it affects the **TextScrollBean**.

Indexed Properties

Indexed properties are similar to the simple properties, but rather than getting and setting single properties, indexed properties represent arrays of values. In the BDK1.0, the BeanBox does not support indexed properties. Typically, indexed properties have methods that support getting and setting the entire array of values, as well as methods to get and set individual elements of the array.

Bound Properties

A bound property is one that notifies other objects when this property's value changes. bound properties are useful when we have a property whose value we would like to be automatically propagated to another property or to another bean. For example, if we were developing a bean

Figure 3-5
Adjusting the
textString
property.

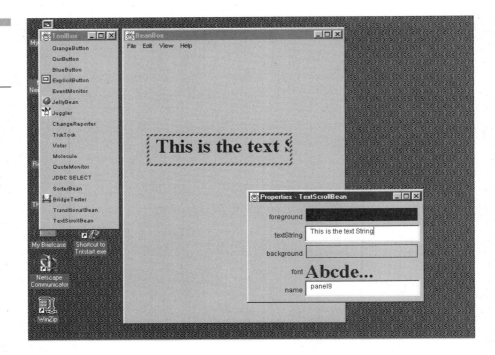

that is a slider control, we would want changes made to that slider to be sent to another bean that will act on those changes.

Bound properties require the addition of a property change object to our bean, methods to add and remove bound property listeners, and finally the change event listener to the property we wish to monitor.

In Listing 3-2, we have added a bound property that changes the speed of the animation of the scrolling text.

Listing 3-2
Adding a bound
property.

```java
import java.awt.event.*;
import java.awt.Graphics;
import java.awt.*;
import java.beans.*;

public class TextScrollBean extends Panel implements
     Runnable {

     String text = null;
     Thread kicker = null;
     int speed=10;
     int x = 0;
     int y = 30;
```

Listing 3-2

```java
    int stringwidth;
    int width = 250;
    int height = 50;
    FontMetrics fm;
    // Offscreen graphics context and image to implement
    // double buffering
    Image offscreen;
    Graphics goffscreen;
    // Declare and instantiate a PropertyChange object
    private PropertyChangeSupport changes =
            new PropertyChangeSupport(this);

    public TextScrollBean() {
            text = "Beans make components easy";
            setFont(new Font("TimesRoman",Font.BOLD,36));

            start();
    }


    public Dimension getPreferredSize() {
            return (new Dimension(width, height));
    }

    public String getTextString() {
            return text;
    }

    public void setTextString(String newtext) {
            text = newtext;
    }

    public int getSpeed() {
            return speed;
    }

    public void setSpeed(int newSpeed) {
            // Send change event to listeners when
            // speed is changed
            changes.firePropertyChange("Speed", "" +
            speed, "" + newSpeed);
            speed = newSpeed;
    }

    // Add a listener.  This will get called by the
    // BeanBox
    public void
    addPropertyChangeListener(PropertyChangeListener l) {
       changes.addPropertyChangeListener(l);
    }
    // Remove a listener.  This will get called by the
```

Continues

Listing 3-2
Continued.

```
// BeanBox
public void
      removePropertyChangeListener
      (PropertyChangeListener 1) {
            changes.removePropertyChangeListener(l);
}

public void start() {
      if(kicker == null) {
            kicker = new Thread(this);
            kicker.start();
      }
}

public void stop() {
      kicker = null;
}

public void run() {
      while (kicker != null) {
            try {
                  Thread.sleep(speed);
            } catch (InterruptedException e) {
                  e.printStackTrace();
            }
            repaint();
      }
kicker = null;
}

public void paint(Graphics g) {
      update(g);
}

public void update(Graphics g) {
      fm = g.getFontMetrics();
      stringwidth = fm.stringWidth(text);

      // Added double buffering to eliminate flashing
      // Create an offscreen graphics context
      if (goffscreen == null) {
            offscreen = createImage(width,height);
            goffscreen = offscreen.getGraphics();
      }
      // Paint to our offscreeen graphics context
      goffscreen.setColor(getBackground());
      goffscreen.fillRect(0,0,width,height);
      goffscreen.setColor(getForeground());
      goffscreen.drawString(text, x, y);


      // Paint our offscreen image to the screen
      g.drawImage(offscreen,0,0,this);
```

Listing 3-2

```
                    if (x <= (-stringwidth)) {
                         x=width;
                    } else {
                         x-;
                    }
               }
          }
```

We now have a new `PropertyChangeSupport` event that will allow us to fire events when the speed property is changed. The painting has been moved to the update method, and flashing has been eliminated by painting our text to an offscreen image, which is then painted to the screen. This technique is known as double buffering.

Let's jar this new class and load it in the BeanBox.

TIP: *To avoid typing in the* `jar` *command every time, we can create a batch file to automate this process. Create a file called* `jarme.bat` *and type the following information into it:*

```
jar cfm TextScrollBean.jar manifest.tmp
TextScrollBean.java
copy TextScrollBean.jar c:\BDK\jars
```

We can now type `jarme` *at the command line to archive the bean and copy it into the* `BDK\jars` *directory. All JAR files stored in this directory will be automatically loaded into the BeanBox when it starts.*

Now we add an instance of the `TextScrollBean` to the BeanBox and add a ChangeReporter bean to the BeanBox as well. Select the `TextScrollBean`, and choose Edit -> Events -> propertyChange -> propertyChange. Bind this event to the ChangeReporter bean. When the EventTargetDialog box pops up, choose reportChange. If the speed is changed in the properties box, it will report it to the ChangeReporter bean. (Figure 3-6)

Constrained Properties

Constrained properties, like bound properties, send out a notification when they have been changed. However, unlike bound properties, objects that are registered as listeners to a constrained property can veto a change. In general, constrained properties should also be bound properties.

Listing 3-3 contains code that changes the speed property into a constrained property.

Again, lets jar the **TextScrollBean** and open it in the BeanBox. If we look at the events for this bean, there is now a **vetoableChange** property (Figure 3-7).

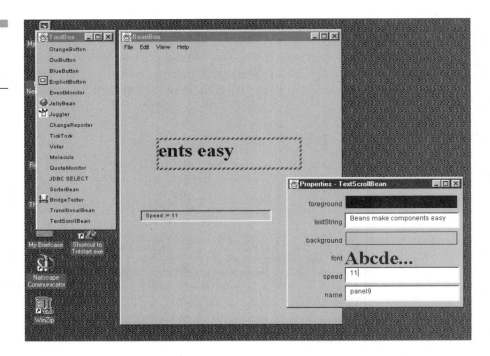

Figure 3-6
Bound properties interacting with the ChangeReporter.

Listing 3-3
Code to change the speed.

```
public class TextScrollBean extends Panel implements
    Runnable {
.......

    private PropertyChangeSupport changes =
        new PropertyChangeSupport(this);
    private VetoableChangeSupport vetos =
        new VetoableChangeSupport(this);

.......

    public void setSpeed(int newSpeed) throws
PropertyVetoException {
        // tell vetoers about the change
vetos.fireVetoableChange("Speed", "" + speed, ""    +
```

Listing 15-1.
A collection example.

```
        newSpeed);

                // Send change event to listeners when
                // speed is changed
changes.firePropertyChange("Speed", "" + speed, "" +
    newSpeed);
                speed = newSpeed;
    }


    // Add a veto listener.  This will get called by the
    // BeanBox
    public void
    addVetoableChangeListener(VetoableChangeListener l) {
        vetos.addVetoableChangeListener(l);
    }

    // Remove a veto listener.  This will get called by
    // the BeanBox
    public void removeVetoableChangeListener(
    VetoableChangeListener l) {
        vetos.removeVetoableChangeListener(l);
    }
```

Figure 3-7
TextScrollBean with a
vetoable change.

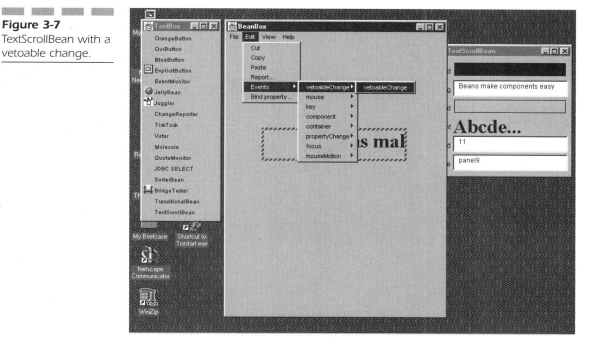

Events

In the first part of this chapter, we connected the **buttonPressed** event of a button to the **startJuggling** and **stopJuggling** events of the Juggler bean. In this section, we will go over how to add events to our code.

When adding event-handling code, it is important to keep in mind which kind of events that the bean should be handling. For the case of events such as **buttonPressed** and **menuSelect**, the **ActionListenerelect** events, it is **ActionEvents** that we should be looking for (see Listing 3-4).

Try adding Start and Stop buttons to the form, as we did in the first example, and link them to the **startScrolling** and **stopScrolling** methods. When the BeanBox links the buttons to the **TextScrollBean**, it scans for methods that accept the **buttonPushed** event, in this case, methods that accept **ActionEvent** (see Figure 3-8).

Customizing Beans—**BeanInfo**

The **BeanInfo** classes enable developers to have stronger control as to how a bean is presented. Inside the **BeanInfo** class, we can define properties, methods, events, and display names and help information for the user. When a bean is analyzed by the builder application, it first looks for the **BeanInfo** file of the bean. If a **BeanInfo** file does not exist, the builder application uses reflection to find basic information for the bean.

The naming convention used to identify the **BeanInfo** file is quite straightforward: if we have a bean called MyBean, the corresponding **BeanInfo** file would be **MyBeanBeanInfo.java**. The string "**BeanInfo**" is simply appended to the name of the bean. Note that if an explicit **BeanInfo** on a

Listing 3-4
Added code to start and stop our text scroller.

```
// This method can be used to connect a Button to
// the TextScrollBean.startScrolling method
public void startScrolling(ActionEvent ex) {
    kicker.resume();
}

// This method can be used to connect a Button to
// the TextScrollBean.stopScrolling method
public void stopScrolling(ActionEvent ex) {
    kicker.suspend();
}
```

class is not found, the builder application will use low-level reflection to study the methods of the class and apply standard design pattern matching to identify property accessors, event sources, or public methods.

The following is the **BeanInfo** file we generate for our sample bean. We have exported the properties and events we want users to see. The file is **TextScrollBeanBeanInfo.java** (Listing 3-5). Note that we extend the **SimpleBeanInfo** class rather than the more elaborate **BeanInfo** class. We go over the **BeanInfo** class in later chapters.

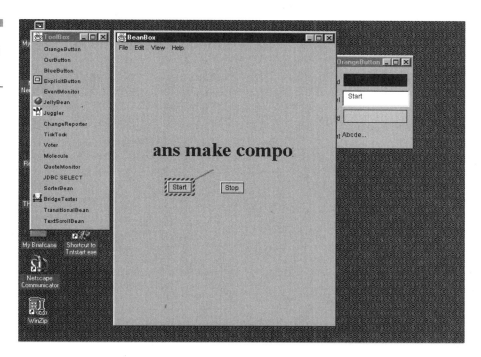

Figure 3-8
Wiring start and stop events to the **TextScrollBean**.

Listing 3-5
TextScrollBeanBeanInfo.java.

```
import java.beans.*;
import java.lang.reflect.*;
import java.awt.*;

public class TextScrollBeanBeanInfo extends SimpleBeanInfo {
    // Define our beanClass that we are working with
    private final static Class beanClass =
    TextScrollBean.class;

    // This method returns standard information about
    // our Bean
```
Continues

Listing 15-1.
Continued.

```
// Currently it is changing the name to Text
// Scroller
public BeanDescriptor getBeanDescriptor() {
        BeanDescriptor bd = new
        BeanDescriptor(beanClass);
        bd.setDisplayName("Text Scroller");
            return bd;
    }


// This method returns the icon to be used in the
// BeanBox.

// Normally we would check for which size of the
// Image we're looking for, but we only have one
// icon

public Image getIcon(int iconKind) {
        return loadImage("TextScroll.gif");
    }


// This method changes the Property Editor to only
// display the properties we want it to.
public PropertyDescriptor[] getPropertyDescriptors() {
        try {
                PropertyDescriptor speedPD =
                    new PropertyDescriptor("speed",
                    beanClass);
                PropertyDescriptor textStringPD =
                    new PropertyDescriptor("textString",
                    beanClass);
                PropertyDescriptor fontStringPD =
                    new PropertyDescriptor("font",
                    beanClass);
                PropertyDescriptor pdArray[] = {
                        speedPD,textStringPD,
                        fontStringPD };

                        return pdArray;
        } catch (IntrospectionException ex) {
                throw new Error(ex.toString());
        }
    }

}
```

Through the use of the **BeanInfo** class, we were able to change several elements of our bean, namely the title, the icon, and the property sheet (Figure 3-9).

Figure 3-9
Use of **BeanInfo**
Class.

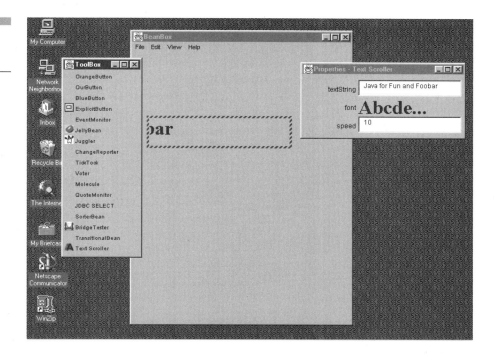

After we created the **BeanInfo** class, the **manifest.txt** will need to be modified as well. It should contain the following information:

```
Manifest-Version: 1.0

Name: TextScrollBean.class
Java-Bean: True

Name: TextScrollBeanBeanInfo.class
```

Note the addition of the **BeanInfo** file. Remember to add the **BeanInfo** file and the GIF file when compressing the files using **jar**.

```
jar cfm TextScrollBean.jar manifest.txt TextScrollBean.class
    TextScrollBeanInfo.class TextScroll.gif
```

The first method, **getBeanDescriptor**, enables us to customize the name of the bean in the BeanBox. In the next method, **getIcon**, we added a small 16×16 pixel icon which shows up in the toolbox. The path to this image is relative to our classes. The final method, **getPropertyDescriptors**, customizes the property sheet so that it only displays three properties: **speed**, **textString**, and **font**. We'll learn more about customizing property sheets using customizers in Chapter 6.

Persistence

The final step in the creation of our bean is to make it persistent. Persistence allows us to save the modified state of the bean, so that it can be restored at a later time. If we were to try creating an applet from our bean in its current state, an error would be thrown because our bean cannot be serialized. To make our applet serializable, there are a couple of items we need to add. To function as a well written bean it should implement the **java.io.Serializable** interface.

```
public class TextScrollBean extends Panel implements
    Runnable,
        java.io.Serializable {
```

This will allow the BeanBox that it can serialize our bean. However, not all objects can be serializable. In our case, **Thread**, **Image**, and **Graphics** cannot be serialized. In JDK1.1 the keyword **transient** indicates that these objects should not be serialized.

By making the following changes we can save the state of our bean in an applet. (Figure 3-10)

Figure 3-10
TextScrollBean
running as an applet.

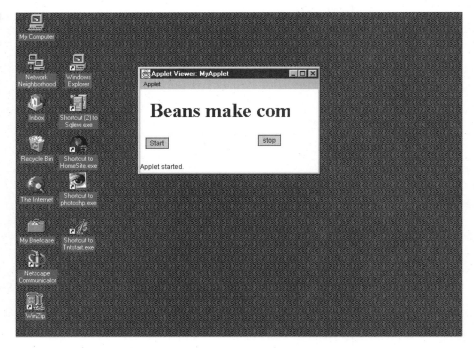

```
transient Thread kicker = null;
transient Image offscreen;
transient Graphics goffscreen;
```

Putting It All Together

Listing 3-6 shows the complete listing for **TextScrollBean**.
Listing 3-7 shows the complete listing for **TextScrollBeanBeanInfo**.

Listing 3-6
Complete
TextScrollBean.java.

```
import java.awt.event.*;
import java.awt.Graphics;
import java.awt.*;
import java.beans.*;

public class TextScrollBean extends Panel implements
        java.io.Serializable,
  Runnable {

        String text = null;
        transient Thread kicker = null;
        int speed=10;
        int x = 0;
        int y = 30;
        int stringwidth;
        int width = 250;
        int height = 50;
        FontMetrics fm;
        // Offscreen graphics context and image to implement
        // double buffering
        transient Image offscreen;
        transient Graphics goffscreen;
        // Declare and instantiate a PropertyChange object
        private PropertyChangeSupport changes =
                new PropertyChangeSupport(this);
        private VetoableChangeSupport vetos =
                new VetoableChangeSupport(this);


        public TextScrollBean() {
                text = "Beans make components easy";
                setFont(new Font("TimesRoman",Font.BOLD,36));

                start();
        }
```

Continues

Listing 3-6
Continued.

```java
public Dimension getPreferredSize() {
     return (new Dimension(width, height));
}

public String getTextString() {
     return text;
}

public void setTextString(String newtext) {
     text = newtext;
}

public int getSpeed() {
     return speed;
}

public void setSpeed(int newSpeed) throws
PropertyVetoException {
     // tell vetoers about the change
     vetos.fireVetoableChange("Speed", "" + speed,
     "" + newSpeed);

     // Send change event to listeners when
     // speed is changed
     changes.firePropertyChange("Speed", "" +
     speed, "" + newSpeed);
     speed = newSpeed;
}

// Add a listener.  This will get called by the
// BeanBox
public void
addPropertyChangeListener(PropertyChangeListener 1) {
     changes.addPropertyChangeListener(1);
}

// Remove a listener.  This will get called by the
// BeanBox
public void
removePropertyChangeListener(PropertyChangeListener 1) {
     changes.removePropertyChangeListener(1);
}

// Add a veto listener.  This will get called by the
// BeanBox
public void
addVetoableChangeListener(VetoableChangeListener 1) {
     vetos.addVetoableChangeListener(1);
}

// Remove a veto listener.  This will get called by
// the BeanBox
```

Listing 3-6

```java
    public void
removeVetoableChangeListener(VetoableChangeListener l) {
        vetos.removeVetoableChangeListener(l);
    }


    // This method can be used to connect a Button to
    // the TextScrollBean.startScrolling method
    public void startScrolling(ActionEvent ex) {
        kicker.resume();
    }

    // This method can be used to connect a Button to
    // the TextScrollBean.stopScrolling method
public void stopScrolling(ActionEvent ex) {
        kicker.suspend();
    }

    public void start() {
        if(kicker == null) {
                kicker = new Thread(this);
                kicker.start();
        }
    }

    public void stop() {
        kicker = null;
    }

    public void run() {
        while (kicker != null) {
                try {
                        Thread.sleep(speed);
                } catch (InterruptedException e) {
                        e.printStackTrace();
                }
                repaint();
        }
kicker = null;
    }

    public void paint(Graphics g) {
        update(g);
    }

    public void update(Graphics g) {
        fm = g.getFontMetrics();
        stringwidth = fm.stringWidth(text);

        // Added double buffering to eliminate
        // flashing
```

Continues

Listing 3-6
Continued.

```
        // Create an offscreen graphics context
        if (goffscreen == null) {
            offscreen = createImage(width,height);
            goffscreen = offscreen.getGraphics();
        }
        // Paint to our offscreeen graphics context
        goffscreen.setColor(getBackground());
        goffscreen.fillRect(0,0,width,height);
        goffscreen.setColor(getForeground());
        goffscreen.drawString(text, x, y);


        // Paint our offscreen image to the screen
        g.drawImage(offscreen,0,0,this);


        if (x <= (-stringwidth)) {
            x=width;
        } else {
            x-;
        }
    }
}
```

Listing 3-7
TextScrollBeanBean-
Info.java.

```
import java.beans.*;
import java.lang.reflect.*;
import java.awt.*;

public class TextScrollBeanBeanInfo extends SimpleBeanInfo
    {
    // Define our beanClass that we are working with
private final static Class beanClass =
    TextScrollBean.class;

    // This method returns standard information about
    // our Bean

    // Currently it is changing the name to Text
    // Scroller
public BeanDescriptor getBeanDescriptor() {
        //BeanDescriptor bd = new
        //BeanDescriptor(beanClass, customizerClass);
BeanDescriptor bd = new BeanDescriptor(beanClass);
        bd.setDisplayName("Text Scroller");
            return bd;
    }

    // This method returns the icon to be used in the
```

Listing 3-7

```
// BeanBox.
// Normally we would check for which size of the
// Image we're looking for, but we only have one
// icon

public Image getIcon(int iconKind) {
        return loadImage("TextScroll.gif");
}


// This method changes the Property Editor to only
// display the properties we want it to.
public PropertyDescriptor[] getPropertyDescriptors()
{
        try {
                PropertyDescriptor speedPD =
                    new PropertyDescriptor("speed",
                    beanClass);
                PropertyDescriptor textStringPD =
                    new PropertyDescriptor("textString",
                    beanClass);
                PropertyDescriptor fontStringPD =
                    new PropertyDescriptor("font",
                    beanClass);
                PropertyDescriptor pdArray[] = {
                        speedPD,textStringPD,
                        fontStringPD };

                return pdArray;
        } catch (IntrospectionException ex) {
                throw new Error(ex.toString());
        }
    }
}
```

CONCLUSION

A good JavaBean has several important features. It should have a constructor that takes no arguments, so it can be created inside bean environments. Beans should also implement the **Serializable** interface, so that their state can be saved and restored.

Beans are intended to be reused and should be designed with this in mind. New beans can be created from old beans by instantiating one or more beans, manipulating them using customizer tools, and finally saving their state and packaging them into new beans.

JavaBeans represent a new paradigm in development for Java. Through beans, developers can package existing code as beans and reuse them in future projects. True visual application development becomes more of a reality as developers can drag-and-drop components and connect them without having to resort to writing code.

Serialization and Introspection

Almost all computer users, from the 10-year-old elementary student to the retired software engineer, are aware of the fundamental problem with today's memory technology: it is not persistent; as soon as the main power switch turns off, the entire contents of the system's memory vanishes. All data becomes an irretrievable mess of random electrical signals, resulting in more than a few horror stories of lost hard work.

Until nonvolatile memory becomes commonplace, one obvious solution to this problem is to write important data to permanent storage, such as a hard disk, before the computer shuts down. When the computer starts again, the data can be read back into main memory. The original version of Java offered developers several core classes for handling this task: **DataOutputStream**, **RandomAccessFile**, **IOException**, and others.

Although each of these I/O classes was based on an object-oriented design, none of them could actually handle the reading and writing of objects. Saving the state of a Java 1.0 object required many tedious steps. Because these steps were not defined in any specification, developers came up with their own proprietary and incompatible object file formats. Exchanging object data among vendors was impossible.

Today, these problems have been solved by a Java feature called "serialization." First introduced in the 1.1 release of Java, serialization provides an extensible, customizable, and standard way to convert a hierarchy of object data into a one-dimensional stream of bits. The serialized data can then be saved to disk, sent through a network, exchanged among processes, and so on. Once transferred, the serialization algorithms can restore the bit stream back to its original form.

Although serialization is extremely important for network communication and file streams, it is equally valuable to the JavaBeans architecture. Development tools, for instance, rely on serialization to save a bean's state when generating applications. When these application are run, the serialization mechanisms are again called upon to restore the bean to its design-time state. This process, which the Java specification affectionately calls "pickling," gives developers the luxury of building complex Java programs without writing a single line of Java code.

In this chapter, we look at the interfaces and classes that make this magic possible. We pay close attention to how serialization affects the development of JavaBeans, and we provide some sample code that gives the abstract concepts a more solid feel. Finally, we'll take a peek at introspection, a relatively new Java feature that lays the groundwork for both serialization and the JavaBeans architecture itself.

This Chapter Covers

- What is object serialization?
- Code generators versus serializers.
- A serializing lava lamp simulator.
- The ins and outs of the core reflection API.
- The `java.beans.Introspector` class.

Serialization

Serialization may be new to Java, but in the world of object-oriented programming, it's a solid and mature concept. Programmers have been using it for years to store and retrieve objects. They write the objects to a stream; move the stream to a network, file system, or separate process; and then read the steam back and reconstruct the objects.

Note that this storage and retrieval involves only object *data*, not object *code*. In other words, serialization has nothing to do with Java class files; it applies only to the state of those classes after they have been instantiated as objects. So when we speak of an object being serialized, we actually mean that the fields of the object are being saved while the code stays behind.

Despite its ignorance of bytecodes, Java serialization is extremely useful for file storage, network communication, and any other situation in which object data has to be passed around. But how does serialization benefit JavaBeans? Well, if you are a developer of JavaBeans, serialization probably won't help you much. The real value of serialization only comes to light if you're a JavaBeans user.

JavaBeans users, whether they realize it or not, love serialization. With it, they can avoid writing code and build Java applications with mere mouse clicks. They can save time by designing their programs visually and letting the Bean builder tool handle the details. Typically, the builder tool provides a feature that actually "builds" the application, generating the event adapter code, packaging the JavaBean class files, and—here's where serialization comes in—storing the state of all beans in the application. When the application runs, its startup code calls on Java serialization to retrieve the saved data, which restores each bean to its original state. The end result: users see the program exactly as the developer designed it. Figure 4-1 provides an illustration of this process.

Although developers who use JavaBeans may love serialization, many developers who create those beans don't share the same affection for it. That's because serialization introduces several dilemmas for bean authors. First, not all Java objects can be serialized. If a bean stores such an object as a field, the entire bean is not serializable. This minor detail can cause major problems when the bean is loaded into a builder tool. Second, because Java threads are not serializable, developers must take extra care when writing multithreaded beans. An unexpected change in a variable due to serialization could corrupt the thread. And third, sensitive infor-

Figure 4-1
Serialization is the key to building Java applications out of JavaBeans.

❶ The developer designs an application by adding Beans to a prototype inside a builder tool.

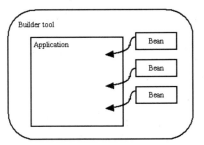

❷ The developer changes properties in the Beans and hooks Bean events together.

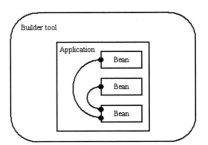

❸ The developer tells the builder tool to create an application from the prototype. The tool generates hookup classes for the connected events and serializes all Bean properties to files, which are stored along with the application and hookup classes. The class files and serialized data are packaged for the target platform.

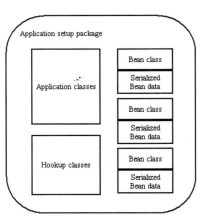

❹ The end user installs the developer's setup package and runs the application. The startup code deserializes the Bean properties and reconnects the event hookups. The resulting application looks identical to the prototype in the builder tool.

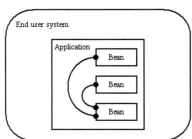

mation should not be serialized. A password, for instance, should be encrypted before serialization occurs (or should simply be left out of the serialization process altogether). We'll see how to handle each of these issues later on in this chapter.

Code Generators Versus Serializers

Thanks to Java's built-in support for serialization, creating a Bean builder tool that generates serialized applications is relatively simple. This support is fairly new, however, and some tools don't rely on serialization to build applications. For example, Borland's JBuilder and Powersoft's PowerJ currently use a technique known as "code generation" to transform prototypes into working applications. Code generation produces Java source code that offers the same functionality of serialization. Instead of reading an object's field from serialized data, JBuilder and PowerJ applications explicitly set the field using a Java statement such as `i = 6` or `foreground = new Color(255, 0, 0)`.

Although Borland and Powersoft have both stated that their tools will eventually support Java serialization, code generators will likely remain popular for years to come. Many developers simply prefer code generation because it gives them a "bottom up" view of their application and enables them to edit any portion of its source code outside of the tool that created it. Serialization, on the other hand, tends to hide the initialization process within a cryptic binary file.

Regardless of your preferred approach to application building, you have a responsibility as a JavaBeans developer to support serialization. The official specification states categorically that all beans must be serializable, which means that any JavaBean that can't serialize its data is not a JavaBean at all. Plus, you never know where your bean will end up. Your customers will surely load your components into all sorts of development tools, and many of those tools expect only serializable beans. If customers discover that your products won't work with their tools, your support costs will go up and your sales will go down—all the more reason to make your beans serializable.

If, for some reason, you know that your bean will not work properly with a code generator and in fact requires serialization, you can force the tool to use serialization when saving and restoring the state of your bean. Simply set the bean's hidden-state attribute to True. This can be done inside the `getBeanDescriptor()` method of the bean's `BeanInfo` class. (See Chapter 5 to learn more about `BeanInfo`.) For example,

```
public BeanDescriptor getBeanDescriptor() {
    BeanDescriptor bd = new BeanDescriptor(MyBean.class);
    bd.setValue("hidden-state", Boolean.TRUE);
    return bd;
}
```

With this code in place, code generators will automatically recognize that your bean requires serialization.

Fortunately, not all aspects of Java serialization are bad news for developers. Creating a serializable JavaBean has a pleasant side effect: that bean is now compatible with ActiveX, DCOM, CORBA, and a variety of other component architectures. Like Java, these architectures rely on serialization; however, their stream formats are totally incompatible. JavaBeans gets around this limitation by bridging via native code each architecture to Java. This code translates serialized data in Java to its native stream format and vice versa automatically. So once we've learned how to write serializable components in Java, we have instantly learned how to write serializable components in any architecture that can be bridged with JavaBeans.

Figure 4-2 demonstrates the advantages of this bridging of serialization formats. On the left side, we see a bean loaded into Sun's BeanBox. A few properties in the bean have been changed, and the states of these properties have been saved using Java serialization. The bean has been packaged with its serialized data and converted using Sun's JavaBeans Bridge for ActiveX to an ActiveX control. On the right side, we see Microsoft Word, an ActiveX container that has loaded the bean into a document. Notice that the Java serialization mechanisms have retrieved the stored properties, putting the bean back to its original state.

Behind the Scenes

To gain a better understanding of Java serialization, let's take a quick look at how it works behind the scenes. The key concept here is that serialization translates a multidimensional structure (the object hierarchy) into a one-dimensional array (the serialized stream of data). To demonstrate this process, we'll walk through serialization of the following Java class:

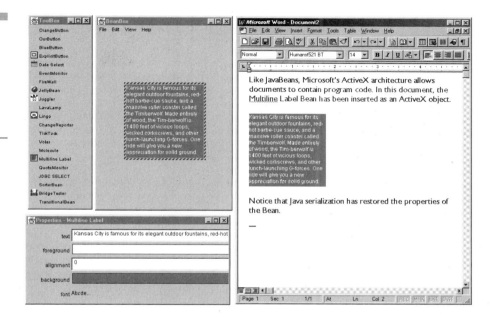

Figure 4-2
Java serialization works with any bridgeable architecture, as shown by this demonstration of ActiveX.

```
class SerialTest
{
    int someInt;
    java.awt.Point someXY;
    String someString;
}
```

When Java serializes an object, it begins with the primitive fields sorted by name and continues with the object fields sorted by name. Thus, for the **SerialTest** class, Java first serializes **someInt**, then **someString**, and finally **someXY**. It constructs a stream of data containing four bytes for the integer, two bytes times the length of the string, plus eight bytes for the **Point** object. Figure 4-3 shows a diagram of the resulting stream.

Notice that the **x** and **y** fields of the **Point** object are serialized, even though they are not (directly) fields of the **SerialTest** class. This illustrates a fundamental feature of Java serialization: Whenever an object field becomes serialized, all fields in that object are serialized as well. Java will recursively parse each field in an object to ensure that all of its subfields, sub-subfields, and so on are accounted for.

In addition to the downward search for subfields, Java's serialization algorithms also search upward through the object hierarchy. In other words, whenever an object becomes serialized, the entire family tree for that object also becomes serialized. The order of serialization begins with

Figure 4-3
Java serialization
translates structured
object data into an
array of bytes.

Class code

```
class SerialTest
{
    int someInt;
    java.awt.Point someXY;
    String someString;
}
```

Class structure

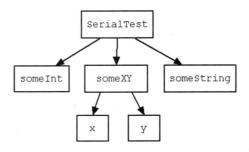

Serialized data

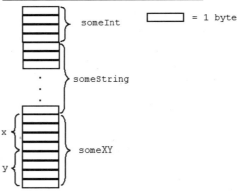

the object itself and proceeds with the object's parent, then its grandparent, and so on.

Let's modify the previous example to see how this works. We will simply create a parent class for the **SerialTest** object and serialize its data. The new code is given in Listing 4-1.

When the **SerialTest** class is serialized, each of its fields—**someInt**, **someXY**, and **someString**—will be serialized, just as in the previous example. However, because **SerialTest** now has a parent, its parent object

Listing 4-1
A sample class
hierarchy for
demonstrating
serialization.

```
class SerialTestParent
{
    float someFloat;
    java.awt.Color someColor;
    byte someByte;
}

class SerialTest extends SerialTestParent
{
    int someInt;
    java.awt.Point someXY;
    String someString;
}
```

Figure 4-4
When an object is
serialized, all its
parents are
appended to the
stream.

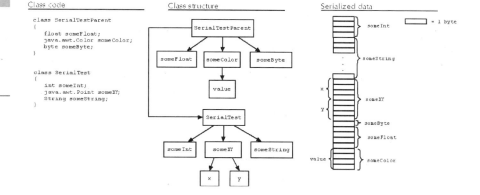

will become serialized too. Java will simply append the parent object to the end of the stream, as shown in Figure 4-4.

A Java serialization stream is, of course, more complex than the simple array of bytes shown in these diagrams. Actual streams contain headers, primitive type flags, and class descriptors. Streams may also contain handles that point to previous references. These handles allow the serialization algorithms to save space that would otherwise be wasted by duplicate field types, duplicate instances, and circular references.

Knowing all about the internals of serialization streams isn't necessary, so we won't look any closer at the details. After all, one of the biggest advantages of serialization in Java is that the virtual machine handles the tedious, low-level tasks automatically, leaving us to concentrate on the implementation of our objects. We only need to concern ourselves with how to make a class serializable, as explained in the following section.

The Serializable Interface

Now that we know what serialization is and why it is necessary, it's time to learn how to use it. First, remember that Java serialization can be looked at from two perspectives: the perspective of one object asking another object to serialize itself and the perspective of one object actually performing the serialization of its fields.

In the world of JavaBeans, development tools view serialization from the first perspective. These tools often ask beans to serialize their data to a file. The tools then package this file along with the bean classes so that the state of each component can be restored. However, this book is about JavaBeans components, not Bean builder tools, so we won't concentrate on this perspective of serialization.

On the other hand, the latter perspective of serialization is absolutely vital for learning how to design a JavaBean. All beans simply must be serializable. Builder tools expect, and often require, the beans that they load to support serialization. So if a bean does not support serialization, not only does it fail to conform to the official JavaBeans specification, but it will also fail to load into standard development tools.

The key to making a bean serializable is a simple one-line interface named, of course, **Serializable**. Located in the java.io package, the interface looks like this:

```
public interface Serializable {};
```

Obviously, this interface has no methods and constants. Its only purpose is to flag an object as supporting serialization. When Java serialization sees this flag on a bean, it knows that the bean can be safely serialized. For example, here's how the **Serializable** interface would look when implemented by the **SerialTest** class from earlier in this chapter:

```
class SerialTest implements java.io.Serializable
{
    int someInt;
    java.awt.Point someXY;
    String someString;
}
```

As you can see, the **Serializable** interface is so easy to use, it's trivial. Just declare your bean as implementing serializable, and you're done. Java serialization handles the work of investigating the class, searching for fields to save or restore, and reading or writing the data.

TIP: *The* **Serializable** *interface isn't always necessary. If a bean is extended from a* **Serializable** *class, that bean automatically becomes serializable, even if it doesn't actually implement* **java.io.Serializable.** *Nevertheless, you should always declare your beans as implementing the* **Serializable** *interface just to remind yourself (and others) that your components can handle serialization properly.*

Customizing Java's Automatic Serialization

The simplicity of the **Serializable** interface is also its disadvantage. The "flag and forget" approach can sometimes make serialization inefficient and may even cause exceptions to be thrown. The solution to these problems is to tweak automatic serialization according to the particular features of your bean. Java provides two features for customizing automatic serialization: transient fields and a pair of methods called **readObject()** and **writeObject()**.

TRANSIENT FIELDS   The first release of Java reserved the keyword **transient**, but it had no meaning. With the advent of Java 1.1 and its support for object serialization, **transient** now has a purpose. It makes any field "invisible" to the serialization process, preventing the field from being read or written. You should always mark a field as transient whenever that field can be calculated from other fields. Consider the following class:

```
class BaseballPlayer implements java.io.Serializable
{
    private int atBats;
    private int hits;
    private transient float average;
}
```

In this case, the **average** field has been marked transient because it can be calculated by dividing hits through **atBats**. This technique saves space in the serialized data stream.

Note that even though all of **BaseballPlayer**'s fields are private, they still get serialized. This feature of Java serialization could prove to be a gaping security hole if the class contains sensitive information, such as a password. The only way to close the hole is to declare the password as transient.

TIP: *The easiest way to check the serialization mechanisms of a bean is to load it into a builder tool. If the tool doesn't complain, the bean is probably working fine. Still, you might not trust the tool to implement serialization completely or perfectly. If that's the case, you can easily test the serialization of a bean yourself. Just run the following code, where* **MyBean** *is the name of the bean you want to debug:*

```
MyBean myBean1 = new MyBean();
FileOutputStream fos = new FileOutputStream("debug");
ObjectOutput oo = new ObjectOutputStream(fos);
oo.writeObject(myBean1);
oo.flush();

FileInputStream fis = new FileInputStream("debug");
ObjectInput oi = new ObjectInputStream(fis);
MyBean myBean2 = (MyBean) oi.readObject();
```

After this code executes, check the values of **MyBean1** *and* **MyBean2**. *If their fields and properties are identical, you can be sure that serialization of* **MyBean** *is alive and well.*

Another important need for the **transient** keyword arises whenever a bean contains a field or property that does not implement the **Serializable** interface. Here's a demonstration of the problem:

```
class Problem {
    private String s;
}

public class ProblemBean implements java.io.Serializable {
    private Problem p = new Problem();
}
```

When a development tool (or any other Java object) attempts to serialize this **ProblemBean**, a **NotSerializableException** will be thrown. **NotSerializableException**, which is defined in the java.io package, is raised at runtime whenever Java determines that an object has requested serialization of a non-serializable class.

Bean developers commonly run into this annoying situation when they work with the standard **java.awt.Image** class, which does not implement the **Serializable** interface. For instance, they might want to display an icon in a bean, so they simply declare an **Image** object as a private field. When the bean is loaded into a development tool, however, the tool will suddenly pop up an error message. Fortunately, the solution is simple: declaring the **Image** field as transient makes the error message disappear.

Remember, though, that the **transient** keyword is not always a magic solution. For instance, if the **ProblemBean** extended the **Problem** class instead of just contained it, **transient** would be of no use. The **Problem** superclass would throw an **InvalidClassException** or, if it contained a no-argument constructor, would simply not be serialized along with the **ProblemBean**. Fixing this problem would require a rewrite of the **Problem** class so that it implements **Serializable**. But if that's not an option, we could define two special methods that perform an explicit serialization of the **Problem** superclass, as explained in the following section.

THE readObject() AND writeObject() METHODS The flexibility of the **transient** keyword is sometimes not enough to properly customize Java's automatic serialization. A bean may require a notification that its fields have been saved or restored, or it may need to append extra information to the serialized stream. For either case, the solution is this pair of methods:

```
private void writeObject(ObjectOutputStream stream) throws
    IOException;
private void readObject(ObjectInputStream stream) throws
    IOException;
```

When a bean implements these methods, the Java serialization mechanisms will detect their signatures and call the appropriate method before a read or write occurs. The bean can then use the given **ObjectOutputStream** or **ObjectInputStream** objects to read or write the data. Both of these objects provide an assortment of methods for sending primitive data types or arrays through a stream. As an example of how to use them, take a look at Listing 4-2.

The **CustomerInfo** class in this listing is serializable, just like all of the other classes up to this point. This new class, however, implements the **writeObject()** and **readObject()** methods. The **writeObject()** method is called whenever an object tries to serialize **CustomerInfo**, and the **readObject()** method is called whenever an object tries to deserialize— that is, restore data from a serialized stream—**CustomerInfo**.

With the **writeObject()** and **readObject()** methods implemented, the **CustomerInfo** class has complete control over its serialization. It can choose what items should be serialized and how to serialize them. It can also choose to append extra data to the serialization stream.

Appending extra data to the stream is exactly what the **CustomerInfo** class does. Note that the implementation of **writeObject()** calls **ObjectOutputStream**'s **defaultWriteObject()** method. This powerful

Listing 4-2
A demonstration
of the
writeObject()
and **readObject()**
methods.

```java
class CustomerInfo implements java.io.Serializable
{
    private String name;
    private int age;
    private transient String password;

    private static final int OFFSET = 6;

    public CustomerInfo(String name, int age, String
      password)
    {
        this.name = name;
        this.age = age;
        this.password = password;
    }

    private void writeObject(ObjectOutputStream stream)
      throws IOException
    {
        stream.defaultWriteObject();

        stream.writeInt(password.length());

        for (int i = 0; i < password.length(); i++)
        {
            stream.writeInt(password.charAt(i) + OFFSET);
        }
    }

    private void readObject(ObjectInputStream stream) throws
      IOException, ClassNotFoundException
    {
        stream.defaultReadObject();

        int length = stream.readInt();
        StringBuffer pw = new StringBuffer();

        for (int i = 0; i < length; i++)
        {
            pw.append((char)(stream.readInt() - OFFSET));
        }

        password = pw.toString();
    }
}
```

method tells Java to perform serialization of `CustomerInfo`'s data as if the `writeObject()` or `readObject()` methods had not been implemented. Therefore, after `defaultWriteObject()` has been called, the **name** and **age** fields have already been written to the stream, and the

CustomerInfo class doesn't have to deal with them. (Also, notice that we have slightly modified the signature of the **readObject()** method from its original declarations in order to accommodate **defaultReadObject()**, which requires handling of the **ClassNotFoundException**.)

The **password** field, however, is transient, so it stays behind. **CustomerInfo**'s **writeObject()** method converts this field to an array of integers, encrypting them in case they are written to a file or serialized by some process that could view the password. The encryption algorithm shown here is overly simplistic for the purposes of this tutorial.

As the encryption algorithm executes, the **writeObject()** method calls **ObjectOutputStream**'s **writeInt()** method to send the integers through the stream. If we needed to write other data types to the stream, we would simply use **ObjectOutputStream**'s comprehensive set of methods. These methods come in all flavors for primitive types, arrays, strings, and full-blown objects. See the JDK documentation for a complete list of methods.

Equally important to the **CustomerInfo** class is the **readObject()** method. (After all, there's no point in serializing an object to a stream if we can't get that stream back to its original object form.) **readObject()** is essentially the reverse of its sibling. It first calls **defaultReadObject()** to deserialize the name and age fields. It then reads the length of the **password** string, which was previously written by the **writeObject()** method. Finally, it calls **ObjectInputStream**'s **readInt()** method to decrypt the password string. The result is a **CustomerInfo** object identical to the object created by **writeInt()**.

TIP: *Be careful what you do inside the **readObject()** and **writeObject()** methods. Just because the serialization stream could be a file stream doesn't mean your bean has file-access privileges. If your serializing algorithm needs to encrypt data, for instance, you shouldn't load an encryption table from the file system. Instead, store and access the table as a Java resource/stream use files only if you know for certain that your bean has permission to leave Java's security sandbox.*

The **writeObject()** and **readObject()** methods are good for more than just customizing data streams. They also show their strength when a class requires notification that its fields have been serialized or deserialized. If, for example, a field's value depends solely on the values of other fields, it should be declared transient for the sake of efficiency. This can cause a problem, though, as shown in Listing 4-3.

When this program executes, we want it to print

```
size = 2000
```

```java
import java.io.*;

class TextDisplayInfo implements Serializable
{
    public int rows;
    public int cols;
    public transient int size;

    public TextDisplayInfo(int rows, int cols)
    {
        this.rows = rows;
        this.cols = cols;
        size = rows * cols;
    }
}

public class test
{
    public static void main(String[] args)
    {
        try
        {
            FileOutputStream fos = new
                            FileOutputStream("test");
            ObjectOutput oo = new ObjectOutputStream(fos);
            oo.writeObject(new TextDisplayInfo(80, 25));
            oo.flush();

            FileInputStream fis = new
                            FileInputStream("test");
            ObjectInput oi = new ObjectInputStream(fis);
            TextDisplayInfo tdi = (TextDisplayInfo)
            oi.readObject();

            System.out.println("size = " + tdi.size);
        }
        catch(Exception e)
        {
            System.out.println(e);
        }
    }
}
```

but instead, it prints

```
size = 0
```

This error occurs because the **size** field is transient and does not get restored from the file stream. Of course, we could easily fix this problem just by removing the **transient** flag. This removal, however, would waste space in the stream and increase the time required to read it and write it. (Actually, space and time factors are almost negligible for the simple example presented here, but they become far more important in a real-world scenario with large objects containing many transient fields.)

The alternative solution to this problem is to implement the **readObject()** and **writeObject()** to act as notifications. In this case, we don't need notification of serialization, so we'll simply make **writeObject()** perform its default serialization tasks. But we do want to be notified when a deserialization occurs, so we'll make **readObject()** do its regular job, and then we'll update the size field using the deserialized values. The new code is shown in Listing 4-4.

Listing 4-4
The **writeObject()** and **readObject()** methods can act as notifications that serialization or deserialization has occurred.

```java
import java.io.*;

class TextDisplayInfo implements Serializable
{
    public int rows;
    public int cols;
    public transient int size;

    public TextDisplayInfo(int rows, int cols)
    {
        this.rows = rows;
        this.cols = cols;
        size = rows * cols;
    }

    private void writeObject(ObjectOutputStream stream)
        throws IOException
    {
        stream.defaultWriteObject();
    }

    private void readObject(ObjectInputStream stream) throws
        IOException, ClassNotFoundException
    {
        stream.defaultReadObject();

        size = rows * cols;
    }
}

public class test
{
    public static void main(String[] args)
```

Continues

Listing 4-4
Continued.

```
{
    try
    {
        FileOutputStream fos = new
                            FileOutputStream("tmp");
        ObjectOutput oo = new ObjectOutputStream(fos);
        oo.writeObject(new TextDisplayInfo(80, 25));
        oo.flush();

        FileInputStream fis = new FileInputStream("tmp");
        ObjectInput oi = new ObjectInputStream(fis);
        TextDisplayInfo tdi = (TextDisplayInfo)
                            oi.readObject();

        System.out.println("size = " + tdi.size);
    }
    catch(Exception e)
    {
        System.out.println(e);
    }
}
}
```

When this code executes, it prints

```
size = 2000
```

just like we wanted.

Building Serialization from Scratch

With its support for customization via the `writeObject()` and `readObject()` methods, the `Serializable` interface packs a lot of power. In case you want an even greater degree of control over the serialization process, Java provides a second interface called `Externalizable`. The source code for `Externalizable`, which can be found in the java.io package, looks like this:

```
public interface Externalizable extends
    java.io.Serializable {
  void writeExternal(ObjectOutput out) throws IOException;
  void readExternal(ObjectInput in) throws IOException,
    ClassNotFoundException;
```

Though it may look significantly different, the `Externalizable` interface is virtually identical to its parent. Like `Serializable`, `Externalizable` tags a class as supporting serialization, and its **writeExternal()** and **readExternal()** methods are analogous to **Serializable**'s **writeObject()** and **readObject()** methods. Unlike **Serializable**, however, **Externalizable** provides absolutely no automatic assistance. It serializes neither fields nor superclasses.

The most important difference between the **Externalizable** and **Serializable** interfaces is that the parameters of **Externalizable**'s methods are **ObjectOutput** and **ObjectInput** interfaces, not the **ObjectOutputStream** and **ObjectInputStream** classes of **Serializable**. The consequence is that the **defaultWriteObject()** and **defaultReadObject()** methods are unavailable.

So why, then, with all these disadvantages does the **Externalizable** interface even exist? Well, there is really little reason to implement **Externalizable**. It is useful in only two circumstances:

- You need to allow serialization of a bean but you want to prevent serialization of its parent class or classes.

- You know that your bean needs to handle all of its serialization itself, and you want to make this fact obvious in your source code by implementing **Externalizable**.

Just in case you happen to run into one of these situations, let's look at some sample code to see how the **Externalizable** interface works. Listing 4-5 shows a sample class that demonstrates **Externalizable**. As required by the interface, the class declares the methods **writeExternal()** and **readExternal()**, implementing them to write and read its fields to the given stream.

Listing 4-5
A demonstration of the **Externalizable** interface.

```
import java.io.*;

class FootballPlayer
{
    protected String name;
    protected java.util.Date birthdate;
    protected int gamesPlayed;

    public FootballPlayer(String name, java.util.Date
      birthdate, int gamesPlayed)
    {
        this.name = name;
        this.birthdate = birthdate;
        this.gamesPlayed = gamesPlayed;
    }
```

Continues

Listing 4-5
Continued.

```
}

class Quarterback extends FootballPlayer implements
    Externalizable
{
    protected int passCompletions;
    protected int passYardage;
    protected int sacks;

    public Quarterback(String name, java.util.Date
        birthdate, int gamesPlayed,
                        int passCompletions, int
                        passYardage, int sacks)
    {
        super(name, birthdate, gamesPlayed);

        this.passCompletions = passCompletions;
        this.passYardage = passYardage;
        this.sacks = sacks;
    }

    public void writeExternal(ObjectOutput stream) throws
        IOException
    {
        stream.writeUTF(name);
        stream.writeObject(birthdate);
        stream.writeInt(gamesPlayed);
        stream.writeInt(passCompletions);
        stream.writeInt(passYardage);
        stream.writeInt(sacks);
    }

    public void readExternal(ObjectInput stream) throws
        IOException, ClassNotFoundException
    {
        name = stream.readUTF();
        birthdate = (java.util.Date) stream.readObject();
        gamesPlayed = stream.readInt();
        passCompletions = stream.readInt();
        passYardage = stream.readInt();
        sacks = stream.readInt();
    }
}
```

As evidenced by this code, designing an **Externalizable** class is no more difficult than designing a **Serializable** class. The methods for writing and reading data are essentially the same, except for the notable lack of **defaultWriteObject()** and **defaultReadObject()**. The important thing to remember is that the **writeExternal()** and **readExternal()**

methods have complete control. Nothing gets serialized or deserialized without their permission.

TIP: *The* `ObjectOutputStream` *and* `ObjectInputStream` *classes perform caching to reduce the number of bytes they send through their streams. This increase in efficiency can also increase your frustration when you discover that a bean you transport to a remote host remains the same even after changing its fields and resending it across the network. Most likely, the problem is a direct result of* `ObjectOutputStream`*'s cache algorithm. To work around the problem, just call the* `ObjectOutputStream.reset()` *method to force an update of the object's state.*

Versioning

Change is inevitable, and, naturally, JavaBeans are not immune to this fact of life. Over the course of its lifetime, a bean could change often to support new methods and properties, and obsolete methods or properties could be removed. Though these changes can bring huge improvements in the quality of the bean, they could spell disaster when the bean is deserialized.

Consider this scenario: A company ships version 1.00 of a JavaBean. Several developers purchase the bean, build an application with it (using Java serialization), and ship the application to their customers. Before long, the company discovers a bug in their bean. Fixing the bug requires the addition of a new field, so the company adds the field and ships version 1.01 of the bean to the developers. The developers, in turn, ship the new component to their customers who install it on their systems. Suddenly, the customers begin to report mysterious error messages that had never appeared before. Apparently, the company's bug fix wasn't much of a fix after all.

For a clearer demonstration of this problem, consider the following Java class:

```
class SomeBean implements java.io.Serializable
{
    public int someField;
}
```

When an object of this class becomes serialized, the stream will contain a single integer value representing the state of the **someField** property. Now, consider what would happen if we added a field to the class:

```
class SomeBean implements java.io.Serializable
{
    public int someField;
    public char anotherField;
}
```

If the original serialized stream were read back into this new version of the class, a **java.io.InvalidClassException** would be thrown. The reason is obvious: Java serialization expects the stream to contain data for the **anotherField** field, but instead it just runs into the end of the stream.

The question now is, "How do we go about fixing this problem?" The answer may surprise you. We simply need to add a single integer field, and the problem goes away. The new version would look like this:

```
class SomeBean implements java.io.Serializable
{
    public int someField;
    public char anotherField;
    static final long serialVersionUID =
        7876863521679305162L;
}
```

With this strange-looking field, deserializing a stream of the original class version produces no errors. The **someField** field becomes its original, pre-serialization value, and the **anotherField** field becomes '\u0000', which is exactly what we wanted and expected in the first place.

STREAM UNIQUE IDENTIFIERS   The secret behind this serialization magic is a 64-bit long integer known as a "stream unique identifier," stored as a field called **serialVersionUID**. It may look like a random value, but it is actually determined by a complex algorithm. This algorithm walks through the attributes of a Java class-name, field names and types, method names and parameters and constructs a hash value based on this information. The resulting integer is unique for all classes and thus avoids conflicts between classes with identical names.

All serialization streams contain this integer; that is, they all contain a stream unique identifier (SUID). If an object does not explicitly define an SUID, it is generated automatically, on-the-fly, as the object is serialized. When the stream is deserialized, Java compares the SUIDs of the saved object and of the class being restored. If the two values are different, Java knows that the classes are different and throws an **InvalidClassException**.

Occasionally, however, two classes may look different but are still compatible for deserialization. For instance, an additional field wouldn't necessarily cause a problem because it could be set to its default value (as was the case in the **SomeBean** example). Likewise, an additional method would not harm Java's capability of deserializing an object stream. Java takes the conservative approach, though, and does not make these assumptions about version compatibility.

Stream unique identifiers provide a fix for Java's conservatism. By giving two versions of a class the same SUID, we can force Java to get liberal when deserializing an object. We can let Java know that the two objects belong to the same version hierarchy. Java will then reconcile the differences between the two versions automatically, but only if the changes are compatible.

We'll look at what constitutes a compatible change later. But first, we need to learn how to obtain the SUID of a root class so that we can give later versions of that class the same SUID. To obtain an SUID, run the serialver program, a utility included with Sun's Java Development Kit. Running serialver with the parameter **-show** displays a user interface. For example, the command

```
serialver -show
```

produces the dialog box in Figure 4-5.

After running serialver, cut and paste the SUID into all versions of your class. Java will then be able to restore serialized objects of the older classes into the newer ones. (Remember that you don't need to paste an SUID into the original version of the class because Java can calculate it for you automatically.)

COMPATIBLE AND INCOMPATIBLE CHANGES Stream unique identifiers are only a partial solution to the versioning problem. That's because the evolution of a class could change it so much that Java can't safely reconcile the differences among its versions. Even with the proper **serialVersionUID** field, Java will still throw an **InvalidClassException**

Figure 4-5

Sun's Serial Version Inspector tool can display the stream unique identifier of any Java class.

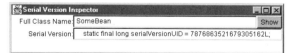

Serial Version Inspector	
Full Class Name: SomeBean	Show
Serial Version: static final long serialVersionUID = 7876863521679305162L;	

when it detects an "incompatible change." If, however, the class contains only "compatible changes," Java will deserialize the stream without errors, just as before.

The compatible changes are:

- Adding fields
- Adding classes to the hierarchy
- Removing classes from the hierarchy
- Changing the access to a field (public, package, protected, private)
- Changing a field from static to nonstatic or transient to nontransient
- Adding `writeObject` and `readObject` methods
- Removing `writeObject` and `readObject` methods
- Implementing `java.io.Serializable`
- Removing implementation of `java.io.Serializable`

The incompatible changes are:

- Deleting fields
- Moving classes up or down the hierarchy
- Changing a nonstatic field to static or a nontransient field to transient
- Changing the declared type of a primitive field
- Changing a `writeObject` or `readObject` method so that it no longer writes or reads the default field data, or changing it so that it attempts to write or read it when the previous version did not
- Changing a class from `java.io.Serializable` to `java.io.Externalizable` or visa-versa
- Removing either `java.io.Serializable` or `java.io.Externalizable`

Refer back to these lists before shipping a new version of a JavaBean. If the changes in the new code fall into the former list, everything's fine. But if the changes fall into the latter list, you've got three choices: one, alter the new version to include only compatible changes; two, use the manual versioning techniques explained in the following section; or three, be prepared for some angry customers and increased support costs.

MANUAL VERSIONING Every once in a while, upgrading the features of a JavaBean requires changes that are incompatible with Java's automatic serialization. The only way to make these changes and still preserve compatibility with older serialized objects is to plan ahead. If you expect to make incompatible changes to a bean at any point during its lifetime, you'll need to handle all the serialization yourself, starting with the first version. Only then can you ensure that changes such as deleting a field won't destroy the bean's backward compatibility for serialization.

The sole requirement for performing manual serialization is that the bean implements `java.io.Externalizable`. Other than that, the serialization format is at the complete discretion of the developer. For the purposes of this tutorial, we'll define a simple format that uses stream unique identifiers to mark sections of the serialization stream. Here's how it works: in the first version, the `writeExternal()` method will write its own SUID to the stream, followed by each of its fields, and finally an integer of value 0, which indicates that the stream contains no further data. In the second version, the `writeExternal()` method will begin by writing data that is compatible with the first version. That is, it will write the first version's SUID and all of its fields to the stream. The second version will then write an integer whose value is the size, in bytes, of its own data. This value will be the sum of the size of the second version's SUID, plus the size of each of its fields, plus the size of an integer. The final data written by the second version will be an integer of value 0. Each new version of the bean will continue in this manner, writing all the data from the previous versions to the stream, then its own data, and finally a zero.

Now that we have defined the format for our manually serialized streams, the `readExternal()` methods become pretty easy. They simply walk through each block of data, using the SUIDs to separate each block. The first version, for example, would read in its own SUID (promptly ignoring it) and continue with each of its fields. It would then read the integer value at the end of the block. If this value is zero, the `readExternal()` method knows that there is no more data and can quit reading the stream. If the value is non-zero, however, the `readExternal()` method will skip the amount of bytes specified by the value because, in this case, the bean is only the first version and doesn't know what to do with the data. In the second version of the bean, the `readExternal()` method performs the same walk-through up to this point, but instead of skipping bytes, it reads them in as its own fields. When it arrives at the final integer value, it performs the same "skip if non-zero" technique in case the stream was created by the third, fourth, or any other future version of the bean. With this approach to manual serialization, both backward and forward compatibility can be maintained for all streams.

All of this reading and writing may seem fairly complicated, so let's look at example to put things in order. We'll begin with a trivial bean called

"Manual Versioning" which contains two fields: a byte and a string. As required by manual serialization, it implements **java.io.Externalizable** and defines the SUID of itself. Its **writeExternal()** method sends the SUID to the stream, followed by the byte and string fields, and finally a 0 integer. The source code for this first version of Manual Versioning is given in Listing 4-6.

Notice that the last line of **writeExternal()** writes a zero to the stream, indicating that no more data exists. In the **readExternal()** method, the last line reads the number of bytes remaining in the stream and then skips that amount. (The **ObjectInput.skip()** method correctly handles zero parameters—good thing, too, in case this version happens to read a serialized stream that was created by itself.)

Now let's add some features to the bean. This second version will remove the original byte field and add a new field of type float. The source code for these changes is shown in Listing 4-7. Note that the new version defines the SUID of the first in order to make Java happy. Without the SUID, Java might throw an **InvalidClassException** in the **readExternal()** method.

Listing 4-6
The first version of the Manual Versioning bean.

```java
class ManualVersioning implements Externalizable
{
    public byte i;
    public String j;

    public ManualVersioning()
    {
        i = 1;
        j = "2";
    }

    public void writeExternal(ObjectOutput stream) throws
        IOException
    {
        stream.writeByte(i);
        stream.writeUTF(j);
        stream.writeInt(0);
    }

    public void readExternal(ObjectInput stream) throws
        IOException
    {
        i = stream.readByte();
        j = stream.readUTF();
        stream.skip(stream.readInt());
    }
}
```

```
class ManualVersioning implements Externalizable
{
    public String j;
    public float k;
    static final long serialVersionUID = -
        5276978260358454107L;

    public ManualVersioning()
    {
        j = "2";
        k = 3;
    }

    public void writeExternal(ObjectOutput stream) throws
        IOException
    {
        // Version 1 block
        stream.writeByte(0);
        stream.writeUTF(j);

        stream.writeInt(4 + 4);   // sizeof(float) +
            sizeof(int)

        // Version 2 block
        stream.writeFloat(k);

        stream.writeInt(0);
    }

    public void readExternal(ObjectInput stream) throws
        IOException
    {
        // Version 1 block
        stream.readByte();
        j = stream.readUTF();

        if ( stream.readInt() != 0 )
        {
            // Version 2 block
            k = stream.readFloat();
            stream.skip(stream.readInt());
        }
    }
}
```

Recall that Java's automatic versioning would not allow the removal of
the byte field, so we are handling all of the serialization ourselves. In the
writeExternal() method, we send version 1's fields to the stream, followed by an integer that reveals the number of bytes in version 2's block.

We then write the new float field and top everything off with a zero. In the **readExternal()** method, we skip the byte field (because the second version does not declare it) and read in the string. Next, we must determine whether the stream is a "version 1 stream" or a "version 2 stream" by reading the next integer. For version 1, the integer will be 0, and we have no more data to read. If the integer is non-zero, however, we read in the float field and, to account for future versions, skip the number of bytes specified by the final integer.

Manual versioning is powerful, but it comes with a caveat. In the above example, note that if version 1 reads a version 2 stream, the byte field will become its default (zero) value, and if version 2 reads a version 1 stream, the float field will become the value provided by the constructor (or zero if the constructor does not provide a value). This means, in more general terms, that beans supporting manual versioning must be prepared for zero and null values after deserialization. Though that may seem like a big disadvantage, it is simply the price we pay to overcome the limitations of automatic serialization.

Putting It All Together: the Lava Lamp

So far, we've seen small, short examples of how to implement serialization. Let's move a step further and see how the **java.io.Serializable** interface looks in a full-fledged component. We'll start with a non-serializable bean and walk through each step required to make it serializable.

STEP 1   The bean we'll be working with is called the Lava Lamp. It's exactly what its name implies: a virtual lava lamp, built from Java code on top of the JavaBeans architecture. It displays a digital liquid, oozing around in colors and patterns defined by the bean's properties. Figure 4-6 shows the Lava Lamp in action, and Listing 4-8 shows its source code.

STEP 2   Even though the JavaBean presented in Listing 4-8 implements neither the **Serializable** nor **Externalizable** interfaces, it is still serializable. This is because the **LavaLamp** class extends the **Canvas** class, which extends the **Component** class, which implements the **Serializable** interface. By induction, then, the Lava Lamp is also serializable. We should, however, declare our class as implementing **Serializable**, just to make it abundantly clear that Lava Lamp objects can indeed be serialized. The new class header looks like this:

```
public class LavaLamp
    extends Canvas
    implements Runnable, ComponentListener,
        java.io.Serializable
```

Figure 4-6
The Lava Lamp
displays vivid colors
in a variable-speed
animation.

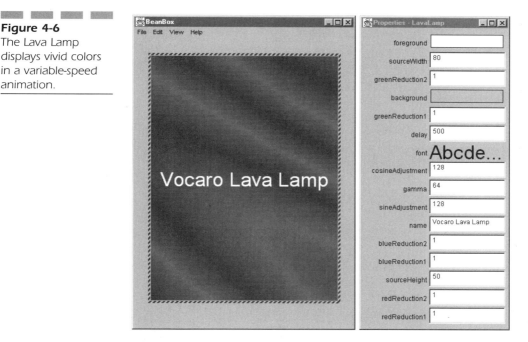

Listing 4-8
The source code to
the Lava Lamp.

```java
import java.awt.*;
import java.awt.image.*;
import java.awt.event.*;

public class LavaLamp extends Canvas implements Runnable,
        ComponentListener
{
    private int m_nSourceWidth = 80;
    private int m_nSourceHeight = 50;
    private int m_nGamma = 64;
    private int m_nDelay = 50;
    private int m_nRedReduction1 = 256;
    private int m_nRedReduction2 = 1;
    private int m_nGreenReduction1 = 256;
    private int m_nGreenReduction2 = 256;
    private int m_nBlueReduction1 = 1;
```
Continues

Listing 4-8
Continued.

```java
private int m_nBlueReduction2 = 1;
private int m_nSineAdjustment = 128;
private int m_nCosineAdjustment = 128;
private int[] m_nSinTable, m_nCosTable;
private byte[] m_byBits;
private IndexColorModel m_cmPalette;
private Image m_imgBuffer;
private int m_i, m_j;
private Thread m_threadLavaLamp = new Thread(this);
private int m_nFontWidth, m_nFontHeight;

public LavaLamp()
{
    setForeground(Color.white);
    setFont(new Font("Dialog", Font.PLAIN, 14));
    setName("Vocaro Lava Lamp");

    addComponentListener(this);
}

public void update(Graphics g)
{
    paint(g);
}

public synchronized void paint(Graphics g)
{
    g.drawImage(m_imgBuffer, 0, 0, m_imgBuffer.
  getWidth(this), m_imgBuffer.getHeight(this), this);
}

public Dimension getPreferredSize()
{
    return new Dimension(160, 100);
}

public void start()
{
    updateFont();
    updateTrigTables();
    updatePalette();
    updateImage();

    m_threadLavaLamp.start();
}

public void stop()
{
    m_threadLavaLamp.stop();
}

public void run()
```

```
{
    while (true)
    {
        repaint();
        renderNextFrame();

        try
        {
            Thread.sleep(m_nDelay);
        }
        catch (InterruptedException e)
        {
            stop();
        }
    }
}

public void componentHidden(ComponentEvent e) {}
public void componentMoved(ComponentEvent e) {}
public void componentShown(ComponentEvent e) {}

public void componentResized(ComponentEvent e)
{
    updateImage();
    updateFont();
}

private synchronized void renderNextFrame()
{
    int x, y, r, s;

    for (y = 0; y < m_nSourceHeight; y++)
    {
        r = m_nSinTable[(y + m_i) % 256];
        s = m_nCosTable[m_j % 256];

        for (x = 0; x < m_nSourceWidth; x++)
        {
            m_byBits[y * m_nSourceWidth + x] = (byte)
            ((m_nSinTable[(x + r) % 256] +
            m_nCosTable[(y + s) % 256]) % 256);
        }
    }

    if (m_i == 0) m_i = 255; else m_i-;
    if (m_j == 255) m_j = 0; else  m_j++;

    Image imgLava = createImage( new MemoryImageSource
                                    (m_nSourceWidth,
                                     m_nSourceHeight,
                                     m_cmPalette,
```

Continues

Listing 4-8
Continued.

```
                                          m_byBits,
                                          0,
                                          m_nSourceWidth) );

    Graphics g = m_imgBuffer.getGraphics();

    int w = getSize().width;
    int h = getSize().height;

    g.drawImage(imgLava, 0, 0, w, h, this);

    g.drawString(getName(),
                 w / 2 - m_nFontWidth / 2,
                 h / 2 + m_nFontHeight / 2);
}

private void updateFont()
{
    FontMetrics fm = getFontMetrics(getFont());

    m_nFontWidth = fm.stringWidth(getName());
    m_nFontHeight = fm.getAscent();
}

private void updateTrigTables()
{
    boolean bAlive = m_threadLavaLamp.isAlive();

    if (bAlive) m_threadLavaLamp.suspend();

    m_nSinTable = new int[256];
    m_nCosTable = new int[256];

    for (int i = 0; i < 256; i++)
    {
        m_nSinTable[i] = (int) (Math.sin(2 * Math.PI * i
                         / 256) * m_nSineAdjustment +
                         256);
        m_nCosTable[i] = (int) (Math.cos(2 * Math.PI * i
                         / 256) * m_nCosineAdjustment +
                         256);
    }

    if (bAlive) m_threadLavaLamp.resume();
}

private void updatePalette()
{
    boolean bAlive = m_threadLavaLamp.isAlive();

    if (bAlive) m_threadLavaLamp.suspend();
```

Listing 4-8

```
byte[] byReds   = new byte[256];
byte[] byGreens = new byte[256];
byte[] byBlues  = new byte[256];
int i;

for (i = 0; i < 64; i++)
{
    byReds[i]          = (byte)(i /
                         m_nRedReduction1);
    byGreens[i]        = (byte)(i /
                         m_nGreenReduction1);
    byBlues[i]         = (byte)(i /
                         m_nBlueReduction1);

    byReds[127 - i]   = (byte)(i / m_nRedReduction1);
    byGreens[127 - i] = (byte)(i /
                         m_nGreenReduction1);
    byBlues[127 - i]  = (byte)(i /
                         m_nBlueReduction1);

    byReds[127 + i]   = (byte)(i / m_nRedReduction2);
    byGreens[127 + i] = (byte)(i /
                         m_nGreenReduction2);
    byBlues[127 + i]  = (byte)(i /
                         m_nBlueReduction2);

    byReds[254 - i]   = (byte)(i / m_nRedReduction2);
    byGreens[254 - i] = (byte)(i /
                         m_nGreenReduction2);
    byBlues[254 - i]  = (byte)(i /
                         m_nBlueReduction2);
}

for (i = 0; i < 256; i++)
{
    if (byReds[i] + m_nGamma > 255)
        byReds[i] = (byte)255;
    else
        byReds[i] += (byte)m_nGamma;

    if (byGreens[i] + m_nGamma > 255)
        byGreens[i] = (byte)255;
    else
        byGreens[i] += (byte)m_nGamma;

    if (byBlues[i] + m_nGamma > 255)
        byBlues[i] = (byte)255;
    else
        byBlues[i] += (byte)m_nGamma;
}
```

Continues

Listing 4-8
Continued.

```java
    m_cmPalette = new IndexColorModel(8, 256, byReds,
                    byGreens, byBlues);

    if (bAlive) m_threadLavaLamp.resume();
}

private void updateImage()
{
    boolean bAlive = m_threadLavaLamp.isAlive();

    if (bAlive) m_threadLavaLamp.suspend();

    m_byBits = new byte[m_nSourceWidth *
                m_nSourceHeight];

    m_imgBuffer = createImage(getSize().width,
                    getSize().height);

    if (bAlive) m_threadLavaLamp.resume();
}

public void setFont(Font f) {
    super.setFont(f);
    updateFont();
}

public void setName(String str) {
    super.setName(str);
    updateFont();
}

public void setBlueReduction1(int n) {
    if ( n < 1 ) return;

    m_nBlueReduction1 = n;

    updatePalette();
    updateImage();
}

public int getBlueReduction1() {
    return m_nBlueReduction1;
}

public void setBlueReduction2(int n) {
    if ( n < 1 ) return;

    m_nBlueReduction2 = n;

    updatePalette();
    updateImage();
}
```

Listing 4-8

```
public int getBlueReduction2() {
    return m_nBlueReduction2;
}

public void setCosineAdjustment(int n) {
    if (n < 1 || n > 255) return;

    m_nCosineAdjustment = n;

    updateTrigTables();
}

public int getCosineAdjustment() {
    return m_nCosineAdjustment;
}

public void setDelay(int n) {
    m_nDelay = n;
}

public int getDelay() {
    return m_nDelay;
}

public void setGamma(int n) {
    m_nGamma = n;

    updatePalette();
    updateImage();
}

public int getGamma() {
    return m_nGamma;
}

public void setGreenReduction1(int n) {
    if ( n < 1 ) return;

    m_nGreenReduction1 = n;

    updatePalette();
    updateImage();
}

public int getGreenReduction1() {
    return m_nGreenReduction1;
}

public void setGreenReduction2(int n) {
    if ( n < 1 ) return;
```

Continues

Listing 4-8
Continued.

```
      m_nGreenReduction2 = n;

   updatePalette();
   updateImage();
}

public int getGreenReduction2() {
   return m_nGreenReduction2;
}

public void setRedReduction1(int n) {
   if ( n < 1 ) return;

   m_nRedReduction1 = n;

   updatePalette();
   updateImage();
}

public int getRedReduction1() {
   return m_nRedReduction1;
}

public void setRedReduction2(int n) {
   if ( n < 1 ) return;

   m_nRedReduction2 = n;

   updatePalette();
   updateImage();
}

public int getRedReduction2() {
   return m_nRedReduction2;
}

public void setSineAdjustment(int n) {
   if (n < 1 || n > 255) return;

   m_nSineAdjustment = n;

   updateTrigTables();
}

public int getSineAdjustment() {
   return m_nSineAdjustment;
}

public void setSourceHeight(int n) {
   m_nSourceHeight = n;

   updateImage();
```

Listing 4-8

```
        }

        public int getSourceHeight() {
            return m_nSourceHeight;
        }

        public void setSourceWidth(int n) {
            m_nSourceWidth = n;

            updateImage();
        }

        public int getSourceWidth() {
            return m_nSourceWidth;
        }
    }
```

STEP 3   As mentioned, a class that implements `java.io.Serializable` may throw a `NotSerializableException` if one or more of its fields is not serializable. This is precisely what happens to the Lava Lamp class when it gets serialized. Listing 4-9 shows the Java error log that is produced when a Bean builder tool attempts to serialize the Lava Lamp.

The quick fix for this problem is to declare the three non-serializable fields—`IndexColorModel`, `Image`, and `Thread`—as transient. The new field declarations look like this:

```
private transient IndexColorModel m_cmPalette;
private transient Image m_imgBuffer;
private transient Thread m_threadLavaLamp = new
        Thread(this);
```

With this new code, the Lava Lamp can be serialized without error.

STEP 4   Of course, making those three fields transient means that their values won't be restored when the Lava Lamp is deserialized. Java's serialization mechanisms will simply leave them alone. Want we want, though, is to bring them back to life, resurrecting their values to their original, pre-serialization state.

To accomplish this feat, we must define the `writeObject()` and `readObject()` methods to act as notifications that serialization or deserialization has occurred. We'll also use them to append some extra data to the stream, allowing us to restore the transient fields. For the non-transient fields, we'll simply let the default serialization mechanisms do the work for us. Here's how the `writeObject()` method will look:

```
java.io.NotSerializableException: sun.awt.windows.
    WOffScreenImage
        at java.io.ObjectOutputStream.outputObject
        (ObjectOutputStream.java:660)
        at java.io.ObjectOutputStream.writeObject
        (ObjectOutputStream.java:225)
        at java.io.ObjectOutputStream.defaultWriteObject
        (ObjectOutputStream.java:325)
        at java.io.ObjectOutputStream.outputObject
        (ObjectOutputStream.java:707)
        at java.io.ObjectOutputStream.writeObject
        (ObjectOutputStream.java:225)
java.io.NotSerializableException: java.awt.image.
    IndexColorModel
        at java.io.ObjectOutputStream.outputObject
        (ObjectOutputStream.java:660)
        at java.io.ObjectOutputStream.writeObject
        (ObjectOutputStream.java:225)
        at java.io.ObjectOutputStream.defaultWriteObject
        (ObjectOutputStream.java:325)
        at java.io.ObjectOutputStream.outputObject
        (ObjectOutputStream.java:707)
        at java.io.ObjectOutputStream.writeObject
        (ObjectOutputStream.java:225)
java.io.NotSerializableException: java.lang.Thread
        at java.io.ObjectOutputStream.outputObject
        (ObjectOutputStream.java:660)
        at java.io.ObjectOutputStream.writeObject
        (ObjectOutputStream.java:225)
        at java.io.ObjectOutputStream.defaultWriteObject
        (ObjectOutputStream.java:325)
        at java.io.ObjectOutputStream.outputObject
        (ObjectOutputStream.java:707)
        at java.io.ObjectOutputStream.writeObject
        (ObjectOutputStream.java:225)
```

```
private void writeObject(ObjectOutputStream stream) throws
    IOException
{
    stream.defaultWriteObject();

    boolean isThreadRunning = m_threadLavaLamp.isAlive();
    stream.writeBoolean(isThreadRunning);
}
```

The first line of this method sends all the non-transient data through
the stream. The rest of the method obtains a Boolean value to determine
whether the Lava Lamp's thread is running and then sends this value
through the stream, as well. We require this step because the thread ob-

Listing 4-10
A **readObject()** method for the Lava Lamp bean.

```
private void readObject(ObjectInputStream stream) throws
    IOException, ClassNotFoundException
{
    stream.defaultReadObject();

    m_threadLavaLamp = new Thread(this);

    boolean wasThreadRunning = stream.readBoolean();

    if (wasThreadRunning)
    {
        m_threadLavaLamp.start();
    }

    updatePalette();
}
```

ject is not serializable, yet we want to reconstruct its state when the bean is deserialized. With the single Boolean value we can do that.

We now need a **readObject()** method to convert the serialized stream back to its original form. Listing 4-10 shows how it will look.

Naturally, the first line of **readObject()** restores the non-transient data that the **writeObject()** created. The rest of the method reconstructs the transient fields to their original state. At this point, things start to get complicated.

First, notice that the Lava Lamp's constructor (see Listing 4-8) adds itself as a component listener by calling **addComponentListener()**. When the Lava Lamp is deserialized, however, this function is never called, because an object's constructor is always skipped during deserialization. Thus, you might think that we should call **addComponentListener()** in the **readObject()** to restore the Lava Lamp's state as a component listener. Actually, we can skip this step altogether. A quick look at the source code for the **java.awt.Component** class shows that its **readObject()** method automatically restores its listener state for all AWT events. So far, so good.

Next, take a look at the declaration of **m_threadLavaLamp**, a non-serializable **Thread** object. This object is initialized the moment it is declared. We would like to restore this initialized state when the Lava Lamp is deserialized; however, the deserialization process skips field initializations of classes just like it skips their constructors. So we'll need to reinitialize **m_threadLavaLamp** during deserialization, and that's exactly what we do in the second statement of **readObject()**.

Although the thread object has been properly initialized, its new, deserialized state might be different than its old, serialized state. If, for example, the Lava Lamp was serialized after its thread was started, the thread would now be stopped. Luckily, we remembered to store the thread's state as a Boolean variable, so the fix for this problem is easy. We simply read back the Boolean variable and, if the variable is true, restart the thread.

Now we must continue restoring the state of the remaining transient fields. First on the agenda is **m_cmPalette**. Because the value of this object can be calculated from other fields, we merely call **updatePalette()** to restore it. Note that if **m_cmPalette** could not have been calculated from other fields, we would have had to preserve its value by appending data to the stream.

Finally, only one non-transient field remains: **m_imgBackground**. Thanks to a quirk in Java serialization, this tiny field turns out to be a large problem. The quirk, in this case, is that a **Component** object's peer does not get restored until after the **readObject()** method returns. This means that calling the Lava Lamp's **updateImage()** method to restore the field will result in a **NullPointerException** because the **createImage()** method (which is called by the **updateImage()** method) expects a valid peer. The workaround is to delay restoring **m_imgBackground** until it is needed. The easiest way to do this is by calling **updateImage()** inside the **paint()** method. The new **paint()** looks like this:

```
public synchronized void paint(Graphics g)
{
    if (m_imgBuffer == null) updateImage();

    g.drawImage(m_imgBuffer, 0, 0,
        m_imgBuffer.getWidth(this),
        m_imgBuffer.getHeight(this), this);
}
```

With this change, the Lava Lamp—including all of its transient fields—can be successfully deserialized.

STEP 5   In Step 4, the Lava Lamp bean is successfully serialized, but it is arguably not correctly serialized. The issue here is that the class contains certain non-transient fields whose values can be obtained from calculations. As mentioned earlier in this chapter, such fields usually should not be written to a serialized stream for the sake of efficiency. They should instead be recalculated when the object becomes deserialized.

The Lava Lamp contains two fields that can be calculated (**m_nSinTable** and **m_nCosTable**) and one field that is used as a temporary buffer (**m_byBits**). Therefore, we will make all three fields transient. The new declarations look like this:

```
private transient int[] m_nSinTable, m_nCosTable;
private transient byte[] m_byBits;
```

We must now update the **readObject()** method to restore the state of the three variables. This step requires only two lines:

```
updateTrigTables();
m_byBits = new byte[m_nSourceWidth * m_nSourceHeight];
```

The result is a bean that serializes itself just as well but requires less space to do so. Figure 4-7 shows how support for serialization allows tools like Taligent's Bean Tester to transform a prototype of the Lava Lamp into a working application.

Introspection

Unlike some other languages, Java was not designed by a standards committee nor did it simply evolve over time. It was built by several teams of programmers at Sun working closely together. The process was not very open or official, but it definitely allowed Java's core features to become

Figure 4-7
Because the Lava Lamp supports serialization, Taligent's Bean Tester can build an application that looks just like the prototype.

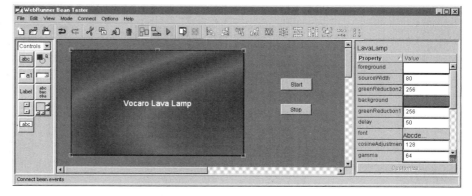

tightly integrated. Java's Remote Method Invocation (RMI), for example, is an API for object-oriented networking that relies heavily on the serialization mechanisms discussed in this chapter. Similarly, JavaBeans depends on both serialization and RMI for enabling visual development and distributed programming. The Java Foundation Classes—a class library built by Sun, Netscape, and others—continues the trend. It includes components built using the JavaBeans architecture. Obviously, the development teams at Sun have paid close attention to what the others were doing.

Object serialization is yet another example of one Java feature relying on some other Java feature. In this case, serialization depends on reflection, an API introduced in Java 1.1. Reflection obtains information about any given class: its constructors, methods, and fields, including private, package, and protected fields. It can also invoke the constructors and methods that it finds, and it can get and set the fields (as long as the system security manager allows it).

Although reflection lies at the heart of Java, its usefulness to bean developers is actually quite limited. Reflection is suited mainly to utility applications that need to discover and use all the features of a given class. Java-based debuggers, interpreters, and class browsers, for instance, perform their duties via reflection.

The question before us now is, "If reflection applies only to these low-level tools, why do we, the component developers, even care about it?" In truth, reflection has only an academic value to JavaBeans programmers. Its inclusion in this chapter is mainly for the sake of completeness, given that object serialization depends on it.

Reflection is not the end the story, however. There exists a second, higher level version of reflection designed exclusively for the JavaBeans architecture. Known as introspection, it wraps the complex reflection API into a friendly, easy-to-use class called **Introspector**. It obtains the methods, properties, and events exposed by a bean and is thus a vital ingredient of most builder tools.

In this section, we'll look at the details of both the core reflection API and the **Introspector** class. We'll also provide an example program that runs the gamut of the reflection classes. Later, we'll peruse some sample code that demonstrates how to perform introspection.

Core Reflection API

Unlike most of Java's feature set, the reflection API is not confined to a single package. The reflection classes are split up between the **java.lang** and `java.lang.reflect` packages, thanks to the ultra-dynamic history of Java. The majority of these classes are nothing more than wrappers for the fundamental elements of Java: classes, fields, methods, primitive types, and so on. The most important wrapper classes are:

- `java.lang.Class`
- `java.lang.reflect.Constructor`
- `java.lang.reflect.Method`
- `java.lang.reflect.Field`
- `java.lang.reflect.Array`
- `java.lang.reflect.Modifier`
- `java.lang.reflect.Member` (interface)

`Class`, `Constructor`, `Method`, `Field`, and `Array` are exactly what their names imply. They represent—indeed, reflect—the Java language elements class, constructor, method, field, and array. The `Modifier` class is just a helper class that provides constants for decoding access modifiers (i.e. private, final, transient, abstract, etc.), and the `Member` class is simply an interface that ties the similarities of the `Constructor`, `Method`, and `Field` classes together.

In addition to these crucial classes, the reflection API also provides wrappers for the primitive data types. The classes are:

- `java.lang.Boolean`
- `java.lang.Byte`
- `java.lang.Character`
- `java.lang.Double`
- `java.lang.Float`
- `java.lang.Integer`
- `java.lang.Long`
- `java.lang.Short`
- `java.lang.Void`

These wrapper classes are necessary because the reflection API deals entirely with object references, not primitive types. Note that the final class in the list, `Void`, is not actually a wrapper but merely an uninstantiable placeholder. It makes possible the description of methods that don't return a value.

The intimate details of these fifteen classes are beyond the scope of this book, and they are well-documented in Sun's Java Development Kit.

Therefore, we will only provide an example of how to use them. For this sample application, we'll demonstrate how the reflection API can expose the internal structure of the Lava Lamp (the example bean from earlier in this chapter). Listing 4-11 is the source code for a program that prints the class name, class hierarchy, interfaces, constructors, fields, and methods in the Lava Lamp. The output of the program is shown in Listing 4-12.

Listing 4-11

A program that uses the reflection API to display the internal structure of the Lava Lamp.

```
import java.lang.reflect.*;

public class LavaLampReflector
{
    public static void main(String[] args)
    {
        Class lavaLamp = null;

        try
        {
            lavaLamp = Class.forName("com.vocaro.
                    freestuff.LavaLamp");
        }
        catch (ClassNotFoundException e)
        {
            System.out.println("ERROR: Could not load com.
                    vocaro.freestuff.LavaLamp");
        }

        // Name...

        System.out.println("NAME:");
        System.out.println(lavaLamp.getName());

        // Family tree...

        System.out.println("HIERARCHY:");

        for ( Class parent = lavaLamp; parent != null;
            parent = parent.getSuperclass() )
        {
            System.out.println(parent.getName());
        }

        // Interfaces...

        System.out.println("INTERFACES:");

        Class[] interfaces = lavaLamp.getInterfaces();

        for (int i = 0; i < interfaces.length; i++)
        {
```

```
                    System.out.println(interfaces[i].getName());
    }

    // Constructors...

    System.out.println("CONSTRUCTORS:");

    Constructor[] constructors = lavaLamp.
    getDeclaredConstructors();

    for (int i = 0; i < constructors.length; i++)
    {
        System.out.println(constructors[i].getName());
    }

    // Fields...

    System.out.println("FIELDS:");

    Field[] fields = lavaLamp.getDeclaredFields();

    for (int i = 0; i < fields.length; i++)
    {
        System.out.println(fields[i].toString());
    }

    // Methods...

    System.out.println("METHODS:");

    Method[] methods = lavaLamp.getDeclaredMethods();

    for (int i = 0; i < methods.length; i++)
    {
        System.out.println(methods[i].toString());
    }
    }
}
```

The output displayed
by the Lava Lamp
Reflector program.

```
NAME:
com.vocaro.freestuff.LavaLamp
HIERARCHY:
com.vocaro.freestuff.LavaLamp
java.awt.Canvas
java.awt.Component
java.lang.Object
INTERFACES:
java.lang.Runnable
```

Continues

Listing 4-12
Continued.

```
java.awt.event.ComponentListener
java.io.Serializable
CONSTRUCTORS:
com.vocaro.freestuff.LavaLamp
FIELDS:
private int com.vocaro.freestuff.LavaLamp.m_nSourceWidth
private int com.vocaro.freestuff.LavaLamp.m_nSourceHeight
private int com.vocaro.freestuff.LavaLamp.m_nGamma
private int com.vocaro.freestuff.LavaLamp.m_nDelay
private int com.vocaro.freestuff.LavaLamp.m_nRedReduction1
private int com.vocaro.freestuff.LavaLamp.m_nRedReduction2
private int com.vocaro.freestuff.LavaLamp.
    m_nGreenReduction1
private int com.vocaro.freestuff.LavaLamp.
    m_nGreenReduction2
private int com.vocaro.freestuff.LavaLamp.m_nBlueReduction1
private int com.vocaro.freestuff.LavaLamp.m_nBlueReduction2
private int com.vocaro.freestuff.LavaLamp.m_nSineAdjustment
private int com.vocaro.freestuff.LavaLamp.
    m_nCosineAdjustment
private transient int[] com.vocaro.freestuff.LavaLamp.
    m_nSinTable
private transient int[] com.vocaro.freestuff.LavaLamp.
    m_nCosTable
private transient byte[] com.vocaro.freestuff.LavaLamp.
    m_byBits
private transient java.awt.image.IndexColorModel
    com.vocaro.freestuff.LavaLamp.m_cmPalette
private transient java.awt.Image com.vocaro.freestuff.
    LavaLamp.m_imgBuffer
private int com.vocaro.freestuff.LavaLamp.m_i
private int com.vocaro.freestuff.LavaLamp.m_j
private transient java.lang.Thread com.vocaro.freestuff.
    LavaLamp.m_threadLavaLamp
private int com.vocaro.freestuff.LavaLamp.m_nFontWidth
private int com.vocaro.freestuff.LavaLamp.m_nFontHeight
METHODS:
private void com.vocaro.freestuff.LavaLamp.writeObject
    (java.io.ObjectOutputStream) throws
    java.io.IOException
private void com.vocaro.freestuff.LavaLamp.readObject
    (java.io.ObjectInputStream) throws
    java.io.IOException,java.lang.ClassNotFoundException
public void com.vocaro.freestuff.LavaLamp.update
    (java.awt.Graphics)
public synchronized void com.vocaro.freestuff.LavaLamp.
    paint(java.awt.Graphics)
public java.awt.Dimension com.vocaro.freestuff.LavaLamp.
    getPreferredSize()
public void com.vocaro.freestuff.LavaLamp.start()
public void com.vocaro.freestuff.LavaLamp.stop()
public void com.vocaro.freestuff.LavaLamp.run()
```

Listing 4-12

```
public void com.vocaro.freestuff.LavaLamp.componentHidden
    (java.awt.event.ComponentEvent)
public void com.vocaro.freestuff.LavaLamp.componentMoved
    (java.awt.event.ComponentEvent)
public void com.vocaro.freestuff.LavaLamp.componentShown
    (java.awt.event.ComponentEvent)
public void com.vocaro.freestuff.LavaLamp.componentResized
    (java.awt.event.ComponentEvent)
private synchronized void com.vocaro.freestuff.LavaLamp.
    renderNextFrame()
private void com.vocaro.freestuff.LavaLamp.updateFont()
private void com.vocaro.freestuff.LavaLamp.
    updateTrigTables()
private void com.vocaro.freestuff.LavaLamp.updatePalette()
private void com.vocaro.freestuff.LavaLamp.updateImage()
public void com.vocaro.freestuff.LavaLamp.setFont
    (java.awt.Font)
public void com.vocaro.freestuff.LavaLamp.setName
    (java.lang.String)
public void com.vocaro.freestuff.LavaLamp.
    setBlueReduction1(int)
public int com.vocaro.freestuff.LavaLamp.getBlueReduction1()
public void com.vocaro.freestuff.LavaLamp.
    setBlueReduction2(int)
public int com.vocaro.freestuff.LavaLamp.getBlueReduction2()
public void com.vocaro.freestuff.LavaLamp.
    setCosineAdjustment(int)
public int com.vocaro.freestuff.LavaLamp.
    getCosineAdjustment()
public void com.vocaro.freestuff.LavaLamp.setDelay(int)
public int com.vocaro.freestuff.LavaLamp.getDelay()
public void com.vocaro.freestuff.LavaLamp.setGamma(int)
public int com.vocaro.freestuff.LavaLamp.getGamma()
public void com.vocaro.freestuff.LavaLamp.
    setGreenReduction1(int)
public int com.vocaro.freestuff.LavaLamp.
    getGreenReduction1()
public void com.vocaro.freestuff.LavaLamp.
    setGreenReduction2(int)
public int com.vocaro.freestuff.LavaLamp.
    getGreenReduction2()
public void com.vocaro.freestuff.LavaLamp.
    setRedReduction1(int)
public int com.vocaro.freestuff.LavaLamp.getRedReduction1()
public void com.vocaro.freestuff.LavaLamp.
    setRedReduction2(int)
public int com.vocaro.freestuff.LavaLamp.getRedReduction2()
public void com.vocaro.freestuff.LavaLamp.
    setSineAdjustment(int)
public int com.vocaro.freestuff.LavaLamp.
    getSineAdjustment()
```

Continues

Listing 4-12
Continued.

```
public void com.vocaro.freestuff.LavaLamp.
    setSourceHeight(int)
public int com.vocaro.freestuff.LavaLamp.getSourceHeight()
public void com.vocaro.freestuff.LavaLamp.
    setSourceWidth(int)
public int com.vocaro.freestuff.LavaLamp.getSourceWidth()
```

Notice that all members of the Lava Lamp bean were printed. This reveals an important characteristic of the low-level reflection API: it can uncover even the private fields and methods of Java classes, although these elements are normally restricted during runtime. Fortunately, Java's security manager can block this potentially dangerous feature. Most Web browsers, for instance, provide security managers that prevent untrusted applets from gaining access to private fields and from invoking private methods. Applets attempting to perform the same tasks as the Lava Lamp Reflector will fail with a security exception.

The Lava Lamp Reflector exhibits the key ideas behind reflection, but it is certainly not comprehensive. Java's reflection API provides a rich set of features that can create instances of any class, modify the data contained in any field, and invoke any method. It can also break down program elements into their basic components. For example, instead of dumping all items to the screen, the Lava Lamp Reflector could have determined which items were public and which were private and then separated the items into two list boxes. The classes necessary for doing this work are fully documented in the Java Development Kit, so the task has been left as an exercise for the reader.

Introspector class

The core reflection API, as noted previously, is of limited value to JavaBeans developers. In fact, programmers of beans and of Bean builder tools should never call the API directly. Instead, they should rely on **java.beans.Introspector**, a class that hides the complexities of reflection. It provides a set of static methods that can obtain the properties, events, and methods inside a bean (see Listing 4-13).

Unlike the reflection API, this class does not offer a dizzying assortment of methods for handling every possible feature of a bean. Instead, **Introspector** takes the simplest route by consolidating its features into a single method: **getBeanInfo()**. This method encapsulates all the infor-

Listing 4-13
The java.beans.
Introspector class.

```
public class Introspector
{
    public static BeanInfo getBeanInfo(Class beanClass)
        throws IntrospectionException;
    public static BeanInfo getBeanInfo(Class beanClass,
        Class stopClass) throws IntrospectionException;
    public static String[] getBeanInfoSearchPath();
    public static void setBeanInfoSearchPath(String path[]);
    public static String decapitalize(String name);
}
```

mation about a bean and wraps it up into a single **BeanInfo** object. **Bean-Info** objects, which are discussed thoroughly in Chapter 5, provide their own methods for getting descriptions of the methods, events, and properties exposed by a bean.

Using **Introspector** is a two-step process. We call **getBeanInfo()** to retrieve the **BeanInfo** object for a particular bean, and then we call the **BeanInfo**'s methods to obtain the actual details about the component. Note that the **Introspector** class uses reflection only when a bean does not provide this **BeanInfo** object. If one cannot be found, the reflection API kicks in, browsing the methods of the bean and its superclasses and allowing **Introspector** to find names that match the standard JavaBeans design patterns. The class then uses this information to construct a new **BeanInfo** object on-the-fly. So although a bean might not always provide a **BeanInfo** object, we can always depend on **Introspector** to give us a proper **BeanInfo**, even if that object is a "fake" created behind the scenes.

The other four methods in the **Introspector** class are only complimentary to **getBeanInfo()**. The second overloaded **BeanInfo** method—the one with two parameters—is identical to the first, except that it can limit the search through the bean's superclasses by stopping at a given class. The **getBeanInfoSearchPath()**/**setBeanInfoSearchPath()** methods specify extra directories in which to look when searching for **BeanInfo** objects. And the **decapitalize()** method is just a utility that helps determine a property name from the names of its **get** or **set** methods.

To illustrate the **Introspector** class, let's look at a sample program that uses it. This program will inspect the Lava Lamp bean and display its properties, methods, and events. The source code of the program is in Listing 4-14, and its output is in Listing 4-15. Note that the program code catches an **IntrospectionException**. This exception is a partner to the **Introspector** and enables us to distinguish between generic problems and problems related directly to introspection.

Listing 4-14
A program that uses introspection to display the properties, methods, and events of the Lava Lamp bean.

```java
import java.beans.*;

public class LavaLampIntrospector
{
    public static void main(String[] args)
    {
        Class lavaLamp = null;

        try
        {
            lavaLamp = Class.forName("com.vocaro.
                    freestuff.LavaLamp");
        }
        catch (ClassNotFoundException e)
        {
            System.out.println("ERROR: Could not load com.
                    vocaro.freestuff.LavaLamp");
        }

        BeanInfo beanInfo = null;

        try
        {
            beanInfo = Introspector.getBeanInfo(lavaLamp,
                    lavaLamp.getSuperclass());
        }
        catch (IntrospectionException e)
        {
            System.out.println("ERROR: Could not obtain
                        BeanInfo object");
        }

        // Properties...

        System.out.println("PROPERTIES:");

        PropertyDescriptor[] properties =
        beanInfo.getPropertyDescriptors();

        for (int i = 0; i < properties.length; i++)
        {

        System.out.println(properties[i].getDisplayName());
        }

        // Methods...

        System.out.println("METHODS:");

        MethodDescriptor[] methods = beanInfo.
                                    getMethodDescriptors();
```

Listing 4-14

```
        for (int i = 0; i < methods.length; i++)
        {
            System.out.println(methods[i].getDisplayName());
        }

        // Events...

        System.out.println("EVENTS:");

        EventSetDescriptor[] events =
        beanInfo.getEventSetDescriptors();

        for (int i = 0; i < events.length; i++)
        {
            System.out.println(events[i].getDisplayName());
        }
    }
}
```

Listing 4-15
The output displayed
by the Lava Lamp
Introspector
program.

```
PROPERTIES:
preferredSize
sourceWidth
greenReduction2
greenReduction1
delay
font
cosineAdjustment
gamma
sineAdjustment
name
blueReduction2
blueReduction1
sourceHeight
redReduction2
redReduction1
METHODS:
getGamma
setRedReduction2
setRedReduction1
getSineAdjustment
getCosineAdjustment
setBlueReduction2
setBlueReduction1
componentShown
setCosineAdjustment
update
getSourceHeight
setSourceHeight
```

Continues

Listing 4-15
Continued.

```
setFont
componentResized
setSineAdjustment
getSourceWidth
setGreenReduction2
setGreenReduction1
setDelay
getPreferredSize
setName
stop
getRedReduction2
getRedReduction1
componentHidden
setSourceWidth
getDelay
componentMoved
run
paint
getBlueReduction2
setGamma
getBlueReduction1
start
getGreenReduction2
getGreenReduction1
EVENTS:
```

As shown in the listing, the Lava Lamp Introspector displays all the properties and methods of the Lava Lamp bean, but no events appear because the bean has no events. If, however, the program had not specified a "stop class" in the call to **getBeanInfo()**, the output would be much longer, given that the Lava Lamp's parents contain additional properties, methods, and events.

Note that the list of methods includes every public method in the Lava Lamp, even though the bean has only two "real" methods (**start()** and **stop()**). This not only reveals a flaw in the implementation of the **Introspector** class (it should be smart enough to recognize that the get/set property methods are not real methods) but it also shows us an excellent reason to implement a **BeanInfo** interface for every bean we create. **BeanInfo** objects, which are described in Chapter 5, can eliminate problems such as these which are inherent in introspection.

Despite the redundancy in its search for methods, it's easy to see that the **Introspector** class saves us quite a bit of work. Without it, we would have to churn through the reflection API, distinguishing between public and non-public elements, deriving property names from **get** and **set** method names, and so on. Another benefit of the `Introspector` class is that it provides a sort of common ground for Bean builder tools. As long as they all use the class, each tool will view all beans in exactly the same way. This standardization is indispensable for the success of the Java-Beans architecture.

CONCLUSION

Object serialization and introspection are called "core" features. And rightly so, because both are integral parts of the JavaBeans architecture and of Java itself. Serialization provides an easy and efficient means of saving an object's state to disk or sending it through a network. Plus, it allows Bean builder tools to take picture-perfect snapshots of application prototypes and bring them back to life on an end-user's system. All of this would not be possible, however, without an assist from the reflection API. It provides the basis for both serialization and introspection. Taken as a whole, these features make the JavaBeans architecture powerful and flexible.

5

Building a **BeanInfo** Interface

In October 1996, Sun Microsystems unleashed the first version of the JavaBeans specification. Only a few weeks later, the company's e-mail server was flooded with messages from Java developers who wanted to learn more about JavaBeans. Sun was forced to install an extra server just to handle the backlog of messages.

To further reduce the strain on the e-mail server, Sun created an Internet mailing list devoted exclusively to the discussion of JavaBeans. Internet mailing lists, unlike their pen-and-paper counterparts, are automated, 24-hour bulletin boards; any developer wanting to view the board or post to it could simply forward her e-mail address to the list server. The server would then send her daily copies of all messages posted to the list.

Although Sun's JavaBeans mailing list is no longer available (having been eclipsed by the comp.lang.java.beans newsgroup), I can recall the last few months of its existence when I was a subscriber. The most common question was, "What makes a JavaBean a JavaBean?"

As you have already learned, the answer is "Not much." Technically, any Java class is also a JavaBean. The only major difference is that bean-style Java classes are structured in such a way that they can be integrated easily with other classes and—more importantly—with development tools such as IBM's Visual Age for Java or Lotus' BeanMachine.

In this chapter, you will learn one of the easiest and yet most important ways to give your JavaBeans this structure. It's called the **BeanInfo** interface, and it's located in the **java.beans** package. The first half of this chapter gets down and dirty with **BeanInfo**, describing all of its facets and digging through its helper classes. The chapter's second half presents a full-blown JavaBean and walks you through all the steps necessary for building its **BeanInfo** interface.

This Chapter Covers

- What is a **BeanInfo** interface?
- Method, property, and event set descriptors
- JavaBean icons
- Default properties and event sets
- A sample **BeanInfo** interface for real-time fire animation

What Is **BeanInfo**?

In chapter 3, we talked about **BeanInfo**. The **BeanInfo** interface is exactly that: an interface. It has no methods, no variables, and no implementation of any kind. It's just a collection of functions that exposes your bean to the outside world. Listing 5-1 shows the Java source code of the interface.

Each method in this interface provides a certain piece of information about the JavaBean, including:

■ The bean descriptor: details about the bean itself, such as its display name and customizer class (see Chapter 6).

■ Event set descriptors: names, attributes, and other details about the events fired by the bean.

■ Property descriptors: names, attributes, and other details about the properties exposed by the bean.

■ Method descriptors: names, attributes, and other details about the methods exposed by the bean.

■ Additional **BeanInfo** objects: Extra **BeanInfo** objects if the bean is derived from another bean.

■ Icon images: images for displaying 32x32- and 16x16-pixel icons of the bean for toolbars and similar gadgets.

You will learn how to provide this information later in this chapter. For now, remember that it is your responsibility to implement every method in **BeanInfo** to return the appropriate values for your particular bean. Java classes and development tools that use the bean automatically call its **BeanInfo** methods to obtain these values.

Listing 5-1
The **BeanInfo** interface exposes your bean to the outside world.

```
public interface BeanInfo
{
    BeanDescriptor getBeanDescriptor();

    EventSetDescriptor[] getEventSetDescriptors();
    int getDefaultEventIndex();

    PropertyDescriptor[] getPropertyDescriptors();
    int getDefaultPropertyIndex();

    MethodDescriptor[] getMethodDescriptors();

    BeanInfo[] getAdditionalBeanInfo();

    java.awt.Image getIcon(int iconKind);

    final static int ICON_COLOR_16x16 = 1;
    final static int ICON_COLOR_32x32 = 2;
    final static int ICON_MONO_16x16 = 3;
    final static int ICON_MONO_32x32 = 4;
}
```

TIP: *Many beans don't need all the features of the* **BeanInfo** *interface. A bean with no parameters and no events, for instance, would implement* **getPropertyDescriptors()** *and* **getEventSetDescriptors()** *to return null. The designers of JavaBeans realized this fact and provided bean developers with a nifty shortcut: the* **SimpleBeanInfo** *class. Located in the java.beans package, this class provides a generic implementation of the* **BeanInfo** *interface. So, instead of creating your own implementation of* **BeanInfo**, *you can just extend* **SimpleBeanInfo**, *override only the methods you need, and let the parent class (that is,* **SimpleBeanInfo**) *handle the rest. See the Fire Wall sample at the end of this chapter for some example code using* **SimpleBeanInfo**.

After you've implemented the **BeanInfo** methods, the rest of your work is easy. Just follow these steps:

1. Make sure that the name of your **BeanInfo** class is "bean name" + "BeanInfo." For example, if your bean is named CalculatorBean, your **BeanInfo** class must be named **CalculatorBeanBeanInfo**.

2. Compile the Java source code containing your **BeanInfo** class.

3. Package the compiled **BeanInfo** class along with the rest of the bean's classes. If your bean is to be shipped as a JAR file, for instance, you must insert your **BeanInfo** class into the JAR. See Chapter 12 to learn how.

That's it! You don't need to register your **BeanInfo** class or take any special steps to enable it. Simply package it with your bean, and you're done.

Behold! Bean Builders Build **BeanInfo** Behavior

In the early months of JavaBeans' existence, most programmers had only one tool to assist them: the Beans Development Kit, available for free from Sun's Web site. Unfortunately, with the BDK, you got what you paid for. The samples and documentation were okay, but the kit offered no tools for automating the process of bean programming.

These days, however, the world of JavaBean development is far better, thanks to more than a dozen bean builder tools that are commercially available. Although each tool provides its own unique blend of features, almost all of them can generate a **BeanInfo** interface automatically. So, instead of creating a **BeanInfo** from scratch, you can let the builder handle the work. You simply define the methods, properties, and events you want, and let the builder do the rest.

IBM's Visual Age for Java is one such tool that can generate `BeanInfo` interfaces automatically. It offers a set of dialog boxes and wizards for helping you define `BeanInfo` data (see Figure 5-1). Although Visual Age's complex user interface is difficult to learn, the tool is fully compliant with the `BeanInfo` standard. It can generate error-free `BeanInfo` source code with just a few clicks of the mouse. In fact, Visual Age makes `BeanInfo` creation so easy, that if you've already invested in a copy, you can probably skip this whole chapter.

Another tool for eliminating the need to write a `BeanInfo` interface is Taligent's WebRunner Bean Wizard. Unlike Visual Age for Java, this bean builder is not a graphical source code *editor*, but rather a step-by-step source code *generator*. You can start by editing an existing bean or creating a new one from scratch. With either option, the Bean Wizard enables you to create methods, properties, and events simply by typing their names into a dialog box (see Figure 5-2). When you're finished, the wizard churns through the information you provided and magically produces the proper source files for the bean—including, of course, a `BeanInfo` interface.

Figure 5-1
IBM's Visual Age for Java.

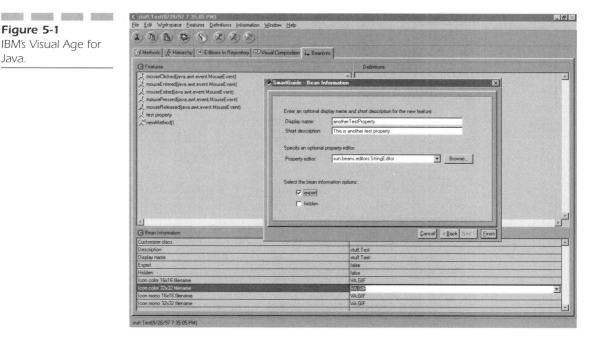

Figure 5-2
Taligent's Bean
Wizard is a source
code generator that
can produce
BeanInfo interfaces
automatically.

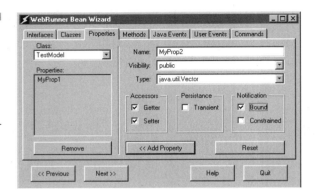

Figure 5-2
Taligent's Bean
Wizard is a source
code generator that
can produce
BeanInfo interfaces
automatically.

Why Do I Need **BeanInfo**?

If you've read Chapter 4, you know all about a Java 1.1 feature called *introspection*. To recap, introspection allows any Java class (but usually a Java development tool, such as Powersoft's PowerJ) to learn about the methods, properties, and events exposed by some other Java class (or JavaBean).

But wait a minute: if introspection can reveal a JavaBean to the world, then why is the **BeanInfo** interface necessary at all? The answer is that introspection is too simple. It can reveal only the names and parameters of the methods, properties, and events in a bean. Quite often, developers want to fine tune the introspection process to provide more details about their bean and to have greater control over how it is exposed. That's where **BeanInfo** comes in. It overrides the introspection process whenever a bean is loaded into a development tool (see Figure 5-3).

Another important reason to use **BeanInfo** comes into play when running the ActiveX Bridge. Available for free from Sun Microsystems, the ActiveX Bridge can transform any JavaBean into an ActiveX control. When beans masquerade as ActiveX controls, they can be brought into non-Java environments such as Visual Basic or C++.

The ActiveX Bridge relies on the same introspection techniques as other JavaBeans tools. And again, the problem of simplicity emerges. For instance, when the introspection process looks at a bean's methods, it assumes that every method in the entire hierarchy of the bean—that is, the bean and all of its parent classes—should be considered a method of that bean. For beans derived from AWT classes (as most are), this can add up to dozens of methods, including ones that are completely irrelevant to the bean's functionality. This issue may cause confusion for users who load the bean into a standard ActiveX development tool (see Figure 5-4) and discover cryptic Java methods that they don't understand.

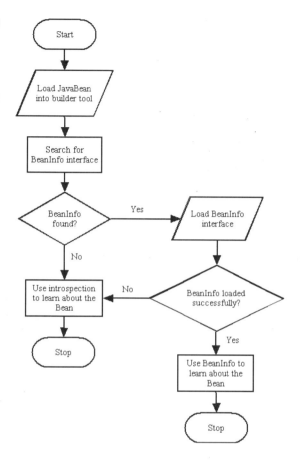

Figure 5-3
If present, the
BeanInfo interface
overrides the
introspection process.

Fortunately, there's an easy solution to this problem: just use **BeanInfo**. It eliminates the potential dangers of introspection and allows only the true methods of your bean to be revealed.

Feature Descriptors

Now that you know the whats and the whys of **BeanInfo**, it's time to pry open the hood and take a closer look inside the interface. First, go back to Listing 5-1 and note the return values of the methods in **BeanInfo**. You will see names such as "BeanDescriptor," "MethodDescriptor," and so on. These data types are classes defined in the java.beans package, and each class encapsulates a certain piece of information about the bean. For example, as you can probably guess, the **MethodDescriptor** class holds the

Figure 5-4

Figure 5-4
When an
ActiveX/bean does
not provide a
BeanInfo interface,
every method in the
bean's class hierarchy
appears in Visual
Basic as methods of
the bean.

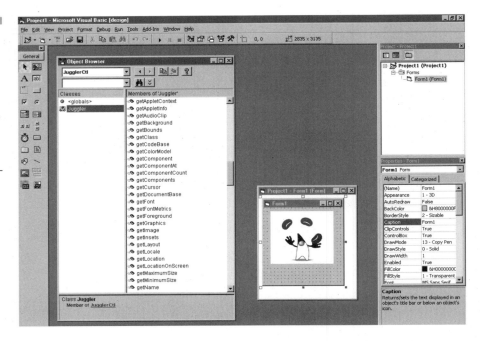

name of a method, its parameter names and types, and other miscellaneous data. Likewise, **PropertyDescriptor** holds the name of a property, its type, and other miscellaneous data.

While designing the JavaBeans architecture, the programmers at Sun Microsystems noticed that this "other miscellaneous data" was identical for all of the descriptor classes. So in keeping true to the object-oriented programming paradigm, they removed the common data, placed it into its own class, and extended (that is, inherited) all descriptor classes from it. They named this new base class **FeatureDescriptor**. The definition is shown in Listing 5-2.

As indicated by the previous listing, the **FeatureDescriptor** class encapsulates the following data:

- **Name**: string value containing the actual Java name of the method, property, or event. This name is identical to the name listed in the bean's source code.

- **DisplayName**: string value containing a user-friendly name of the method, property, or event. In this case, "user-friendly" means a name that is not restricted to the rules of Java source code, which allow only alphanumeric identifiers with no spaces. Thus, a property named **readOnlyColorVal** in the source code might have a display name of "Read-only Color Value." Bean builder tools can detect this friendlier

Listing 5-2
The **Feature Descriptor** class is the parent of all other descriptor classes.

```
public class FeatureDescriptor
{
    public FeatureDescriptor();

    public String getName();
    public void setName(String name);

    public String getDisplayName();
    public void setDisplayName(String displayName);

    public String getShortDescription();
    public void setShortDescription(String text);

    public boolean isExpert();
    public void setExpert(boolean expert);

    public boolean isHidden();
    public void setHidden(boolean hidden);

    public void setValue(String attributeName, Object
        value);
    public Object getValue(String attributeName);
    public java.util.Enumeration attributeNames();
}
```

name and display it in place of the programmatic name. More importantly, the **DisplayName** value also allows for localization. For instance, if you expect to market your bean to German developers, you could override the **getDisplayName** method to return *Schreibgeschützter Farbwert* if the Java VM is set for a German locale. (Remember that a display name is entirely optional. If you don't specify one, then the source code name will be used.)

▧ **ShortDescription**: string value containing a sentence or two of quick help text for the method, property, or event. As with **DisplayName**, **ShortDescription** can be localized for particular languages. If not specified, the short description will default to the programmatic name.

▧ **Expert**: boolean value that informs bean builders whether the method, property, or event should be used only by expert developers. This value is rather esoteric, as very few bean builder tools provide normal/expert modes.

▧ **Hidden**: boolean value that informs bean builders not to display the method, property, or event. Typically, you would hide an object if it is only used internally. A suite of beans, for example, might share hidden properties to exchange information.

■ **Value**: the designers of JavaBeans provided **Expert** and **Hidden** as built-in tags for all methods, properties, and events. They realized, however, that JavaBeans developers may require additional tags for their own use, and so instead of merely guessing what those other tags might be, they provided a generic tag called **Value**. **Value** is not a single tag but rather a dictionary of tags. You can add an entry to the dictionary by calling **setValue()**, passing it the unique name of the tag along with the tag itself (a **java.lang.Object** value). To retrieve a set tag, you simply call the **getValue()**, passing it the name of the tag you want. You can obtain a list of all **Value** tag names by calling **attributeNames()**.

With the **FeatureDescriptor** class well defined, the creators of Java-Beans were ready to extend classes from it to get the actual functionality they desired. The following four sections examine each of these classes in detail.

Method Descriptors

MethodDescriptor does exactly what its name implies—it describes a JavaBeans method. The class definition is given in Listing 5-3.

Methods without Parameters

To create an instance of **MethodDescriptor**, you must always pass a handle to the method through the **MethodDescriptor**'s constructor. This is typically done by calling the **java.lang.Class.getMethod()**. For example, the

Listing 5-3
The **Method Descriptor** class describes the features of a method.

```
public class MethodDescriptor extends FeatureDescriptor
{
    public MethodDescriptor(Method method);
    public MethodDescriptor(Method method,
                            ParameterDescriptor
                            parameterDescriptors[]);

    public Method getMethod();
    public ParameterDescriptor[] getParameterDescriptors();
}
```

following code would get a handle to a method called **doSomething()** in
class **MyBean**:

```
Method m;

try {
    m = MyBean.class.getMethod("doSomething", null);
}
catch (Exception e) {
    throw new Error("Missing method: " + e);
}
```

Once you've got a handle to the method, you can pass it directly to
MethodDescriptor's constructor, like this:

```
MethodDescriptor mDesc = new MethodDescriptor(m, null);
```

Creating a **MethodDescriptor** is really the only thing you ever have to
do with the class. (After all, you built the method yourself, so you don't
need a description of it.) You only have to return the object in your **Bean-
Info**'s **getMethodDescriptors()** function so that JavaBeans development
tools can learn about the method. For an example of how this is done, see
the section "Putting It All Together" later in this chapter.

Methods with Parameters

If your bean method has parameters, creating a **MethodDescriptor** for it
is a little more complicated. First, you will need to specify the parameter
types when obtaining a handle to the method. For example, if the previous "**doSomething**" example method had two parameters, an integer and
a string, the code to get a handle to it would look like this:

```
Method m;

try {
    Class args[] = { java.lang.Integer.class,
        java.lang.String.class };
    m = MyBean.class.getMethod("doSomething", args);
}
catch (Exception e) {
    throw new Error("Missing method: " + e);
}
```

Second, you must specify descriptions of the parameters by using the
ParameterDescriptor class, located in the java.beans package. The complete source code for **ParameterDescriptor** is given in Listing 5-4.

Listing 5-4
The **Parameter Descriptor** class describes the features of a parameter.

```
public class ParameterDescriptor extends FeatureDescriptor
{
}
```

No, you haven't found a typo in this book. The **ParameterDescriptor** class actually has no implementation. Through the magic of object-oriented programming, all of the code for this class comes from its parent, **FeatureDescriptor**. The designers of JavaBeans decided that **ParameterDescriptor** needed no extra functionality (beyond what was provided by its parent) and simply left it alone.

Thus, if you know how to use **FeatureDescriptor**, then you already know how to use **ParameterDescriptor**. Going back to the same "**doSomething**" example, here's how you might create a **MethodDescriptor** object for parameters called **myInteger** (and integer) and **myString** (a string).

```
ParameterDescriptor myInteger = new ParameterDescriptor();
myInteger.setName("myInteger");
myInteger.setShortDescription("This is my integer.");

ParameterDescriptor myString = new ParameterDescriptor();
myString.setName("myString");
myString.setShortDescription("This is my string.");

ParameterDescriptor[] pd = { myInteger, myString };
MethodDescriptor mDesc = new MethodDescriptor(m, pd);
```

TIP: *Okay, pop quiz: You have a bean. You have a bean builder. And you don't have any methods in the bean. How do you tell the builder that your bean has zero methods? If you answered, "Return null in the* **getMethodDescriptors()** *function," then you flunked the quiz. Returning null causes the introspection process to kick in, and, as was mentioned earlier in this chapter, introspection assumes that the methods of all parents of your bean are actually methods of your bean. To get rid of that assumption, try this little trick:*

```
public MethodDescriptor[] getMethodDescriptors() {
    MethodDescriptor rv[] = {};
    return rv;
}
```

Property Descriptors

Another descendant of **FeatureDescriptor** is a class called **Property Descriptor**. As you can surely guess, **PropertyDescriptor** describes the features of a property in a JavaBean. The class definition for **Property Descriptor**, which you can find in the **java.beans** package, is shown in Listing 5-5.

Using the **PropertyDescriptor** class is fairly straightforward. Creation is simply a matter of passing the following data to the **Property Descriptor**'s constructor:

- The programmatic name of the property
- The class where the property is located
- The names of the methods for getting and setting the property's value

Listing 5-5
The **Property Descriptor** class describes the features of a property.

```
public class PropertyDescriptor extends FeatureDescriptor
{
    public PropertyDescriptor(String propertyName, Class
                             beanClass)
    public PropertyDescriptor(String propertyName, Class
                             beanClass,
                             String getterName, String
                             setterName)
    public PropertyDescriptor(String propertyName, Method
                             getter,
                             Method setter)

    public boolean isBound();
    public void setBound(boolean bound);

    public boolean isConstrained();
    public void setConstrained(boolean constrained);

    public void setPropertyEditorClass(Class
       propertyEditorClass);
    public Class getPropertyEditorClass();

    public Class getPropertyType();

    public Method getReadMethod();
    public Method getWriteMethod();
}
```

For the last item, you have the choice of providing either the string names of the methods or handles to the methods (as java.lang.Method objects). For instance, the following code creates two **PropertyDescriptor**s for a single integer property called **MyProp**, the first one by specifying method names and the second by specifying method handles:

```
PropertyDescriptor myProp1 = new
      PropertyDescriptor("myProp", MyBean.class,
      "getMyProp", "setMyProp");

Method mGet, mSet;
try {
   mGet = MyBean.class.getMethod("getMyProp", null);
   Class args[] = { java.lang.Integer.class };
   mSet = MyBean.class.getMethod("setMyProp", args);
}
catch (Exception e) {
   throw new Error("Missing method: " + e);
}

PropertyDescriptor myProp2 = new
      PropertyDescriptor("myProp", mGet, mSet);
```

Note that providing method information, either by name or by handle, is entirely optional. If you don't supply this information, JavaBeans uses introspection to obtain it.

TIP: *Keep Your Hands Off My Props. Normally, a property is public. It can be read and written without restriction. You can, however, make a property read-only or write-only simply by leaving out its* **get** *or* **set** *method. If you do, remember to reflect this change in your* **BeanInfo**. *Just pass a null value for the appropriate method name when constructing the* **PropertyDescriptor**.

After you have constructed a **PropertyDescriptor**, check your source code implementation of the property it represents. If you have made the property bound or constrained, you must also mark the **Property Descriptor** to reflect this. You do this, as you might expect, by calling the **setBound()** or **setConstrained()** methods, passing them a Boolean value. If your property is neither bound nor constrained, then you can simply leave the **PropertyDescriptor** alone because it defaults to false for both values.

The only other **PropertyDescriptor** method you need to worry about is **setPropertyEditorClass()** (the others are handled for you automatically). This method sets the Java class that will be used for editing of the property in a JavaBeans development tool. To learn more about setPropertyEditorClass() and property editors in general, turn to Chapter 6, where they are covered in detail.

Indexed Property Descriptors

Indexed properties require slightly different handling for their descriptor class because indexed properties can have two pairs of **get** or **set** methods: one for the entire array of indexes, and one for a single element in the array. Rather than create a whole new descriptor class just to handle this one discrepancy, the JavaBeans architects simply extended from **PropertyDescriptor** and named the new class **IndexedProperty Descriptor**. Its definition is shown in Listing 5-6.

Like **PropertyDescriptor**, the methods in **IndexedPropertyDescriptor** are pretty self-explanatory. In fact, these two classes are so similar that no example code is necessary. Just remember that the first pair of **get** or **set** methods—that is, the "normal" methods—deal with the entire array of

Listing 5-6
The **Indexed Property Descriptor** class describes the features of an indexed property.

```
public class IndexedPropertyDescriptor extends
        PropertyDescriptor
{
    public IndexedPropertyDescriptor(String propertyName,
                                Class beanClass);

    public IndexedPropertyDescriptor(String propertyName,
                                Class beanClass,
                                String getterName,
                                String setterName,
                                String
                                indexedGetterName,
                                String
                                indexedSetterName);

    public IndexedPropertyDescriptor(String propertyName,
                                Method getter,
                                Method setter,
                                Method indexedGetter,
                                Method indexedSetter);

    public Method getIndexedReadMethod();
    public Method getIndexedWriteMethod();

    public Class getIndexedPropertyType();
}
```

indexes, whereas the second pair—the ones with the "indexed" prefix—deal with only one element of the array. (For a review of what indexed properties are and how to use them, see Chapter 2.)

Event Set Descriptors

The fourth and final descriptor class is the **EventSetDescriptor**, and, of course, this class describes event sets. Packaged along with its siblings in java.beans, the **EventSetDescriptor** class definition can be found in Listing 5-7.

Don't be intimidated by the constructors in this class. Although you might see several constructors and a bewildering array of parameters, they are actually quite easy to use. You will see how in a moment, but first, recall that an event set has four components:

- The name of the set
- The name(s) of the event(s) in the set
- A listener interface
- A pair of methods for adding and removing listeners of the set

This information is what you must supply to one of **EventSetDescriptor**'s constructors. Occasionally, however, your event set might be extremely simple. It might contain only one event, the event might contain only one parameter (of the standard event object type), and the **add** or **remove** methods might conform to the standard JavaBeans naming conventions. For this special case, the first constructor in **EventSetDescriptor** is the most appropriate. It requires fewer parameters than the other constructors due to the simple form of your event set. For example, here's how you might create an **EventSetDescriptor** for a set called **timer** containing a single event called **timeOut**:

```
EventSetDescriptor timer;

try {
    timer = new EventSetDescriptor(MyBean.class,
                    "timer", TimerListener.class,
                    "timeOut");
}
catch (IntrospectionException e) {
    throw new Error(e.toString());
}
```

Listing 5-7
The **EventSet**
Descriptor class
describes the features
of an event set.

```java
public class EventSetDescriptor extends FeatureDescriptor
{
    public EventSetDescriptor(Class sourceClass, String
        eventSetName,
        Class listenerType, String listenerMethodName);

    public EventSetDescriptor(Class sourceClass, String
        eventSetName,
        Class listenerType, String listenerMethodNames[],
        String addListenerMethodName, String
        removeListenerMethodName);

    public EventSetDescriptor(String eventSetName,
        Class listenerType, Method listenerMethods[],
        Method addListenerMethod, Method
        removeListenerMethod);

    public EventSetDescriptor(String eventSetName,
        Class listenerType,
        MethodDescriptor listenerMethodDescriptors[],
        Method addListenerMethod, Method
        removeListenerMethod);

    public Class getListenerType();
    public Method[] getListenerMethods();
    public MethodDescriptor[]
        getListenerMethodDescriptors();
    public Method getAddListenerMethod();
    public Method getRemoveListenerMethod();

    public void setUnicast(boolean unicast);
    public boolean isUnicast();

    public void setInDefaultEventSet(boolean
        inDefaultEventSet);
    public boolean isInDefaultEventSet();
}
```

The first parameter is the Bean class containing the event; the second parameter is the name of the event set; the third is the class containing the event set listener interface; and the final parameter is the name of the sole event in the set. These four pieces of data are all that is necessary to construct the descriptor. The implementation of **EventSetDescriptor** uses introspection to determine everything else it needs.

Simple events are not the only events your bean may have, of course. Your sets might contain more than one event, or your **add** or **remove**

listener methods might not conform to the standard naming conventions. In this case, the second **EventSetDescriptor** constructor is the best choice. It is similar to the first constructor, but instead of requiring a single string for the event name, it requires an array of strings for the multiple event names. It also provides two extra strings for passing the names of the **add** or **remove listener** methods. (Note that if your event set has multiple events but uses standard listener method names, you must still provide the method names because **EventSetDescriptor** has no constructors that can handle multiple events *and* use introspection to determine the method names.) Here is an example of using the second constructor for an event set called **select** with events **selectChar**, **selectWord**, and **selectSentence**:

```
EventSetDescriptor select;

try {
    String[] events = { "selectChar", "selectWord",
                        "selectString" };
    select = new EventSetDescriptor(MyBean.class,
                "select", SelectListener.class, events,
                "addSelectListener",
                "removeSelectListener");
}
catch (IntrospectionException e) {
    throw new Error(e.toString());
}
```

The remaining two constructors in **EventSetDescriptor** are essentially identical to the second. The only difference is that the third and fourth constructors take **MethodDescriptor** or **Method** handles, as opposed to simple strings. This feature enables you to create events that are not limited to a single event object parameter, but rather any number of parameters of any Java type. Because this feature is esoteric and non-standard, examples are not provided here.

Like **PropertyDescriptor**, the **EventSetDescriptor** class contains several methods that you do not need to worry about. Namely, all of the **getXxx()** methods can be ignored because they merely obtain information that you have already passed to the constructor.

The last two pairs of methods, however, are important. These methods are used to get and set two flags: **unicast** and **inDefaultEventSet**. After creating an **EventSetDescriptor**, simply call **setUnicast()** and **setInDefaultEventSet()** according to how you have implemented your event. (That is, if the event is unicast but not the default set, call **setUnicast(true)** and **setInDefaultEventSet(false)**.) Note that the unicast flag defaults to false and that the **inDefaultEventSet** flag defaults to true, so explicitly setting these flags is not always necessary.

Bean Icons

A picture is worth a thousand words, right? The designers of JavaBeans must have thought so. They provided a feature for representing beans as tiny pictures. Better known as icons, these pictures are typically displayed in a toolbox when the bean is loaded into a development tool. The idea is that identifying a bean by its icon is easier and more aesthetic.

To specify an icon for your bean, you should first design it using a graphics program of your choice. Any program will do as long as it can save pictures in the industry-standard GIF format. When designing the icon, note that JavaBeans allows only four picture formats:

- 16x16-pixel monochrome
- 16x16-pixel color
- 32x32-pixel monochrome
- 32x32-pixel color

You can specify any combination of these formats that you like. However, because most computers these days support color, most JavaBeans developers decide to leave out the monochrome formats. Also, if you choose to provide only one format, you should provide the 16x16-pixel format because it is the most common.

After you have created your icons and saved them as GIF files, you must declare them in your **BeanInfo** interface by implementing the **getImage()** method. This method has a single parameter, iconKind of type int, which specifies the icon format that is being requested. It may have one of the following values:

- **ICON_COLOR_16x16** for 16x16-pixel color
- **ICON_COLOR_32x32** for 32x32-pixel color
- **ICON_MONO_16x16** for 16x16-pixel monochrome
- **ICON_MONO_32x32** for 32x32-pixel monochrome

In your implementation of **getImage()**, you must check for these values and return a handle to the image being requested (or null if you choose not to provide the requested format). For example, let us say that you have provided two icons for your bean—one in 16x16-pixel monochrome format and one in 32x32-pixel color format—and that you have loaded them as **java.awt.image.Image** handles named "icon16x16" and "icon32x32," respectively. Your implementation of **getImage()** would then look like this:

```
public Image getIcon(int iconKind)
{
    if (iconKind == BeanInfo.ICON_MONO_16x16) return
                   icon16x16;
    if (iconKind == BeanInfo.ICON_COLOR_32x32) return
                   icon32x32;
    return null;
}
```

After creating the icon pictures and implementing **getIcon()**, you are still not quite finished. You must also package the GIF files inside the JAR file containing your bean. To learn how to package files into a JAR, refer to Chapter 12.

TIP: *Offload Your Work with* **loadImage()***. Loading GIF images from JAR files is a tedious task. To assist you, the creators of JavaBeans provide a utility function called* **loadImage()***. This method handles all the work of loading the image; the only catch is that you must extend from the* **java.beans.SimpleBeanInfo** *class in order to use it. See the section "Putting It All Together" for an example.*

Additional **BeanInfo**

If you want to become a true hard-core JavaBeans developer, you should know about a **BeanInfo** method called **getAdditionalBeanInfo()**. This method is necessary only if the source code for your bean is extended from some other bean. If this is the case, you can save work by combining the **BeanInfo** of the original bean with the **BeanInfo** of your new bean. For example, an original bean might expose events and properties, whereas the new bean might only add new methods. Then, instead of writing a whole new **BeanInfo** for the new bean, you could combine the old with the new, like this:

```
public BeanInfo[] getAdditionBeanInfo()
{
    try {
        BeanInfo[] bi = {
```

```
        (BeanInfo)OriginalBeanBeanInfo.class.newInstance() };

    return bi;
        }
        catch (Exception e) {
            throw new Error(e.toString());
        }
    }
```

This example shows one-level inheritance. You could, of course, specify multiple **BeanInfo**s if the new bean is inherited from multiple parents.

Default Properties and Events

A somewhat unique feature of the JavaBeans architecture is its concept of default properties and default events. A "default," in this case, is a property or event that you assume will be used more often than any other. Bean builder tools can detect the defaults and, for example, put the default property at the top of a list of properties.

Specifying default properties and events is accomplished through the **BeanInfo** interface and requires only a single line of code. The two relevant methods are called **getDefaultPropertyIndex()** and **getDefault EventIndex()**. Both methods return a zero-based integer index that denotes which property or event is the default. For instance, if your bean has three properties and you want the second one marked as the default, you would implement **getDefaultPropertyIndex()** as follows:

```
public int getDefaultPropertyIndex()
{
    return 1;  // the second property
}
```

The order of property and event indexes is given by the order you specified them in your **BeanInfo**'s **getPropertyDescriptors()** and **getEventSetDescriptors()** methods.

Putting It All Together

Now is the time to roll up your sleeves and get your hands dirty with a full-blown example. In this section, you will walk through each step of

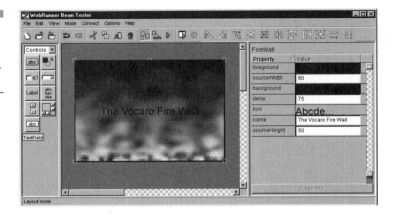

building a complete **BeanInfo** interface for a real JavaBean. The bean is called "The Fire Wall," and a picture is shown in Figure 5-5.

The FireWall's function is rather trivial. It simply displays an animation of orange flames on a black background. The FireWall's design, however, is just the right complexity to make it an interesting case study in how to implement **BeanInfo**.

Step 1: The Raw Bean

First, take a quick look at Listing 5-8. It's the complete source code to the FireWall. (Notice that a **BeanInfo** interface is missing.)

```java
import java.applet.*;
import java.awt.*;
import java.awt.image.*;
import java.awt.event.*;

public class FireWall extends Applet implements Runnable,
        ComponentListener
{
    private int m_nSourceWidth = 80;
    private int m_nSourceHeight = 50;
    private int m_nBufferWidth = 80;
    private int m_nBufferHeight = 52;
    private int m_nDelay = 75;

    // Private member variables
    private int[] m_nBits;
    private IndexColorModel m_cmPalette;
```

Listing 5-8

```
private Image m_imgBuffer;
private Thread m_threadFireWall = new Thread(this);
private int m_nFontWidth, m_nFontHeight;

public FireWall()
{
    addComponentListener(this);
}

public void update(Graphics g)
{
    paint(g);
}

public synchronized void paint(Graphics g)
{
    g.drawImage(m_imgBuffer, 0, 0,
    m_imgBuffer.getWidth(this),
    m_imgBuffer.getHeight(this), this);
}

public Dimension getPreferredSize()
{
    return new Dimension(m_nSourceWidth * 2,
    (m_nSourceHeight - 2) * 2);
}

public void init()
{
    setBackground(Color.black);
    setForeground(Color.black);
    setFont(new Font("Dialog", Font.PLAIN, 14));
    setName("The Vocaro Fire Wall");

    // Initialize the palette...

    byte[] pbyColors = {
        /* RED   GREEN   BLUE    RED   GREEN   BLUE */
            0,     0,     0,      0,     0,    24,
            0,     0,    24,      0,     0,    28,
            0,     0,    32,      0,     0,    32,
            0,     0,    36,      0,     0,    40,
            8,     0,    40,     16,     0,    36,
           24,     0,    36,     32,     0,    32,
           40,     0,    28,     48,     0,    28,
           56,     0,    24,     64,     0,    20,
           72,     0,    20,     80,     0,    16,
           88,     0,    16,     96,     0,    12,
          104,     0,     8,    112,     0,     8,
          120,     0,     4,   -128,     0,     0,
         -128,     0,     0,   -124,     0,     0,
```

Continues

Listing 5-8
Continued.

```
-120,      0,     0,   -116,      0,     0,
-112,      0,     0,   -112,      0,     0,
-108,      0,     0,   -104,      0,     0,
-100,      0,     0,    -96,      0,     0,
 -96,      0,     0,    -92,      0,     0,
 -88,      0,     0,    -84,      0,     0,
 -80,      0,     0,    -76,      0,     0,
 -72,      4,     0,    -68,      4,     0,
 -64,      8,     0,    -60,      8,     0,
 -56,     12,     0,    -52,     12,     0,
 -48,     16,     0,    -44,     16,     0,
 -40,     20,     0,    -36,     20,     0,
 -32,     24,     0,    -28,     24,     0,
 -24,     28,     0,    -20,     28,     0,
 -16,     32,     0,    -12,     32,     0,
  -4,     36,     0,     -4,     36,     0,
  -4,     40,     0,     -4,     40,     0,
  -4,     44,     0,     -4,     44,     0,
  -4,     48,     0,     -4,     48,     0,
  -4,     52,     0,     -4,     52,     0,
  -4,     56,     0,     -4,     56,     0,
  -4,     60,     0,     -4,     60,     0,
  -4,     64,     0,     -4,     64,     0,
  -4,     68,     0,     -4,     68,     0,
  -4,     72,     0,     -4,     72,     0,
  -4,     76,     0,     -4,     76,     0,
  -4,     80,     0,     -4,     80,     0,
  -4,     84,     0,     -4,     84,     0,
  -4,     88,     0,     -4,     88,     0,
  -4,     92,     0,     -4,     96,     0,
  -4,     96,     0,     -4,    100,     0,
  -4,    100,     0,     -4,    104,     0,
  -4,    104,     0,     -4,    108,     0,
  -4,    108,     0,     -4,    112,     0,
  -4,    112,     0,     -4,    116,     0,
  -4,    116,     0,     -4,    120,     0,
  -4,    120,     0,     -4,    124,     0,
  -4,    124,     0,     -4,   -128,     0,
  -4,   -128,     0,     -4,   -124,     0,
  -4,   -124,     0,     -4,   -120,     0,
  -4,   -120,     0,     -4,   -116,     0,
  -4,   -116,     0,     -4,   -112,     0,
  -4,   -112,     0,     -4,   -108,     0,
  -4,   -104,     0,     -4,   -104,     0,
  -4,   -100,     0,     -4,   -100,     0,
  -4,    -96,     0,     -4,    -96,     0,
  -4,    -92,     0,     -4,    -92,     0,
  -4,    -88,     0,     -4,    -88,     0,
  -4,    -84,     0,     -4,    -84,     0,
  -4,    -80,     0,     -4,    -80,     0,
  -4,    -76,     0,     -4,    -76,     0,
  -4,    -72,     0,     -4,    -72,     0,
```

Listing 5-8

```
  -4,    -68,     0,          -4,    -68,      0,
  -4,    -64,     0,          -4,    -64,      0,
  -4,    -60,     0,          -4,    -60,      0,
  -4,    -56,     0,          -4,    -56,      0,
  -4,    -52,     0,          -4,    -48,      0,
  -4,    -48,     0,          -4,    -48,      0,
  -4,    -48,     0,          -4,    -48,      0,
  -4,    -44,     0,          -4,    -44,      0,
  -4,    -44,     0,          -4,    -44,      0,
  -4,    -40,     0,          -4,    -40,      0,
  -4,    -40,     0,          -4,    -40,      0,
  -4,    -40,     0,          -4,    -36,      0,
  -4,    -36,     0,          -4,    -36,      0,
  -4,    -36,     0,          -4,    -32,      0,
  -4,    -32,     0,          -4,    -32,      0,
  -4,    -32,     0,          -4,    -28,      0,
  -4,    -28,     0,          -4,    -28,      0,
  -4,    -28,     0,          -4,    -28,      0,
  -4,    -24,     0,          -4,    -24,      0,
  -4,    -24,     0,          -4,    -24,      0,
  -4,    -20,     0,          -4,    -20,      0,
  -4,    -20,     0,          -4,    -20,      0,
  -4,    -16,     0,          -4,    -16,      0,
  -4,    -16,     0,          -4,    -16,      0,
  -4,    -16,     0,          -4,    -12,      0,
  -4,    -12,     0,          -4,    -12,      0,
  -4,    -12,     0,          -4,     -8,      0,
  -4,     -8,     0,          -4,     -8,      0,
  -4,     -8,     0,          -4,     -4,      0,
  -4,     -4,     4,          -4,     -4,      8,
  -4,     -4,    12,          -4,     -4,     16,
  -4,     -4,    20,          -4,     -4,     24,
  -4,     -4,    28,          -4,     -4,     32,
  -4,     -4,    36,          -4,     -4,     40,
  -4,     -4,    40,          -4,     -4,     44,
  -4,     -4,    48,          -4,     -4,     52,
  -4,     -4,    56,          -4,     -4,     60,
  -4,     -4,    64,          -4,     -4,     68,
  -4,     -4,    72,          -4,     -4,     76,
  -4,     -4,    80,          -4,     -4,     84,
  -4,     -4,    84,          -4,     -4,     88,
  -4,     -4,    92,          -4,     -4,     96,
  -4,     -4,   100,          -4,     -4,    104,
  -4,     -4,   108,          -4,     -4,    112,
  -4,     -4,   116,          -4,     -4,    120,
  -4,     -4,   124,          -4,     -4,    124,
  -4,     -4,  -128,          -4,     -4,   -124,
  -4,     -4,  -120,          -4,     -4,   -116,
  -4,     -4,  -112,          -4,     -4,   -108,
  -4,     -4,  -104,          -4,     -4,   -100,
  -4,     -4,   -96,          -4,     -4,    -92,
```

Continues

Listing 5-8
Continued.

```
                    -4,    -4,    -88,      -4,    -4,    -88,
                    -4,    -4,    -84,      -4,    -4,    -80,
                    -4,    -4,    -76,      -4,    -4,    -72,
                    -4,    -4,    -68,      -4,    -4,    -64,
                    -4,    -4,    -60,      -4,    -4,    -56,
                    -4,    -4,    -52,      -4,    -4,    -48,
                    -4,    -4,    -48,      -4,    -4,    -44,
                    -4,    -4,    -40,      -4,    -4,    -36,
                    -4,    -4,    -32,      -4,    -4,    -28,
                    -4,    -4,    -24,      -4,    -4,    -20,
                    -4,    -4,    -16,      -4,    -4,    -12,
                    -4,    -4,    -8,       -4,    -4,    -4     };

        m_cmPalette = new IndexColorModel(8, 256, pbyColors,
                                          0, false);
    }

    public void start()
    {
        updateFont();
        updateImage(m_nSourceWidth, m_nSourceHeight,
        m_nBufferWidth, m_nBufferHeight);

        m_threadFireWall.start();
    }

    public void stop()
    {
        m_threadFireWall.stop();
    }

    public void run()
    {
        while (true)
        {
            repaint();
            renderNextFrame();

            try
            {
                Thread.sleep(m_nDelay);
            }
            catch (InterruptedException e)
            {
                stop();
            }
        }
    }

    public void componentHidden(ComponentEvent e) {}
    public void componentMoved(ComponentEvent e) {}
    public void componentShown(ComponentEvent e) {}
```

Listing 5-8

```java
public void componentResized(ComponentEvent e)
{
    updateImage(m_nSourceWidth, m_nSourceHeight,
    m_nBufferWidth, m_nBufferHeight);
    updateFont();
}

private synchronized void renderNextFrame()
{
    int x, y;

    for (y = 1; y < m_nBufferHeight - 1; y++)
    {
        for (x = 0; x < m_nBufferWidth; x++)
        {
            if (x == 0)
            {
                m_nBits[(y - 1) * m_nBufferWidth + x] = (
                    m_nBits[y * m_nBufferWidth + x] +
                    m_nBits[(y - 1) * m_nBufferWidth +
                    m_nBufferWidth - 1] +
                    m_nBits[y * m_nBufferWidth + x + 1] +
                    m_nBits[(y + 1) * m_nBufferWidth + x] )
                    / 4;
            }
            else
            {
                if (x == m_nBufferWidth - 1)
                {
                    m_nBits[(y - 1) * m_nBufferWidth + x] =
                    (
                        m_nBits[y * m_nBufferWidth + x] +
                        m_nBits[y * m_nBufferWidth + x - 1] +
                        m_nBits[(y + 1) * m_nBufferWidth] +
                        m_nBits[(y + 1) * m_nBufferWidth +
                        x] ) / 4;
                }
                else
                {
                    m_nBits[(y - 1) * m_nBufferWidth + x] =
                    (
                        m_nBits[y * m_nBufferWidth + x] +
                        m_nBits[y * m_nBufferWidth + x - 1] +
                        m_nBits[y * m_nBufferWidth + x + 1] +
                        m_nBits[(y + 1) * m_nBufferWidth +
                        x]) / 4;
                }
            }

            if (m_nBits[y * m_nBufferWidth + x] > 11)
                m_nBits[y * m_nBufferWidth + x] -= 12;
```

Continues

Listing 5-8
Continued.

```
            else
            {
                if (m_nBits[y * m_nBufferWidth + x] > 3)
                    m_nBits[y * m_nBufferWidth + x] -= 4;
                else
                {
                    if (m_nBits[y * m_nBufferWidth + x] >
                    0) m_nBits[y * m_nBufferWidth + x]-;
                    if (m_nBits[y * m_nBufferWidth + x] >
                    0) m_nBits[y * m_nBufferWidth + x]-;
                    if (m_nBits[y * m_nBufferWidth + x] >
                    0) m_nBits[y * m_nBufferWidth + x]-;
                }
            }
        }
    }

    // Set two new bottom lines with random white or
    // black...

    for (x = 0; x < m_nBufferWidth; x++)
    {
        int byRandom = Math.random() < 0.5 ? 0 : 255;

        m_nBits[(m_nBufferHeight - 2) * m_nBufferWidth +
        x] = byRandom;
        m_nBits[(m_nBufferHeight - 1) * m_nBufferWidth +
        x] = byRandom;
    }

    Image imgFire = createImage(
        new MemoryImageSource(m_nSourceWidth,
        m_nSourceHeight - 2,
            m_cmPalette, m_nBits, 0, m_nSourceWidth) );

    Graphics g = m_imgBuffer.getGraphics();

    int w = getSize().width;
    int h = getSize().height;

    g.drawImage(imgFire, 0, 0, w, h, this);

    g.drawString(getName(),
                    w / 2 - m_nFontWidth / 2,
                    h / 2 + m_nFontHeight / 2);
}

private void updateFont()
{
    FontMetrics fm = getFontMetrics(getFont());

    m_nFontWidth = fm.stringWidth(getName());
```

Listing 5-8

```
        m_nFontHeight = fm.getAscent();
    }

    private void updateImage(int nSourceWidth, int
        nSourceHeight, int nBufferWidth, int nBufferHeight)
    {
        boolean bAlive = m_threadFireWall.isAlive();

        if (bAlive) m_threadFireWall.suspend();

        m_nSourceWidth = nSourceWidth;
        m_nSourceHeight = nSourceHeight;
        m_nBufferWidth = nBufferWidth;
        m_nBufferHeight = nBufferHeight;

        m_nBits = new int[m_nBufferWidth * m_nBufferHeight];

        m_imgBuffer = createImage(getSize().width,
        getSize().height);

        if (bAlive) m_threadFireWall.resume();
    }

    public void setFont(Font f)
    {
        super.setFont(f);

        updateFont();
    }

    public void setName(String str)
    {
        super.setName(str);

        updateFont();
    }

    public void setDelay(int n)
    {
        m_nDelay = n;
    }

    public int getDelay()
    {
        return m_nDelay;
    }

    public void setSourceWidth(int n)
    {
        updateImage(n, m_nSourceHeight, m_nBufferWidth,
        m_nBufferHeight);
```

Continues

Listing 5-8
Continued.

```
    }

    public int getSourceWidth()
    {
        return m_nSourceWidth;
    }

    public void setSourceHeight(int n)
    {
        updateImage(m_nSourceWidth, n, m_nBufferWidth, n +
        2);
    }

    public int getSourceHeight()
    {
        return m_nSourceHeight;
    }
}
```

Step 2: Adding `SimpleBeanInfo`

Next, you will add a `BeanInfo` interface for the FireWall. This step requires you to create a separate file to hold the interface because of Java's requirement that all public classes reside in their own files. For starters, keep the FireWall's `BeanInfo` simple. This step only implements the `getBeanDescriptor()` and `getIcon()` methods, as shown in Listing 5-9.

The `BeanInfo` source code in this step does only two things: It returns a `BeanDescriptor` object for setting the Bean's user-friendly display name, and it returns `Image` handles to the Beans icons. Listing 5-14 shows how these two changes affect the BeanBox's toolbar.

Notice that in the `FireWallBeanInfo` class, you didn't actually implement the `BeanInfo` interface. Instead, you simply derived from `SimpleBeanInfo` a helper class located in the `java.beans` package. `SimpleBeanInfo` implements an "empty" `BeanInfo` interface, allowing you to override only the `BeanInfo` methods you need.

Figure 5-6
The BeanBox's
toolbar before and
after adding a
BeanInfo interface
to the FireWall.

Listing 5-9
The beginnings of a
BeanInfo interface
for the FireWall.

```java
import java.beans.*;
import java.awt.*;

public class FireWallBeanInfo extends SimpleBeanInfo
{
    public BeanDescriptor getBeanDescriptor()
    {
        BeanDescriptor bd = new
                            BeanDescriptor(FireWall.class);
        bd.setDisplayName("The Vocaro Fire Wall");
        return bd;
    }

    public Image getIcon(int iconKind)
    {
        if (iconKind == BeanInfo.ICON_COLOR_16x16)
        {
            Image img = loadImage("FireWallIcon_16x16.gif");
            return img;
        }

        if (iconKind == BeanInfo.ICON_COLOR_32x32)
        {
            Image img = loadImage("FireWallIcon_32x32.gif");
            return img;
        }

        return null;
    }
}
```

Step 3: Adding Method Descriptors

In this step, you inform Bean builders about the methods in the FireWall. There are only two: `start()` and `stop()`. Listing 5-10 shows how to override `getMethodDescriptors()` to handle these two methods.

The code in this example is relatively simple because the `start()` and `stop()` methods require no parameters. If methods have parameters, remember to create the appropriate `ParameterDescriptor` objects for them, as explained in the section "Method Descriptors" earlier in this chapter.

Step 4: Adding Property Descriptors

Now add some `PropertyDescriptors` for the five properties in the FireWall. The new additions to the `FireWallBeanInfo` class are shown in Listing 5-11.

Listing 5-10
Adding a
**getMethod
Descriptors()**
method returns
information about
the methods in the
FireWall.

```java
public MethodDescriptor[] getMethodDescriptors()
{
    Method mStart, mStop;

    try
    {
        mStart = FireWall.class.getMethod("start", null);
        mStop  = FireWall.class.getMethod("stop", null);
    }
    catch (Exception e)
    {
        throw new Error("Missing method: " + e);
    }

    MethodDescriptor start = new MethodDescriptor(mStart,
                                null);
    MethodDescriptor stop = new MethodDescriptor(mStop,
                                null);

    start.setDisplayName("Start");
    start.setShortDescription("Begins animation of the
                                FireWall");

    stop.setDisplayName("Stop");
    stop.setShortDescription("Stops animation of the
                                FireWall");

    MethodDescriptor rv[] = { start, stop };

    return rv;
}
```

Like the previous step, the code shown here is relatively simple. None of the properties are bound or constrained, so we simply left the **Property Descriptors** at their defaults.

Also, note that we overrode the **getDefaultPropertyIndex()** method to tell JavaBeans development tools that **name** is the FireWall's default property.

Step 5: Adding Event Set Descriptors

For the fifth and final step, override the **getEventSetDescriptors()** method to tell Bean builders about the events in the FireWall. Of course, if you looked carefully at the FireWall source code, you noticed that there are no events to talk about. So, for the purposes of this tutorial, add an

Listing 5-11
The implementation
of the
**getProperty
Descriptors()**
method.

```
public PropertyDescriptor[] getPropertyDescriptors()
{
   try
   {
      PropertyDescriptor font =
         new PropertyDescriptor("font", FireWall.class);
      PropertyDescriptor name =
         new PropertyDescriptor("name", FireWall.class);
      PropertyDescriptor delay =
         new PropertyDescriptor("delay", FireWall.class);
      PropertyDescriptor sourceWidth =
         new PropertyDescriptor("sourceWidth",
                                    FireWall.class);
      PropertyDescriptor sourceHeight =
         new PropertyDescriptor("sourceHeight",
                                    FireWall.class);

      font.setDisplayName("Font");
      font.setShortDescription("The font for displaying the
                                 caption");

      name.setDisplayName("Name");
      name.setShortDescription("The caption inside the
                                 FireWall");

      delay.setDisplayName("Delay");
      delay.setShortDescription("The speed of the animation
                                 (lower=faster)");

      sourceWidth.setDisplayName("Source Width");
      sourceWidth.setShortDescription("The horizontal
   resolution of the flames");

      sourceHeight.setDisplayName("Source Height");
      sourceHeight.setShortDescription("The vertical
   resolution of the flames");

      PropertyDescriptor rv[] =
         { font, name, delay, sourceWidth, sourceHeight };

      return rv;
   }
   catch (IntrospectionException e)
   {
      throw new Error(e.toString());
   }
}

public int getDefaultPropertyIndex()
{
   return 1;  // the "name" property
}
```

event set right now. Call the set `fireWall` and give it a single event: `fireAtMaximumHeight`. The event is sent whenever the fire animation is at its maximum height. To implement the event, first create two Java source code files containing the following classes (each class belongs in its own file):

```java
public class FireWallEvent extends java.util.EventObject {
    public FireWallEvent(Object source) {
        super(source);
    }
}

public interface FireWallListener extends
        java.util.EventListener {
    void fireAtMaximumHeight(FireWallEvent event);
}
```

Next, add the following code somewhere in the main `FireWall` class:

```java
transient private Vector m_eventListeners = new Vector();

public synchronized void
        addFireWallListener(FireWallListener l) {
    m_eventListeners.addElement(l);
}

public synchronized void removeFireWallListener
        (FireWallListener l) {
    m_eventListeners.removeElement(l);
}
```

Then add the following code to the `renderNextFrame()` method:

```java
for (x = 0; x < m_nBufferHeight; x++) {
    if (m_nBits[x] > 0) {
        Vector l;
        synchronized(this) { l = (Vector)
                               m_eventListeners.clone(); }
        for (int i = 0; i < l.size(); i++) {
            FireWallListener listener = (FireWallListener)
                                        l.elementAt(i);
            listener.fireAtMaximumHeight(new
                                         FireWallEvent(this));
        }
    }
}
```

Finally, describe the new event by adding the following code in Listing 5-12 to the `FireWallBeanInfo` class:

Listing 5-12
The implementation
of the
getEventSet Descriptors()
method.

```java
public EventSetDescriptor[] getEventSetDescriptors()
{
    EventSetDescriptor fireWall;

    try
    {
        fireWall = new EventSetDescriptor(FireWall.class,
                "fireWall", FireWallListener.class,
                "fireAtMaximumHeight");
    }
    catch (IntrospectionException e)
    {
        throw new Error(e.toString());
    }

    EventSetDescriptor[] rv = { fireWall };

    return rv;
}

public int getDefaultEventIndex()
{
    return 0;
}
```

Because the **fireWall** event set contains only one event, constructing the **EventSetDescriptor** object is as simple as it could possibly be. For more complicated sets containing multiple events, you would need to declare an array of strings that hold the event names, then pass that name to **EventSetDescriptor**'s constructor.

CONCLUSION

Though not essential, the **BeanInfo** interface is an important part of the JavaBeans architecture. Its primary function is to fine-tune the occasionally clumsy introspection process. It also offers some nifty features like Bean icons and quick-and-dirty help text. Creating the interface can be tedious, but with a little help from this chapter—or from a JavaBeans development tool that automates the entire process—the extra work is worth it, especially considering the benefits of a well-written **BeanInfo**.

Property Editors and Customizers

Everyone loves to customize! Just take a Saturday night cruise through any town in America, and you will see proof of this: souped-up hotrods with chrome hubcaps, torn jeans decorated with magic marker, faded rainbows of illicit graffiti. Some folks even like to customize their own flesh. Tattoos, unusual hair colors, and face piercings are increasingly popular as people search for new ways to customize their property.

Although computer programmers might not be the type for wearing nose rings and orange hair, they still like to customize. Most programmers enjoy changing desktop wallpaper to suit their tastes, screen colors to match their moods, and software settings to fit their needs. In more practical terms, many programmers make a living providing highly customized applications that solve specific problems for companies with unique software requirements.

The love and need to customize plays a key role in developing JavaBeans components. Whether you plan to create beans for in-house use by your own company or want to sell them commercially (or both), the programmers who use your beans will certainly want to customize them. They will need to change the look, feel, and functionality of your components to match the applications in which they are used.

The JavaBeans architecture provides two features that allow customization of components: property editors and customizers. *Property editors* offer easy editing of user-defined data types; *customizers* provide graphical, automated assistance in changing a bean's properties. Both features apply only to design-time customization.

Because end-users never see either of these features, you might think that they are not important. Don't fall into this trap. Good property editors and customizers can greatly improve the developer's view of your components. And remember: developers, not end-users, are your customers. If they become frustrated just trying to customize your beans, they might switch to one of your competitors.

This chapter shows you how to avoid this potential problem. Revealed are the powerful yet easy-to-use interface for property editors, as well as a few ideas for crafting well-designed customizers. We will also provide a comprehensive example and a couple of real-world property editors that you can plug directly into your own beans.

This Chapter Covers

- What are property editors and customizers?
- Tips and tricks for building property editors and customizers
- Real-world property editors for pasting into your own projects
- When not to follow the JavaBeans specification
- A step-by-step example bean that uses property editors and a customizer

Property Editors

Typically, the process of integrating JavaBeans with Java applications works like this:

1. Load the bean into a bean builder tool.
2. Configure the bean's properties.
3. Serialize the bean's properties to disk.

These three tasks are so common and so necessary that every bean builder tool—from the simplest to the most complex—provides assistance in helping the user perform them. Lotus' BeanMachine, for instance, displays a "property sheet" that allows Step 2 to be completed without writing a single line of Java code (see Figure 6-1).

BeanMachine is not the only tool that can display a property sheet. In fact, all commercially available JavaBeans development environments display some sort of graphical interface for viewing and editing the properties of a bean. Most tools provide built-in support in their property sheets for all of the standard property types: `int`, `boolean`, `String`, `java.awt.Color`, and so on.

The creators of JavaBeans realized that support of only these standard types would not suffice. They knew that programmers inevitably would define their own property types to handle their own special needs. They also knew that most bean builder tools would not provide support for Java data types that are standard but seldom used, such as `java.util.Locale` or `java.net.URL`.

To solve these problems, the JavaBeans architects designed an interface called `PropertyEditor`. This interface, which is located in the java.beans package, lets any `Java` class act as a custom property editor and be integrated with the property sheet of any bean builder. Thus, when

Figure 6-1
Lotus' BeanMachine, like nearly all bean builder tools, displays a property sheet for viewing and editing a bean's properties.

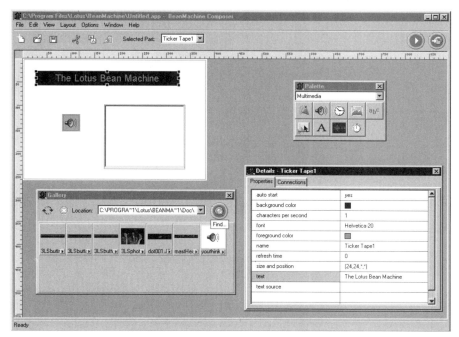

Figure 6-2
Vocaro Technologies'
Date Select provides
its own
java.util.Date
editor because most
JavaBeans
development tools
do not supply one.

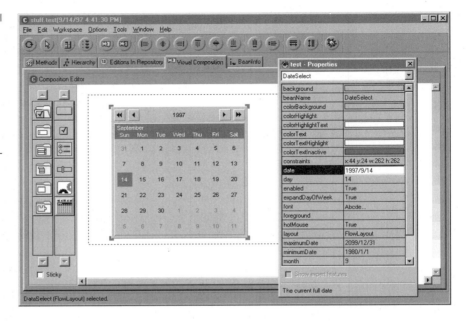

component developers create a non-standard property, they can design a class that conforms to the **PropertyEditor** interface, package the class with their beans, and know that the custom data type will be viewable and editable in any JavaBeans-compliant development tool.

Figure 6-2 shows the **PropertyEditor** interface action. In this example, a bean from Vocaro Technologies, called the Date Select, is loaded into IBM's Visual Age for Java. Notice that the property sheet on the right-hand side contains an element called **date**, which is a property of type **java.util.Date**. Normally, Visual Age cannot display this property type (because it provides no **java.util.Date** editor) but because the programmers at Vocaro packaged their own property editor with the Date Select, their **date** property can be viewed and edited under IBM's or any other company's bean builder tool.

The **PropertyEditor** Interface

The **PropertyEditor** interface is the contract that binds a property sheet to a custom property editor. Shown in Listing 6-1, it allows up to three different ways of editing a property: as text, as a component, or as an enumeration. Each of these techniques is explained in detail in the following three sections.

Before moving on, however, take note of the **setValue()** and **getValue()** methods because they are required for all three types of property editors. This pair of methods is nothing more than a wrapper for the data type represented by the property editor class. They block potentially dangerous direct access to the data, and they allow the property editor to know when its value has been changed externally. Listing 6-2 offers a quick example of how we might implement the two methods.

Listing 6-1
The
PropertyEditor
interface is the key to integrating custom property editors with property sheets.

```
public interface PropertyEditor
{
    void setValue(Object value);
    Object getValue();

    String getAsText();
    void setAsText(String text) throws
        IllegalArgumentException;

    java.awt.Component getCustomEditor();
    boolean supportsCustomEditor();

    boolean isPaintable();
    void paintValue(java.awt.Graphics gfx,
        java.awt.Rectangle box);

    String[] getTags();

    String getJavaInitializationString();

    void addPropertyChangeListener(PropertyChangeListener
        listener);
    void removePropertyChangeListener(PropertyChangeListener
        listener);
}
```

Listing 6-2
This code snippet shows how the
setValue() and
getValue()
methods are mere wrappers for the property editor's data type.

```
public class MyPropertyEditor implements PropertyEditor
{
    private MyProperty myprop;

    public void setValue(Object value)
    {
        myprop = (MyProperty)value;

        // Handle the property change if necessary...
    }
```

Continues

Listing 6-2
Continued.

```
pubilc Object getValue()
{
    return myprop;
}
    .
    .
    .
}
```

TIP: *Get Support From* `PropertyEditorSupport`. *By decree of the Java Language Specification, any Java class that implements an interface must implement every single method in that interface. Sometimes, however, this requirement can make our programming tasks a bit too tedious—especially when it comes to the* `PropertyEditor` *interface. A property editor that only supports text editing, for instance, must still implement the other methods for component and enumeration editing. The designers of JavaBeans were aware of this inconvenience and built a* `helper` *class to simplify our implementation of the* `PropertyEditor` *interface. Called* `PropertyEditorSupport`, *this class provides default code for every method in* `PropertyEditor`. *So, instead of implementing* `PropertyEditor` *and its methods, we can simply extend from* `PropertyEditorSupport` *and override only the methods we need. For an example of how this is done, see the BigInteger example in the section, "Property Editors As Text."*

Property Editors as Text

The simplest, easiest, and most common type of property editor is the text-based editor. This type works only for properties that can be viewed and edited as a string of characters. All bean builder tools provide text editors for Java's standard number types (that is, **byte**, **int**, **float**, and so on) and for the **String** type. Even the most basic of bean development tools—the BeanBox, supplied with Sun's Java Development Kit—comes pre-loaded with a set of text-based editors. Figure 6-3 shows the Bean-Box's numeric property editors.

Creating a text-based property editor is surprisingly easy. In fact, if we extend our property editor from the **java.beans.PropertyEditorSupport** class, we usually need to write only a couple dozen lines of code. A property editor for the **java.math.BigInteger** class, for instance, requires only

Figure 6-3
All bean tools, including the BeanBox shown here, provide text-based property editors for Java's standard types.

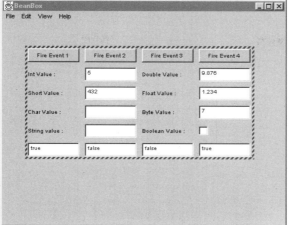

Listing 6-3
A fully functioning text-based property editor, such as this one for the **BigInteger** class, requires only a few lines of code.

```java
import java.math.*;

public class BigIntegerEditor extends
        java.beans.PropertyEditorSupport
{
    public String getAsText()
    {
        return getValue().toString();
    }

    public void setAsText(String text) throws
        IllegalArgumentException
    {
        setValue(new BigInteger(text));
    }
}
```

14 lines. As shown in Listing 6-3, we merely override the **setAsText()** and **getAsText()** methods.

We now have our complete text-based property editor and are able to view and change **BigInteger**s, even though the property sheets of most bean tools, such as Taligent's Bean Tester (see Figure 6-4), do not support them.

Implementing the **getAsText()** and **setAsText()** methods is pretty straightforward, so there is not much to say about them. Just remember the following tips:

■ Check for invalid user input in the **setAsText()** method, throwing an **IllegalArgumentException** if it is detected.

Figure 6-4
After creating a text-based property editor for the
BigInteger, we can edit
BigInteger
properties in Taligent's Bean Tester and all other JavaBeans development environments.

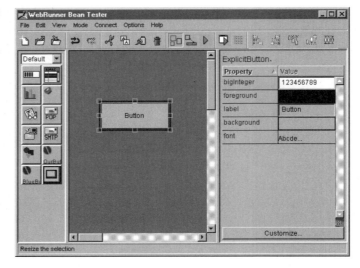

- Make sure that your **setAsText()** method can handle any value that your **getAsText()** might return—without throwing any exceptions.

- Use **setValue()** and **getValue()** as safe shortcuts to the property data.

- If a property editor supports both text-based and component-based editing, most bean builder tools will use only the text-based version. Therefore, you should implement **setAsText()** and **getAsText()** only if your property type does not require component-based editing.

Property Editors as Components

Although text-based property editors work fine for most data types, they do have their limitations. First, not all data types can be represented adequately as text. Icons and colors, for instance, would make poor choices for simple text-based editors. Second, certain properties require more advanced editing than a text box, even though they might be translated easily into text. For example, we might want to display fonts, dates, or locales by using lists, graphics, and buttons.

Fortunately, the programmers at Sun have granted our wish. They have provided a powerful hook into the JavaBeans architecture that lets property editors display a full-blown **java.awt.Component** object for editing the property's data. These components can contain any number of

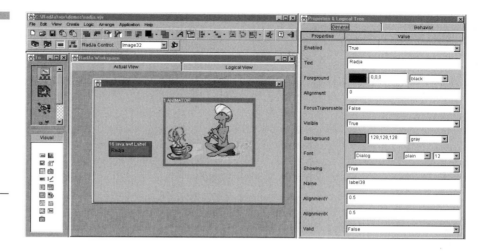

Figure 6-5
Like most bean builders, Applicom Software Industries' Radja ships with component-based property editors for the
`java.awt.Font`
and
`java.awt.Color`
data types.

other Java components, such as check boxes, choices, images, and so on. When properly combined, they provide an easier and more intuitive way of editing properties (see Figure 6-5).

Creating component-based property editors is a two-step process. In addition to building the component itself, you must also write a method that draws the property in a window. The second step is necessary simply due to the way most property sheets work. Typically, these sheets want to display a graphical representation of the property instead of the component. Only when the user clicks on the graphic does the sheet display a dialog box that reveals the component. Thus, to create a component-based editor, you must design both the component itself and a Java routine that draws the property.

TIP: *The JavaBeans Spec Is Not the JavaBeans Bible. The JavaBeans spec, which can be downloaded from* `http://java.sun.com/beans`*, contains the formal specification of the JavaBeans architecture. It describes every aspect of JavaBeans, from API definitions to ZIP formats. Because of its official status, it has gained a reputation as the "Beans Bible." It acts as a central authority that allows all JavaBeans products to conform to the same standard.*

Of course, the JavaBeans spec is not holy gospel. It is always changing, and it cannot sufficiently answer all of your questions. Sometimes, it can even be downright misleading. The section on property editors is a prime example. The spec implies that if you create a component-based property editor, you do not need to write a method that draws the property. Not true! Although bean builders are free to decide how to display a component-based property editor, many tools won't display it at all unless it also exposes a method for painting itself; if you create a component-based editor, always remember to implement the **paintValue()** *method, no matter what the JavaBeans spec tells you. (For more information on* **paintValue()**, *see the section "Drawing The Property.")*

Before we delve into more details, let us first define our own custom data type. We will use this type as a foundation for learning how to design component-based property editors. The type is not complex; it is just a simple Java class that holds generic information about a network user. Called **UserInfo**, its source code is given in Listing 6-4.

As you can see, the **UserInfo** class is nothing more than a wrapper for three variables: name, password, and access. The *name* is the name of the network user, the *password* is her password, and the *access* is her level of access to network resources. The **getAccessString()** method is a helper function that translates the access code to a friendly name.

Of course, in a real-world scenario, more information about the network user would be required. For the purposes of this tutorial, however, we have kept the **UserInfo** property type as simple as possible. We are much more interested in designing an editor for the property, rather than the property itself. Continue with the following two sections to learn how to create a component-based property editor for the **UserInfo** class.

DRAWING THE PROPERTY   Drawing a graphical representation of a property is not difficult. If you are already familiar with Java graphics, the steps are fairly trivial. First, you need to implement the **PropertyEditor. isPaintable()** method to return true. For example:

```
public boolean isPaintable()
{
    return true;
}
```

The return value of true notifies bean builder tools that your property editor knows how to paint itself.

Next, implement the **PropertyEditor.paintValue()** method. This method handles the actual painting of the property in a property sheet. bean builder tools call **paintValue()** whenever they need to display your editor. They pass two parameters to the method—a **java.awt.Graphics** object and a **java.awt.Rectangle** object—which you must use for rendering the property. As an example, Listing 6-5 shows how you might implement **paintValue()** for the **UserInfo** data type.

Listing 6-4
UserInfo is an example of a property type that requires a component-based property editor.

```java
public class UserInfo
{
    public String name = new String();
    public String password = new String();
    public int access;

    public UserInfo() {}

    public UserInfo(String name, String password, int
        access)
    {
        this.name = name;
        this.password = password;
        this.access = access;
    }

    public String getAccessString()
    {
        switch (access)
        {
            case 0: return "Guest";
            case 1: return "Power User";
            case 2: return "Backup Operator";
            case 3: return "Administrator";
            default: return "";
        }
    }
}
```

Listing 6-5
An implementation of **paintValue()** for the **UserInfo** data type.

```java
public void paintValue(Graphics g, Rectangle rc)
{
    UserInfo info = (UserInfo)getValue();

    Font oldFont = g.getFont();
    Rectangle oldClip = g.getClipBounds();

    g.setFont(new Font(oldFont.getName(), Font.BOLD,
        oldFont.getSize()));
    g.setClip(rc.x, rc.y, rc.width, rc.height);

    g.drawString(info.name, rc.x, rc.y + rc.height / 2 +
        g.getFontMetrics().getAscent() / 2);

    g.setFont(oldFont);
    g.setClip(oldClip.x, oldClip.y, oldClip.width,
        oldClip.height);
}
```

Although it might look complex, this implementation simply draws the **UserInfo.name** field. It calls **setValue()** to obtain the field, sets the current font to bold, and then draws the string. Notice that the drawing algorithm follows two important rules:

1. *Never draw outside the Rectangle parameter.* It is your responsibility to keep all drawing operations within the provided rectangle. If you do not, you might corrupt other areas of the bean builder's property sheet. An easy way to meet this requirement is to force automatic clipping by calling **Graphics.setClip()**.

2. *Always restore the state of the Graphics object.* The JavaBeans specification explicitly states that you do not need to restore changes made to **paintValue()**'s **Graphics** parameter. This, however, is another instance where the spec is not quite correct. Some bean builder tools mistakenly expect your algorithm not to change the color, font, and other settings stored by the **Graphics** object. To ensure compatibility with all bean builder tools, you should practice good housekeeping and always leave the object in the same state you found it. (In our **UserInfo** example, note that the font and the clip rectangle are reverted to their original values before exiting the method.)

If you remember to follow these rules, your component-based property editors should work properly in all bean builder tools. Figure 6-6 shows the results of **UserInfo**'s **paintValue()** method in one such tool: Taligent's WebRunner Bean Tester.

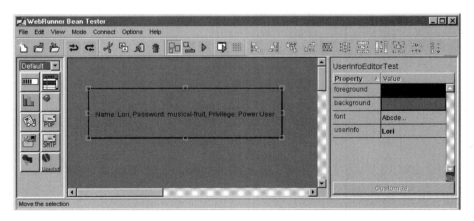

Figure 6-6
Bean builder tools such as Taligent's Webrunner Bean Tester call
PropertyEditor. paintValue() to render a component-based property editor in a property sheet.

CREATING THE COMPONENT   Once your editor can draw itself, you are ready to create the actual component of the component-based property editor. First, implement the `PropertyEditor.supportsCustomEditor()` method to return true. For example:

```
public boolean supportsCustomEditor()
{
    return true;
}
```

The return value of true notifies bean builder tools that your property editor can display a custom editor—that is, a user interface component—for viewing and changing the property.

Next, we must implement the `PropertyEditor.getCustomEditor()` method. This method returns a `java.awt.Component` value that bean builder tools display to the user. Thanks to Java's object-oriented nature, however, property editors are not required to return an actual `Component` object; they can return any descendant of `Component`. In fact, most property editors return a `java.awt.Panel` object, allowing them to store an entire group of `Components` (and any other classes derived from `Component`) as a single object. This technique is often a necessity for complex property types that require more advanced editing by the user.

We will use the same tactic for building our `UserInfo` editor. We will return a `Panel` object containing a text field for the name, a masked text field for the password, and a list box for the access level. The result will look like Figure 6-7.

At this point, we must decide how to create the `Panel` object for the property editor. We have two choices. We could either create a class that extends from `Panel` and implements `PropertyEditor`, or we could create a class that extends from `PropertyEditorSupport` and bring in a `Panel` object from a separate class. Both choices would achieve the same end result, but the latter choice is the better one because it provides the benefits of the `PropertyEditorSupport` class.

Figure 6-7
This **Panel** object will act as the **Component** for the **UserInfo** property editor.

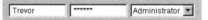

Listing 6-6 shows an example of this latter choice. It is the complete source code for the component-based **UserInfo** property editor, and it demonstrates how to bring in a **Panel** object from a separate class. Notice how this technique simplifies the **getCustomEditor()** method to a single statement.

Listing 6-6
The complete source code for the **UserInfo** property editor.

```java
import java.awt.*;
import java.awt.event.*;

public class UserInfoEditor extends
    java.beans.PropertyEditorSupport
{
    public boolean isPaintable()
    {
        return true;
    }

    public void paintValue(Graphics g, Rectangle rc)
    {
        UserInfo info = (UserInfo)getValue();

        Font oldFont = g.getFont();
        Rectangle oldClip = g.getClipBounds();

        g.setFont(new Font(oldFont.getName(), Font.BOLD,
                    oldFont.getSize()));
        g.setClip(rc.x, rc.y, rc.width, rc.height);

        g.drawString(info.name, rc.x, rc.y + rc.height / 2 +
                    g.getFontMetrics().getAscent() / 2);

        g.setFont(oldFont);
        g.setClip(oldClip.x, oldClip.y, oldClip.width,
                    oldClip.height);
    }

    public boolean supportsCustomEditor()
    {
        return true;
    }

    public Component getCustomEditor()
    {
        return new UserInfoEditorPanel();
    }

    /* - Inner class - */
    private class UserInfoEditorPanel extends Panel
        implements TextListener, ItemListener
    {
        private TextField name = new TextField();
        private TextField password = new TextField();
```

Listing 6-6

```
private Choice access = new Choice();

public UserInfoEditorPanel()
{
    setLayout(null);
    setSize(300, 40);

    UserInfo info = (UserInfo)getValue();

    name.setBounds(5, 9, 90, 21);
    name.setText(info.name);
    name.addTextListener(this);
    add(name);

    password.setEchoChar('*');
    password.setBounds(100, 9, 90, 21);
    password.setText(info.password);
    password.addTextListener(this);
    add(password);

    access.add("Guest");
    access.add("Power User");
    access.add("Backup Operator");
    access.add("Administrator");
    access.setBounds(195, 5, 100, 30);
    access.select(info.access);
    access.addItemListener(this);
    add(access);
}

public Dimension getPreferredSize()
{
    return new Dimension(300, 40);
}

public void itemStateChanged(ItemEvent e)
{
    UserInfo info = (UserInfo)getValue();

    info.access = access.getSelectedIndex();
    setValue(info);
}

public void textValueChanged(TextEvent e)
{
    UserInfo info = (UserInfo)getValue();

    if ( e.getSource() == name )
    {
        info.name = name.getText();
    }
    else if ( e.getSource() == password )
```

Continues

Listing 6-6
Continued.

```
    {
        info.password = password.getText();
    }

    setValue(info);
    }
  }
}
```

As the listing shows, the `UserInfoEditorPanel` class is a standard `java.awt.Panel` that adds two text fields and a list box to itself. The only unique thing about this class is the handling of "item state changed" and "text value changed" messages. Upon receipt of either message, the `UserInfoEditorPanel` class calls `setValue()` to update the `UserInfo` property with the new data. The `setValue()` method, in turn, sends a message to the bean builder tool, telling it to update all properties. The result is a dynamic redraw that lets users see changes to properties as they make them.

Property Editors as Enumerations

So far, we have seen two types of property editors. First, there is the text-based editor. It is easy to implement, but it works only for the simplest types of properties. And there is the component-based property editor. It is extremely powerful, but it requires more work to create.

Thankfully, the JavaBeans architecture provides a third type that combines the features of both text-based and component-based property editors. Known as the "enumerated" or "tagged" property editor, this type is designed specifically for properties that are limited to a finite range of values.

Let us say, for example, that you have written a bean that conducts a reader-response survey for a Web site. This bean contains an integer property that holds the reader's overall opinion of the site, with 1 signifying "poor," and 5 signifying "excellent." Normally, this property type would appear in a property sheet as a simple (but dangerous) integer value. Users could set the property to values outside the given range, such as 0 or 6. They might also become confused about the various values, perhaps thinking that 1 means "best."

To prevent these problems, we could create a component-based property editor that displays a list box with all possible values for the property type (see Figure 6-8). Users would be forced to select from the list, thus

Figure 6-8

A list box displays all possible values for an enumerated "opinion" property type.

preventing errors due to invalid values. Plus, they would easily see the various values and be sure that they were selecting the right one. Of course, building this sort of component-based editor would require extra effort on our part, such as implementing the **paintValue()** and **getCustomEditor()** methods.

But why do all that work? Enumerated property editors can handle those nasty chores for you. They can display the list box directly inside the property sheet, and, with a little help from **PropertyEditorSupport**, require very few lines of code. The only catch is that whenever you design a property editor for tagged values, you must design **getAsText()** and **setAsText()** methods for the editor, as well.

The key to creating enumerated property editors is the **PropertyEditor. getTags()** method. You must implement this method to return an array of **String**s that corresponds to all possible values of the enumerated type. Going back to our reader survey example, the string array for the opinion property might contain the values Poor, Fair, Average, Good, and Excellent.

After implementing **getTags()**, your next step is to implement the **getAsText()** and **setAsText()** methods, as explained in the section "Property Editors As Text." bean builder tools use these methods to translate values to tags and tags to values. This approach enables you to write enumerated property editors for any data type, not just integers.

With those three methods implemented, your enumerated property editor is complete. Check out Listing 6-7 for the source code to an enumerated editor for our "opinion" property. (Remember that this type is actually just an integer limited to the values 1 through 5.)

As you can see, an enumerated property editor requires about the same amount of code as a text-based editor, but it wields the power of a full-blown component-based editor.

Initialization Strings

A primary goal of many bean builder tools is to generate the source code of a complete Java application automatically. The idea is that application

Listing 6-7
A property editor for
an enumerated
integer property
called "opinion."

```
public class OpinionEditor extends java.beans.
    PropertyEditorSupport
{
    private static final String[] opinions = { "Poor",
        "Fair", "Average", "Good", "Excellent" };

    public String getAsText()
    {
        Integer opinion = (Integer)getValue();
        return opinions[opinion.intValue() - 1];
    }

    public void setAsText(String s)
    {
        for (int i = 0; i < 5; i++)
        {
            if ( s.equals(opinions[i]) )
            {
                setValue(new Integer(i + 1));
                return;
            }
        }

        throw new IllegalArgumentException();
    }

    public String[] getTags()
    {
        return opinions;
    }
}
```

developers use the tool to wire beans together and design their products visually, avoiding most of the complexities of hand-coding the program from scratch.

When generating this source code, bean builder tools know exactly how to handle standard types such as **string**, **int**, and **boolean**. Custom properties, though, can confuse them. For instance, an off-the-shelf tool would not know how to create source code for our **UserInfo** data type.

The solution to this problem is the **PropertyEditor** interface's **getJavaInitializationString()** method. By implementing this method, you can get intimate with builder tools and let them know the exact Java code necessary to initialize your property type. The code always depends on the current value of the property, which means you cannot hard-code the return value as a single, static string. Instead, you must combine it with calls to the `getAsText()` or `getValue()` methods. For example, the implementation of `getJavaInitializationString()` for the `BigInteger` editor (from the section "Property Editors As Text") would look like this:

```
public String getJavaInitializationString()
{
    return "new BigInteger(" + getAsText() + ")";
}
```

Likewise, the implementation of `getJavaInitializationString()` for the `UserInfo` editor (from the section "Property Editors As Components") would look like this:

```
public String getJavaInitializationString()
{
    UserInfo info = (UserInfo)getValue();
    return "new UserInfo(" + info.name + ", " +
                            info.password + ", " +
                            info.access + ")";
}
```

You may have noticed that previous examples in this chapter have not included an implementation of the `getJavaInitializationString()` method. This was only for the sake of simplicity, not because the method is optional. You must always write a `getJavaInitializationString()` method for all property editors. Otherwise, your components won't work properly in many bean builder tools.

TIP: *All property editor examples in this chapter contain the suffix "Editor" in their names. You might think this suffix is a requirement. Actually, editor classes can be named anything you like. The "Editor" suffix is just a nice convention to follow because it makes the classes easy to identify.*

Property Change Events

At this point, we have looked at every method in the `PropertyEditor` interface except for two:

- `void addPropertyChangeListener(PropertyChangeListener listener);`

- `void removePropertyChangeListener(PropertyChangeListener listener);`

We have not touched on these methods because the **PropertyEditor Support** class handles them fine without our help. For the sake of completeness, however, we should explain them, just in case you run into a situation where you do not want to extend from **PropertyEditorSupport**.

As suggested by their names, these methods serve the same purpose for property editors that they serve for regular beans: they allow external objects to detect changes to a property. In this case, the external object is the bean builder tool that has loaded your custom property editor and displayed the property in a property sheet. The tool wants to detect property changes that your editor makes, so it will implement the **PropertyChangeListener** interface and call your **addPropertyChangeListener()** method to register itself as a listener.

When implementing **addPropertyChangeListener()**, your job is to save a copy of the listener object that the bean builder tool (or any other object) passes to you. Now, as we mentioned, you can save yourself from this responsibility by extending from **PropertyEditorSupport**. If you do not, handling the job yourself is not too tough.

First, you will need a private **Vector** variable to hold a list of the objects that are passed to you via **addPropertyChangeListener()**:

```
private java.util.Vector listeners;
```

Next, you must implement **addPropertyChangeListener()** so that it appends the property listener objects to the **Vector**. The algorithm, shown in Listing 6-8, is no different than the **addPropertyChangeListener()** method for bound properties in actual beans.

Finally, implement the **removePropertyChangeListener()** method as shown in Listing 6-9. Bean builder tools will call this method when they

Listing 6-8
A standard implementation of PropertyEditor's **add PropertyChange Listener()** method.

```
public void addPropertyChangeListener(PropertyChangeListener
    listener)
{
   synchronized (this)
   {
      if (listeners == null)
      {
         listeners = new java.util.Vector();
      }

      listeners.addElement(listener);
   }
}
```

Listing 6-9
A standard
implementation of
PropertyEditor's
**remove
PropertyChange
Listener()**
method.

```
public void removePropertyChangeListener
    (PropertyChangeListener listener)
{
    synchronized (this)
    {
        if (listeners == null)
        {
            return;
        }

        listeners.removeElement(listener);
    }
}
```

are no longer interested in changes to your property. Again, this algorithm is identical to the version for bound properties.

With both methods implemented, you still have one more step to complete: you must call the **propertyChanged()** method of each saved listener whenever you make a change to your property. As before, you can basically cut and paste the Java code for bound property handling into your **PropertyEditor** implementation. The easiest way to do this is by restricting all access of the property to the **getValue()** and **setValue()** methods. In other words, never modify the property data directly; always use **setValue()** to make changes. By following this rule of thumb, firing the **propertyChanged()** method requires only a minor addition to **setValue()**, as shown in Listing 6-10.

Remember that the steps outlined in this section are often unnecessary. You only need to perform them when your property editor class does not extend from **PropertyEditorSupport**.

Registering Property Editors

Unlike **BeanInfo** interfaces, which are always automatically recognized and loaded by development tools (see Chapter 5), property editors must sometimes be explicitly registered before bean builder tools can find them. Registration is a somewhat complex process, and the JavaBeans spec fails to describe it completely. In this section, we will clear up any confusion you might have and tell you exactly how to register property editors.

The core of the registration process is a class in the **java.beans** package called **PropertyEditorManager**, which keeps track of a list of property

Listing 6-10
A standard
implementation of
PropertyEditor's
setValue()
method, modified to
fire property change
events.

```java
public void setValue(Object value)
{
    this.value = value;

    java.util.Vector targets;

    // Make a copy of the listeners vector, synchronized to
    // avoid problems with multithreaded access.
    synchronized (this)
    {
        if (listeners == null)
        {
            return;
        }

        targets = (java.util.Vector) listeners.clone();
    }

    // Fire the propertyChange() method on each listener
    // in the vector.
    PropertyChangeEvent evt = new
        PropertyChangeEvent(source, null, null, null);

    for (int i = 0; i < targets.size(); i++)
    {
        PropertyChangeListener target =
        (PropertyChangeListener)targets.elementAt(i);
        target.propertyChange(evt);
    }
}
```

editor classes. The list maps each class to its corresponding property type, and it is global to each instance of the Java Virtual Machine.

The methods, fields, and other details of **PropertyEditorManager** are unimportant to us component developers. (The class is of interest mainly to designers of JavaBeans development environments.) We only need to concern ourselves with how **PropertyEditorManager** searches for property editors.

SEARCHING FOR PROPERTY EDITORS   Searching for an editor is a three-part process, as shown by the flowchart in Figure 6-9. First, **PropertyEditorManager** searches its internal list to determine whether it contains an entry for a given property type. If not, the manager looks for a class with the same name as the type but with the word "Editor" at the end. So for a property named **UserInfo** whose class resides in the package **com.vocaro.freestuff**, the manager will search for a property

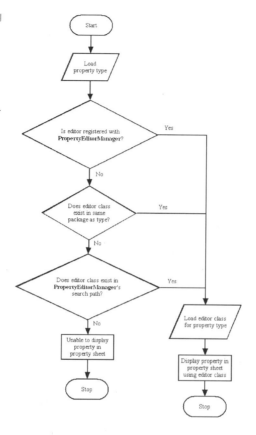

Figure 6-9
PropertyEditor Manager performs three steps to search for property editor classes.

editor called **com.vocaro.freestuff.UserInfoEditor.** If the class still cannot be found, the manager will look for the same "type + Editor" class in a list of packages. (The **PropertyEditorManager** class contains methods for adding and removing package names to and from this search path.) If, after all that work a property editor still cannot be located, the manager assumes that the editor does not exist, and the bean builder tool won't display the property in its property sheet.

If you find this process confusing, just remember the following three rules. You should always register your property editor if:

■ the editor is for a standard Java type (such as **int**, **BigDecimal**, or **Calendar**).

■ the editor and its property type reside in different packages.

■ the editor and its property type reside in the same package, but the editor class does not conform to the "type + Editor" naming convention.

Now that you know when to register a property editor, it is time to learn how. Fortunately, this is the easy part. You simply call the **setPropertyEditorClass()** method. This method is a member of **java.beans.PropertyDescriptor**, which means your components must define a **BeanInfo** interface in order to register their property editors. (For detailed information on **BeanInfo**, see Chapter 5.) After the **BeanInfo** interface is packaged along with the editor class, your property editor will appear on the property sheet as if it were built-in to the development environment.

DATE EDITOR EXAMPLE   As an example of how to register a property editor, we will look at the **java.util.Date** class. Although relatively common, this class is almost never supported by bean builder tools. Therefore, if your bean contains a property of type **Date**, it will not appear on a property sheet unless you write and register a property editor for it. Listing 6-11 contains the complete source code of a text-based property editor for the **java.util.Date class.**

Listing 6-11
A text-based property editor for the
java.util.Date
class.

```
import java.beans.*;
import java.util.*;

public class DateEditor extends PropertyEditorSupport
{
    public void setAsText(String text)
    {
        StringTokenizer tokenizer = new StringTokenizer(text,
                                                         "/");
        GregorianCalendar calendar = new GregorianCalendar();

        try
        {
            calendar.set(Calendar.YEAR, Integer.valueOf
                        (tokenizer.nextToken()).intValue());

            int i;

            i = Integer.valueOf(tokenizer.
                                nextToken()).intValue();

            if (i < Calendar.JANUARY || i > Calendar.DECEMBER)
                return;

            calendar.set(Calendar.MONTH, i - 1);

            i = Integer.valueOf(tokenizer.
```

Listing 15-1.
A collection example.

```
                                    nextToken()).intValue();

        if (i < 1 || i > 31) return;

        calendar.set(Calendar.DAY_OF_MONTH, i);

        setValue(calendar.getTime());
        }
    catch (NoSuchElementException e) {}
    catch (NumberFormatException e) {}
    }

public String getAsText()
{
    GregorianCalendar calendar = new GregorianCalendar();
    calendar.setTime((Date)getValue());

    return Integer.toString(calendar.get(Calendar.YEAR))
    + "/" +
            Integer.toString(calendar.get(Calendar.MONTH)
                            + 1) + "/" +
            Integer.toString(calendar.get(Calendar.
                                        DAY_OF_MONTH));
    }

public String getJavaInitializationString()
{
    return "new java.util.Date(" +
    Long.toString(((Date)getValue()).getTime()) + ")";
    }
}
```

To register this editor, you must compile it, package it with your bean, and then add a call to **setPropertyEditorClass()** somewhere inside the **getPropertyDescriptors()** method of the bean's **BeanInfo** interface. For instance, if the **Date** property is named "startDate," the **getPropertyDescriptors()** method would contain the following code:

```
PropertyDescriptor startDate = new PropertyDescriptor
        ("startDate", MyBean.class);
startDate.setPropertyEditorClass(DateEditor.class);
```

The parameter to **setPropertyEditorClass()** is just a hard-coded reference to the **DateEditor** class. Bean builder tools will use the reference to locate and load the property editor.

Although the previous code will work, it is not quite correct. Imagine what would happen if a bean builder tool were pre-packaged with its own **java.util.Date** editor. This editor would likely be more powerful and more capable than our simple text-based editor. However, because we have explicitly registered our date editor by calling **setPropertyEditorClass()**, the builder tool might mistakenly think that our particular editor is somehow required for our bean. This assumption could deny users the benefits of the tool's own date editor.

Luckily, there is an easy fix for this troublesome scenario. We simply need to call on **PropertyEditorManager** to search for a date editor class. If it finds one, we can safely skip registration of our own editor. If not, we can go ahead and call **setPropertyEditorClass()** as before. The new code would look like this:

```
PropertyDescriptor startDate = new PropertyDescriptor
    ("startDate", MyBean.class);

if ( PropertyEditorManager.findEditor(java.util.Date.class)
    == null )
{
    startDate.setPropertyEditorClass(DateEditor.class);
}
```

With this code in place, bean builder tools can always load our date properties into their property sheets, no matter who provides the editor. Figure 6-10 shows the **DateEditor** inside the property sheet of Taligent's WebRunner Bean Tester.

Customizers

As powerful as they are, property editors cannot handle every situation. Times arise when you require a greater degree of control over how developers configure your beans. You may, for example, want to display a step-by-step, automated guide that walks the user through the configuration process. Or you might want to replace the bean builder tool's property sheet with your own, just to be sure that your bean's properties are displayed completely and correctly.

For either scenario, the JavaBeans architecture provides a solution known as a customizer. Like property editors, *customizers* are nothing more than specialized **java.awt.Component** objects (or any descendant

Figure 6-10
Because it is packaged with and registered by Vocaro Technologies' Date Select, the date editor looks like it is built-in to Taligent's WebRunner Bean Tester.

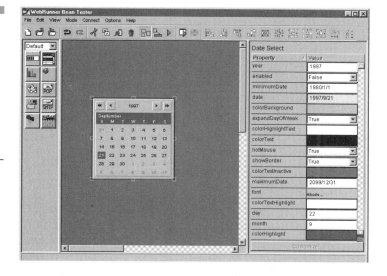

Figure 6-11
The BeanBox, like most bean builder tools, display a bean's customizer in a separate dialog window.

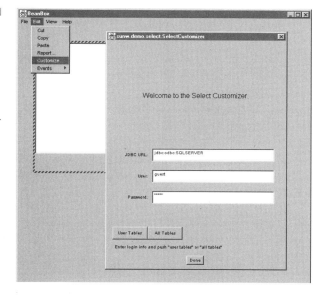

of **`java.awt.Component`**). JavaBeans development environments usually provide a button or menu item that lets the user display a bean's customizer. Sun's BeanBox, for instance, appends "Customizer..." to its Edit menu whenever it detects a customizer in the selected bean (see Figure 6-11).

Listing 6-12
The **java.beans.**
Customizer
interface.

```
public interface Customizer
{
    void setObject(Object bean);
    void addPropertyChangeListener(PropertyChangeListener
        listener);
    void removePropertyChangeListener(PropertyChangeListener
        listener);
}
```

The Customizer Interface

To create a customizer, you must design a Java class that implements the **java.beans.Customizer** interface. Because customizers come in only one flavor, the interface is far less complex than **java.beans.PropertyEditor**. It contains only three methods, as shown in Listing 6-12.

The **setObject()** method is called by the bean builder tool just before it displays your customizer. The tool passes a reference of the selected bean as the Object parameter in **setObject()**. You should save this parameter as a private variable, casting it to the type of your bean. This gives you easy access to the instance of the bean that the user is customizing. We will look at an example of how to implement **setObject()** later in this chapter.

The last two methods in the **Customizer** interface should hardly need an explanation. They have the same format and purpose as the **add/ removePropertyChangeListener()** methods in regular beans and in property editors. That is, they allow external objects (in this case, bean builder tools) to detect changes that your **Customizer** class makes to properties. We will take a closer look at these methods later on.

TIP: *ActiveX Will Not Activate without Customizers. JavaBeans are not only cross-platform; they are cross-architecture. By installing "bean bridges," you can deploy Java components in LiveConnect, ActiveX, and other non-Java architectures.*

Sun Microsystems currently provides a bridge for Microsoft's ActiveX architecture. This bridge, which you can download for free from **http://java.sun.com/beans**, *does its best to transform any standard JavaBean into an ActiveX control. However, due to limitations in ActiveX, the bridge is unable to convert property editors to their ActiveX equivalents.*

If you use the ActiveX bridge and run into this problem, don't sweat it. Just send in a customizer to the rescue. Most ActiveX control containers are perfectly capable of displaying bean customizers—with a little help from Sun's bridge, of course. So the workaround for the problem is pretty simple: simply load your property editors inside your customizer.

Registering Customizers

Unlike typical property editors, customizers must be registered before bean builder tools can recognize them. Registration is a simple one-line statement, though this statement must reside in a **BeanInfo** interface that could span many lines. The statement is merely the construction of a **BeanDescriptor** object inside the **BeanInfo.getBeanDescriptor()** method. For example:

```
public BeanDescriptor getBeanDescriptor()
{
    return new BeanDescriptor(MyBean.class,
        MyBeanCustomizer.class);
}
```

MyBean is the class name of the bean, and **MyBeanCustomizer** is the class name of the customizer. When placed inside the bean's **BeanInfo** class, this statement is all that is necessary to register the customizer.

Implementing a Customizer

After that whirlwind tour, let us look at some sample code to get a better feel for how to implement a customizer. In this section, we will build a customizer class for a JavaBean called "The Lingo." This bean translates any string of English text into one of four "lingos": pig latin, Elmer Fudd-speak, Morse code, or mock Swedish. Figure 6-12 shows the Lingo bean loaded into Taligent's WebRunner Bean Tester. The complete source code for the bean can be found on this book's CD-ROM.

To make a customizer for the Lingo bean, we will need to extend a new class from **java.awt.Component** and implement **java.beans.Customizer** in that class. Any ancestor of **Component** will work equally well, so we will extend from **java.awt.Panel**, allowing us to put components inside the customizer. The source code for this customizer class is shown in Listing 6-13.

Notice a peculiarity in this code: we initialized the customizer's components not in the constructor, but rather in the **setObject()** method. We

Figure 6-12
The Lingo bean can
translate English text
into various lingos.

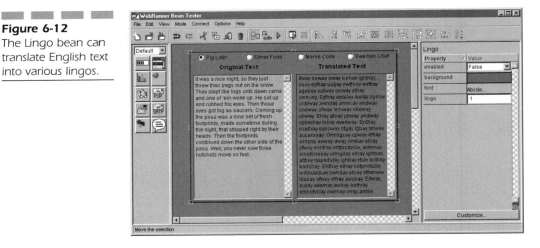

Listing 6-13
The source code to
the Lingo bean's
customizer class.

```java
import java.awt.*;
import java.awt.event.*;
import java.beans.*;

public class LingoCustomizer extends Panel implements
      Customizer, KeyListener, ItemListener
{
    private Lingo m_target;
    private Choice m_choiceLingo;
    private TextField m_tfSource, m_tfDest;
    private PropertyChangeSupport m_pcs = new
      PropertyChangeSupport(this);

    public LingoCustomizer()
    {
        setLayout(null);
    }

    public void setObject(Object obj)
    {
        m_target = (Lingo) obj;

        Label label;

        // Lingo property

        label = new Label("Lingo:", Label.RIGHT);
        add(label);
        label.setBounds(5, 5, 105, 25);

        m_choiceLingo = new Choice();
        m_choiceLingo.add("Pig Latin");
```

Listing 6-13

```
        m_choiceLingo.add("Elmer Fudd");
        m_choiceLingo.add("Morse Code");
        m_choiceLingo.add("Swedish Chef");
        add(m_choiceLingo);
        m_choiceLingo.setBounds(115, 5, 88, 25);
        m_choiceLingo.addItemListener(this);
        m_choiceLingo.select(m_target.getLingo() - 1);

        // Source text property

        label = new Label("Source Text:", Label.RIGHT);
        add(label);
        label.setBounds(5, 38, 105, 25);

        m_tfSource = new TextField();
        add(m_tfSource);
        m_tfSource.setBounds(115, 38, 88, 25);
        m_tfSource.addKeyListener(this);
        m_tfSource.setText(m_target.m_taSource.getText());

        // Translated text property

        label = new Label("Translated Text:", Label.RIGHT);
        add(label);
        label.setBounds(5, 73, 105, 25);

        m_tfDest = new TextField();
        add(m_tfDest);
        m_tfDest.setBounds(115, 73, 88, 25);
        m_tfDest.setEditable(false);
        m_tfDest.setText(m_target.getTranslatedText());
    }

    public Dimension getPreferredSize()
    {
        return new Dimension(220, 105);
    }

    public void keyTyped(KeyEvent e) {}
    public void keyPressed(KeyEvent e) {}

    public void keyReleased(KeyEvent e)
    {
        if (e.getComponent() == m_tfSource)
        {
            String str = m_tfSource.getText();
            m_target.setSourceText(str);
            m_pcs.firePropertyChange("sourceText", null,
                                      null);
            m_tfDest.setText(m_target.getTranslatedText());
```

Continues

Listing 6-13
Continued.

```
        }
    }

    public void itemStateChanged(ItemEvent e)
    {
        if (e.getStateChange() == ItemEvent.SELECTED)
        {
            m_target.setLingo((short)(m_choiceLingo.
                            getSelectedIndex() + 1));
            m_pcs.firePropertyChange("lingo", null, null);
            m_tfDest.setText(m_target.getTranslatedText());
        }
    }

    public void addPropertyChangeListener
        (PropertyChangeListener l)
    {
        m_pcs.addPropertyChangeListener(l);
    }

    public void removePropertyChangeListener
        (PropertyChangeListener l)
    {
        m_pcs.removePropertyChangeListener(l);
    }
}
```

were forced to delay initialization because we had no bean to initialize! Only after the call to **setObject()** do we receive the handle to the bean we are customizing.

Also notice that we define a **PropertyChangeSupport** object to keep track of property change listeners and to fire property change events. Performing these duties lets the bean builder tool update its property sheet whenever the user makes a change in the customizer.

As was mentioned, simply creating the Lingo bean's customizer class is not enough. We must also register the class inside the Lingo bean's **BeanInfo** interface. The necessary code looks like the following:

```
public BeanDescriptor getBeanDescriptor()
{
    return new BeanDescriptor(Lingo.class,
        LingoCustomizer.class);
}
```

After compiling, packaging, and reloading this new code, the Bean Tester's Customize... button becomes enabled. Clicking it produces the dialog box shown in Figure 6-13.

Figure 6-13
The Bean Tester can display the Lingo bean's customizer with the click of a button.

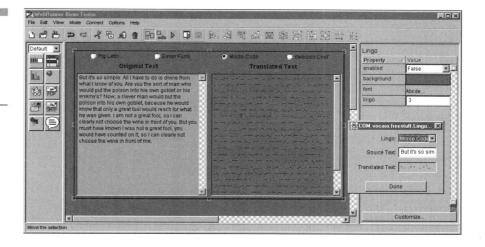

Putting It All Together

We now know when, how, and why to build property editors and customizers. Let us take what we have learned and apply it to a raw JavaBean in order to observe, step by step, how customization can improve the overall design-time quality of a component.

Step 1: The Magic Lens Class

In this section, we will look at a bean called "The Magic Lens." It is a relatively simple component that displays an image in its container. As the mouse moves across the bean, a spherical "lens" appears, magnifying a square of pixels underneath the mouse cursor (see Figure 6-14). The size and strength of the lens, as well as the underlying image, are exposed as properties that users can modify. Listing 6-14 contains the source code to the bean.

Step 2: Add a **BeanInfo** Interface

Our final goal is to add property editors for the Magic Lens's **diameter** and **magnification** properties, as well as a customizer for selection of the background image. Before we can do that, however, we must implement a **BeanInfo** interface for the Magic Lens. This class is required for registration of both the property editors and the customizer. Listing 6-15 shows the source code of a **BeanInfo** class for the Magic Lens.

Figure 6-14
The Magic Lens is a JavaBean that generates real-time spherical magnification of any 256-color image.

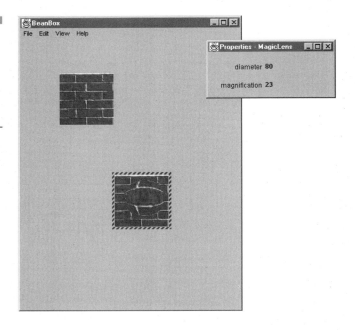

Listing 6-14
The source code for the Magic Lens.

```
import java.awt.*;
import java.awt.event.*;
import java.awt.image.*;

public class MagicLens extends java.applet.Applet
       implements MouseListener, MouseMotionListener
{
    private int nDiameter = 100;
    private int nMagnification = 25;
    private int nRadius = 50;
    private Image imgBackground, imgLens;
    private int nWidth, nHeight;
    private int[] nTransform;
    private byte[] byPixels;
    private IndexColorModel cmPalette;

    public void init()
    {
        addMouseListener(this);
        addMouseMotionListener(this);

        try
```

Listing 6-14

```
        {
            java.net.URL url = getClass().getResource
                                ("MagicLensIcon_32x32.gif");
            java.awt.Toolkit tk = java.awt.Toolkit.
                                getDefaultToolkit();
            setImage( tk.createImage((java.awt.image.
                    ImageProducer) url.getContent()) );
        }
        catch (Exception ex)
        {
            System.out.println("ERROR: Could not load default
                                image");
        }
    }

    public void paint(Graphics g)
    {
        if (imgBackground != null)
            g.drawImage(imgBackground, 0, 0, this);
    }

    public Dimension getPreferredSize()
    {
        return new Dimension(nWidth, nHeight);
    }

    public void mouseExited(MouseEvent e)
    {
        if (imgBackground != null)
            getGraphics().drawImage(imgBackground, 0, 0,
                                this);
    }

    public void mouseMoved(MouseEvent e)
    {
        Point ptMouse = e.getPoint();

        fixCoordinates(ptMouse);
        drawLens(ptMouse);
    }

    public void mouseClicked(MouseEvent e) {}
    public void mousePressed(MouseEvent e) {}
    public void mouseReleased(MouseEvent e) {}
    public void mouseDragged(MouseEvent e) {}
    public void mouseEntered(MouseEvent e) {}

    private void getIndexColorData(Image img, byte[]
                                byPixels, byte[] byReds,
                                byte[] byGreens, byte[]
                                byBlues)
```

Continues

Listing 6-14
Continued.

```java
{
    int nWidth         = img.getWidth(this);
    int nHeight        = img.getHeight(this);
    int nPaletteIndex = 0;
    int[] nPixels      = new int[nWidth * nHeight];
    int[] nPalette     = new int[256];
    PixelGrabber pg    = new PixelGrabber(img, 0, 0,
                            nWidth, nHeight, nPixels, 0,
                            nWidth);

    try
    {
        pg.grabPixels();
    }
    catch (InterruptedException e) {}

    // Loop through each pixel in the image...
    for (int y = 0; y < nHeight; y++)
    {
        for (int x = 0; x < nWidth; x++)
        {
            int nIndex = -1;

            // Search for the palette index of the current
            //    pixel's color...
            for (int i = 0; i <= nPaletteIndex; i++)
            {
                if ( nPalette[i] == nPixels[y * nWidth +
                    x] )
                {
                    nIndex = i;
                    break;
                }
            }

            // If the current pixel's color is not in the
            //    palette, add it
            // to the palette.
            if ( nIndex == -1 )
            {
                nPalette[nPaletteIndex] = nPixels[y *
                nWidth + x];
                nIndex = nPaletteIndex;
                nPaletteIndex++;
            }

            // Change the pixel from a color value to an
            //    index value.
            byPixels[y * nWidth + x] = (byte) nIndex;
        }
    }
```

```
            for (int i = 0; i < 256; i++)
            {
                int red   = (nPalette[i] >> 16) & 0xff;
                int green = (nPalette[i] >> 8 ) & 0xff;
                int blue  = (nPalette[i]      ) & 0xff;

                byReds[i]   = (byte)red;
                byGreens[i] = (byte)green;
                byBlues[i]  = (byte)blue;
            }
        }

        private void calculateTransform()
        {
            nTransform = new int[ nDiameter * nDiameter ];
            double dSphereRay = Math.sqrt( nRadius * nRadius -
                                           nMagnification *
                                           nMagnification );
            int x, y, a, b;

            for (y = -nRadius; y < -nRadius + nDiameter; y++)
            {
                for (x = -nRadius; x < -nRadius + nDiameter; x++)
                {
                    if ( x * x + y * y < dSphereRay *
                        dSphereRay )
                    {
                        double z = Math.sqrt( nRadius * nRadius -
                                              x * x - y * y );
                        a = (int)((double)x *
                            (double)nMagnification / z + 0.5);
                        b = (int)((double)y *
                            (double)nMagnification / z + 0.5);
                    }
                    else
                    {
                        a = x;
                        b = y;
                    }

                    nTransform[(y + nRadius) * nDiameter +
                               (x + nRadius)] = (b + nRadius) *
                               nDiameter + (a + nRadius);
                }
            }
        }

        /**
        This function uses the transformation array and a
        double-buffer to draw the lens on the applet window.
        */
```

Continues

Listing 6-14
Continued.

```java
private void drawLens(Point pt)
{
    if (imgBackground == null)
        return;

    byte[] bySrcPixels  = new byte[ nDiameter *
                            nDiameter ];
    byte[] byDestPixels = new byte[ nDiameter *
                            nDiameter ];

    // Grab the pixels from the area to be transformed
    // and put them in a buffer...
    for (int y = pt.y - nRadius; y < pt.y - nRadius +
                nDiameter; y++)
    {
        System.arraycopy(byPixels,
                            y * nWidth + (pt.x - nRadius),
                            bySrcPixels,
                            (y - (pt.y - nRadius)) *
                             nDiameter,
                             nDiameter);
    }

    // Transform the pixels...
    for (int i = 0; i < nDiameter * nDiameter; i++)
    {
        byDestPixels[i] = bySrcPixels[ nTransform[i] ];
    }

    imgLens = createImage( new MemoryImageSource
                            (nDiameter,
                             nDiameter,
                             cmPalette,
                             byDestPixels,
                             0,
                             nDiameter) );

    // Create a double-buffer...
    Image imgBuffer = createImage(nWidth, nHeight);
    Graphics gBuffer = imgBuffer.getGraphics();

    gBuffer.drawImage(imgBackground, 0, 0, this);
    gBuffer.drawImage(imgLens, pt.x - nRadius, pt.y -
                nRadius, this);
    getGraphics().drawImage(imgBuffer, 0, 0, this);
}

/**
This function changes the mouse coordinates so that the
lens lies within the applet window.
```

Listing 6-14

```
*/
private void fixCoordinates(Point ptMouse)
{
    ptMouse.x = Math.min(ptMouse.x, getSize().width -
                nRadius);
    ptMouse.x = Math.max(ptMouse.x, nRadius);
    ptMouse.y = Math.min(ptMouse.y, getSize().height -
                nRadius);
    ptMouse.y = Math.max(ptMouse.y, nRadius);
}

public void setMagnification(int nMagnification)
{
    this.nMagnification = nMagnification;

    if ( this.nMagnification > nRadius )
        this.nMagnification = 0;
    else
        this.nMagnification = nRadius -
                              this.nMagnification;

    calculateTransform();
}

public int getMagnification()
{
    return nRadius - nMagnification;
}

public void setDiameter(int nDiameter)
{
    this.nDiameter = nDiameter;

    if ( this.nDiameter > Math.min(nWidth, nHeight) )
        this.nDiameter = Math.min(nWidth, nHeight);

    nRadius = this.nDiameter / 2;

    calculateTransform();
}

public int getDiameter()
{
    return nDiameter;
}

public void setImage(Image img)
{
    imgBackground = img;
```

Continues

Listing 6-14
Continued.

```java
      MediaTracker tracker = new MediaTracker(this);
      tracker.addImage(imgBackground, 0);

      try
      {
         tracker.waitForAll();
      }
      catch (InterruptedException e) {}

      nWidth = imgBackground.getWidth(this);
      nHeight = imgBackground.getHeight(this);

      if ( nDiameter > Math.min(nWidth, nHeight) )
         nDiameter = Math.min(nWidth, nHeight);

      nRadius = nDiameter / 2;

      if (nMagnification > nRadius)
         nMagnification = 0;
      else
         nMagnification = nRadius - nMagnification;

      byte[] byReds = new byte[256];
      byte[] byGreens = new byte[256];
      byte[] byBlues = new byte[256];

      byPixels = new byte[nWidth * nHeight];

      getIndexColorData(imgBackground, byPixels, byReds,
                        byGreens, byBlues);

      cmPalette = new IndexColorModel(8, 256, byReds,
                                      byGreens, byBlues);

      imgBackground = createImage( new MemoryImageSource
                                      (nWidth,
                                       nHeight,
                                       cmPalette,
                                       byPixels,
                                       0,
                                       nWidth) );
      calculateTransform();

      resize(nWidth, nHeight);
   }

   public Image getImage()
   {
      return imgBackground;
   }
}
```

Listing 6-15
This **BeanInfo** class
is required for
registering the
property editors and
the customizer for
the Magic Lens.

```java
import java.beans.*;
import java.awt.*;
import java.lang.reflect.*;

public class MagicLensBeanInfo extends SimpleBeanInfo
{
    public PropertyDescriptor[] getPropertyDescriptors()
    {
        try
        {
            PropertyDescriptor image =
                new PropertyDescriptor("image",
                                       MagicLens.class);

            PropertyDescriptor diameter =
                new PropertyDescriptor("diameter",
                                       MagicLens.class);

            PropertyDescriptor magnification =
                new PropertyDescriptor("magnification",
                                       MagicLens.class);

            image.setShortDescription("The background
                                      image");
            diameter.setShortDescription("Diameter of the
                                         lens in pixels");
            magnification.setShortDescription("Magnification
                                              strength of the
                                              lens (must be
                                              less than half
                                              the diameter)");

            PropertyDescriptor rv[] =
                { image, diameter, magnification };

            return rv;
        }
        catch (IntrospectionException e)
        {
            throw new Error(e.toString());
        }
    }

    public int getDefaultPropertyIndex()
    {
        return 0; // image property
    }

    public EventSetDescriptor[] getEventSetDescriptors()
    {
        EventSetDescriptor[] rv = {};
```

Continues

Listing 6-15
Continued.

```
      return rv;
   }

   public int getDefaultEventIndex()
   {
      return -1;
   }

   public MethodDescriptor[] getMethodDescriptors()
   {
      MethodDescriptor rv[] = {};

      return rv;
   }

   public Image getIcon(int iconKind)
   {
      if (iconKind == BeanInfo.ICON_COLOR_16x16)
      {
         Image img = loadImage("MagicLensIcon_16x16.gif");
         return img;
      }

      if (iconKind == BeanInfo.ICON_COLOR_32x32)
      {
         Image img = loadImage("MagicLensIcon_32x32.gif");
         return img;
      }

      return null;
   }
}
```

Step 3: Add a Property Editor

Now we are ready to add property editors for the **diameter** and **magnification** properties. Both of these properties are integers, so we need only one editor class. Called **IntCircleEditor**, this component-based editor displays a circle that contains the integer value. The user can drag the circle with the mouse to change its size, which increases or decreases the property value. Listing 6-16 shows the **IntCircleEditor**'s complete source code.

Because the **IntCircleEditor** overrides the default integer property editor, we cannot simply package it with the Magic Lens bean. We must register it in the **BeanInfo** class's **getPropertyDescriptors()** method, like this:

```
diameter.setPropertyEditorClass(IntCircleEditor.class);
magnification.setPropertyEditorClass(IntCircleEditor.class);
```

With this new code, bean builder tools will skip their default integer editor and use ours instead.

Listing 6-16
The source code for the IntCircleEditor.

```
package COM.vocaro.freestuff;

import java.awt.*;
import java.awt.event.*;

public class IntCircleEditor extends
      java.beans.PropertyEditorSupport
{
    public boolean isPaintable()
    {
        return true;
    }

    public void paintValue(Graphics g, Rectangle rc)
    {
        Font oldFont = g.getFont();
        Rectangle oldClip = g.getClipBounds();

        g.setFont(new Font(oldFont.getName(), Font.BOLD,
                        oldFont.getSize()));
        g.setClip(rc.x, rc.y, rc.width, rc.height);

        g.drawString(((Integer)getValue()).toString(), rc.x,
                        rc.y + rc.height / 2 +
                        g.getFontMetrics().getAscent() / 2);

        g.setFont(oldFont);
        g.setClip(oldClip.x, oldClip.y, oldClip.width,
                oldClip.height);
    }

    public boolean supportsCustomEditor()
    {
        return true;
    }

    public Component getCustomEditor()
    {
        return new IntCircleEditorCanvas();
    }

    private class IntCircleEditorCanvas extends Canvas
        implements MouseListener, MouseMotionListener
```

Continues

Listing 6-16
Continued.

```
{
    private Point lastMousePoint = new Point();

    public IntCircleEditorCanvas()
    {
        setSize(400, 400);

        addMouseListener(this);
        addMouseMotionListener(this);
    }

    public Dimension getPreferredSize()
    {
        return new Dimension(400, 400);
    }

    public void paint(Graphics g)
    {
        Rectangle r = getBounds();

        g.setColor( getBackground() );
        g.fillRect(r.x, r.y, r.width, r.height);

        g.setColor( getForeground() );
        g.drawString("Click and drag to change integer
                     value", 0, g.getFontMetrics().
                     getHeight());

        int i = ((Integer)getValue()).intValue();

        g.setColor( Color.red );
        g.fillOval( r.width / 2 - i / 2, r.height / 2 -
                    i / 2, i, i);

        g.setColor( Color.white );
        g.drawString(i + "", r.width /
        2 - g.getFontMetrics().stringWidth(i + "") /
        2, r.height / 2 + g.getFontMetrics().getAscent()
        / 2);
    }

    public void mouseDragged(MouseEvent e)
    {
        int i = ((Integer)getValue()).intValue();

        if ( e.getY() > lastMousePoint.y )
        {
            i -= e.getY() - lastMousePoint.y;

            if ( i < 0 ) i = 0;
        }
        else
```

Listing 6-16

```
                    {
                        if ( e.getY() < lastMousePoint.y )
                        {
                            i += lastMousePoint.y - e.getY();

                            if ( i > 400 ) i = 400;
                        }
                    }

                    setValue( new Integer(i) );

                    repaint();

                    lastMousePoint = e.getPoint();
                }

                public void mousePressed(MouseEvent e)
                {
                    lastMousePoint = e.getPoint();
                }

                public void mouseMoved(MouseEvent e) {}
                public void mouseClicked(MouseEvent e) {}
                public void mouseEntered(MouseEvent e) {}
                public void mouseExited(MouseEvent e) {}
                public void mouseReleased(MouseEvent e) {}
            }
        }
```

Step 4: Add a Customizer

To complete our improvements to the Magic Lens, we will add a customizer that displays the current value of the **Image** property. We will also put a Browse button in the customizer that will enable the user to load images from the file system. The result will look like Figure 6-15. Listing 6-17 is the complete source code for our customizer class.

The preceding code uses the **java.awt.FileDialog** class to retrieve a file name from the user. Note that that although **FileDialog** requires a **java.awt.Frame** object, we are still able to display it, even though our customizer is a Panel, not a Frame, because we create an invisible Frame window to act as a surrogate parent for our **FileDialog**. We simply initialize the window, leave it in its invisible state, and set its bounds to match the bounds of our customizer. You can use this trick in any customizer, property editor, or other class where you need a Frame window but don't have one.

Figure 6-15
The Magic Lens's
customizer, shown
here running in IBM's
Visual Age for Java,
lets users browse for
different images.

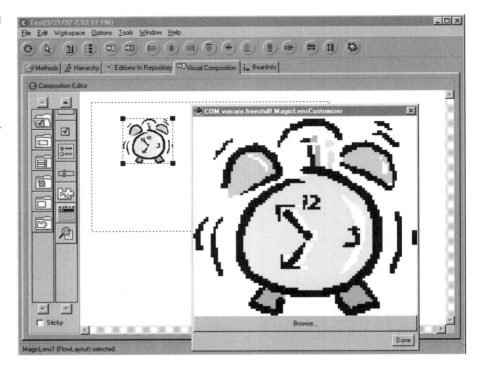

Listing 6-17
The source code to
the Magic Lens's
customizer class.

```java
import java.awt.*;
import java.awt.event.*;
import java.beans.*;

public class MagicLensCustomizer extends Panel implements
     Customizer, ActionListener
{
   private MagicLens target;
   private Button browse = new Button("Browse...");
   private PropertyChangeSupport pcs = new
     PropertyChangeSupport(this);

   public MagicLensCustomizer()
   {
      setLayout(null);
   }

   public void setObject(Object obj)
   {
      target = (MagicLens) obj;
```

Listing 6-17

```
        add(browse);
        browse.setBounds(0, 370, 400, 30);
        browse.addActionListener(this);
    }

    public Dimension getPreferredSize()
    {
        return new Dimension(400, 400);
    }

    public void paint(Graphics g)
    {
        Image img = target.getImage();

        g.drawImage(img, 0, 0, 400, 370, 0, 0,
                    img.getWidth(this), img.getHeight(this),
                    this);
    }

    public void actionPerformed(ActionEvent e)
    {
        Frame frame = new Frame();
        frame.setBounds(getLocationOnScreen().x,
                        getLocationOnScreen().y,
                        getSize().width,
                        getSize().height);

        FileDialog fd = new FileDialog(frame);
        fd.setMode(FileDialog.LOAD);
        fd.show();

        if ( fd.getFile() != null )
        {
            target.setImage(Toolkit.getDefaultToolkit().
                            getImage(fd.getDirectory( ) +
                            fd.getFile()));
            repaint();
        }
    }

    public void addPropertyChangeListener
        (PropertyChangeListener l)
    {
        pcs.addPropertyChangeListener(l);
    }

    public void removePropertyChangeListener
        (PropertyChangeListener l)
    {
        pcs.removePropertyChangeListener(l);
    }
}
```

One final step is necessary before our Magic Lens modifications are complete: we must register the customizer in our **BeanInfo** class. This step involves only one line of code inside the **getBeanDescriptor()** method. The new method looks like this:

```
public BeanDescriptor getBeanDescriptor()
{
    return new BeanDescriptor(MagicLens.class,
        MagicLensCustomizer.class);
}
```

With our customizer registered, it can be recognized and displayed by any bean builder tool that loads the Magic Lens.

CONCLUSION

Regardless of how you like to customize components, the JavaBeans architecture probably has a feature for you. Choose property editors for handling user-defined data types or go the customizer route for the ultimate in power and flexibility. Either way, you should pay close attention to the ease at which developers can customize your beans. If they have trouble using your products, they might think twice about purchasing from you again. After all, the developer is your customer, and the customer is king.

7

Runtime Containment and Services Protocol

As you have seen, Java beans are powerful through the use of the interface. Part of the complexity of this type of architecture is the low-level bindings to the underlying Java Virtual Machine, which in turn ultimately binds to the object code to the underlying machine code. It is easy for a Java program to rely on any information that can be generated from a call to the underlying Java API or from the Virtual Machine (VM) from which it is executing. The initial reason for creating a specification for runtime containment is in part to solve that problem. Further, it is meant to help in establishing a hierarchy within the beans framework.

This Chapter Covers

- The problems of containment within the beans abstraction.
- The nesting and nestability of beans.
- The increasing need for beans to be able to interact and provide services.
- The **BeanContext** interface.
- The **BeanContextListener** interface.
- The abstract **BeanContextEvent** class.
- The **BeanContextChild** interface.
- New ways of overloading the beans **instantiate()** method.
- Java bean contexts and their relation to the applet.
- The bean context support "helper" class.
- The six standard conventions for bean context delegates.
- The Java Development Kit 1.2 implementation of bean contexts.
- A code example of a bean context using the JDK 1.2.

Problems of Containment

JavaSoft thinks of this problem in terms of "containers." Containers by this definition are nothing more than an execution environment or "context" from which a bean is instantiated, used, and eventually deallocated.

For us to be able to view and discuss this problem correctly, we must start by further defining what we mean by container. A container can be thought of as an environment that a bean lives in. It would not be fair to assume that it is only a desktop, because it is possible to instantiate a bean remotely on a different machine and therefore a different environment than the machine that is executing the program that caused it to be instantiated. That is to say through the use of CORBA or RMI, one can execute a program on one machine, A, and that program makes a remote call or naming service lookup of a bean that resides on machine B. Machine B then instantiates the bean and passes a reference back to machine A. In this way, the container for that bean is on machine B. However the container for any beans instantiated or used by machine A, particularly by the graphical user interface (GUI), are contained by machine A.

Because the word "container" is about as overused as the word "object," JavaSoft decided to refer to this phenomenon strictly as a context or **Bean Context**. Different facilities or functionalities that are provided by the container to its underlying beans are referred to as "services." The most important part of this activity is again the interface. The interface of the context in which a bean operates and creates a relationship between the bean, its underlying context, and any services that are provided within that context.

So to summarize what JavaSoft outlined it would provide with the extensible runtime containment and services protocol specification, the following are outlined:

- Creation of a generic environment abstraction context, where a Java bean executes through its lifecycle and also is a hierarchical structure within the beans specification

- Allow for services to be added during runtime execution (dynamically)

- Provide a mechanism by which a bean can contact its environment to discover the availability of services and use them if necessary

- Provide a means by which to push an environment from one bean to another

- Provide better support for JavaBean applet programs

In the above list, a bean lifecycle is defined as the time between when it is instantiated all the way through the time when it as a resource is freed from memory and all the execution between those two events. Figure 7-1 shows an illustration of how beans and their associated contexts could interoperate.

Figure 7-1
Interoperation with beans and their associated contexts.

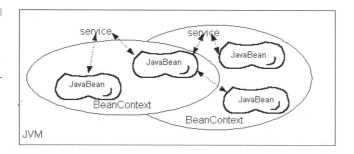

The Need for the "Nesting" of Beans

To address the issue of the possibility of being able to nest beans within bean contexts and to be able to nest bean contexts within each other, Java-Soft provided the specification for the **BeanContextChild** interface, outlined in Listing 7-3. In this fashion, a bean context contains a collection, or set, of nested contexts and/or beans. A developer must be careful in using or employing this abstraction in terms of recursion.

The Need for Beans to Interact to Provide Services

The key behind services is the thinking that goes behind the paradigm. The paradigm is further trying to simplify the complex task of disambiguating between platforms during the execution of a bean. To continue in this vein, when we break our software solution up in terms of objects and beans within our execution context, a convenient way to think about functionalities anything else it relies on as a service, it more closely resembles the real world. This helps out a lot in identifying solutions to problems within a distributed domain as well. If we think of a service as an interface method that takes specific parameters and returns a specific value, it doesn't matter what machine we are executing on anymore.

Both CORBA and RMI provide this type of relationship. RMI specifies the remote object and interface nomenclature, and CORBA specifies the Interface Definition Language (IDL), which forces the developer to think of the interfaces in terms of clients and servers. The goal in the end is to make both the virtual machine and the underlying computer ambiguous to the developer, such that they can specify in terms of beans, objects, services, and environments and expect to execute the same types of functionalities regardless.

The **BeanContext**

The **BeanContext** interface is the center of this specification. It provides the key elements of the runtime containment and services from which the **BeanContextChild** and listener build off of. Following in Listing 7-1 is a specification of the interface definition.

Listing 7-1
Specification of the
interface definition

```
public interface java.beans.BeanContext
    extends java.beans.BeanContextChild,
           java.util.Collection {

    Object instantiateChild(String beanName)
      throws IOException, ClassNotFoundException;
    Object getService(Class serviceClass,
                       BeanContextChild requestor);
    boolean hasService(Class serviceClass,
                       BeanContextChild requestor);
    public InputStream getResourceAsStream
                        (String name, BeanContextChild
                         requestor);
    public java.net.URL getResource(String name,
                            BeanContextChild
                            requestor);
    void addPropertyChangeListener
      (String name,PropertyChangeListener pcl);
    void removePropertyChangeListener
      (String name, PropertyChangeListener pcl);
    void removeBeanContextListener
      (BeanContextListener bcl);
    void addBeanContextListener(BeanContextListener bcl);
}
```

First, note how this interface extends **BeanContextChild**. It turns out that **BeanContextChild** extends interface **java.util.Eventlistener**. Recall that the **EventListener** interface is a "tagging" type interface that all **EventListeners** must extend. In this way, it was mandatory that the **BeanContextChild** extend this interface because of its relation to the **BeanContextListener** interface. It also extends the **java.util.Collection** interface. That interface is defined as the root of the collection hierarchy, which defines methods on collections that are implementation-independent.

The first method, **instantiatChild(String)**, allows a **BeanContext** to instantiate a child bean instance depending on the string name variable sent. The means by which this is accomplished is through the overloadable **java.beans.Beans.instantiate()** method and call-back.

The **getService(Class, BeanContextChild)** method serves to look up and obtain a reference to a service for a supported bean child of that context and to pass that reference back to the caller so that the caller can then invoke discovery or other methods on the service object. The **hasService()** method is a boolean method that returns "True" if a service exists within a **BeanContext** for a child to call on. These services are intended to be dynamic in nature and are supposed to be discovered and used at runtime.

The `getResourceAsStream()`, and `getResource()` methods are similar to their counterpart in `java.lang.Classloader`. It is intended that these methods will be called in place of the underlying class loader to allow the overarching `BeanContext` to interfere with the semantics of the resources. This allows for the context to further define or hone a resource before it is used by any of its children.

The `addPropertyChangeListener()` and `removePropertyChange Listener()` methods are the same as previously mentioned in this book. The `add` and `removeBeanContextListener()` methods allow a bean context to add and remove listeners specific to the runtime environment outlined in this chapter.

The `BeanContextListener`

Following is the specification of the `BeanContextListener`:

```
public interface BeanContextListener
   extends java.util.EventListener {
   void beanContextChanged(BeanContextEvent bce);
}
```

First, note that it extends `java.util.eventListener`. This interface serves the purpose of allowing bean contexts to notify listeners that are monitoring them when they experience any state changes. The only method defined in this interface is `beanContextChanged()`, which is called whenever a state change occurs in a particular bean context, where the `BeanContextEvent` parameter will contain the state information of the actual change.

The `BeanContextEvent`

Following, in Listing 7-2, is the specification for the inheritance hierarchy of `BeanContextEvents`.

The first outlined interface, `BeanContextEvent`, is the interface at the center of the context event interfaces. It builds off of `java.util.EventObject` and adds some new functionalities to aid in the use of bean contexts. The overall purpose of this class is to allow the listeners that are registered to hear this event to determine whether it was sent by its associated nested bean context.

Listing 7-2
Specification for the
inheritance hierarchy
of **BeanContext**
Events

```
public abstract class BeanContextEvent
    extends java.util.EventObject {
      public BeanContext getBeanContext();
      public synchronized void
        setPropagatedFrom(BeanContext bc);
      public synchronized BeanContext getPropagatedFrom();
      public synchronized boolean isPropagated()
  }

  public abstract class BeanContextMembershipEvent
    extends BeanContextEvent {
      public boolean isDeltaMember(Object o);
      public Object[] getDeltas();
      public boolean isChildrenAddedEvent();
      public boolean isChildrenRemovedEvent()
  }

  public BeanContextAddedEvent
    extends BeanContextMembershipEvent {
    BeanContextAddedEvent(BeanContext bc, Object[] bccs);
  }

  public BeanContextRemovedEvent
    extends BeanContextMembershipEvent {
      BeanContextRemovedEvent(BeanContext bc, Object[]
      bccs);
  }
```

The **getPropagatedFrom()** and **boolean isPropagated()** methods are intended to serve this purpose. The **getBeanContext()** method is intended to return the bean context which is currently handling the event.

The **BeanContextChild**

The **BeanContextChild** interface definition is intended for use within bean contexts. It allows the specification of child objects that are to be used within a bean context. Listing 7-3 outlines the **BeanContextChild**.

This is similar to what you are already used to seeing within this book as far as how a Java bean is defined. The **add** and **removeVetoableChange Lister()** methods, as well as the **add** and **removePropertyChange Listener()** methods act as you would expect. They allow beans to register interest in the properties and vetoable changes of the underlying bean context. One additional method is **addBeanContext()**, which allows the child to create a reference to its underlying bean context.

Listing 7-3
BeanContext
Child outline

```
public interface java.beans.BeanContextChild
   extends BeanContextListener {
      void setBeanContext(BeanContext bc)
         throws PropertyVetoException;
      BeanContext getBeanContext();
      void addPropertyChangeListener
         (String name, PropertyChangeListener pcl);
      void removePropertyChangeListener
         (String name, PropertyChangeListener pcl);
      void addVetoableChangeListener
         (String name, VetoableChangeListener pcl);
      void removeVetoableChangeListener
         (String name, VetoableChangeListener pcl);
}
```

Overloading `java.beans.instantiate`

One of the problems in defining the context abstraction is that there needs to be some facility of tracking the new **BeanContext** information. Java beans are specified to initially instantiate or instantiate more than once through the **java.beans.instantiate** method. The solution to our problem of tracking the additional piece of information is to extend the **instantiate** method to accommodate as follows:

```
public static Object instantiate(ClassLoader cl, String
                                 beanName,
                                 BeanContext beanContext);
```

Now, the appropriate containing **BeanContext** class is passed as the third parameter to the bean that is about to instantiate as a child to that context.

Java Bean Contexts and Their Relation to the Applet

It has been a long-standing problem within the beans Application Programmers Interface (API) that sufficient support does not yet exist for applets in relation to beans. The bean context seeks to solve this problem by further outlining how the **AppletContext** and **AppletStub**s are to be used. The new specified interface to the **instantiate** method of a bean that is also an applet is as follows in Listing 7-4.

There is an additional parameter passed to the bean's **initialize** method, which is the underlying **AppletInitializer**. The **Applet**

```
public static Object instantiate(ClassLoader cl, String
                                 beanName,
                                 BeanContext bCtxt,
                                 AppletInitializer ai);

public interface AppletInitializer {
   void initialize(Applet newApplet, BeanContext bCtxt);
   void activate(Applet newApplet);
}
```

Initializer is defined as an interface to two methods. The first method, **initialize**, takes the applet itself and the underlying bean context in as parameters and is responsible for setting the stage of operations between the applet and possible bean context.

The second argument of a **BeanContext** instance to the **initialize** method is optionally Null. In case it is Null, this **initialize** method is responsible for setting up the applets container and calling the associated **add()** method on the container. However, if the **BeanContext** argument is non-Null, that **BeanContext** is responsible for creating the underlying applet container and adding the applet.

The **activate()** method is responsible for setting the underlying applet in execution as "active" and optionally calling the **start()** method on the applet.

The **BeanContextSupport**

There is a provision and specification for the **java.beans.beancontext. BeanContextSupport** class, which provides a facility to handle the fairly complex "help" protocol (in relation to **BeanContext**). This class can either be created specifically as a reference from another class, or subclassed and then used.

Standard Conventions for **BeanContext** Delegates

A **BeanContext** delegate is defined as an implementation that should support the objectives of the bean context specification—that is, the bean context satisfies the introduction or use of the technology within the Java and beans frameworks. There are six set delegates:

- **BeanContext**s that support InfoBus technology

- **BeanContext**s used in conjunction with printing

- **BeanContext**s that provide design and/or runtime support

- **BeanContext**s that provide visibility support

- **BeanContext**s that can expose locale information

- **BeanContext**s that have associated presentation

The Infobus technology was created by Lotus Development Corporation, and is an extension to the Java Core API that allows for the exchange of *dynamic self-describing data*. It is an extension meaning it is not intended to be a part of the Java Core platform API release. Infobus allows for dynamic self-describing data through the use of publish and subscribe methods. A **BeanContext** will expose an Infobus to its child through the service API specified herein, more specifically the **hasService()** and **getService()** methods. This allows a **BeanContextChild** to use the **BeanContext** relationship as a cross-reference point to obtain Infobus information.

A suitable purpose of a **BeanContext** is using it in conjunction with printing. In that, the **BeanContext** can pass information dynamically to its children regarding its print services so that those children can then capitalize on those printing facilities in the future, or if they are nested **BeanContext**s, they can use and pass the print information to their children. This becomes an increasingly attractive alternative when combined with the JNDI specification to create a global name space to address print services both locally and abroad.

BeanContexts can also provide design or runtime support. The idea behind design support is thinking of it in terms of rapid application development and modes, where the developer may wish to develop with the bean interactively in a BeanBox or some such. A problem was stated with the first version of this specification, whereby whether the bean was in design or runtime mode was declared as a global variable in the JVM. This proved to be a problem because of the possibility that beans could be used in an integrated development environment (IDE) as design mode, but the IDE itself could well be using beans in its execution, which would require runtime mode. This of course was impossible because the variable was global, and that the same VM would probably be in use in both the IDE and the beans being interactively developed within the IDE.

The specification currently scopes this down at a level below the JVM global attribute level. The **BeanContext** can create and propagate the state of the design mode through the use of the class **java.beans. BeansContextMode** and more specifically with the following method:

```
public interface java.beans.DesignMode {
  void setDesignTime(boolean isDesignTime);
  boolean isDesignTime();
}
```

The Java beans specification provides the visibility package and classes to allow for individual beans to specify at runtime whether or not they can be rendered or used within a GUI. Although this is fine for beans at an individual level, there is no mechanism to help automate this process through the containment of a **BeanContext** to all of its children. To aid with this, the **BeanContext**s can create a reference to a visibility state class as follows:

```
public interface java.beans.VisibilityState {
  boolean isOkToUseGui();
}
```

In the cases that **BeanContext**s may include with them information about their locale, it becomes necessary to create a means by which the locale information can be propagated to its children. The property named **locale** is used for this purpose. The associated **BeanContext**s are required to fire off event changes of this type when any pertinent locale information is to be pushed to the children.

Lastly, beans and **BeanContext**s that are used in conjunction directly with GUIs and widgets are to be associated with an appropriate container or component from the java.awt class library. This is further associated with the **add()** and **remove()** functions of that container or component. When these functions are performed, the associated actions should be mirrored within the **BeanContext**. This includes any and all children that this particular **BeanContext** is associated with and all the potential nesting hierarchy.

Java Development Kit (JDK) 1.2 BeanContext Implementation

The JDK 1.2 release provides an implementation of **BeanContext** via its **java.beans.beancontext** package. The package is intended to provide the interface definitions outlined in this chapter as well as a reference release implementation of some of the interfaces as classes. This is very similar to what JavaSoft has done with the Beans Development Kit (BDK), in that the classes provided are meant to be used in a research capacity only. They are to be treated as a proof of concept.

The JDK 1.2 package `java.beans.beancontext` defines the following interfaces:

- `BeanContext`
- `BeanContextChild`
- `BeanContextMemborshipListener`

The package further defines these classes:

- `BeanContextAddedEvent`
- `BeanContextEvent`
- `BeanContextMembershipEvent`
- `BeanContextRemovedEvent`
- `BeanContextSupport`
- `BeanContextSupport.BCSChildInfo`

The `BeanContextAddedEvent` extends the `BeanContextMembershipEvent` and implements its interface. Its purpose is to fire events through this interface when one or more of its children are added to the set of children nested by this instance.

The `BeanContextEvent`, `BeanContextMembershipEvent`, and `BeanContextRemovedEvent`, as you would expect, implements the specified `BeanContextEvent` as outlined above in this chapter.

Finally, the most important part of the JDK 1.2 release is the provision of the `BeanContextSupport` classes. These classes are meant to either be used through subclassing or through implicit creation of an instance of this class by another. This class provides what JavaSoft refers to as a "utility" implementation of the `BeanContext` interface. In different words, this means that the class is not meant for heavy use and won't solve all the world's problems concerning runtime contexts, but will provide enough implementation to learn from and provide a good example. Listing 7-5 provides the full listing of this utility implementation.

Listing 7-5
The **BeanContext Support** class from JDK 1.2.

```
public class BeanContextSupport extends Object
    implements BeanContext, Serializable,
        PropertyChangeListener,
    VetoableChangeListener, Visibility, DesignMode,
        VisibilityState {

    // Constructors:

    public BeanContextSupport(BeanContext peer, Locale lcle,
```

Listing 7-5

```
                                        boolean dTime, boolean
                                        visible);

public BeanContextSupport(BeanContext peer, Locale lcle,
                                boolean dtime);

public BeanContextSupport(BeanContext peer, Locale lcle);

public BeanContextSupport(BeanContext peer);

public BeanContextSupport();

// Methods:

public BeanContext getBeanContextPeer();
public void setBeanContext(BeanContext nbc)
  throws PropertyVetoException;
public BeanContext getBeanContext();

public void addVetoableChangeListener
   (VetoableChangeListener pcl);
public void removeVetoableChangeListener
   (VetoableChangeListener vcl);

public void addPropertyChangeListener
   (PropertyChangeListener pcl);
public void removePropertyChangeListener
   (PropertyChangeListener pcl);

public Object instantiateChild(String beanName) throws
   IOException,
  ClassNotFoundException;

public int size();
public boolean isEmpty();
public boolean contains(Object o);
public Iterator iterator();
public Object[] toArray();
protected BeanContextSupport.BCSChildInfo
   createBCSChildInfo(
  Object targetChild);

public boolean add(Object targetChild);
public boolean remove(Object targetChild);
protected boolean remove(Object targetChild,
                          boolean callChildSetBC);
public boolean containsAll(Collection c);
public boolean addAll(Collection c);
public boolean removeAll(Collection c);
public boolean retainAll(Collection c);
public void clear();
```

Continues

Listing 7-5
Continued.

```
public void addBeanContextMembershipListener(
   BeanContextMembershipListener bcml);
public void removeBeanContextMembershipListener(
   BeanContextMembershipListener bcml);

public void membershipChanged(BeanContextMembershipEvent
                                      bcme);
public Object getService(Class serviceClass,
                         BeanContextChild bcc);
public boolean hasService(Class serviceClass);
public InputStream getResourceAsStream(String name,
                                       BeanContextChild
                                       bcc);
public URL getResource(String name, BeanContextChild
                       bcc);
public void setDesignTime(boolean dTime);
public boolean isDesignTime();
public void setLocale(Locale newLocale);
public Locale getLocale();

public boolean needsGui();
public void dontUseGui();
public void okToUseGui();
public boolean avoidingGui();
public boolean isOkToUseGui();

public void vetoableChange(PropertyChangeEvent pce)
   throws PropertyVetoException;
public void propertyChange(PropertyChangeEvent pce);
protected boolean validatePendingAdd(Object targetChild);

protected boolean validatePendingRemove(Object
                                         targetChild);
protected void addChildComponentToContainer(Object child,
                                            Component
                                            component,
                                            Container
                                            container);
protected void removeChildComponentFromContainer(Object
                                                 child,
                                                 Component
                                                 component,
                                                 Container
                                                 container)
                                                 ;
protected void registerChildListeners(Object
                                       targetChild);
protected void unregisterChildListeners(Object
                                         targetChild);
protected Container getBeanContextPeerContainer();
```

```
protected static final Visibility getChildVisibility
    (Object child);
protected static final Serializable getChildSerializable(
    Object child);
protected static final Component getChildComponent(Object
                                                   child);
protected static final PropertyChangeListener
    getChildPropertyChangeListener(Object child);
protected static final VetoableChangeListener
    getChildVetoableChangeListener(Object child);
protected static final BeanContextMembershipListener
    getChildBeanContextMembershipListener(Object child);
protected static final BeanContextChild
    getChildBeanContextChild(Object child);

protected final void fireVetoBeanContextChange
    (BeanContext
    previousValue, BeanContext currentValue) throws
    PropertyVetoException;
protected final void fireBeanContextChanged(BeanContext
    previousValue, BeanContext currentValue);
protected final void fireChildrenAdded(Object[]
                                       childrenAdded);
protected final void fireChildrenRemoved(Object[]
                                         childrenRemoved);
protected final void fireVetoLocaleChange(Locale
                                          previousValue,
    Locale currentValue) throws PropertyVetoException;
protected final void fireLocaleChanged(Locale
                                       previousValue,
                                       Locale
                                       currentValue);
protected final void fireDesignModeChanged(boolean
                                           currentValue);
protected final void fireVisibilityStateChanged(boolean
    currentValue);
protected final void fireBeanContextMembershipEvent(
    BeanContextMembershipEvent bcme);
protected final void fireVetoableChange
    (String propertyName,
    Object previousValue, Object newValue)
    throws PropertyVetoException;

protected final void firePropertyChange(String
                                        propertyName,
                                        Object
                                        previousValue,
                                        Object newValue);
```

Continues

Listing 7-5
Continued.

```
    protected final Object[] copyChildren();
    protected final boolean containsChild(Object
                                    targetChild);

    protected boolean isDelegated();
    protected static final boolean classEquals(Class first,
                                        Class second);


// Attributes:

    protected transient BeanContext beanContext;
    protected transient Hashtable children;
    protected transient Vector bcmListeners;
    protected transient Vector bcsListeners;
    protected transient Hashtable services;
    protected Locale locale;
    protected boolean okToUseGui;
    protected boolean designTime;
    protected PropertyChangeSupport pcSupport;
    protected VetoableChangeSupport vcSupport;


}
```

As you can see, there are several constructors outlined. They take various arguments and therefore various degrees of specification within the application that instantiates it. This means that you have the ability to call a constructor without any arguments if you wish, and Null values (to be replaced by defaults) will be filled in. If you wish to spell out more tightly the initial variables, you have the ability to do so. Examples of some variables include whether this context is starting within a design mode or not, whether it is visible, the type of locale (see **java.util. Locale**), and so forth.

There are a whole host of methods available. They range from simple access functions, such as obtaining the size of the number of children nested within the context or an array (of type Object) of all the children to the various firing functions for **Bean**, **Property**, and **BeanContext** events to adding and deleting listeners. You can of course add and delete children beans or **BeanContext**s, and you can obtain information about the services for this context as well. You also can test and check the containment of children beans during execution.

Once established, a **BeanContext** can fire events through and to its children, and if chosen, the children beans or **BeanContext**s can fire events to it. In this way, the containment mechanism can keep track of necessary events with its children by registering itself as interested and vice-versa. The dependencies can be on the runtime environment and therefore much more diversified and dynamic.

TIP: *Please note that a* `BeanContextSupport` *class can use a set of GUI access functions that bind how and if the context can be used within a GUI—that is, a Beanbox, or another visual tool. A developer now has the ability to limit the use of graphical component beans within one of these environments based on the context of the runtime environment, a feature that was previously not available without much more implementation.*

An Example of a `BeanContext` in Action

For our example in this chapter, we will implement a simple button bar that can be lain out across the top of a GUI screen. The special behavior of this button bar is that it can change across different platforms or, more importantly, relies on the runtime environment for its configuration. This button bar will act as a nestable container for button widgets. Besides containment, it will provide member-based services to the GUI application that it is used in.

The first thing that we need to be able to do is define and implement a bean or `BeanContext` that is meant to be contained by our button bar. For this example, the `OurButton` class provided with JavaSoft's Beans Development Kit works fine (see Listing 7-6).

Listing 7-6
The
OurButton.java
class file from the
JavaSoft Bean
Development Kit 1.0.

```
package sunw.demo.buttons;

import java.awt.*;
import java.awt.event.*;
import java.beans.*;
import java.io.Serializable;
import java.util.Vector;

/**
 * A simple Java Beans button.  OurButton is a "from-
 * scratch" GUI component that's derived from Canvas.  It's
 * a good example of how to implement bound properties and
 * support for event listeners.
 *
 * Parts of the source are derived from
 * sun.awt.tint.TinyButtonPeer.
 */
public class OurButton extends Canvas implements
```
Continues

Listing 7-6
Continued.

```
                             Serializable,
                   MouseListener, MouseMotionListener {

  /**
   * Constructs a Button with the a default label.
   */
  public OurButton() {
    this("press");
  }

  /**
   * Constructs a Button with the specified label.
   * @param label the label of the button
   */
  public OurButton(String label) {
    super();
    this.label = label;
    setFont(new Font("Dialog", Font.PLAIN, 12));
    setBackground(Color.lightGray);
    addMouseListener(this);
    addMouseMotionListener(this);
  }

  //---------------------------------

  /**
   * Paint the button: the label is centered in both
   * dimensions.
   *
   */
  public synchronized void paint(Graphics g) {
    int width = getSize().width;
    int height = getSize().height;

    g.setColor(getBackground());
    g.fill3DRect(0, 0, width - 1, height - 1, !down);

    g.setColor(getForeground());
    g.setFont(getFont());

    g.drawRect(2, 2, width - 4, height - 4);

    FontMetrics fm = g.getFontMetrics();
    g.drawString(label, (width - fm.stringWidth(label))
                 / 2, (height + fm.getMaxAscent() -
                 fm.getMaxDescent())
                 / 2);
  }

  //---------------------------------

  // Mouse listener methods.
```

Listing 7-6

```
public void mouseClicked(MouseEvent evt) {
}

public void mousePressed(MouseEvent evt) {
  if (!isEnabled()) {
      return;
  }
  down = true;
  repaint();
}

public void mouseReleased(MouseEvent evt) {
  if (!isEnabled()) {
      return;
  }
  if (down) {
      fireAction();
      down = false;
      repaint();
  }
}

public void mouseEntered(MouseEvent evt) {
}

public void mouseExited(MouseEvent evt) {
}

public void mouseDragged(MouseEvent evt) {
  if (!isEnabled()) {
      return;
  }
  // Has the mouse been dragged outside the button?
  int x = evt.getX();
  int y = evt.getY();
  int width = getSize().width;
  int height = getSize().height;
  if (x < 0 || x > width || y < 0 || y > height) {
      // Yes, we should deactivate any pending click.
      if (down) {
        down = false;
        repaint();
      }
  } else if (!down) {
      down = true;
      repaint();
  }
}

public void mouseMoved(MouseEvent evt) {
}
```

Continues

Listing 7-6
Continued.

```
//--------------------------------

// Methods for registering/deregistering event
// listeners

/**
 * The specified ActionListeners actionPerformed method
 * will be called each time the button is clicked.
 * The ActionListener object is added to a list of
 * ActionListeners managed by this button, it can be
 * removed with removeActionListener.
 * Note: the JavaBeans specification does not require
 * ActionListeners to run in any particular order.
 *
 * @see #removeActionListener
 * @param l the ActionListener
 */

public synchronized void
  addActionListener(ActionListener l) {
    pushListeners.addElement(l);
}

/**
 * Remove this ActionListener from the buttons
 * internal list.  If the ActionListener isn't on the
 * list, silently do nothing.
 *
 * @see #addActionListener
 * @param l the ActionListener
 */

public synchronized void
  removeActionListener(ActionListener l) {
    pushListeners.removeElement(l);
}

/**
 * The specified PropertyChangeListeners propertyChange
 * method will be called each time the value of any
 * bound property is changed.  The PropertyListener
 * object is addded to a list of
 * PropertyChangeListeners managed by this button, it
 * can be removed with removePropertyChangeListener.
 * Note: the JavaBeans specification does not require
 * PropertyChangeListeners to run in any particular
 * order.
 *
 * @see #removePropertyChangeListener
 * @param l the PropertyChangeListener
 */
```

Listing 7-6

```java
public void addPropertyChangeListener
  (PropertyChangeListener l) {
    changes.addPropertyChangeListener(l);
}

/**
 * Remove this PropertyChangeListener from the buttons
 * internal list.
 * If the PropertyChangeListener isn't on the list,
 * silently do nothing.
 *
 * @see #addPropertyChangeListener
 * @param l the PropertyChangeListener
 */
public void removePropertyChangeListener
  (PropertyChangeListener l) {
    changes.removePropertyChangeListener(l);
}

//--------------------------------

/**
 * This method has the same effect as pressing the
 * button.
 *
 * @see #addActionListener
 */

public void fireAction() {
    if (debug) {
        System.err.println("Button " + getLabel() + "
                            pressed.");
    }
    Vector targets;
    synchronized (this) {
        targets = (Vector) pushListeners.clone();
    }
    ActionEvent actionEvt = new ActionEvent(this, 0,
                                            null);
    for (int i = 0; i < targets.size(); i++) {
        ActionListener target = (ActionListener)
                                targets.elementAt(i);
        target.actionPerformed(actionEvt);
    }

}

/**
 * Enable debugging output.  Currently a message is
 * printed each time the button is clicked.  This is a
 * bound property.
```

Continues

Listing 7-6
Continued.

```
     *
     * @see #getDebug
     * @see #addPropertyChangeListener
     */
    public void setDebug(boolean x) {
      boolean old = debug;
      debug = x;
      changes.firePropertyChange("debug", new Boolean(old),
                                 new Boolean(x));
    }

    /**
     * Returns true if debugging output is enabled.
     *
     * @see #setDebug
     */
    public boolean getDebug() {
      return debug;
    }

    /**
     * Set the font size to 18 if true, 12 otherwise.
     * This property overrides the value specified with
     * setFontSize.  This is a bound property.
     *
     * @see #isLargeFont
     * @see #addPropertyChangeListener
     */
    public void setLargeFont(boolean b) {
      if (isLargeFont() == b) {
          return;
      }
      int size = 12;
      if (b) {
          size = 18;
      }
      Font old = getFont();
      setFont(new Font(old.getName(), old.getStyle(),
                       size));
      changes.firePropertyChange("largeFont", new
                                 Boolean(!b), new
                                 Boolean(b));
    }

    /**
     * Returns true if the font is "large" in the sense
     * defined by setLargeFont.
     *
     * @see #setLargeFont
     * @see #setFont
     */
    public boolean isLargeFont() {
```

Listing 7-6

```
           if (getFont().getSize() >= 18) {
               return true;
       } else {
           return false;
       }
   }


   /**
    * Set the point size of the current font.  This is a
    * bound property.
    *
    * @see #getFontSize
    * @see #setFont
    * @see #setLargeFont
    * @see #addPropertyChangeListener
    */
   public void setFontSize(int x) {
     Font old = getFont();
     setFont(new Font(old.getName(), old.getStyle(), x));
     changes.firePropertyChange("fontSize", new
        Integer(old.getSize()), new Integer(x));
   }

   /**
    * Return the current font point size.
    *
    * @see #setFontSize
    */
   public int getFontSize() {
       return getFont().getSize();
   }

   /**
    * Set the current font and change its size to fit.
    * This is a bound property.
    *
    * @see #setFontSize
    * @see #setLargeFont
    */
   public void setFont(Font f) {
     Font old = getFont();
     super.setFont(f);
     sizeToFit();
     changes.firePropertyChange("font", old, f);
   }

   /**
    * Set the buttons label and change it's size to fit.
    * This is a bound property.
    *
    * @see #getLabel
```

Listing 7-6
Continued.

```
  */
public void setLabel(String newLabel) {
  String oldLabel = label;
  label = newLabel;
  sizeToFit();
  changes.firePropertyChange("label", oldLabel,
                             newLabel);
}

/**
 * Returns the buttons label.
 *
 * @see #setLabel
 */
public String getLabel() {
  return label;
}

public Dimension getPreferredSize() {
  FontMetrics fm = getFontMetrics(getFont());
  return new Dimension(fm.stringWidth(label) +
                  TEXT_XPAD, fm.getMaxAscent() +
                  fm.getMaxDescent() + TEXT_YPAD);
}

/**
 * @deprecated provided for backward compatibility
 * with old layout managers.
 */
public Dimension preferredSize() {
  return getPreferredSize();
}

public Dimension getMinimumSize() {
  return getPreferredSize();
}

/**
 * @deprecated provided for backward compatibility
 * with old layout managers.
 */
public Dimension minimumSize() {
  return getMinimumSize();
}

private void sizeToFit() {
  Dimension d = getPreferredSize();
  setSize(d.width, d.height);
  Component p = getParent();
  if (p != null) {
      p.invalidate();
      p.doLayout();
```

Listing 7-6

```
      }
    }

    /**
     * Set the color the buttons label is drawn with.
     * This is a bound property.
     */
    public void setForeground(Color c) {
      Color old = getForeground();
      super.setForeground(c);
      changes.firePropertyChange("foreground", old, c);
    }


    /**
     * Set the color the buttons background is drawn with.
     * This is a bound property.
     */
    public void setBackground(Color c) {
      Color old = getBackground();
      super.setBackground(c);
      changes.firePropertyChange("background", old, c);
    }


    private boolean debug;
    private PropertyChangeSupport changes = new
      PropertyChangeSupport(this);
    private Vector pushListeners = new Vector();
    private String label;
    private boolean down;
    private boolean sized;

    static final int TEXT_XPAD = 12;
    static final int TEXT_YPAD = 8;
}
```

The next thing that we wish to do is add these button beans to our context container class. For this example we chose to extend the **BeanContextSupport** class that is provided in the JDK1.2 outlined above because it contains the functional capabilities for us to be able to create this example case. Listing 7-7 shows how we will do this.

In this file, we first create a button bar context and the associated button beans. We then get a diagnostic piece of information about the context, its locale, and print it out. Then we add the button beans to the context to take advantage of its containment capabilities. We check by printing out whether we are still empty, which at this point is False. Finally, we notify

Listing 7-7
The **buttonBar**
Context class.

```
import java.beans.*;
import java.beans.beancontext.*;
import java.io.*;
import OurButton;

public class buttonBarContext
   extends BeanContextSupport{

  // Constructor
  public buttonBarContext(){
    super();
  }

  public static void main( String args[] ){

    System.out.println( "In test case for buttonBar." );

    System.out.println( "Allocating OurButton's." );

    OurButton button1 = new OurButton( "button1" );
    OurButton button2 = new OurButton( "button2" );
    OurButton button3 = new OurButton( "button3" );

    System.out.println( "Allocating buttonBarContext." );
    buttonBarContext myContext = new buttonBarContext();

    System.out.println( "Locale is: " +
      myContext.getLocale().toString() );
    System.out.println( "It is " + myContext.isEmpty() + "
                        that we are empty." );

    System.out.println( "Adding OurButton Beans to
                        buttonBarContext.");

    myContext.add( button1 );
    myContext.add( button2 );
    myContext.add( button3 );

    System.out.println( "It is " + myContext.isEmpty() + "
                        that we are empty." );

    System.out.println( "Firing that children were
                        added." );

    myContext.fireChildrenAdded( myContext.toArray() );

    System.out.println( "end." );
  }

} // end class buttonBar
```

all our children button beans—in this case three—that we have added them to our context—so that if they are set up to take advantage or act on being added to a context, they can.

The reason that we use beans-type buttons instead of just regular objects is two-fold. First, we want the ability to be able to exchange, and fire event information to that child, and second, we want to be able to rely in the ingrained beans functionalities if called on by a service or something else within the context, such as serialization.

At this point we have a executing context that contains three buttons. From here, we can implement any number of service classes that we wish to, that take advantage of the buttons. We can also take advantage of the instantiate method provided by this context instead of within the Java-Beans package class. Applications could include only showing and instantiating certain buttons based on runtime decisions and environments or providing different services that returned different values depending on the environment or even events that had been fired upon it.

Note how we also have the option to manipulate if and how the button bar is displayed in a GUI with the functions: `avoidingGui()`, `dontUseGui()`, and so forth if we wanted to be more interactive with a potential runtime editing environment, such as IBM's VisualAge, or SunSoft's Java WorkShop.

CONCLUSION

In conclusion, there were a series of strong needs that lead to the design and implementation of the bean context set of classes and interfaces and the runtime containment and services specification. To recap, those were

- The need for beans to be able to be nestable and allow for the propagation of events from containers to their children
- The need for beans to be able to specify, manipulate, discover, and use services during the process of their lifecycle
- The need for beans to be able to discover information at runtime from the environment that surrounds them so that they could execute and interact with each other better having learned this information
- The need to maintain the "write once, run anywhere" promise

It was not an easy problem to solve, but over the last year, through requests for comments (RFCs), JavaSoft has been able to specify and implement in the 1.2 JDK a paradigm that addresses these needs. Obviously, a lot of work still needs to be done, and there needs to be a widespread acceptance of this paradigm before it will really start paying off. Used with distributed systems, and in conjunction with other Java or related facilities, such as the Java Naming and Directory infrastructure (JNDI), these concepts become even more powerful.

8

JavaBeans
Activation
Framework

The JavaBeans Activation Framework (JAF) is designed to provide standard services to access typed data, to discover the operations available on the data, and to execute these operations by invoking JavaBeans. A typical example of its use is in a file system explorer similar to the Windows 95 Explorer. This application provides the functionality for the user to select the file, view a list of operations such as View, Edit, Print, etc. that are allowed on the file, and execute a selected operation. Applications can register themselves to execute these operations on standard data types. Typically, a word processor would register itself for the operations View or Edit for text files, a paint application for picture files, and so on. A Web browser is another example of an application that can discover the data type of an incoming data stream and then bind the data to helper applications that could view or edit the data.

Most of the basic facilities required for data typing and registry, as well as facilities for passing data to JavaBeans are already available in JDK 1.1. The Uniform Data Transfer Mechanism introduced in Chapter 9 defines the basic interfaces for data typing. The serialization and externalization APIs enable JavaBeans to read and write binary data to and from streams. The JAF essentially integrates and further standardizes these various APIs into an easy-to-use and extensible framework.

The JAF offers developers facilities to

■ Encapsulate arbitrary data and represent its data type

■ Discover operations or commands available for a given data type

■ Execute an operation or command on a given data

This Chapter Covers

■ Using the framework for processing data.

■ Creating JAF compatible beans.

■ Creating new JAF data sources.

Using the Framework for Operating on Data

As a preview, let us first look at a diagrammatic representation, shown in Figure 8-1, of how the data is handled by the various JAF components.

As we see in Figure 8-1, data from various sources can be introduced into the framework. Incoming data is shown at the top. The individual components of the framework ultimately pass the data to the Java bean that acts on the data. The JavaBeans are shown at the bottom.

As such, there are two ways in which the framework can be used. It can be used to bind data sources to JavaBeans for operating on the data. The second way to use it is to extend the framework by adding custom components at various places in the framework.

In this first section, we will see how to use the framework. The later sections will illustrate how to extend the framework.

To understand how to use the JAF, let us consider a simple example called FileExplorer. The entire listing of **FileExplorer.java** is included

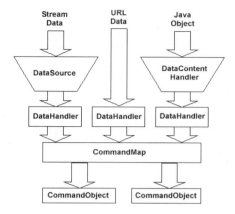

Figure 8-1
A diagrammatic
representation of the
JAF classes.

at the end of this section in Listing 8-1. This application will take the name of a single file as a parameter, display a menu of all available operations for the given file and then let the user select and execute one of the operations.

Let us break down the behavior into the following three steps:

1. Creating the data source: the application opens the file, the source of data.

2. Querying available operations: the application queries the JAF for a list of available operations on the data and displays a menu.

3. Executing an operation: the user selects an operation to perform on the file. The application is invoked to carry out the selected operation.

Creating the Data Source

In the FileExplorer example, the data source is the specified file, which is a stream. This method of introducing data into the JAF is shown in Figure 8-1 at the top left. The JAF defines an interface called **DataSource** that encapsulates stream-based data and its MIME type (see Table 8-1).

A concrete implementation of this interface is provided for file streams and is called the **FileDataSource** class. This class encapsulates file streams and assigns MIME types by looking at the filename extension.

In the FileExplorer, we create a **FileDataSource** for the specified file as follows:

Table 8-1

The **DataSource**
interface.

`public abstract String` `    getContentType()`	This method returns the MIME type of the data in the form of a String.
`public String getName();`	This method returns the domain specific name of this object, such as the file name for file data sources.

`public abstract InputStream`
`    getInputStream()`
`    throws IOException`
	This method returns an InputStream representing the data or throws the appropriate exception if it cannot do so.

`public abstract OutputStream`
`    getOutputStream()`
`    throws IOException`
	This method returns an OutputStream where the data can be written to, or throws the appropriate exception if it cannot do so.

```
FileDataSource fds = new FileDataSource(filename);
```

The DataSource represents one of the extensible components of the JAF. We can define new **DataSource** classes to correspond to new types of stream data. However, note that the **DataSource** class is useful only for stream-based data as per the present definition of the class. If the source of data is not a stream, we cannot use the **DataSource** class.

The two other ways of introducing data are shown at the top right of Figure 8-1 and correspond to data from an URL or from any Java object. We will illustrate with an example how data from a Java object can be used in the JAF.

The second class we need to use is the **DataHandler** class. This is the main class in the JAF that exposes the various subsystems of the framework. We create a **DataHandler** from the **FileDataSource** as follows:

```
DataHandler dh = new DataHandler(fds);
```

Because one instance of **DataHandler** corresponds to a single data source instance, there may be a need for several **DataHandler** objects, one for each piece of data being processed. For simplicity, our FileExplorer application deals with only one piece of data—a single file. But if we were to extend the same application to handle, say, a list of files, we would need to create a **DataHandler** for each file. This is reflected in Figure 8-1, which shows a separate **DataHandler** for each different source of data coming into the JAF.

The **DataHandler** can be constructed in three ways, corresponding to the three methods in which data can be introduced into the JAF. These three constructors are described in Table 8-2.

Table 8-2	`public DataHandler(DataSource ds)`	This constructor creates a DataHandler with the specified DataSource.
The **DataHandler** constructors.	`public DataHandler(Object obj, String mimeType)`	This constructor is used when the application already has in memory representations of the data in the form of Java objects.
	`public DataHandler(URL url)`	This constructor creates a **DataHandler** with the data from a URL

Table 8-3	`public CommandInfo(String verb, String className);`	The constructor that takes a command name or verb and the class name of the bean that implements the command.
The **CommandInfo** class.	`public String getCommandName(); public Object getCommandObject (DataHandler dh, ClassLoader cl);`	This method returns the command name or verb. This method instantiates and returns the command bean. In case the bean implements the **CommandObject** interface, it also passes a reference to the specified **DataHandler**. This method is invoked by the **getBean** method of the **DataHandler**.

Querying Available Operations

The **DataHandler** has methods that return the list of commands available for the associated data. The command information is returned as an array of **CommandInfo** objects.

```
CommandInfo[] ci = dh.getAllCommands();
```

The **CommandInfo** class encapsulates the name of the operation or "verb" that describes the operation and the JavaBean class that implements the operation. Using the array of **CommandInfo** objects, we create a list of possible commands that can operate on the specified file. We do this by using the **getCommandName** method on the **CommandInfo** objects.

```
String[] cmdNames=new String[ci.length];
for (int i=0;i<ci.length;i++) {
  cmdNames[i]=ci[i].getCommandName();
}
```

We can then use this array to present a menu or choice of available operations of the file (see Table 8-3).

HOW THE MAPPING WORKS   The `DataHandler` actually uses another JAF class called `CommandMap` to map operations to data types. This is shown in Figure 8-1. The default `CommandMap` used by the `DataHandler` is a concrete implementation called `MailcapCommandMap`. This class maps MIME types to a set of operations based on the `mailcap` standard defined in RFC 1524.

The `MailcapCommandMap` has default mappings for the MIME type: text and plain. Operations View and Edit are mapped into two beans, `com.sun.activation.viewers.TextViewer` and `com.sun.activation.viewers.TextEditor` respectively. Hence the `CommandInfo` array that is returned in the code above actually contains two entries for these two commands.

We can also create a custom `CommandMap` based on any other registration method and make the `DataHandler` use this map by invoking the `setCommandMap` method of the `DataHandler`. However, in our FileExplorer example, we will rely on the default `MailcapCommandMap`. Note that as shown in Figure 8-1, a single instance of the `CommandMap` can be used by several `DataHandler` instances (see Table 8-4).

Table 8-4

The `CommandMap` abstract class.

`public static CommandMap getDefaultCommandMap();`	This method returns the static default CommandMap, which is initially set to the MailcapCommandMap.
`public static void setDefaultCommandMap(CommandMap map);`	This method sets or changes the default CommandMap.
`abstract public CommandInfo[]getPreferredCommand(String mimeType);`	This method returns the preferred command list for the specified mimeType. Typically this will return one bean (info) for each defined command for the mimeType.
`abstract public CommandInfo[]getAllCommands(String mimeType);`	This method returns an array of all commands that accept the specified mimeType.
`abstract public CommandInfo getCommand(String mimeType, String cmdName);`	This method attempts to find the specified command named cmdName that can accept the specified `mimeType`.

Executing an Operation

When the user selects one of the displayed operations, we can execute the operation by first retrieving the bean representing the operation and then presenting it to the user.

To retrieve an instance of the bean that implements the selected operation, we use the **getBean** method of the **DataHandler** class. The parameter passed to it is an element of the **CommandInfo** array that we retrieved from the **getAllCommands** method: **Object bean=dh.getBean(ci[selectedIndex]);**. This method retrieves the bean corresponding to the specified command.

Having instantiated the bean, we also need to pass the data to it. We could have done this using serialization or externalization. However, the JAF defines a new interface called **CommandObject**. This interface basically allows a bean to use the **DataHandler** for retrieving data from the JAF. When we invoke the **getBean** method on a **DataHandler**, it automatically sends a reference to itself (the **DataHandler**) to the newly instantiated bean. This eliminates the need to serialize or externalize the data.

But if the newly created bean is not a **CommandObject**, we have to explicitly pass data to the bean using some other scheme such as serialization or externalization. We implement this logic by using the following code:

```
if (!(bean instanceof CommandObject)) {
if (my_bean instanceof Externalizable) {
try {
      InputStream is=dh.getInputStream();
      ObjectInputStream os=new ObjectInputStream(is);
((Externalizable)my_bean).readExternal(os);
} catch(Exception e) {
System.out.println("Error constructing Object:"+e);
}
}
}
```

In this code fragment, we first check whether the retrieved bean is a **CommandObject**. If it is, we don't need to do anything special to pass data to it, because the **getBean** method has already done the job. If it is not a **CommandObject**, we check to see whether the bean implements Externalizable. If it does, we retrieve the **InputStream** from the **DataHandler** by using the **getInputStream** method, and we also use it to pass an **Object InputStream** to the **readExternal** method of the bean.

The **DataHandler**'s **getInputStream** method gets the **InputStream** by invoking **getInputStream** method of the associated **DataSource**. Refer to Table 8-1 for **DataSource** methods. In the FileExplorer case, the **DataSource** is a **FileDataSource** instance, which returns an **InputStream** for the associated file. Hence in effect, the file's `InputStream` is used to read an externalized version of the bean.

Once the bean is instantiated and the corresponding data is passed to it, we can present it to the user if it is a visible bean. Not all operations may need visible beans. For example, a print bean might not need to display anything. In such cases, instantiating the bean and passing data to should result in the operation being performed.

```
if (bean instanceof Component) {
   add(bean);
}
```

The complete code for this example is included in Listing 8-1.

Listing 8-1
FileExplorer.
java.

```
import java.awt.*;
import java.awt.event.*;
import java.io.*;
import java.beans.*;
import javax.activation.*;

public class FileExplorer implements
       WindowListener,ActionListener {
       private Frame choiceFrame=null;
       private Window beanWindow=null;
       private FileDataSource fds=null;
       private DataHandler dh=null;
       // private CommandInfo[] ci=null;
       private BeanInfo[] bi=null;
       // CommandInfo is not implemented at the time of
       // writing
       // BeanInfo is used in its place in the reference
       // implementation
       private Choice verbsChoice=null;
       private Button execButton=null;
       private Object bean=null;
       private boolean isOperating=false;


public static void main(String args[]) throws Exception {
if (args.length == 0) {
System.out.println("usage: FileExplorer filename");
System.exit(1);
}
FileExplorer f = new FileExplorer(args[0]);
}


public FileExplorer(String filename) throws Exception {
       // Step 1: Creating the Data Source
```

Listing 8-1

```
        fds = new FileDataSource(filename);
        dh = new DataHandler(fds);

        // Step 2: Querying available operations
        // ci=dh.getAllCommands();
        bi = dh.getAllCommands();

        // if (ci == null || ci.length ==0) {
        if (bi == null || bi.length==0) {
        System.out.println("no operations found, exiting");
        System.exit(1);
}

        choiceFrame = new Frame("Operations on "+filename);
        choiceFrame.setLayout(new BorderLayout());
        verbsChoice=new Choice();
        // for (int I=0;I<ci.length;I++) {
        for (int i=0;i<bi.length;i++) {
            // verbsChoice.add(ci[i].getCommandName());
        verbsChoice.add(bi[i].getBeanDescriptor().getName());
        }
        choiceFrame.add(verbsChoice,"South");
        execButton=new Button("Execute");
        choiceFrame.add(execButton,"North");
        execButton.addActionListener(this);
        choiceFrame.setSize(new Dimension(400,300));
        choiceFrame.show();
        choiceFrame.addWindowListener(this);
}

public void actionPerformed(ActionEvent e) {

        if ( isOperating && bean!=null) {
            // remove old bean if any
            choiceFrame.remove((Component)bean);
            isOperating=false;
        }

        if (verbsChoice==null ||
            verbsChoice.getSelectedIndex()<0) return;

        // Step 3: Executing the operation
        // bean = dh.getBean(ci[verbsChoice.
        //                  getSelectedIndex()]);
        bean = dh.getBean(bi[verbsChoice.
                        getSelectedIndex()]);
        // Passing data to the non-JAF bean
        if (!(bean instanceof CommandObject)) {
            if (my_bean instanceof Externalizable) {
        try {
            InputStream is=dh.getInputStream();
```

Continues

Listing 8-1
Continued.

```
            ObjectInputStream os=new ObjectInputStream(is);
                ((Externalizable)my_bean).
                    readExternal(os);
            } catch(Exception e) {
                System.out.println("Error constructing
                                    Object:"+e);
            }
            }
    }

    // Display the bean
    if (bean instanceof Component) {
            choiceFrame.add((Component)bean,"Center");
            isOperating=true;
            choiceFrame.invalidate();
            choiceFrame.validate();
            choiceFrame.doLayout();
    }
}

public void windowOpened(WindowEvent e){}
public void windowClosing(WindowEvent e) {
    System.exit(1);
}
public void windowClosed(WindowEvent e){}
public void windowIconified(WindowEvent e){}
public void windowDeiconified(WindowEvent e){}
public void windowActivated(WindowEvent e){}
public void windowDeactivated(WindowEvent e){}

}
```

In this example, we have covered the basic usage of the Java Activation Framework using the built-in classes only. The framework is designed in such a way that most components can be extended to provide for additional functionality or customization. In the following sections, we will see how some of these components can be customized.

Creating JAF-Compatible Beans

The Java Activation Framework is designed in such a way that any standard JavaBean can be used as an operator on typed data. However, as explained in the previous section, the preferred method of writing beans for the JAF is for the bean to implement the **CommandObject** interface. This interface simplifies the process of passing data to the bean that implements it. The `CommandObject` interface is extremely simple, having a single method.

```
public interface CommandObject {
    public void setCommandContext(String verb, DataHandler
        dh);
}
```

NOTE: *In the reference JAF implementation available at the time of this writing, the* `CommandObject` *is defined with a different method.*

```
public void setDataHandler(DataHandler);
```

This essentially does the same task but does not have the name of the operation. We will define this method, too, in the example.

This method is invoked by the `getBean` method of `DataHandler`. The `getBean` method instantiates the bean first and then calls this method so as to let the bean know where its data is coming from. The bean can then access all the `DataHandler` functionality that allows it to retrieve data from the `DataSource`, modify it, or write to it.

The `DataHandler` class also implements the Uniform Data Transfer Mechanism's Transferable interface. This makes it possible for the `CommandObject` to retrieve the data in any supported DataFlavor.

A Simple JAF-Compatible Bean

As a simple example, let us create a bean that counts line numbers while displaying the contents of a text file. Listing 8-2 shows how we design this bean.

Listing 8-2
FileCountLines.
java

```
import java.awt.*;
import java.awt.event.*;
import java.io.*;
import java.beans.*;
import javax.activation.*;

public class FileCountLines extends Container implements
        CommandObject {
    TextArea fileViewArea=null;

    public FileCountLines() {
```
Continues

Listing 8-2
Continued.

```
        super();
        fileViewArea=new TextArea();
        setLayout(null);
        add(fileViewArea);
    }

    public void doLayout() {
        fileViewArea.setSize(getSize().width,
                             getSize().height);
    }

    public Dimension getMinimumSize() {
        return new Dimension(50,50);
    }

    public Dimension getPreferredSize() {
        return getMinimumSize();
    }

    public void setCommandContext(String verb,
                                  DataHandler dh) {
        setDataHandler(dh);
    }

    public void setDataHandler(DataHandler dh) {
        try {
        InputStream is=dh.getInputStream();
            countLines(is);
        } catch (IOException e) {

    }
    }

    private void countLines(InputStream is) {
        fileViewArea.setText("");
        // get the file
        int lineNum;
        String line;
        try {
            InputStreamReader isr=new
            InputStreamReader(is);
                LineNumberReader rd=new
                LineNumberReader(isr);
            do {
                lineNum=rd.getLineNumber();
                line=rd.readLine();
                if ( line!=null ) fileViewArea.
                append(""+lineNum+":"+line+"\n");
            } while ( line!=null );
        } catch (IOException e) {
            fileViewArea.append("IOException:"+e);
        }
    }
}
```

The FileCountLines bean created in the Listing 8-2 is designed to read the contents of a text file and display it in a text area, with each line prepended with the corresponding line number. This functionality is implemented by the **countLines** method that takes an **InputStream** as a parameter.

The bean display consists of a text area. It implements the **CommandObject** interface by defining the method **setCommandContext**. This method takes two parameters. The first parameter is a string that indicates the name of the operation to be performed, and the second parameter is the actual **DataHandler** that gives access to the source of the data. The **setCommandContext** method simply calls the **setDataHandler** method. The **setDataHandler** method is implemented as

```
public void setDataHandler(DataHandler dh) {
      try {
              InputStream is=dh.getInputStream();
      countLines(is);
} catch (IOException e) {
}
}
```

We use the **DataHandler**'s **getInputStream** method to get access to the **InputStream** for the file. This is passed on the **countLines** method that creates a **LineNumberInputReader** from this stream, reads its contents, and puts each line prepended with its line number in the text area.

Integrating the Bean into the JAF

To integrate the FileCountLines bean we created into the JAF, we define two meta-information files—a **mime.types** file and a **mailcap** file as follows:

The **mime.types** file contains

```
type=text/plain desc="Text" exts=txt
```

The **mime.types** file is used to inform the JAF about the MIME type that this bean can accept. In this case it is the "text/plain" MIME type. The **exts** parameter indicates the file extension used. In particular, the **FileDataSource** is supposed to use this file to map file extensions to MIME types.

The **mailcap** (RFC 1524) file contains

```
text/plain; ; x-java-count=FileCountLines; \
x-java-view=com.sun.activation.viewers.TextViewer; \
x-java-edit=com.sun.activation.viewers.TextEditor
```

The `mailcap` file is used by the default `MailcapCommandMap` to map operations for the specified MIME type.

We package the three files,

```
META-INF/mime.types
META-INF/mailcap
FileCountLines.class
```

into the JAR file for the bean.

If we execute the FileExplorer application created in the previous section, we will notice that we get a choice of three operations with the previous View and Edit operations and a new third Count operation, mapped to our new FileCountLines bean.

This example illustrates how we can create JAF-compatible beans by simply implementing the `setCommandContext` method of the `CommandObject`. Essentially this makes it easy for the bean to access data from the `DataHandler`. If a bean that does not implement the `CommandObject` were to be used, data would have to be explicitly passed on to it by using serialization or externalization.

Creating New JAF Data Sources

We have seen in the examples so far that dealing with data in files is quite straightforward by using the pre-built `FileDataSource` class. Now we will see how to integrate other sources of data into the JAF.

There are two categories that have been made based on where the data comes from. Based on which of these two categories our data falls in, the method of integrating it into the JAF will change.

- For stream-based data, we need to either use the existing `FileDataSource` or create our own new `DataSource` implementation.

- For data that comes directly from Java objects, we need to create a `DataContentHandler`, which is responsible for converting an object to a stream and vice-versa.

The `DataHandler` itself has constructors that enable us to specify either a `DataSource` or a URL or directly an object with an associated MIME type. Refer Table 8-2 for a list of constructors.

Hence depending on where the data comes from, we need to create the appropriate `DataHandler` using the constructor that either takes a `DataSource` or a Java object.

We have already seen how the **FileDataSource** is used in the FileExplorer example. The **FileDataSource** is an example of how stream-based data is used in the JAF. Now let us create another example that illustrates passing data from a Java object.

We divide the procedure into four steps:

1. Create a **Line** class.
2. Create a **LineDataHandler** class that can read and write data files for the **Line** class.
3. Create a LineViewer bean that can be mapped onto the View command for the **Line** object.
4. Integrate these components into the JAF.

Creating the **Line** Class

We define a new class called **Line** as in Listing 8-3 below. This represents a line between two points, **(x1,y1)** and **(x2,y2)**. We create **setter** and **getter** methods for the four coordinates, and simple constructors.

Listing 8-3
Line.java.

```
import javax.activation.*;
import java.awt.datatransfer.*;

public class Line {
        int x1,y1,x2,y2;

        public Line() {
                x1=0;y1=0;x2=0;y2=0;
        }

        public Line(int x1,int y1,int x2,int y2) {
                this.x1=x1;
                this.y1=y1;
                this.x2=x2;
                this.y2=y2;
        }

        public void setX1(int x) {
                x1=x;
        }
        public void setY1(int y) {
                y1=y;
        }
        public void setX2(int x) {
```

Continues

Listing 8-3
Continued.

```
            x2=x;
    }
    public void setY2(int y) {
        y2=y;
    }
    public int getX1() {
        return x1;
    }
    public int getY1() {
        return y1;
    }
    public int getX2() {
        return x2;
    }
    public int getY2() {
        return y2;
    }
}
```

Creating the DataContentHandler for the Line Class

Next, we define the DataContentHandler that can convert a Line object into a stream or vice-versa. We do this by creating a class called LineDataContentHandler, which will implement the DataContentHandler interface. The main methods that we need to implement are

▪ public Object getContent(DataSource ds): this method takes the InputStream from the specified DataSource and converts it into a Line object that is returned. The implementation is quite simple. We get the InputStream from the DataSource by using the getInputStream method of the DataSource and then read the four coordinates from the stream and create a new Line object.

▪ public void writeTo(Object line, String mimeType, OutputStream os): this method takes a Line object and writes it into the specified OutputStream. The implementation writes the four coordinates into the output stream.

The complete listing of LineDataContentHandler is included in Listing 8-4.

The other two methods in DataContentHandler, namely getTransfer Flavors and getTransferData are primarily provided in case we want to present data in more than one DataFlavor. We will not implement these for this example.

Listing 8-4
LineDataContent
Handler.java

```java
import java.awt.*;
import java.awt.datatransfer.*;
import java.awt.event.*;
import java.io.*;
import java.beans.*;
import javax.activation.*;
import Line;

class LineDataContentHandler implements DataContentHandler {

public Object getContent(DataSource ds) {

    Line l=new Line();

    try {
        InputStream is=ds.getInputStream();
            StreamTokenizer st=new StreamTokenizer(new
            InputStreamReader(is));

        st.parseNumbers();
        if (st.nextToken()==StreamTokenizer.TT_NUMBER)
            l.setX1((int)st.nval);
        if (st.nextToken()==StreamTokenizer.TT_NUMBER)
            l.setY1((int)st.nval);
        if (st.nextToken()==StreamTokenizer.TT_NUMBER)
            l.setX2((int)st.nval);
        if (st.nextToken()==StreamTokenizer.TT_NUMBER)
            l.setY2((int)st.nval);
    } catch (Exception e) {
    }

    return l;
}

public void writeTo(Object obj, String mimeTye,
    OutputStream os) throws IOException {
    if ( !(obj instanceof Line) ) return;
    Line l=(Line)obj;
    PrintWriter pw=new PrintWriter (os);
    pt.print(l.getX1());pt.print(" ");
    pt.print(l.getY1());pt.print(" ");
    pt.print(l.getX2());pt.print(" ");
    pt.print(l.getY2());

public DataFlavor[] getTransferDataFlavors() {
    return null;
}

public Object getTransferData(DataFlavor df, DataSource ds)
    {
    return getContent(ds);
}

}
```

Creating the LineViewer Bean for Viewing Line Objects

The next class we need to make is a bean that can be mapped to some operation on the **Line** object. Let us say we define a LineViewer bean, which maps onto the View operation. We do this by first creating the LineViewer bean as in listing 8-5.

This bean is implemented similarly to the **FileCountLines** example, in the previous section, in that it implements the **CommandObject** interface so that the bean is able to use the **DataHandler** for retrieving data. However, instead of using the **getInputStream** method of the **DataHandler** like in the previous case, this time we use the **getContent** method to directly get a Line object from the DataHandler as follows:

```
try {
        this.line=(Line)dh.getContent (Line.dataFlavor);
} catch (IOException e) {
        System.out.println(e);
} catch(UnsupportedFlavorException ue) {
        System.out.println(ue);
}
```

What happens when we call the **getContent** method of the **Data Handler** is that it will pass the call to the **getContent** method of our **Line DataContentHandler**, which will read the stream and create a **Line** object for us.

In Listing 8-5, the LineViewer bean actually displays the line passed to it via the **DataHandler**.

Integrating the Line Classes into the JAF

To integrate all these components into the JAF, we define the meta-information files—**mime.types** and **mailcap**. The **mime.types** file contains

```
type=application/x-line desc="Line" exts=lin
```

As explained in the previous section, the **mime.types** file is used to inform the JAF about the MIME type that this bean can accept. In this case we define a new MIME type: **application/x-line**. We also assign the **.lin** extension for data files. The **mailcap** (RFC 1524) file contains

```
application/x-line; ; x-java-view=LineViewer; \
x-java-ContentHandler=LineDataContentHandler
```

Listing 8-5
LineViewer.java

```java
import java.awt.*;
import java.awt.event.*;
import java.io.*;
import java.beans.*;
import javax.activation.*;
import java.awt.datatransfer.*;
import Line;

public class LineViewer extends Component implements
        CommandObject {
    Line line=null;

    public LineViewer() {
        super();
    }

    public LineViewer(Line l) {
        super();
        this.line=l;
    }

    public Dimension getMinimumSize() {
        return new Dimension(Math.abs(line.getX2()-
        line.getX1()),Math.abs(line.getY2()-
        line.getY1()));
    }

    public Dimension getPreferredSize() {
        return getMinimumSize();
    }

    public void setCommandContext(String verb,
                                        DataHandler dh) {
        setDataHandler(dh);
    }

    public void setDataHandler(DataHandler dh) {
        try {
                this.line=(Line)dh.getContent
                (Line.dataFlavor);
        } catch (IOException e) {
            System.out.println(e);
        } catch(UnsupportedFlavorException ue) {
            System.out.println(ue);
        }
    }
}
```

As explained in the previous section, the **mailcap** file is used by the default **MailcapCommandMap** to map operations for the specified MIME type.

The first line in the **mailcap** file assigns the LineViewer bean to the new MIME type for the operation called View. The second line specifies that the **LineDataContentHandler** be used for data of this MIME type.

We package the files,

```
META-INF/mime.types
META-INF/mailcap
Line.class
LineDataContentHandler.class
LineViewer.class
```

into the JAR file for the bean.

Let us now create a sample data file for the **Line** object, named say **data.lin**, containing the four coordinates: **100**, **120**, **200**, and **300**. We now execute the FileExplorer application and pass the **data.lin** in the command line. We will notice that we get a choice of one View operation, mapped to our new LineViewer bean.

NOTE: *This example does not work under the presently available pre-release of the JAF but should work according to the documentation. It is hoped that it actually does so.*

CONCLUSION

We have seen in this chapter how to use the JAF for applications that handle data sources so as to be able to bind data to JavaBeans that can operate on the data. The FileExplorer example illustrates this by reading a specified file and displaying all available operations on it. When a particular operation is selected, the associated bean is invoked, and the operation carried out.

The JAF works by associating a **DataHandler** with each piece of data. The **DataHandler** provides a common interface to the JAF subclasses. Data can be represented by a **DataSource**, which encapsulates the data and its MIME type. The **DataHandler** uses the **CommandMap** to map operations to registered MIME types. The default registration process is based on **mailcap** (RFC 1524) implemented by the **MailcapCommandMap**.

Next we saw how the default behavior of the JAF can be extended by

- Adding new beans that can operate on MIME type data. The FileCountLines example bean does this by implementing the **CommandObject** interface. This essentially allows the bean to access the data via the **DataHandler** rather than by conventional means such as serialization or externalization.

- Adding new MIME types with associated classes. To implement a new MIME type based on a Java object we need a class that can carry out conversion between streams and the object. In our example we implemented the **LineDataContentHandler** class that can read and write the **Line** object. We also created a LineViewer bean to View the object.

In cases where we extend the functionality of the JAF for either integrating new operator beans or new data sources, we need to define registration information for the JAF to be able to map operations to MIME types. There are two files presently used. The **mime.types** file is used by the **FileDataSource** to map file extensions to MIME types. The **mailcap** file is used by the default **MailcapCommandMap** to map operations on a specified MIME type to beans.

There are two more parts of the JAF that can be extended. We can create new **DataSources** for new stream-based data, and we can create special **CommandMaps** for mapping operations to data types based on a new registration method. However, for all practical purposes, the default classes provided are sufficient for normal uses of the JAF.

Drag-and-Drop Subsystem

Drag-and-drop is a facility that is commonly available in most Window-based graphical user interface (GUI) systems. Typically such GUI systems enable multiple windows to be opened on the screen with one or more applications running in them. Drag-and-drop enables the user to drag an object from one place or application on the screen and drop it into another place or application. It is a highly intuitive operation for transferring data or objects.

Commonly available drag-and-drop operations are copying or moving files from one folder to another or dragging a document in an application so as to view it. The Windows 95 Desktop Explorer is an excellent example of drag-and-drop functionality. We can open several folders on the desktop and then click on any file in one folder and drag it to another folder on the desktop. This initiates a file copy or move operation between the two folders. This example illustrates a drag-and-drop operation within the same application or different instances of the same application—both applications in this case being the Windows

Explorer. Another example from Windows is the ability to drag a file from a folder in Explorer into a word-processing application like Microsoft Word. This results in the particular document being opened in the word processor. This is an example of two different applications exchanging information using drag-and-drop.

Because drag-and-drop facilities are used by different applications to exchange information in a consistent and mutually understandable manner, drag-and-drop support needs to be provided by the operating system itself. Hence drag-and-drop is a platform-specific facility. Because Java applets or applications are platform-independent, they cannot access a platform-specific facility such as drag-and-drop. To enable drag-and-drop in Java, the facility has to be made available within the Java Virtual Machine framework itself. JDK 1.2 introduces this platform-independent mechanism for Java applets or applications so that they can have drag-and-drop capability of transferring data from one application to another. This means, potentially, Java applications could also exchange information through drag-and-drop to and from non-Java applications. We shall cover the drag-and-drop functionality introduced in the *Java Development Kit version 1.2* released by JavaSoft.

To clearly understand all the concepts explained in this chapter, you will need 1) familiarity with the Java language and 2) familiarity with the Java Event Model as defined in JDK1.1.

This Chapter Covers

- The Uniform Data Transfer Mechanism.
- Drag-and-drop concepts.
- Drag-and-drop from the sender's point of view.
- Drag-and-drop from the receiver's point of view.

NOTE: *If you are already familiar with the Uniform Data Transfer Mechanism, skip the first section and go straight to the "Drag-and-Drop Concepts" section. However, do have a look at the examples, because they are used later in the drag-and-drop examples.*

The Uniform Data Transfer Mechanism

The capability of Java applications to exchange information with other applications (Java or non-Java) is not new. JDK 1.1 introduced a facility called the Uniform Data Transfer Mechanism that allows applications to exchange information through the clipboard, another commonly available platform-specific mechanism. The design of the basic classes for the Uniform Data Transfer Mechanism included a preliminary plan for drag-and-drop. But the actual implementation is only available in the JDK 1.2. However, the basic classes introduced remain valid. To understand how drag-and-drop is to be used in Java, we have to understand these basic classes in the Uniform Data Transfer Mechanism. There are two main classes that encapsulate the Uniform Data Transfer Mechanism. These are the **DataFlavor** class and the **Transferable** interface.

The **DataFlavor** Class

One important issue in transferring data between applications is the data format or flavor. Both the applications need to have a common flavor of data that they can interpret. The word "flavor" is appropriately used because the same data could be exchanged in different ways, possibly varying in detail or format. For example, when transferring a document from one application to another, the data could be in HTML so as to include character formatting information or alternatively in plain text. Here HTML is one flavor, whereas plain text is another flavor of the same data. Similarly if the object being transferred is an image, the data could be formatted as either a GIF or JPG format and transferred.

The **DataFlavor** class defines this property of the data being transferred. It encapsulates all necessary information about a particular flavor to enable negotiation and transfer between applications. This information includes

- A logical name of the DataFlavor that acts as an identification string for programs
- A human-presentable form which can be presented to the user
- A representation class that defines the class of the actual object to be transferred

The JDK currently uses MIME type names as logical names. MIME type names were originally defined for sharing information via mail but are now universally recognized type names. MIME type specifications can be found in RFC 2045. Basically, MIME types are specified as a type/subtype pair followed by a set of parameters. Typical MIME types are "text/html," "image/gif," "audio/au," etc. The first part of the name specifies the general type, and the second part specifies the format of the data. Parameters may follow that give additional information about the data type. Parameters are specified as "attribute/value" pairs. There are seven standard main types defined in the MIME specification. Custom types can be defined by prepending an "x-" to the main type.

For maintaining the flexibility of transferring arbitrary data between applications, the **DataFlavor** can specify any Java object as a representation class for the data. For transferring standard data types such as "text/html" the **DataFlavor** can use an **InputStream** as a representation class. For non-standard data types such as a Java component, the **DataFlavor** expects a MIME type **"application/x-java-serialized-object; class=java.awt. Component"**. In such cases, the representation class can be any arbitrary Java class. The **DataFlavor** thus has three main constructors, as shown in the following list.

▨ The first constructor is for constructing a fully specified **DataFlavor** with all the parameters:

```
public DataFlavor(
        String primaryType,              // the primary
                                         MIME type
        String subType,                  // the MIME
                                         subtype
        MimeTypeParameterList params,    // MIME parameters
        Class representationClass,       // the
                                         representation
                                         class
        String humanPresentableName)     // a readable name
```

▨ The second constructor is for defining a **DataFlavor** that represents a Java class.

```
Public DataFlavor(
        Class representationClass,       // the
                                         representation
                                         class
        String humanPresentableName)     // a readable name
```

▨ The third constructor is for constructing a **DataFlavor** for representing a MIME type.

```
public DataFlavor(
        String mimeType,               // the MIME type
        String humanPresentableName)   // a readable name
```

An important observation here is that in the first constructor the MIME parameters are specified as a `MimeTypeParameterList`. This comes from a java.util.mime package, which is a new utility interface defined in JDK 1.2. It is used to represent key-value pairs. In the third constructor, the implied representation class is an `InputStream`. For convenience, two pre-defined `DataFlavor`s are defined:

1. `public static final DataFlavor plainTextFlavor`: this represents a `DataFlavor` for representing plain text using Unicode encoding. The representation class is `InputStream`, and the MIME type is "`text/plain; charset=unicode`". It is equivalent to the following `DataFlavor`:

   ```
   new DataFlavor("text/plain; charset=unicode", "Plain
   Text")
   ```

2. `public static final DataFlavor stringFlavor`: this represents a `DataFlavor` for a Java Unicode String class, the representation class is `java.lang.String`, and the MIME type is "`application/x-java-serialized-object`". It is equivalent to the following data flavor:

   ```
   new DataFlavor(java.lang.String.class, "Unicode String")
   ```

We illustrate the `DataFlavor` class by defining two new data flavors, called `intDataFlavor` and `floatDataFlavor` that are encapsulated in a class called `NumberFlavors`. Listing 9-1 follows.

Listing 9-1
NumberFlavors.
java.

```
public class NumberFlavors {
    /**
     * a private method to create a constant DataFlavor
     */
    static private DataFlavor createConstant(Class rc,
                                             String prn) {
        try {
                return new DataFlavor(rc, prn);
            } catch (MimeTypeParseException mtpe) {
                return null;
            }

    }

    /**
                                              Continues
```

Listing 9-1
Continued.

```
     * A DataFlavor that represents the Integer Number
     */
    public static DataFlavor intDataFlavor=
          createConstant(java.lang.Integer.class,
                         "An Integer Number");
    /**
     * A DataFlavor that represents the Float Number
     */
    public static DataFlavor floatDataFlavor=
        createConstant(java.lang.Float.class,
                       "A Floating Point Number");

}
```

In Listing 9-1, the **NumberFlavors** class is a placeholder for the new **DataFlavor**s and has a single method that creates constant **DataFlavor**s. This method, **createConstant** uses the constructor that takes a representation class and a human presentable name as parameters. The MIME type and subtype are automatically set to be "application" and "x-java-serialized-object," respectively. As for the representation class, we use the **java.lang.Integer** class to represent the integer **DataFlavor**, and **java.lang.Float** class to represent the float **DataFlavor**.

The **Transferable** Interface

A single Java object might represent more than one **DataFlavor**. For example, a class representing a number may be transferred either as an integer or as a floating-point number. In this case, the transfer can use one of the two **DataFlavor**s we have defined in the above example, namely **intDataFlavor** or **floatDataFlavor**. To encapsulate such multiplicity, an interface called **Transferable** has been provided. To define a Java object that can be transferred using the Uniform Data Transfer Mechanism, that object needs to implement the **Transferable** interface. This interface contains methods that represent the **DataFlavor**s that the class can transfer, as well as a method to retrieve the data for a specified **DataFlavor**. The **Transferable** interface definition is quite simple, with only three methods as described in the following list.

▨ **public DataFlavor[] getTransferDataFlavors()**

Returns an array of DataFlavor objects indicating the flavors the data can be provided in. The array should be ordered according to preference for providing the data from most richly descriptive to least descriptive. It returns an array of data flavors in which this data can be transferred.

■ **`public boolean isDataFlavorSupported(DataFlavor flavor)`**

Returns whether or not the specified data flavor is supported for this object. The flavor passed is the requested flavor for the data. It returns a boolean indicating whether or not the data flavor is supported.

■ **`public Object getTransferData(DataFlavor flavor) throws UnsupportedFlavorException, IOException`**

Returns an object that represents the data to be transferred. The representation class of the flavor defines the class of the object returned. The flavor passed is the requested flavor for the data. It throws an IOException if the data is no longer available in the requested flavor. It throws UnsupportedFlavorException if the requested data flavor is not supported. The returned Object is the one representing the data to be transferred.

Though this last method returns a generic object class for flexibility, the user of this method has the responsibility of forcing the type to the representation class of the **`DataFlavor`** that it asked for. For example, in Listing 9-2, we define a **`Transferable`** class that represents a number; this class could transfer data using the data flavors **`intDataFlavor`** or **`floatDataFlavor`** that we have already created.

Listing 9-2
`NumberData.java`.

```java
import java.lang.*;
import java.io.*;
import java.util.*;
import java.awt.datatransfer.*;
import NumberFlavors;

/**
 * NumberData class demonstrates a Transferable object that
 *     represents<BR>
 * more than one DataFlavor.
 */
public class NumberData implements Transferable {

    /**
     * Creates a number from an float
     * @param num a float
     */
    public NumberData(float num) {
```

Continues

Listing 9-2
Continued.

```java
          this.num=num;
}

    /**
     * Creates a number from a String
     * @param num a float
     */
    public NumberData(String snum) throws
       NumberFormatException {
       Float flt=new Float(snum);
       this.num=flt.floatValue();
    }

    /**
     * returns the supported data flavors
     * NumberFlavors.intDataFlavor and
     * NumberFlavors.floatDataFlavor
     */
    public DataFlavor[] getTransferDataFlavors() {
       DataFlavor[] dfArray = new DataFlavor;
dfArray[0]=NumberFlavors.floatDataFlavor;
       dfArray=NumberFlavors.intDataFlavor;
       return dfArray;
    }

    /**
     * returns true for
     * NumberFlavors.intDataFlavor or
 * NumberFlavors.floatDataFlavor
     * and false for any other DataFlavor
     */
    public boolean isDataFlavorSupported(DataFlavor
    flavor) {
    return ( flavor.equals(NumberFlavors.floatDataFlavor)
             ||
       flavor.equals(NumberFlavors.intDataFlavor) );
    }

    /**
     * returns the specified data
     */
    public Object getTransferData(DataFlavor flavor)
                   throws UnsupportedFlavorException,
             IOException {
    if (flavor.equals(NumberFlavors.floatDataFlavor)) {
       return new Float(this.num);
    } else if
    (flavor.equals(NumberFlavors.intDataFlavor)) {
       return new Integer((int)this.num);
    } else {
       throw new UnsupportedFlavorException(flavor);
    }
```

Listing 9-2

```
        }

            /**
             * returns a string value
             */
            public String toString() {
                    return ""+num;
            }

            /**
             * Variables
             */
            float num=0.0f;
    }
```

In Listing 9-2, the **NumberData** class implements the **Transferable** interface by supporting the two data flavors **floatDataFlavor** and **intDataFlavor** and can be requested to return data in either of the two flavors. We create two constructors for the **NumberData** class. One uses a float number and another a string.

```
public NumberData(float num)
```

and

```
public NumberData(String snum)
```

They simply initialize the same internal variable.

The method **public DataFlavor[] getTransferDataFlavors()** returns an array of data flavors that this class supports. We create an array with the two elements—**intDataFlavor** and **floatDataFlavor**.

The method **public boolean isDataFlavorSupported(DataFlavor flavor)** tests whether the **DataFlavor** parameter passed is supported. We test whether it is either **intDataFlavor** or **floatDataFlavor** and return True if we get a match.

The method **public Object getTransferData(DataFlavor flavor)** returns the actual **Transferable** data in the specified data flavor. We implement it by checking whether the flavor is one of the supported flavors and if so return an object corresponding to the data flavor. If the requested flavor is **intDataFlavor**, we create and return a **java.lang.Integer** object. If the requested flavor is **floatDataFlavor**, we create and return a **java.lang.Float** object. If the requested flavor is neither of the supported data flavors, we raise an **UnsupportedFlavorException**.

Uniform Data Transfer Protocols

There are two main protocols supported in the JDK under the Uniform Data Transfer Mechanism. One is the **Clipboard** protocol and another the **drag and drop**. Any class that implements the **Transferable** interface can be transferred using one of these two protocols. The **Clipboard** is a simple protocol that provides cut, copy, and paste operations that are now universally available in all GUI applications. Understanding the **Clipboard** API will help getting a feel for the Uniform Data Transfer Mechanism and pave the way for the more complex **drag and drop** protocol.

The Clipboard Protocol

The **Clipboard** API is in the form of a class **java.awt.datatransfer. Clipboard** and an interface **java.awt.datatransfer.ClipboardOwner**. Though multiple custom **Clipboard**s may be created, there is a single **Clipboard** instance for data transfer to and from non-java native applications. This is available from java.awt.Toolkit by using the method **Clipboard getSystemClipboard()**.

This method returns the system **Clipboard** that can be used to transfer data to other applications that may or may not be in Java. The **Clipboard** class has one constructor and four methods, as described in the following list.

▣ **public Clipboard(String name)**

This Constructs a named Clipboard

▣ **public String getName()**

This method returns the Clipboard's name

▣ **public synchronized void setContents(Transferable contents, ClipboardOwner owner)**

Sets the contents of the Clipboard to a specified Transferable object. The ClipboardOwner represents the object that generated the Transferable object.

▣ **public synchronized Transferable getContents(Object requestor)**

Returns the contents of the Clipboard.

A **Clipboard** has three entities associated with it.

▣ A name that identifies the **Clipboard**

- A **Transferable** object representing the actual data to be transferred
- A **ClipboardOwner** object, which generates the **Transferable** data

The **ClipboardOwner** interface has a single method **public void lostOwnership(Clipboard clipboard, Transferable contents)**. This method is invoked to notify the object that it is no longer the owner of the contents of the **Clipboard**. Whenever the **Clipboard**'s owner changes, it notifies the old owner that it no longer owns the **Clipboard**.

Implementing the clipboard Operations

To implement copy or cut operations, the sender needs to implement the **ClipboardOwner** interface so as to keep track of the cut or copied data. The data to be transferred needs to implement the **Transferable** interface. Invoking **Clipboard.setContents**, which takes the **Transferable** object and the **ClipboardOwner** as parameters, does the actual cut or copy.

To implement paste, we need to invoke **Clipboard.getContents**, which will return the contents of the **Clipboard**, which is a **Transferable** object. As an example, we shall modify our **NumberData** class to implement **ClipboardOwner** by redefining it as

```
public class NumberData implements
        Transferable,ClipboardOwner
```

and adding a dummy method

```
public void lostOwnership(Clipboard clipboard, Transferable
        contents) {
}
```

This method does nothing because we don't need to do anything special when we lose ownership of the **Clipboard**. Listing 9-3 illustrates how we use the **Clipboard** to do copy or paste operations.

Listing 9-3
ClipboardTest.
java.

```
import java.awt.*;import java.awt.*;import
        java.awt.event.*;import java.awt.datatransfer.*;import
        java.awt.dnd.*;import NumberData;
import NumberFlavors;

/**
                                                        Continues
```

Listing 9-3
Continued.

```
   * Demonstrates the Clipboard API<BR>
   */
public class ClipboardTest extends Frame
                                implements ActionListener {

   TextField sourceNumber;
      // the textbox containing the source Number
      TextArea destinationText;
         // the text area to paste the contents to
   Button copyButton;
      // copies the source into a NumberData object into
   the clipboard
   Button pasteIntButton;
         // pastes the contents into the destination as an
         // Integer, received by requesting a
         // intDataFlavor
   Button pasteFloatButton;
      // pastes the contents into the destination as a
      // Float, received by requesting a
      // floatDataFlavorClipboard clipboard = new
      // Clipboard("My Clipboard");
      // creates a clipboard named "My Clipboard"
      /**
       * Constructs the user interface consisting of a
         textbox for the
    * source, a text area for the destination, and three
      buttons.          */public ClipboardTest() {
      super("Clipboard Test");
      setLayout(new FlowLayout());

      sourceNumber = new TextField(32);
      add(sourceNumber);

      copyButton = new Button("Copy Number");
      copyButton.setActionCommand("copy");
      copyButton.addActionListener(this);
      add(copyButton);

      pasteIntButton = new Button("Paste Int");
      pasteIntButton.setActionCommand("paste int");
      pasteIntButton.addActionListener(this);
      pasteIntButton.setEnabled(false);
      add(pasteIntButton);

      pasteFloatButton = new Button("Paste Float");
      pasteFloatButton.setActionCommand("paste float");
      pasteFloatButton.addActionListener(this);
      pasteFloatButton.setEnabled(false);
      add(pasteFloatButton);

      destinationText = new TextArea(8, 32);
      add(destinationText);
```

Listing 9-3

```
        }

/**
 * Event handler for button action events.
 * This is where the actual copy and paste operations
 * are implemented
 */
    public void actionPerformed(ActionEvent evt) {
        String cmd = evt.getActionCommand();

        if (cmd.equals("copy")) {
            // Implement Copy operation
            String srcData = sourceNumber.getText();
            if (srcData != null) {
                NumberData contents=new NumberData(srcData);
            clipboard.setContents(contents, contents);
                pasteIntButton.setEnabled(true);
                pasteFloatButton.setEnabled(true);
                System.out.println("Clipboard
                contents="+contents);
            }
        } else if (cmd.equals("paste int")) {
            // Implement Paste Int operation
            Transferable content = clipboard.getContents
                                    (this);
            if (content != null) {
                try {
                            Integer dstData =
                        (Integer)content.getTransferData(
                            NumberFlavors.intDataFlavor);
                destinationText.append(""+dstData.intValue());
                } catch (Exception e) {
                    System.out.println("Couldn't get contents in
                                    format: "+
                    NumberFlavors.intDataFlavor.
                    getHumanPresentableName()
                        );
                }
            }
        } else if (cmd.equals("paste float")) {
            // Implement Paste Float operation
            Transferable content = clipboard.getContents
                                    (this);
            if (content != null) {
                try {
                    Float dstData =
                    (Float)content.getTransferData(
                        NumberFlavors.floatDataFlavor);
                    destinationText.append
                    (""+dstData.floatValue());
                } catch (Exception e) {
```

Continues

Listing 9-3
Continued.

```
                        System.out.println("Couldn't get contents
                                    in format: "+
                   NumberFlavors.floatDataFlavor.
                   getHumanPresentableName());
                   }
             }
         }
     }
/**
 * main method for the application to start
 */
     public static void main(String[] args) {
         ClipboardTest test = new ClipboardTest();
         test.show();
         test.setSize(300,300);
     }
}
```

You will note that the constructor sets up the user interface components. We have **sourceNumber**, a TextField for entering a source Number-Data to copy, and another TextField **destinationText** as a destination for paste. There are three buttons. The **copyButton** is for doing the copy operation, and the **pasteIntButton** is for pasting the number from the **Clipboard** in the **intDataFlavor**. The **pasteFloatButton** will paste the contents of the **Clipboard** in **floatDataFlavor**. The actual clipboard operations are implemented in the **actionPerformed** method. The first operation is the copy operation. To copy or cut a **NumberData** from the **sourceNumber** component, we do the following:

```
NumberData contents=new NumberData(srcData);
clipboard.setContents(contents, contents);
```

The first statement constructs a **NumberData** object, which is the **Transferable** class we have defined earlier. The second statement passes this **NumberData** to the clipboard.

```
number = new NumberData(10.0);
        // create a NumberData
clipboard =new Clipboard("Test Clipboard");
        // Create a named Clipboard
clipboard.setContents(number,number);
        // put the Transferable object, number into the
Clipboard,
        // and set the ClipboardOwner to the same number.
```

Here the number object acts as the **Transferable** object as well as the **ClipboardOwner**. Then to do a paste, we do the following:

```
NumberData clipboardContents = (NumberData)clipboard.
                                    getContents(window);
```

Most certainly, the same clipboard object needs to be used to copy and paste the number object.

Drag-and-Drop Concepts

The protocol for drag-and-drop involves support from both ends—the data transmitter's end as well as the data receiver's end (see Figure 9-1). A typical drag-and-drop operation involves the following steps:

As shown in Figure 9-1,

1. The user clicks on a GUI element at one location on the screen and starts dragging the mouse (moves the cursor by keeping the mouse button pressed).

2. The cursor shape changes to indicate that a drag-and-drop operation has begun.

3. The cursor moves across other GUI elements on the screen. When it moves over components that cannot accept a drop, the cursor changes shape to indicate an invalid drop target.

4. When the cursor moves onto a component that can accept the dropped object, the shape of the cursor changes to indicate a valid drop target.

5. The user releases the mouse button over the target component, thus carrying out the drop.

6. If the element on which the drop has occurred can accept the dropped object, the actual data transfer begins. If the element cannot accept the dropped object, an error is indicated.

As seen from this sequence, there are two main participants in the drag-and-drop process: the data sender from which the data is dragged and the data receiver into which the data is dropped. In the `clipboard`

Figure 9-1

A typical drag-and-drop operation.

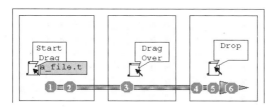

protocol the source and the target of the transfer operation carry out the transfer to or from the **Clipboard** asynchronously. In the drag-and-drop protocol, the entire sequence starting from the drag to the drop involves constant feedback to the user and hence the source and target needed to synchronously monitor the operation.

The implementation of drag-and-drop in Java uses the Uniform Data Transfer Mechanism classes and interfaces, **DataFlavor** and **Transferable**. Data to be transferred is coded as a **Transferable** object and the actual data transferred by using the **DataFlavor** that is suitable for the source and the target of the transfer. The following sections contain the main concepts and terminologies used in relation to the drag-and-drop operation in Java.

Source, Target, Sender, Receiver

The terms **Source** and **Target** have been used to name classes that coordinate the operation on the respective sides and are not really the source or target of the transfer. Hence to avoid confusion, we shall define two terms **Sender** and **Receiver** to refer to the actual objects or components that wish to send data on one side and receive the data on the other.

Actions and the DnDConstants Class

Every drag-and-drop operation does a transfer of an object. The type of operation could be

- Copy operation: where the **Transferable** object is copied from the **Sender** to the **Receiver**
- Move operation: where the **Transferable** object is moved from the **Sender** to the **Receiver**
- Reference operation: where the object's reference is passed from the **Sender** to the **Receiver**. This type of operation is meaningful only between two Java applications.

These actions are coded as constants in the **DnDConstants** class. The constants defined are

- **ACTION_NONE**
- **ACTION_COPY**
- **ACTION_MOVE**

▒ **ACTION_COPY_OR_MOVE**

▒ **ACTION_REFERENCE**

Cursors

Cursors have relevance to the drag-and-drop operation because the feedback to the user about the state of the drag-and-drop operation is normally given via the cursor shape. Typically, such feedback is necessary to tell the user whether the component above which the hotspot is currently moving is a valid drop target or not. We refer to the location of the cursor as "hotspot."

Image

Another feedback mechanism in the drag-and-drop operation is an image associated with the object that is being transferred and actually moves along with the cursor.

Auto Scrolling

Auto scrolling is a feature that lets the **Receiver** component automatically scroll when the hotspot is positioned over it within specified "insets" and is not being dragged (paused).

Drag-and-Drop from the **Sender's** Point of View

Any Java object can act as a **Sender** or initiator of a drag-and-drop operation. To implement a drag-and-drop **Sender** component, we need to do the following:

1. Create a **DragSource** object, which allows us to start a drag-and-drop operation, and coordinates the drag-and-drop operation for the **Sender** object.

2. Implement the **DragSourceListener** interface, which allows us to respond to the drag-and-drop events generated while the operation is in progress.

Figure 9-2
Drag-and-drop from
the sender's point of
view

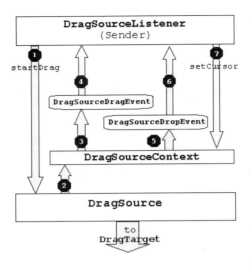

Figure 9-2
Drag-and-drop from
the sender's point of
view

A diagrammatic view of the drag-and-drop operation from the **Sender**'s point of view can be created as shown in Figure 9-2.

Instantiating the DragSource

The first step is to instantiate the **DragSource** object. The lifetime of the **DragSource** object can vary, but the default is a single instance that can be obtained from a static method **DragSource.getDefaultDragSource()**.

Because this is a static object, we can instantiate it at any time before the first drag-and-drop operation starts. This single instance can spawn multiple drag-and-drop operations. Each operation is kept track of by using a **DragSourceContext** object. As an example, we declare a class, **DnDSender** as follows:

```
class DnDSender extends Frame implements
    DragSourceListener,
    MouseMotionListener {
```

The **DnDSender** should have some **Transferable** data that represents the object to be dragged. We shall use the **NumberData** class defined in the previous section. We create a **NumberData** object as follows:

```
NumberData num=new NumberData(100.0f);
```

Next, we declare a static **DragSource** as follows:

```
static DragSource dragSource=DragSource.
        getDefaultDragSource();
```

Recognizing a Drag Request from the User and Starting the DnD Operation

A drag-and-drop operation starts when the user does a predefined gesture, such as click, and drags the mouse on the **Sender** component. Thus the component's **MouseMotionListener** will recognize the beginning of a drag-and-drop operation. The **MouseEvent**, which is an **AWTEvent**, is responsible for starting the operation and will be referred to as the "trigger" event. So we implement the **MouseMotionListener**'s **mouseDragged** callback method:

```
boolean dragStarted=false;         // variable to make sure
                                   we start only once
public void mouseDragged(MouseEvent e) {
    if ( !dragStarted ) {
        try {
            System.out.println("Start Drag");
        dragSource.startDrag(this,e,
                        DnDConstants.ACTION_COPY|
                        DnDConstants.ACTION_MOVE,
                        DragSource.getDefaultCopyDrop
                        Cursor(), null,null, number,
                        this);
        } catch(InvalidDnDOperationException ex) {
                System.out.println("Invalid DnD
                                Operation:"+ex);
        } catch(SecurityException sx) {
            System.out.println("Security Exception:"+sx);
        }
        dragStarted=true;
    }
}
```

To actually start the **DnD** operation, we invoke the **startDrag** method of the **DragSource** object that we have already instantiated. This method is declared as follows:

```
DragSourceContext DragSource.startDrag(
                        Component component, AWTEvent
                        trigger, int actions,
                        Cursor dragCursor,
                        Image dragImage,
                        Point imageOffset,
                        Transferable transferable,
                        DragSourceListener dsl)
```

Table 9-1

`startDrag`
parameters.

Parameter	Description	Example
`component`	A reference to the Component in which the trigger event occurred in	We pass the current instance of the DnDSender in which the event has occurred.
`Trigger`	The actual **AWTEvent** that acted as the trigger.	In this case the **MouseEvent** received by the listener.
`Actions`	A list of valid actions that the Sender can perform, which is a combination of the standard actions defined in **DnDConstants**.	We use copy or move by combining **DnDConstants.ACTION_COPY** | **DnDConstants.ACTION_MOVE**
`dragCursor`	The initial Cursor to use while dragging. Can be set to null if the default cursor is to be used.	We pass the default cursor provided by the **DragSource**'s static method, **GetDefaultCopyDropCursor()** See the reference for DragSource for methods that return other default cursors.
`DragImage`	An Image that is carried with the hotspot, which represents the object being transferred. This can be null if no image is required.	We don't use this facility, and pass null.
`ImageOffset`	An offset between the image and the hotspot of the mouse cursor.	Since no image is passed, this too can be null.
`Transferable`	The actual Transferable object that is to be transferred	We pass the **NumberData** object created earlier.
`Dsl`	A reference to the **DragSourceListener** object that will receive event notifications	We pass a reference to the current **DnDSender** object instance, since it implements the **DragSourceListener** interface.

The parameters are described in Table 9-1.

This method creates a *DragSourceContext* object, as in Step 2 in Figure 9-1. The **DragSourceContext** object is used to convey information to the **Sender** object about a particular drag-and-drop operation. The **DragSource** object is a single static object and hence the **DragSourceContext** is the per-instance object created to maintain information about each operation. We shall see later how this object can be accessed and used.

Keeping Track of the Drag-and-Drop Operation

Once the operation is started, the **Sender** is notified of the status of the operation via the callback methods of the **DragSourceListener** interface. The callback methods are passed a **DragSourceEvent**. The two kinds of **DragSourceEvent**s trapped by the **DragSourceContext** object follow and are shown in Steps 3 and 5 in Figure 9-1:

- The DragSourceDragEvent
- The DragSourceDropEvent

These are passed on to the **Sender**, as in Steps 4 and 6, via the **DragSourceListener**'s callback methods. The **DragSourceListener** has the following callback methods, as described in the following list.

- **void dragEnter(DragSourceDragEvent dsde)**

  Called when the hotspot of the cursor enters a new component that is a potential drop site.

- **void dragOver(DragSourceDragEvent dsde)**

  Called when the hotspot moves within a drop site.

- **void dragGestureChanged(DragSourceDragEvent dsde)**

  Called when the user changes some input device states, such as mouse buttons or keyboard modifiers.

- **void dragExit(DragSourceDragEvent dsde)**

  Called when the hotspot moves out of a drop site

- **void dragDropEnd(DragSourceDropEvent dsde)**

  Called when the drag and drop operation ends.

The **DragSourceContext** object provides default functionality for all these methods. This includes checking for consistency between the actions of the **Sender** and the **Receiver**. Hence the simplest implementation of a **Sender** can only implement dummy versions of all these callback methods that do nothing.

Giving User Feedback

The user is given feedback about the state of the operation by two visual cues described in the following list:

■ By moving an image with the hotspot to indicate that the drag-and-drop operation is in progress. This is achieved by passing an image to the **DragSource.startDrag** method. This mechanism is not guaranteed to work in all operating environments, because it depends on the native drag-and-drop capabilities.

■ By changing the shape of the cursor to indicate whether the component over which the hotspot is positioned is a valid drop site or not. This is achieved by invoking the **setCursor** method in **DragSourceContext**, as shown in Step 7 in Figure 9-1.

We can implement these visual cues in the callback methods as in this example:

```
public void dragEnter(DragSourceDragEvent dsde) {
   java.awt.dnd.DragSourceContext
      dt=dsde.getDragSourceContext();
            // get the DragSourceContext object
      if (
      (dt.getSourceActions()&dsde.getTargetActions())!=0 ) {
                  // compatible actions
                  dt.setCursor(dragSource.
                  getDefaultCopyDropCursor());
                                       // Set cursor to
                                          show drop okay
            } else { // incompatible drop site
                  dt.setCursor(dragSource.
                  getDefaultCopyNoDropCursor());
                                       // Set cursor to
                                          show drop not
                                          okay
            }
   }
```

This method is called when the hotspot of the cursor enters another component that is a potential drop site, or **Receiver**, for the current operation. We handle the event by first retrieving the **DragSourceContext** object associated with the current **DnD** operation. We do two things with this object.

1. Get the **DnD** actions valid for the **Sender** via the **getSourceActions** method. This we compare with the actions valid for the **Receiver** into which the cursor has just entered. The valid operations for the **Receiver** are available via the **getTargetActions** method of the **DragSourceDragEvent**.

2. If the two actions are compatible, we can change the cursor to a "drop" cursor. Otherwise we change the cursor to a "no drop" cursor. Changing the cursor means calling the **setCursor** method of the **DataSourceContext** object.

The other callback methods can be handled similarly.

Cancelling the Operation

If the user gesture indicates an aborted operation, such as releasing the mouse key, or for any other reason relating to the availability of the **Transferable** object, the operation may need to be cancelled. The **Sender** can cancel the operation by using the method **void DragSourceContext. cancelDrag()**. We can do this in the **dragGestureChanged** callback method as follows:

```
public void dragGestureChanged(DragSourceDragEvent dsde) {
     java.awt.dnd.DragSourceContext
     dt=dsde.getDragSourceContext();
     dt.cancelDrag();
}
```

Recognizing the End of the Drag-and-Drop Operation

When the **Receiver** has completed the data transfer or has rejected the drop, the result is notified to the **Sender** via the method **void dragDropEnd(DragSourceDropEvent dsde)**. The actual action that the **Receiver** used to receive the **Transferable** object can be retrieved using the method **boolean DragSourceDropEvent.getDropAction ()**. The result of whether the operation was successful or not can be checked by invoking the method **boolean DragSourceDropEvent.getDropSuccess()**.

NOTE: *At the time of writing this chapter, there is an inconsistency between the beta implementation and the specifications in the name of the above method.*

We implement the **dragDropEnd** method as follows:

```
public void dragDropEnd(DragSourceDropEvent dsde) {
     String dropAction="none";
     if ((dsde.getDropAction()&DnDConstants.
        ACTION_COPY)!=0) {
          dropAction="Copy";          // Dopr action is
                                          COPY
     } else if
     ((dsde.getDropAction()&DnDConstants.ACTION_MOVE)!=0) {
```

```
                    dropAction="Move";         // Drop action is
                                                         MOVE
            } else if ((dsde.getDropAction()
                    &DnDConstants.ACTION_REFERENCE)!=0) {
                    dropAction="Reference";       // Drop action
                                                     is REFERENCE
        }
        if ( dsde.getDropSuccess() ) {
                System.out.println("Drop Successfull");
        } else {
                System.out.println("Drop Unsuccessfull");
        }
        dragStarted=false;
    }
```

All the code for the `DnDSender` class is in Listing 9-4.

Listing 9-4
DnDSender.java

```java
import java.awt.*;
import java.awt.event.*;
import java.awt.dnd.*;
import NumberData;
import java.lang.reflect.*;

class DnDSender extends Frame implements
    DragSourceListener,MouseMotionListener {
    NumberData number=new NumberData(0.0f);
    static DragSource
    dragSource=DragSource.getDefaultDragSource();
    boolean dragStarted=false;
    int lastDragEvent=-1;

    public DnDSender(String title,float num) {
            super(title);
            number=new NumberData(num);
            addMouseMotionListener(this);
    }

    public void mouseDragged(MouseEvent e) {
            if ( !dragStarted ) {
                try {
                    System.out.println("Start Drag");
                    dragSource.startDrag(this,e,
                                    DnDConstants.ACTIO
                                    N_COPY,
                                    DragSource.
                                    DefaultCopyNoDrop,
                                    null,null,number,
                                    this);
                } catch(InvalidDnDOperationException ex) {
                    System.out.println("Invalid DnD
                                        Operation:"+ex);
```

Listing 9-4

```
                              } catch(SecurityException sx) {
                                  System.out.println("Security
                                                      Exception:"+sx);
                              }
                                  dragStarted=true;
                          }
          }

          public void mouseMoved(MouseEvent e) {
          }

          public void dragEnter(DragSourceDragEvent dsde) {
                  if (lastDragEvent!=1) {System.out.
                  println("DragSource:Drag
                          Enter");lastDragEvent=1;}
                      java.awt.dnd.DragSourceContext
                      dt=dsde.getDragSourceContext();
                  if ( (dsde.getTargetActions()&dt.
                      getSourceActions())==0 ) { //
                      incompatible actions
                      System.out.println("Incompatible Drop");
                      dt.setCursor(dragSource.
                                  DefaultCopyNoDrop);
                  } else {
                          System.out.println("Compatible Drop");
                          dt.setCursor(dragSource.
                                      DefaultCopyDrop);
                  }
          }

          public void dragOver(DragSourceDragEvent dsde) {
                  if (lastDragEvent!=2) {System.out.println
                  ("DragSource:Drag Over");lastDragEvent=2;}
          }

          public void dragGestureChanged(DragSourceDragEvent
                                          dsde) {
                  if (lastDragEvent!=3) {System.out.
                  println("DragSource:Drag Gesture
                          Changed");lastDragEvent=3;}
                      java.awt.dnd.DragSourceContext
                      dt=dsde.getDragSourceContext();
                  dt.cancelDrag();
          }

          public void dragExit(DragSourceEvent dse) {
                  if (lastDragEvent!=4) {System.out.
                  println("DragSource:Drag
                          Exit");lastDragEvent=4;}
          }
```

Continues

Listing 9-4
Continued.

```
public void dragDropEnd(DragSourceDropEvent dsde) {
    if (lastDragEvent!=5) {System.out.
    println("DragSource:Drag Drop
            End");lastDragEvent=5;}
    dragStarted=false;
String dropAction="none";
if ((dsde.getDropAction()&DnDConstants.
    ACTION_COPY)!=0) {
    dropAction="Copy";          // Drop action is
                                       COPY
} else if ((dsde.getDropAction()&DnDConstants.
            ACTION_MOVE)!=0) {
    dropAction="Move";          // Drop action is
                                       MOVE
} else if ((dsde.getDropAction()&DnDConstants.
            ACTION_REFERENCE)!=0) {
    dropAction="Reference";        // Drop action
                                      is REFERENCE
}
if ( dsde.getDropSuccess() ) {
    System.out.println("Drop Successfull");
} else {
    System.out.println("Drop Unsuccessful");
}
}

public static void main(String[] args) {
DnDSender test = new
                DnDSender("DnDSender",100.0f);
test.show();
    test.setSize(300,300);
}
}
```

Drag-and-Drop from the Receiver's Point of View

Any object can act as a **Receiver**, or target, of a drag-and-drop operation. To implement a drag-and-drop **Receiver** component, we need to do the following:

1. Have the ability to interpret some data flavor represented by **Transferable** objects that can be received via drag-and-drop operations. This is because drag-and-drop operations in Java use the Uniform Data Transfer Mechanism introduced in the first section of this chapter.

2. Create a **DropTarget** object and associate it with the **Receiver** component. This exposes the component to receive any drag-and-drop operations that may occur in the operating environment

3. Implement the **DropTargetListener** interface, which enables us to respond to the drag-and-drop events generated while the operation is in progress.

We define a new class **DnDReceiver** as follows:

```
class DnDReceiver extends Frame implements
    DropTargetListener {
```

and keep a placeholder for a **NumberData** object,

```
NumberData number=new NumberData(0.0f);
```

The **NumberData** class is a **Transferable** object that represents data flavors defined in the **NumberFlavors** class. These classes are explained in the section of this chapter called "Uniform Data Transfer Mechanism." A diagrammatic view of the drag-and-drop operation from the **Sender**'s point of view can be created as shown in Figure 9-3.

Associating a **DropTarget** with a Component

The **DropTarget** encapsulates all the platform-specific handling of the drag-and-drop protocol from the **Receiver**'s point of view. Unlike the

Figure 9-3
Drag-and-drop from the receiver's point of view.

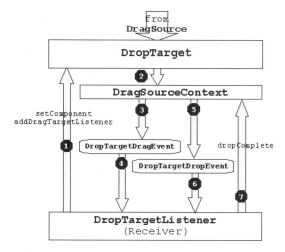

DragSource (a single instance of **DragSource** can take care of multiple operations from the source's point of view) in the case of **DropTarget**, one instance is required for each component that is to be exposed as a drop site. A new **DropTarget** can be constructed by invoking one of its constructors, such as **public DropTarget()**.

The association with the component can be established, as in Step 1 in Figure 9-3, by invoking the method **void DropTarget.setComponent(Component c)**. Alternatively, the same association can be established by invoking the method **void Component.setDropTarget(DropTarget d)** of the component. This is a new method introduced in the **Component** class. The simplest way, however, is to use the constructor: **public DropTarget(Component c, int actions, DropTargetListener dtl)**.

This does four things in a single step:

- It creates the **DropTarget**.
- Associates a component with it.
- Declares the allowed actions for the drag-and-drop operation.
- Registers a **DropTargetListener** to receive drag-and-drop events.

We use this in the constructor for the **DnDReceiver** class as shown below.

```
DropTarget dropTarget=null;
int allowedActions=DnDConstants.
    ACTION_MOVE|DnDConstants.ACTION_COPY;
public DnDReceiver(String title) {
    super(title);
    dropTarget=new DropTarget(this,allowedActions,this);
}
```

Here we first declare an instance variable **dropTarget** and initialize it to Null. Then we declare a variable **allowedActions** and set it to a combination of the MOVE and COPY actions. Next, as part of the constructor for **DnDReceiver**, we create a new **DropTarget** by passing the current object as both the associated component as well as the **DropTargetListener**.

Recognizing the Start of a Drag-and-Drop Operation

Once a component is associated with a **DropTarget**, its geometry is exposed to the client desktop as being receptive to drag-and-drop operations when the hotspot location intersects it. We can recognize the start of a drag-and-drop operation when the following callback method is called

void dragEnter(DropTargetDragEvent dtde). A **DropTargetContext** object that keeps track of the status of the operation on behalf of the receiver generates the **DropTargetDragEvent**.

Checking Compatibility and Accepting or Rejecting the Operation

The **dragEnter** callback method is responsible for checking compatibility of the operation and either accepting or rejecting the operation. Compatibility of the drag-and-drop operation depends on two factors:

- Whether the **Transferable** object associated with the operation represents a data flavor that the **Receiver** can interpret. This is done by getting the array of data flavors associated with the operation by calling the **getCurrentDataFlavors** method of the **DropTargetDragEvent** class.

- Whether the actions represented by the operation are acceptable to the **Receiver**. This is done by:

  1. Retrieving the actions represented by the operation by calling the **getSourceActions** method of the DropTargetDragEvent class.

  2. Comparing these actions with those allowed by the **DropTargetContext**, which are retrieved by calling its **getTargetActions** method. If these actions are not acceptable, the operation is treated as incompatible.

We implement this logic in a method **checkCompatible** as follows:

```
private boolean checkCompatible(DropTargetDragEvent dtde) {
    DataFlavor[]
    dataFlavors=dtde.getCurrentDataFlavors();
                    // get the array of data flavors of the
                       object
        // associated with the operation
    Boolean isCompatible=false;
                    // variable to indicate a compatible
                       operation
    for(int i=0;i<dataFlavors.length;i++) {
        if (number.isDataFlavorSupported(dataFlavors[i]))
        {
                isCompatible=true;
        }
    }
    // check whether the action is compatible
    if ((dtde.getSourceActions()&allowedActions)==0) {
```

```
            isCompatible=false;
    }
    // check whether both compatibility conditions are
       satisfied
    // and accept or reject the operation
    if (isCompatible) {
            dtde.acceptDrag(allowedActions);
    } else {
            dtde.rejectDrag();
    }
    return isCompatible;
}
```

This method checks compatibility of the operation and accepts or rejects the operation. It is used by the **dragEnter** and **dragOver** callback methods of the **DropTargetListener** interface. The operation is accepted or rejected by calling the **acceptDrag** or **rejectDrag** methods of the **DropTargetDragEvent**. We implement the **dragEnter** callback method as follows:

```
public void dragEnter(DropTargetDragEvent dtde) {
    checkCompatible();
}
```

Keeping Track of the Drag-and-Drop Operation and Providing Feedback

Once the operation is accepted, the **Receiver** is notified of the status of the operation via the other callback methods listed:

■ When the hotspot is dragged over the associated component, the method invoked is **public abstract void dragOver (DropTargetDragEvent dtde)**

■ This method is also responsible to validate the compatibility of the operation and either accept or reject it. We implement this method similar to the dragEnter method as:

```
public void dragOver(DropTargetDragEvent dtde) {
    checkCompatible();
}
```

■ When the hotspot intersects the auto-scroll insets of the component and is stationary for a pre-defined period of time, the method invoked is **public abstract void dragScroll(DropTargetDragEvent dtde)**. This method can be used to provide auto-scrolling.

■ When the hotspot exits the associated Component, the method invoked is `public abstract void dragExit(DropTargetDragEvent dtde)`.

Accepting or Rejecting a Drop

When the user initiates a drop, typically by releasing the mouse button, the `Receiver` is notified by the drop method `public abstract void drop(DropTargetDropEvent dtde)`. When this is invoked, the `Receiver` must check whether the operation is compatible and notify the `DropTargetContext`, as in Step 7 of Figure 9-3, whether or not the drop is accepted. Because basic compatibility is guaranteed by the previously called methods, there may be an instance where other factors deem the operation invalid. In such as case, the drop method shall reject the drop by calling `void DropTargetDropEvent.rejectDrop()`. Otherwise, it can accept the drop by calling `void DropTargetDropEvent.acceptDrop()`.

Transfering the Data and Ending the Operation

Once the drop is accepted, the `Receiver` can retrieve the `Transferable` object from the method `Transferable DropTargetDropEvent. getTransferable()`. The `Transferable` object has the method `Object Transferable.getTransferData(DataFlavor flavor)` to retrieve the data associated with any `DataFlavor` that is mutually acceptable by the `Sender` and the `Receiver`.

Once the data transfer is completed, the `Receiver` can notify the `DropTargetContext`, as in Step 7 of Figure 9-3, that the operation has completed by invoking the method `void DropTargetContext. dropComplete(boolean success)`. The parameter indicates the success of the data transfer.

We implement these steps in the drop callback method as follows:

```
public abstract void drop(DropTargetDropEvent dtde) {
        dtde.acceptDrop(allowedActions);
        Transferable transObject=dtde.getTransferable();

        DropTargetContext dt=dtde.getDropTargetContext();
                // retrieve the DropTargetContext associated
                   with the operation
        dt.dropComplete(true);
}
```

All the code for the DnDReceiver class is in Listing 9-5.

```java
import java.awt.*;
import java.awt.event.*;
import java.awt.datatransfer.*;
import java.awt.dnd.*;
import NumberData;
import java.lang.reflect.*;

class DnDReceiver extends Frame implements
    DropTargetListener {

  DropTarget dropTarget=null;
    int lastDropEvent=-1;
    NumberData number=null;
  int allowedActions=DnDConstants.ACTION_MOVE|
   DnDConstants.ACTION_COPY;

    public DnDReceiver(String title) {
        super(title);
        dropTarget=new DropTarget(this,allowedActions,
                                  this);
    }

    private boolean checkCompatible(DropTargetDragEvent
                                    dtde) {
      DataFlavor[] dataFlavors=dtde.
      getCurrentDataFlavors();
        // get the array of data flavors of the
        // object associated with the operation
      boolean isCompatible=false;
        // variable to indicate a compatible operation
      for(int i=0;i<dataFlavors.length;i++) {
          if (number.isDataFlavorSupported
          (dataFlavors[i])) {
              isCompatible=true;
          }
      }
      // check whether the action is compatible
      if ((dtde.getSourceActions()&allowedActions)==0) {
          isCompatible=false;
      }
      // check whether both compatibility conditions are
      // satisfied and accept or reject the operation
      if (isCompatible) {
          dtde.acceptDrag(allowedActions);
      } else {
          dtde.rejectDrag();
      }
      return isCompatible;
    }
```

Listing 9-5

```java
public void dragEnter(DropTargetDragEvent dtde) {
        if (lastDropEvent!=6)
        {System.out.println("DropTarget:Drag
        Enter");lastDropEvent=6;}
        if (checkCompatible(dtde)) {
                if (lastDropEvent!=7)
                {System.out.println("DropTarget:Accept
                Drag");lastDropEvent=7;}
        }
    }

public void dragOver(DropTargetDragEvent dtde) {
        if (lastDropEvent!=8)
        {System.out.println("DropTarget:Drag
        Over");lastDropEvent=8;}
        checkCompatible(dtde);
    }

public void dragScroll(DropTargetDragEvent dtde) {
        if (lastDropEvent!=9)
        {System.out.println("DropTarget:Drag
        Scroll");lastDropEvent=9;}
        checkCompatible(dtde);
    }

public void dragExit(DropTargetEvent dte) {
        if (lastDropEvent!=10)
        {System.out.println("DropTarget:Drag
        Exit");lastDropEvent=10;}
    }

public void drop(DropTargetDropEvent dtde) {
        if (lastDropEvent!=11) {System.out.println
        ("DropTarget:Drop");lastDropEvent=11;}
        dtde.acceptDrop(allowedActions);
        DropTargetContext
        dt=dtde.getDropTargetContext();
            // retrieve the DropTargetContext
                associated with the operation number=
                (NumberData)dtde.getTransferable();
        dt.dropComplete(true);
            if (lastDropEvent!=12)
            {System.out.println("DropTarget:Accept
            Drop");lastDropEvent=12;}
    }

public static void main(String[] args) {
    DnDReceiver test = new DnDReceiver("DnDReceiver");
    test.show();
        test.setSize(300,300);
   }
}
```

CONCLUSION

We have seen in this chapter how drag-and-drop functionality can be provided in a step-by-step manner. The basic functionality illustrated in the code developed in this chapter can be applied to any component so as to provide drag-and-drop functionality. To summarize, a component can either implement drag-and-drop as a sender or a receiver or both. To provide sender functionality, we can use a static **DragSource** object and implement the **DragSourceListener** interface. This interface provides all the callback methods, which allows the component to keep track of the drag-and-drop operation.

To provide receiver functionality, we need to create a **DropTarget** intance for each component that can receive drag-and-drop operations. A **DropTarget** object when associated with the component exposes the component to act as a drag-and-drop receiver. We need to implement the **DropTargetListener** interface, which contains callback methods for handling drag-and-drop events.

At the time of this writing, the JDK 1.2 beta 2 is the latest version released. Unfortunately, drag-and-drop is supposed to be completed only in beta 3. Hence, though the structures and classes have been provided, they do not completely work as expected. Therefore we have not been able to create a better example that demonstrates an actual working application. The sources of **DnDSender** and **DnDReceiver** have been provided, and it is hoped that they will work when compiled in beta 3.

10

Creating an Advanced Java Bean Component

In this chapter we will be using the skills learned in previous chapters to create an advanced JavaBean with Beans 1.1-specific features, such as drag-and-drop, the Java Activation Framework, and the Runtime Containment and Services Protocol. These new features build on the existing capabilities of JavaBeans, adding important capabilities to the existing ones provided by JavaBeans. These new services are designed with the original goals of JavaBeans—developers should be able to quickly start using these new controls without the steep learning curves of other component architectures common in the computer industry.

In this chapter, we will be using the skills learned in previous chapters to create an advanced JavaBeans 1.1 application. This application will be a "smart" file browser, with the capability to load different editors and viewers, depending on the MIME type of the file being loaded. We will also develop our own custom file format, a simple graphics file format with an associated viewer. This file browser applet will be packaged and digitally signed using the JAR tool.

Note that at the time of writing, JDK 1.2 was still in Beta, and not all features were present. Unfortunately, because most visual development environments (such as IBM's VisualAge for Java, or Symantec's Visual Cafe Pro) do not support JDK 1.2 yet, we will not be able to use them for this demonstration.

This Chapter Covers

- The application architecture
- The **BoxImage** Viewer
- The File Viewer
- Adding Drag and Drop Functionality

The Application Architecture

The architecture of the application is quite simple. It is split into the following components:

- The **FileViewer** application is our main application, and it enables us to list and view files on our system. Depending on the MIME type of the file, it launches and displays the appropriate file viewer. The **FileViewer** also enables us to drag-and-drop files to launch the viewers.
- The **BoxImage** bean is a custom file format, which defines a **BoxImage** and provides classes for viewing the **BoxImage** files.

Following is a screenshot of the **FileViewer** in action, with text indicating pertinent areas.

The **BoxImage** Viewer

This example has some parts to it. Let's see them seperately.

Figure 10-1
Important areas of
the **FileViewer**
application.

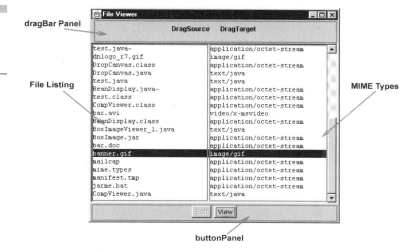

Listing 10-1
A **BoxImage** file.

```
window 200 300
rect 5 5 10 10 125 125 125
rect 20 105 100 100 15 88 200
rect 150 100 50 60 89 200 125
The structure of the file is as follows:
The size of the window to display the BoxImage, in Pixels
window WIDTH HEIGHT
        One or more rectangles, and their color.
            rect X Y WIDTH HEIGHT RED GREEN BLUE
```

The **BoxImage** File Format

The custom application viewer we will develop in this chapter is a simple
raster graphics file format consisting of colored rectangles. This type of
graphics format is quite common—Postscript is an ASCII file format that
consists of graphics primitives and instructions to a preprocessor that ras-
terizes the image into something a screen or printer can understand. This
example is much simpler than PostScript, but it should give you an idea
of what is involved in developing this kind of image file. Listing 10-1
shows a sample **BoxImage** file.

Colors for the rectangles are specified in standard RGB format, with
integers ranging from 0–255. It would not be difficult to extend this file
format to include several other types of shapes, such as ovals or lines.

The BoxImage File

After the file format has been decided, we can now create the BoxImage class, which reads these BoxImage files and constructs an object based on the BoxImage file information. Listing 10-2 shows BoxImage.java.

Listing 10-2
Source to
BoxImage.java,
the class that reads
the **BoxImage** file.

```java
import java.io.*;
import java.awt.*;
import java.util.StringTokenizer;
import java.util.Vector;

public class BoxImage {
    public Dimension windowSize;
    public Vector rectInfo = new Vector();
    public Vector rectColors = new Vector();

    // Main method for testing purposes
    public static void main(String args[]) {
        File boxfile = new File("test.box");
        BoxImage bi = new BoxImage(boxfile);
    }


    // Constructor for our class
    public BoxImage(File filename) {
        String line;
        int i = 0;

        try {
            FileReader fr = new
                            FileReader(filename);
            BufferedReader bf = new
                            BufferedReader(fr);

            line = bf.readLine();

            // Takes the first line and sets the
               size
            setSize(line);

            // Loads the next section of rectangles
            line = bf.readLine();
            while (line != null) {
                addRectangle(line);
                line = bf.readLine();
            }
        } catch (Exception e) {
            e.printStackTrace();
        }
```

Listing 10-2

```
        }

        // Method to add rectangles
        private void addRectangle(String line) {
            Rectangle tempRect;
            Color tempColor;
            int x,y,w,h,r,g,b;

            // Parse file
            StringTokenizer parser = new
        StringTokenizer(line);
            try {
                if ( !(parser.nextElement().equals
                    ("rect")) ) {
                    throw new IllegalArgumentException
                    ("Bad file format");
                }

                x = Integer.parseInt( (String)
                    parser.nextElement());
                y = Integer.parseInt( (String)
                    parser.nextElement());
                w = Integer.parseInt( (String)
                    parser.nextElement());
                h = Integer.parseInt( (String)
                    parser.nextElement());
                r = Integer.parseInt( (String)
                    parser.nextElement());
                g = Integer.parseInt( (String)
                    parser.nextElement());
                b = Integer.parseInt( (String)
                    parser.nextElement());

            } catch (Exception e) {
                    throw new IllegalArgumentException
                    ("Bad file format");
            }

            tempRect = new Rectangle(x,y,w,h);
            tempColor = new Color(r,g,b);

            rectInfo.addElement(tempRect);
            rectColors.addElement(tempColor);


        }

        // Method to set window size
        private void setSize(String line) {
            int x, y;

            StringTokenizer parser = new
```

Continues

Listing 10-2
Continued.

```
                          StringTokenizer(line);
    try {
        if ( !(parser.nextElement().
            equals("window")) ) {
            throw new IllegalArgumentException
            ("Bad file format");
        }

        x = Integer.parseInt( (String) parser.
                            nextElement());
        y = Integer.parseInt( (String) parser.
                            nextElement());


    } catch (Exception e) {
            throw new IllegalArgumentException
            ("Bad file format");
    }

    windowSize = new Dimension(x,y);

}

// Return Window information
public Dimension getSize() {
    return windowSize;
}

// Return vector of rectangles
public Vector getRectInfo() {
    return rectInfo;
}

// Return vector of rectangle colors
public Vector getRectColors() {
    return rectColors;
}
}
```

Let's take a look at this code to see what is happening.

The first thing we do is declare our variables. In this case, we have a **Dimension** object that contains the size of our **BoxImage,** and two Vectors, **rectInfo** and **rectColors,** which contain the information for the rectangles contained within our **BoxImage.** Following this we have a main method used for testing purposes.

The constructor for our **BoxImage** class takes a file as an argument. This file should correspond to the **BoxImage** file we are working with. We use a **BufferedReader** to load the file because a **BufferedReader** enables us to look at each file line by line.

TIP: *By adding a* **main** *method to the various classes as you are developing them, we greatly speed up the testing and debugging process. We can in this way ensure that the individual components work as expected outside of their intended environments, and we can know they will work after we have connected them together. This also speeds up development for programmers who will "inherit" your code because they will quickly be able to see how each component is expected to perform.*

The first line in the file should be the definition for the size of the **BoxImage**. We use a method called **setSize** to set the **windowSize** variable, and we then iterate over the rest of the file, loading the rectangle information into the Vectors. The **addRectangle** method uses a **StringTokenizer** to break the line on spaces into the individual elements, and through an **IllegalArgumentException** error if there is a problem with the file format. After this information has been successfully retrieved, the Rectangle is added to our **rectInfo** Vector.

Following these methods, we have the necessary **get** and **set** methods for our bean. These allow classes that are planning to read the **BoxImage** file format the capability to retrieve information on the **BoxImage** file structure.

The **BoxImage** Viewer

Now that we have an object that can read the information presented in the **.box** file, we need a way to display the information to the screen. The **BoxImageViewer** component enables us to do this by instantiating a **BoxImage** Canvas and adding it to the screen.

As the code indicates, **BoxImageCanvas** extends Canvas and takes a **BoxImage** object and paints it onto itself. The constructor takes one argument, a **BoxImage** object. The bulk of the work is performed by the **paint** method, which takes our **BoxImage** object and reads in the Vectors containing the rectangle information. The **paint** method then iterates through each of the Rectangles in the Vector and paints them to the screen.

Note how we are developing these classes: **BoxImage** stores the information on the structure of the files, **BoxImageCanvas** knows how to paint them, and **BoxImageViewer** brings it all together in a bean that can display these files. It is good practice to split these roles across several different classes.

```
import java.awt.*;
import java.util.Vector;


class BoxImageCanvas extends Canvas {
    BoxImage bi;

    public BoxImageCanvas(BoxImage boximg) {
        bi = boximg;
    }

    public void paint(Graphics g) {
        Vector rectInfo = bi.getRectInfo();
        Vector rectColor = bi.getRectColors();
        Color tempColor;
        Rectangle tempRect;


        // Iterate through the vector of rectangles,
        // // painting each one
        for (int i=0; i < rectInfo.size(); i++) {
            try {
                tempColor = (Color)
                rectColor.elementAt(i);
                tempRect = (Rectangle)
                rectInfo.elementAt(i);

                // Set the color from the rectangle
                // colors vector
                g.setColor(tempColor);
                g.fillRect(tempRect.x,tempRect.y,
                        tempRect.width,
                        tempRect.height);
            } catch (Exception e) {
                e.printStackTrace();
            }
        }
    }
}
```

The **BoxImageViewer** brings together all the elements we have constructed so far and finishes off our bean. This viewer extends several objects: **ActionListener**, **CommandObject**, and **java.io.Serializable**. The first and the last aren't too surprising, but **CommandObject** is new. **CommandObject** is a part of the Java Activation framework, and it is this object that gives us the capability to determine at run time how the object is being called.

Listing 10-4
BoxImageViewer.
java

```java
import java.awt.*;
import java.awt.event.*;
import java.io.File;
import javax.activation.*;
import java.beans.*;

public class BoxImageViewer extends Frame implements
        ActionListener,
    CommandObject, java.io.Serializable {
    DataHandler dh;
    String verb;

    // Implement the CommandObject interface to get
    // information from the application framework
    public void setCommandContext(String _verb,
    DataHandler _dh) {
        verb = _verb;
        dh = _dh;
    }

    // Main method for testing purposes
    public static void main(String args[]) {
        if (args.length == 0 ) {
            System.out.println("usage: LineImage
                        file.box");
            System.exit(1);
        }

        File boxFile = new File(args[0]);
        BoxImage boxImg = new BoxImage(boxFile);
        BoxImageViewer biv = new BoxImageViewer(boxImg);
    }

    // Create a new instance of our viewer
    public BoxImageViewer() {
        try {
            BoxImage tempBI = (BoxImage)
                        dh.getContent();
            BoxImageViewer biv = new
                        BoxImageViewer(tempBI);

        } catch (Exception e) {
            e.printStackTrace();
        }
    }


    // Main Constructor for our class
    public BoxImageViewer(BoxImage bi) {
```

Continues

Listing 10-4
Continued.

```
        Button okButton;

        BoxImageCanvas boxCanvas = new
                            BoxImageCanvas(bi);
        add("Center", boxCanvas);

        Panel p = new Panel();
        p.setBackground(Color.lightGray);
        okButton = new Button("OK");
        okButton.addActionListener(this);
        p.add(okButton);

        add("South", p);

        this.setTitle("Box Image");
        this.setSize(bi.getSize());
        this.setVisible(true);
        enableEvents(AWTEvent.WINDOW_EVENT_MASK);
    }

    // Handle the window close event
    protected void processWindowEvent (WindowEvent e) {
        if (e.getID() == WindowEvent.WINDOW_CLOSING) {
                this.setVisible(false);
        }
        super.processWindowEvent(e);
    }

    // Handle the button click event
    public void actionPerformed(ActionEvent e) {
        this.setVisible(false);
    }
}
```

The first method, `setCommandContext`, is from the `CommandObject` interface and is called through the activation framework. This call tells our object information on its environment; in our case, it informs the Viewer the name of the `BoxImage` it is being called to view.

After our `main` method (used again for testing purposes) we have our `constructor` method, which takes no arguments and is required for proper implementation of the `CommandObject` interface. Following the null argument constructor, we have our main constructor that takes a `BoxImage` object as an argument. This constructor then proceeds to add a `BoxImageCanvas` to itself, and an OK button to dismiss the viewer when the user is ready to close the window. The event handling code for the window close and the button push follows.

Packaging our Bean

Now that we have our viewer, we need to package it as a bean, along with some ancillary files, so that the Java Activation Framework can access the viewer. The first file we need is the **mime.types** file, containing information on the MIME types. Create this in the META-INF subdirectory from where the Java files are created.

Type the following into a file called mime.types in the META-INF subdirectory:

```
type=application/x-boximage desc="Box Image" exts=box
```

Type the following into the mailcap file in the META-INF subdirectory:

```
application/x-boximage; ; x-java-View=BoxImageViewer
```

Finally, we need the manifest.tmp file for our bean:

```
Manifest-Version: 1.0

Name: BoxImageViewer.class
Java-Bean: True

Name: BoxImage.class

Name: BoxImageCanvas.class

META-INF/mailcap
META-INF/mime.types
```

Now that we have created the necessary files for our bean, we jar up the files using the following jar command:

```
jar cfm BoxImage.jar manifest.tmp BoxImageViewer.class
        BoxImage.class BoxImageCanvas.class META-
        INF/mime.types META-INF/mailcap
```

We now have a bean capable of reading and viewing **BoxImage** files, but in order for others to guarantee it's authenticity, we are now going to sign it digitally.

Signing the Bean

To sign our bean digitally, we are going to use the keytool and jarsigner utilities that ship as a part of the JDK 1.2. Note that these tools replace the javakey tool from JDK 1.1—keytool and jarsigner add more functionality, but, unfortunately, the key storage mechanisms are not backward-compatible.

A digital signature is composed of two elements: an object being signed (in this case, our `.jar` file), and a private key of the entity signing the jar file. Combined, the digital signature has the following characteristics:

- *Authenticity:* after a file has been signed digitally, it is possible to verify who signed it.
- *Security:* assuming that the private key is kept private, a digital signature cannot be forged.
- *Tamper-proof:* after data has been signed, it cannot be changed without destroying the signature.

Clearly, digital signatures are an important addition to a developer's arsenal. Digital signatures enable end users to have assurances that the code was developed by a trusted third party, and that it has not been modified in any way. The technology used by JavaBeans is similar to Microsoft's Authenticode technology and Netscape's Object Signing. Unfortunately, although the design of each of these technologies is similar, the implementations are slightly different.

Jar files use a technology known as **Public/Private key cryptography**. This type of cryptography, created by RSA, is currently the most popular on the Internet. It is used by secure web browsers, and by applications such as PGP (Pretty Good Privacy). Briefly, the technology works as follows:

1. A user generates a public and private key. The public key is used for verification; the private key is used for encryption.

2. When it comes time to encrypt a file, the user uses the private key to scramble the contents of the file digitally. Technically speaking, public key cryptography uses the products of very large prime numbers to prevent decryption.

3. When another user receives the file, they are able to use the combination of the original user's public key and the signed code to verify that the user is indeed who they say they are.

In step 1, the public key needs to be verified by a trusted third party. This allows a "web of trust" to be built, which works under the following assumption: if I "trust" entity A, I also trust anyone entity A entrusts. For the case of digital signatures, the company most relied on for trust typically has been the commercial company Verisign. If Verisign is not necessary (for example, a digitally signed applet that is only needed to run within an organization), the certificate can be signed internally.

THE keytool   For the management of keys, a key must first be created using **keytool**. **keytool** gives users the ability to manage their public/private key pairs and associated authentication certificates. Remember that the key pair is generated by the user, and the certificate is generated by a certificate authority, which states that a public key has a particular attribute (typically verifying the authenticity of the user). The **keytool** stores keys in a **keystore**, where they can be accessed by the **jarsigner** tool.

To create a new self-signed certificate (external verification not required —useful for testing purposes), type the following at the command line:

```
keytool -genkey -alias beancert -storepass keystorepass
    -keypass beancertpasswd
```

The **keytool** then prompts you for information for this certificate and saves it with the alias "beancert," and the password "beancertpasswd." The password for the keystore is defined as "keystorepass." All certificates are accessed through unique case-insensitive aliases. This certificate is stored in the **keystore**, which is kept in a file, **.keystore**, located either in a directory specified by concatenating the HOMEDRIVE and HOMEPATH environment variables, or, if they don't exist, in the root directory of the JDK. On Unix systems, the file is stored in the user's home directory.

The keys are stored using the DSA with SH-1 signature algorithm as a default. Although this is the only format currently supported, there may be more in the future. The size of the key defaults to 1,024 bits, but may range between 512 and 1,024 and must be a multiple of 64 bits.

To display a list of entries in the keystore, type the following on the command line:

```
keytool -list
```

This displays the entire contents of the **keystore**. To view a specific certificate, you can specify it with the **-alias** switch. For example, the following displays only the beancert certificate:

```
keytool -list -alias beancert
```

THE jarsigner TOOL   The **jarsigner** tool has two main functions: to sign JAR files and to verify the integrity and the signatures of JAR files.

Currently, **jarsigner** can only sign JAR files created by the Sun JAR program.

When using **jarsigner** to sign a file, the alias of certificate to be signed with is used. For example, to sign our JAR file using the self-signed certificate **beancert** we created above using **keytool**, we would use the following command:

```
jarsigner -storepass keystorepass  -keypass
      beancertpass -signedjar sBoxImage.jar
BoxImage.jar beancert
```

The file **sBoxImage.jar** will contain our signed JAR file. We could have left this option out, which would have caused our **BoxImage**.jar to be overwritten with the signed JAR file.

VERIFYING SIGNED JAR FILES   We can now verify the JAR file if we want by using the **-verify** option if the verification is successful or else an error message will be displayed.

```
jarsigner -verify sBoxImage.jar
```

should return

```
jar verified
```

If additional output is required, the **-verbose** option can be used, which prints out additional debugging information.

It should be noted that this process does not encrypt the JAR file; simply, it digitally signs the jar for verification. This JAR file can still be used by any JavaBean-enabled tool.

The File Viewer

The next step is to create our main application, the file viewer. This application uses the JavaBeans Activation Framework to decide which viewer to load and display the information.

The **FileViewer** application brings together the beans that we have put together so far and performs the bulk of the work for our application. The first method is our **main** method, required because our **FileViewer** is an application.

Listing 10-5
FileViewer.java

```java
import java.awt.*;
import java.io.*;
import java.beans.*;
import javax.activation.*;
import java.awt.event.*;


public class FileViewer extends Frame implements
      ItemListener, ActionListener {
      Panel dragSrcPanel, dragTgtPanel, dragPanel, dragBar,
      buttonPanel;
      Panel dragSrcBox, dragTgtBox;
      Label dragSrcLbl, dragTgtLbl;
      Button editButton, viewButton;
      List listing;
      File currentDir;
      DataHandler dh[];
      int tabStop = 30;

      // Start up our application
      public static void main(String args[]) {
          FileViewer fv = new FileViewer();
          fv.setTitle("File Viewer");
          fv.setSize(450,400);
          fv.setVisible(true);
      }


      public FileViewer() {
          int i;
          String itemName, itemType, padSpaces;

          createUI();


          currentDir = new File(".");

          // Load our default command map
          MailcapCommandMap cmdmap =
            (MailcapCommandMap)CommandMap.
            getDefaultCommandMap();
          cmdmap.addMailcap("application/x-int;
                        jaf.viewers.IntViewer");

          // Get a directory listing
          String dirFiles[] = currentDir.list();
          MimetypesFileTypeMap map = new
                                    MimetypesFileTypeMap
                                    ();
```

Continues

Listing 10-5
Continued.

```java
        // Add additional mime types
        map.addMimeTypes("text/java java\n");
        map.addMimeTypes("application/x-boximage
                        box\n");
        FileTypeMap.setDefaultFileTypeMap(map);

        dh = new DataHandler[dirFiles.length];

        for (i=0; i < dirFiles.length; i++) {

            // For each of the files, find out their
            // mime type and create the datahandler
            // object for them
            FileDataSource fds =
                new FileDataSource
                (currentDir.getAbsolutePath() +
                currentDir.separator + dirFiles[i]);
            dh[i] = new DataHandler(fds);
            dh[i].setCommandMap(cmdmap);
            itemName = dh[i].getName();
            itemType = dh[i].getContentType();
            if (itemType == null) {
                itemType = "unknown";
            }

            // Calculate the number of spaces
            // necessary to line up the mime types
            padSpaces = calcSpaces(itemName);

            // Add the file and mime type to the list
            listing.add(dh[i].getName() + padSpaces +
            itemType);
        }

    }


// This is a helper method to build the user
// interface
public void createUI() {

    // Create the dragsource box

    Font labelFont = new Font("Times", Font.BOLD,
                            12);
    Font listingFont = new Font("Courier",
                                Font.PLAIN, 12);

    // These panels will be where the files can be
    // dragged and dropped to/from.  This is
    // currently not implemented.
    dragSrcPanel = new Panel();
```

Listing 10-5

```
dragSrcPanel.setLayout(new BorderLayout(0,0));
dragSrcPanel.setBackground((new Color(85, 160,
                           90)).brighter());
dragSrcLbl = new Label("DragSource");
dragSrcLbl.setFont(labelFont);
dragSrcLbl.setAlignment(Label.CENTER);
dragSrcBox = new Panel();

dragSrcPanel.add("North", dragSrcLbl);
dragSrcPanel.add("Center", dragSrcBox);

// Create the dragtarget box

dragTgtPanel = new Panel();
dragTgtPanel.setLayout(new BorderLayout(0,0));
dragTgtPanel.setBackground((new Color(85, 160,
                           90)).brighter());
dragTgtLbl = new Label("DragTarget");
dragTgtLbl.setFont(labelFont);
dragTgtLbl.setAlignment(Label.CENTER);
dragTgtBox = new Panel();

dragTgtPanel.add("North", dragTgtLbl);
dragTgtPanel.add("Center", dragTgtBox);

// Create and add to our top frame.

dragBar = new Panel();
dragBar.setBackground(Color.lightGray);
dragBar.add("East", dragSrcPanel);
dragBar.add("West", dragTgtPanel);
dragBar.setSize(300,800);


// Add to our frame
add("North", dragBar);


// Create our file list window
listing = new List();
listing.setBackground(Color.white);
listing.setFont(listingFont);

add("Center", listing);


// Create our bottom Buttonbar
buttonPanel = new Panel();
buttonPanel.setBackground(Color.lightGray);
editButton = new Button("Edit");
viewButton = new Button("View");
```

Continues

Listing 10-5
Continued.

```
            buttonPanel.add("East", editButton);
            buttonPanel.add("West",viewButton);

            add("South", buttonPanel);

            // Bind our listeners
            enableEvents(AWTEvent.WINDOW_EVENT_MASK);
            listing.addItemListener(this);
            editButton.addActionListener(this);
            viewButton.addActionListener(this);


    }


    // Helper method to space out the display of the
    // files
    public String calcSpaces(String name) {
        String tempString = "";
        int nameLength = name.length();

        for (int i=0; i < (tabStop - nameLength); i++) {
            tempString = tempString + " ";
        }
        return tempString;
    }


    // Window Listener
    protected void processWindowEvent (WindowEvent e) {
        if (e.getID() == WindowEvent.WINDOW_CLOSING) {
            System.exit(0);
        }
        super.processWindowEvent(e);
    }


    // Item Listener - Gets called whenever an item is
    // selected.
    public void itemStateChanged(ItemEvent evt) {

        Integer id = (Integer) evt.getItem();

        if (evt.getStateChange() == ItemEvent.SELECTED)
                                    {
            String mime_type = dh[id.intValue()].
                            getContentType();
            viewButton.setEnabled(false);
            editButton.setEnabled(false);

            if (mime_type != null) {
                // Object has a mime type
                CommandInfo cmdInfo[] = null;

                cmdInfo = dh[id.intValue()].
```

Listing 10-5

```
                                    getPreferredCommands();
                   if (cmdInfo != null && cmdInfo.length
                                 > 0) {
                       // A command exists

                       for (int i = 0; i <
                       cmdInfo.length; i++) {
                              // Enable view button if
                                 view command exists
                              if ((cmdInfo[i].
                              getCommandName()).
                              equals("view")) {
                                   viewButton.
                                   setEnabled(true);
                              } else if ((cmdInfo[i].
                              getCommandName()).
                              equals("edit")) {
                                     // Enable edit button
                                        if edit command
                                        exists
                                     editButton.
                                     setEnabled(true);
                              }
                       }
                   }
               }
       }


       // Action listener - handles view or edit button
       // pushes
       public void actionPerformed(ActionEvent evt) {
            BeanDisplay bd;
            Object itemBean = null;
            Object source = evt.getSource();
            int listItem = listing.getSelectedIndex();

            if ((source == editButton) || (source ==
                                            viewButton)) {
                 CommandInfo cmdInfo[] = dh[listItem].
                                         getPreferredCommands
                                         ();

                 if (cmdInfo.length > 0) {

                      // Get a handle on the appropriate
                      // bean
                      for (int i = 0; i < cmdInfo.length;
                           i++) {
                          if (((cmdInfo[i].
                          getCommandName()).equals
```

Continues

Listing 10-5
Continued.

```
                                    ("view")) &&
                                      (source == viewButton)) {
                                        itemBean = dh[listItem].
                                                      getBean(cmdInfo
                                                        [i]);
                                   } else if (((cmdInfo[i].
                                   getCommandName()).
                                   equals("edit")) &&
                                      (source == editButton)) {
                                        itemBean = dh[listItem].
                                                      getBean(cmdInfo
                                                        [i]);
                                    }
                                }


                                // Open the bean if it is an
                                // externalizable object
                                if (!(itemBean instanceof javax.
                                      activation.CommandObject)) {
                                    if (itemBean instanceof
                                        java.io.Externalizable) {
                                        try {
                                            ((Externalizable)
                                            itemBean).
                                            readExternal(
                                              new
                                              ObjectInputStream(
                                                dh[listItem].
                                                getInputStream())
                                                );
                                        } catch (Exception e) {
                                            e.printStackTrace();
                                        }
                                    }
                                }


                                // Once we have a valid bean, pass it
                                // to the BeanDisplay
                                // class which will display the Bean.
                                bd = new BeanDisplay();
                                bd.loadBean((Component) itemBean);
                                bd.show();
                            }
                        }
                    }
                }
```

The constructor for the **FileViewer** sets up our application. The first call, **createUI()**, is a helper method that lays out the components of

FileViewer. Our **FileViewer** application works only within the current directory. It is left as an exercise to the reader to add the capability to view arbitrary directories.

TIP: *Rather than use the sometimes unwieldy* **GridBag** *layout, we have used a combination of nested layouts to perform the same function. Obviously, this will not work for all layout situations, but it can sometimes speed up GUI design considerably because it enables us to build our GUI from several small pieces, rather than one giant call to* **GridBag.**

The next step is to load our default command map, which is done via a call to the **getDefaultCommandMap()** method of **CommandMap.** We then cast this to a **MailcapCommandMap** object and add our **Mailcap.** After we have this, we can create our array of files in the current directory and create a **MimetypesFileTypeMap.** This provides us with a set of default MIME types, to which we add additional MIMEtypes. These MIME types are added through the **addMimeTypes** call. In this case, we are adding two new MIME types: Java files, with a MIME type of text/java and an extension of **.java,** and **BoxImage** files, with a MIME type of application/x-**boximage,** and a **.box** extension. Now that we have defined our **MimetypesFileTypeMap,** we can set it as our default file map through a call to **setDefaultFileTypeMap.**

The next step is to move through our array of files and determine the MIME type of each of the files. This is done in a **for** loop that steps through each of the files. For each file, a new **FileDataSource** is created, and a DataHandler is set up from this. The **DataHandler** class enables us to determine the types of each of the files. From the **DataHandler** object **dh,** we can get the name of the file and its MIME type.

The file listing is using a standard AWT listbox, which does not have the capability to set columns. To get around this, we switch the font to Courier, a fixed-space font, and use spaces to pad the files out to the correct size. To find out the correct number of spaces to use, we create a helper method called **calcSpaces,** which takes the **itemName** string and returns a string containing enough spaces to evenly pad out the MIME-type display.

The event-handling code for the Window Listener is pretty straightforward—it simply closes our application if the Close button is clicked. The **ItemListener** code is a little more complicated. This code gets called whenever an item is selected. The first thing it does is to get the Integer ID of the item that was selected. It then enables or disables the View or Edit button depending if there exists a viewer for that individual MIME type. It does this by first disabling the **viewButton** and the **editButton,** and then using the **dataHandler** classes to find out which commands the viewer supports. If a viewer exists, the call to **getPreferredCommands()** returns a **CommandInfo** object, which describes the supported commands. If the **commandName** is "view," a viewer bean exists and the **viewButton** is enabled. The same process is then performed for the Edit button.

The **actionPerformed** method handles the cases when either the Edit or View button is pushed. It uses a **BeanDisplay** object (defined below) to handle the actual displaying of the file. The same process as above is performed to ensure that there exists a handler for the type of file that is being displayed. The following call retrieves a reference to our bean object:

```
itemBean = dh[listItem].getBean(cmdInfo[i]);
```

This bean may be an externalizable object, in which case instantiating it will be slightly different. The following code reads in our **Externalizable** object and instantiates it:

```
((Externalizable)itemBean).readExternal(new
        ObjectInputStream(
                dh[listItem].getInputStream()));
```

In most cases, however, the bean will not be **Externalizable**, and we will simply be able to load it. In this case, we are using the **BeanDisplay** method to load our bean.

```
bd = new BeanDisplay();
bd.loadBean((Component) itemBean);
bd.show();
```

The **FileViewer** application uses the **BeanDisplay** object to perform the actual displaying of the beans.

BeanDisplay

BeanDisplay extends Frame and is simply passed a bean, to which it adds to itself and displays the following:

**Listing 10-6
BeanDisplay**

```
import java.awt.*;
import java.awt.event.*;
import java.beans.*;
import java.lang.reflect.Method;
import java.io.*;
import java.awt.event.*;
```

Listing 10-6

```java
public class BeanDisplay extends Frame {

    // Default constructor
    public BeanDisplay(){
        this.setSize(400,400);
        this.setTitle("Bean Component");
        this.setVisible(true);
        enableEvents(AWTEvent.WINDOW_EVENT_MASK);
    }


    // The loadBean method takes the bean that is passed
    // to it, puts a frame around it, and opens it up.
    public void loadBean(Component bean)
    {

        Dimension beanSize;

        // Add the bean to the BeanDisplay Frame
        add("Center", (Component)bean);

        // Check to see if the bean has an preferred
        // size
        beanSize =   ((Component)bean).getPreferredSize();

        if (beanSize.width != 0 && beanSize.height != 0)
        {
                beanSize.height += 40;
                beanSize.width += 15;


                // Set the bean size
                this.setSize( beanSize );
                ((Component) bean).invalidate();
                ((Component)bean).validate();
                ((Component)bean).doLayout();
                show();
        } else {
            this.setSize(this.getSize());
            validate();
        }
    }


    // Handle the window close event
    public void processWindowEvent (WindowEvent e) {
        if (e.getID() == WindowEvent.WINDOW_CLOSING) {
                this.setVisible(false);
        }
        super.processWindowEvent(e);
    }
}
```

Figure 10-2
The **FileViewer** in
action.

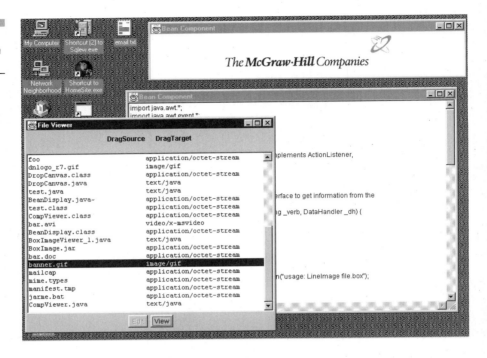

The BeanDisplay object's primary function is **loadBean**, which takes a **Component** as an argument, which is determined through the Activation framework. If the bean has a preferred size, the **BeanDisplay** class changes its size to match the values requested by the bean.

After these files have been compiled, you are able to load a directory of information and view and edit certain files. Be sure to test the file viewer on GIF and JPG files because it has built-in support for these formats (see Figure 10-2).

Adding Drag-and-Drop Functionality

At the time of writing, drag-and-drop was not fully implemented in JDK 1.2 beta 2. Using the methods that are available, the following code example is a good starter. Note that it works only under Windows NT—the same code does not run under Windows 95. These problems should be fixed by the time you read this. To test this bean, select text from an application that supports text dragging and drop it into the main window of the applet. A text viewer should pop up to display the information.

Listing 10-7
DnDTest.java

```java
import java.awt.*;
import java.awt.dnd.*;
import java.awt.datatransfer.*;
import java.awt.event.*;
import java.io.*;

public class DnDTest extends Frame implements
        DropTargetListener {

    DropTarget target;
    TextArea text;
    Panel mypanel;


    // Create our test object
    public Test () {
        mypanel = new Panel();
        target = new DropTarget(mypanel,
                DnDConstants.ACTION_COPY, this);
        target.setActive (true);
        add ("Center", mypanel);
        enableEvents(AWTEvent.WINDOW_EVENT_MASK);
        this.setTitle("Drop items here");
    }

    // Start our application
    public static void main (String args[]) {
        Test f = new Test();
        f.setSize (200, 200);
        f.setVisible (true);
    }

    /// methods in Interface DropTargetListener

    public  void dragEnter (DropTargetDragEvent dtde) {
        System.out.println ("dragEnter");

        // Check to see if we can handle the type of
        // data being dropped
        DataFlavor df[] = dtde.getCurrentDataFlavors();
        for (int i = 0; i < df.length; i++)   {
            // Put code here for handling different
            // flavors of drop
            if ((df[i].getMimeType().
            indexOf("text/plain")) != -1) {
                System.out.println("type is text");
```
Continues

Listing 10-7
Continued.

```
                              dtde.acceptDrag
                              (DnDConstants.ACTION_COPY);
                    return;
              }
         }
         // Reject the drop if we can't handle it.
         dtde.rejectDrag ();

    }

    /// These methods are just for testing purposes.
    /// Note that they must be here in order to fully
    /// implement DropTargetListener

    public  void dragOver (DropTargetDragEvent dtde) {
         // System.out.println ("dragOver");
    }

    public  void dragScroll (DropTargetDragEvent dtde) {
         // System.out.println ("dragScroll");
    }

    public  void dragExit (DropTargetEvent dte) {
         // System.out.println ("dragExit");
    }

    // A drop has occurred
    public  void drop (DropTargetDropEvent dtde) {
         dtde.acceptDrop (DnDConstants.ACTION_COPY);
          System.out.println ("dropped");


         // Get the transferable information
         Transferable trans = dtde.getTransferable();
         DataFlavor df[] = dtde.getCurrentDataFlavors();
         Object obj = null;
         String type = null;

         try {
             for (int i = 0; i < df.length; i++)    {
                 // Put code here for handling
                 // different flavors of drop
                 if ((df[i].getMimeType().
                 indexOf("text/plain")) != -1) {
                     // Type is text
                     System.out.println("type is
                                           text");
                     type = "text";
                     obj = trans.
                           getTransferData(df[i]);
                 }
             }
```

Listing 10-7

```java
                         // Load the text if our type has been
                         // called
                         if (type.equals("text")) {
                              loadText(obj);
                         }


               } catch (Exception e) {
                      e.printStackTrace();
               } finally {
                      try {
                              target.getDropTargetContext().
                              dropComplete(true);
                      } catch (Exception ignore) {}
               }
        }


        // Load our text into separate bean
        private void loadText(Object obj) {
              if (obj != null && obj instanceof InputStream) {
                      InputStream input = (InputStream) obj;
                      StringBuffer str = new StringBuffer();
                      byte[] buffer = new byte[64];

                      try {
                              int count = input.read(buffer);
                              while (count != -1) {
                                      str.append (new String (buffer,
                                             0, count));
                                      count = input.read(buffer);
                              }
                              input.close();
                              TextBean textBean = new TextBean();
                              textBean.setDisplayText
                              (str.toString());

                      } catch (java.io.IOException e) {
                              e.printStackTrace();
                      }
              }
        }

        // Handle the window close event
        protected void processWindowEvent (WindowEvent e) {
              if (e.getID() == WindowEvent.WINDOW_CLOSING)
                      System.exit(0);
              super.processWindowEvent (e);
        }

}
```

TextBean

TextBean supports the displaying of the text from the drag-and-drop operation.

Listing 10-8
TextBean.java

```java
import java.awt.*;
import java.awt.event.*;
import java.io.*;

public class TextBean extends Frame implements
      ActionListener,
  java.io.Serializable {
    // These bean pops up to display the dropped text

    TextArea text;
    Button okButton;

    // Create and layout our bean
    public TextBean () {
        text = new TextArea();
        add ("Center", text);

        Panel p = new Panel();
        p.setBackground(Color.lightGray);
        okButton = new Button("OK");
        okButton.addActionListener(this);
        p.add(okButton);

        add("South", p);

        this.setTitle("Text Information");
        this.setSize(400,200);
        this.setVisible(true);
        enableEvents(AWTEvent.WINDOW_EVENT_MASK);
    }


    // Change the text
    public void setDisplayText(String textString) {
        text.setText(textString);
    }


    // Handle the window close event
    protected void processWindowEvent (WindowEvent e) {
        if (e.getID() == WindowEvent.WINDOW_CLOSING) {
            this.setVisible(false);
        }
        super.processWindowEvent (e);
    }
```

Listing 10-8

```
// Handle the button pushed event
public void actionPerformed(ActionEvent e) {
        this.setVisible(false);
}

}
```

CONCLUSION

In this chapter, we provided you ideas on how to create beans using the JavaBeans 1.1 spec. You have to understand that JavaBeans is an ever-changing technology. As more specs and changes become available, you should customize your beans using those changes. That way, you will be on top of new and interesting features of JavaBeans.

The next two chapters talk about distributed programming with JavaBeans.

RMI and JavaBeans

JavaBeans will be used pervasively to implement both the client and server sides of future distributed applications. At some level, beans running on the client side need to communicate with beans running on the server side and vice versa. Thus RMI (remote method invocation) will play an important role in many of the JavaBeans you write or purchase. You can think of RMI as the object model equivalent of RPC (remote procedure call). A **remote procedure call** allows one application to call another running on a remote platform—that is, the server. If Java is running on the server also, methods can be invoked directly on the server objects via RMI instead of having to resort to RPC or CORBA. Although CORBA provides language-neutral access to remote objects, RMI will suffice nicely because we are concerned here only with Java-to-Java interaction.

RMI allows methods of remote objects to be invoked just as if they were executing locally in the same Java VM (virtual machine). Without the RMI abstraction, an application would have to develop specific protocols for communicating via sockets to remote applications or perhaps resort to JNI (Java Native Interface) for RPC, or IDL and CORBA. RMI eliminates these complications, greatly simplifying remote programming by using an object model for remote objects that is essentially the same as that which is used with local objects. RMI utilizes internally both the object serialization API to marshal parameters and the network transport API to communicate between platforms.

Traditionally, client/server architecture has been two-tiered, meaning the client or first tier embodied not only the GUI presentation code but the business rules as well. The application's data resided in databases back on one or more servers constituting the second tier. With various client screens all containing similar business logic, there is a great deal of redundancy—that is, poor encapsulation—with this approach. Thus client/server architecture based on two-tier is inherently difficult to maintain or extend because required changes to business logic for any one screen may effect a multiple of screens. Replicating these changes in a variety of client views is not only tedious but time-consuming and error-prone.

The three-tiered architectural approach instead takes the business logic formerly held within the client and places it in the middle on application servers. With three-tiered architecture, the GUI views, business rules, and data representation are minimally coupled to one another and maximally factored. Factoring has to do with extracting common behavior and encapsulating it at a common point. The business rules are factored out of the client view and encapsulated in an application server layer—that is, the middle tier. Minimal coupling and encapsulation make applications much easier to maintain, and factoring encourages reuse of code.

The three-tiered approach also enhances security, especially when client views lie outside the firewall, such as is the case with extranet applications. Corporate databases should never be indiscriminately exposed to either intranets or extranets. By forcing client views to feed through application servers, security can be tighter than that provided simply by the DBMS.

The three-tiered approach may also reduce the number of licenses required for accessing DB servers. Instead of requiring one license per client, only one license per application server accessing the DB is required. This could prove to be a substantial savings, at least until the DB vendors catch on.

Figure 11-1
N-tier with RMI

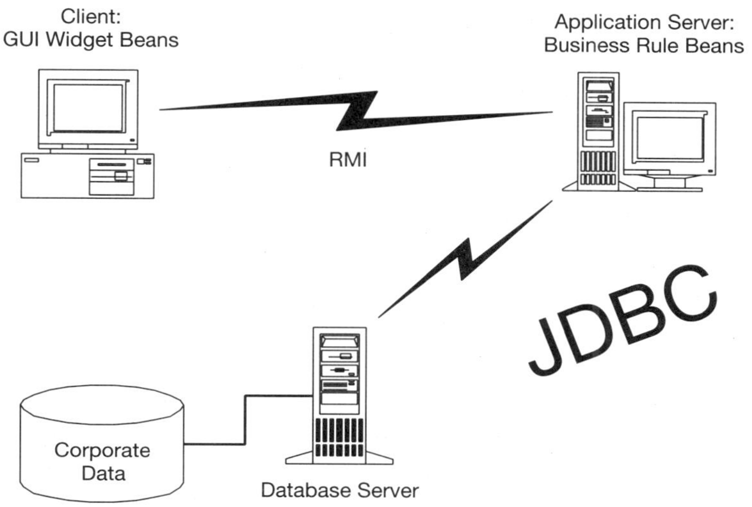

Client:
GUI Widget Beans

RMI

Application Server:
Business Rule Beans

JDBC

Corporate
Data

Database Server

It is not uncommon for the middle tier of the three-tier architecture to unfold into a community of application servers, thus giving rise to *n*-tier architecture.

JavaBean components are destined to become the major building blocks of *n*-tier distributed applications. RMI will be used extensively for inter-platform, bean-to-bean communication (see Figure 11-1). IBM is currently developing an extensive catalog of reusable beans with their San Francisco Project. Currently with more than 150 supporting and contributing vendors, the project promises to leverage programmer productivity greatly. Likewise, as Netscape's crossware vision takes hold, JavaBeans will be everywhere!

This Chapter Covers

- Steps to using RMI
- Generic remote wrappers
- Chat
- Chat as an applet
- Other remote paradigms

Steps to Using RMI

In the example that follows, we will develop a remotely accessible **TextArea** widget in order to demonstrate the use of RMI. The **TextArea** server will allow one or more clients to write to its display area. The several steps necessary to use RMI in any application are outlined below.

Declaring a Remote Interface

The first step necessary in making an object remotely accessible is to define its remote interface. The methods of this interface are precisely those methods on the server object that can be remotely invoked by a client. The fields of a remote object may not be remotely accessed, but neither can fields be specified in an interface except as constants. An interface, therefore, is the perfect language mechanism for representing the client's view of a remote object.

The **RemoteTextArea** interface (see Listing 11-1) has only the **getText()** and **setText()** methods, which is sufficient to demonstrate RMI fundamentals and yet still be reasonably useful. A complete remote interface would include all the methods of **TextArea** that might need to be called remotely. Implementing such a complete remote interface could prove to be a laborious task, especially for a more sophisticated component. (The **RemoteView** and **RemoteModel** classes developed in a later example will show a way to get around this problem.)

Notice that a remote interface must extend the **java.rmi.Remote** interface either directly or indirectly (see Listing 11-1). The **Remote** interface is simply a tagging interface (that is, no methods) to indicate programmatically that an interface may be invoked remotely. This is similar to the **Serializable** interface, which is also a tagging interface with-

Listing 11-1
RemoteTextArea
Interface.

```
import java.rmi.*;

public interface RemoteTextArea
   extends Remote
{
   public String getText() throws RemoteException;
   public void setText(String text) throws RemoteException;
}
```

out which an object may not be serialized. Programmatically, the **instanceof** operator can be used to determine whether an object implements a tagging interface.

Each method of a remote interface must declare the throwing of the **RemoteException**. If an error occurs during the execution of a remote call, it is caught and rewrapped in an instance of **RemoteException** that is subsequently thrown to the calling client. For example, an exception thrown by the underlying network transport is rewrapped in this manner. Because it is not always possible to determine when an exception is thrown —before, during, or after the remote call has completed, for example—it is necessary to keep this in mind when designing or using remote interfaces. Suppose that **increment()** is a remote method that returns its associated value after incrementing. If an **RemoteException** were thrown, was the value incremented or not? Does it even matter in your design?

It is conceivable that a remotely invoked method could throw other exceptions. These must be declared along with their respective methods in the remote interface. The RMI mechanism takes care of capturing these exceptions and transporting them back to the client where they are rethrown just as if they had occurred on the local machine.

Implementing the Remote Interface

The second step in making an object remotely accessible is to implement the remote interface declared in the previous step. Our **TextAreaServer** class implements the **RemoteTextArea** interface while extending the **java.rmi.server.UnicastRemoteObject** (see Listing 11-2). The constructor of **UnicastRemoteObject** automatically exports the **TextAreaServer** object to the RMI runtime thread. The act of exporting causes the server object to be assigned a unique object ID from which it can be identified later by incoming remote method calls. When an object ID is combined with the IP address of the server platform, it naturally forms a globally unique object ID. Conceptually, the **UnicastRemoteObject** class supports peer-to-peer active object references; that is, the server object must be actively executing when a remote method call comes in. It is envisioned that later versions of RMI will support the dynamic loading and load balancing (replication) of server objects. The **UnicastRemoteObject** class is so named to distinguish it from these anticipated cases. The constructor of **TextAreaServer** must declare the throwing of **RemoteException** because the inherited constructor of **UnicastRemoteObject** does.

```
import java.awt.*;
import java.awt.event.*;
import java.rmi.*;
import java.rmi.server.*;

public class TextAreaServer
  extends UnicastRemoteObject
  implements RemoteTextArea
{
  public final TextArea textArea = new TextArea();

  public TextAreaServer() throws RemoteException
    {}

  public String getText() throws RemoteException
  {
    return textArea.getText();
  }

  public void setText(String text) throws RemoteException
  {
    textArea.setText(text);
  }

  public static void main(String args[])
  {
    try {
      TextAreaServer server = new TextAreaServer();
      Naming.rebind("TextAreaServer",server);
      Frame f = new Frame("TextAreaServer");
      f.addWindowListener
        (
          new WindowAdapter()
          {
            public void windowClosing(WindowEvent e)
              { System.exit(0); }
          }
        );
      f.add("Center",server.textArea);
      f.pack();
      f.setVisible(true);
    } catch (Exception e)   {
      e.printStackTrace();
      System.exit(0);
    }
  }
}
```

Because **TextAreaServer** is derived from **UnicastRemoteObject**, it naturally cannot be derived from **TextArea**. Instead of being inherited, the

TextArea is aggregated as a public final field of this class. It is thus directly accessible by the local application, but at the same time the variable reference itself is guaranteed not to change. The **TextAreaServer** simply passes **getText()** and **setText()** calls through to the aggregated, underlying **TextArea** object. An alternative is to derive **TextAreaServer** from **TextArea**, which will be shown shortly.

The **main()** method of **TextAreaServer** demonstrates the use of this class. The **java.rmi.Naming** class is used to bind the name "TextAreaServer" to the **TextAreaServer** stub object. This key-value pair is stored in the RMI registry running on the local platform. The **java.rmi.Naming** class has two methods for binding a name to its associated server, **bind()** and **rebind()**. If a name is already bound, the **bind()** method throws the **AlreadyBoundException**, whereas **rebind()** simply replaces the old binding with the new. Because the example may be run several times without clearing the RMI Registry, the example uses the **rebind()** method to avoid throwing this exception.

The RMI Registry is sometimes referred to as a **bootstrapping registry**. In order to get a conversation started between two platforms, a known point for retrieving the client stub of a remote server must be agreed upon. The RMI Registry serves as this rendezvous point. After the two applications are on speaking terms, subsequent stubs can be returned from other RMI calls without having to resort to an RMI registry. But in order to get the ball rolling, so to speak, the RMI registry allows a distributed application to pull itself up by its bootstraps.

The RMI registry is not to be confused with the RMI runtime. The RMI registry acts like a hashtable, associating names with servers. The RMI registry is itself a remote server returning client stubs for named servers upon request. The RMI runtime, on the other hand, is used to export a server's skeleton so that it can process incoming remote method calls from client stubs. The stub is the representation (proxy) of the server on the client side, whereas the skeleton completes the connection to the actual server object on the server side of the pipe. The client stub marshals the actual parameters to a remote method invocation onto a object stream and then makes the call to the remote server platform. The skeleton on the server side of the pipe unmarshals those parameters and completes the call by invoking the actual method on the server object. The skeleton then marshals the return value, if any, passing it or any exception back over the pipe to the calling stub. The stub completes the call either by returning the return value or throwing the appropriate exception.

The rest of the **main()** method is concerned with constructing a frame in which the **TextArea** activity can be viewed. The **WindowAdapter** added to the frame forces the Java VM to exit upon closing of the demo frame.

Client Access

In order to access the **TextAreaServer** from a client, it is first necessary for the client to install the RMI security manager (see Listing 11-3). This allows the **RMIClassLoader** to load bytecode over the network. Remember the client stub for the **TextAreaServer** must be loaded from the server platform. Installing an RMI security manager was not necessary on the server side because it is only passively awaiting incoming calls and not calling out. (This would not be the case, however, if any of the remote methods on the server take remote parameters. In order to carry out the method call, the stubs of those parameters would then have to be loaded by the server.) Next the client stub for the remote server—that is, **TextAreaServer**—must be obtained from either a returned value from another remote call or via the bootstrapping RMI Registry on the server platform. Once again, the **java.rmi.Naming** class is used—specifically the **lookup()** method—to fetch the **TextAreaServer** stub. Notice that the returned object from **lookup()** is cast to **RemoteTextArea**, the only interface that is allowed to be invoked on the **TextAreaServer** from a remote location.

In this example both the client and server are running on the same platform. Recall in the **TextAreaServer** code that only the name "TextAreaServer" was passed to **Naming.rebind()**:

```
Naming.rebind("TextAreaServer",server);
```

The first parameter passed to the **Naming.rebind()** method is essentially a URL with its suffix segment specifying the name associated with the server object. The prefix of this URL specifies the protocol and the IP address of the platform hosting the RMI registry. In our example, this prefix is conspicuously absent, implying that the local host is where the RMI registry is running. We could have explicitly indicated this by using a fully qualified URL, such as **rmi://127.0.0.1/TextAreaServer**, or **rmi://localhost/TextAreaServer**. Recall in TCP/IP speak that the IP address of the local host is always 127.0.0.1. There is usually a "hosts" file on the local platform that acts as a local DNS (domain naming service) that maps "localhost" to 127.0.0.1. Please note that **bind()**, **rebind()**, and **unbind()** may be called only for the local RMI registry. In other words, servers may only be bound in their local RMI registries.

On the client side, and because both the client and server are presumable running on the same host for demonstration purposes, **Naming.lookup()** is simply called with "TextAreaServer" as the URL.

Listing 11-3
TextAreaClient

```java
import java.rmi.*;
import java.awt.*;
import java.awt.event.*;

public class TextAreaClient
{
  public static void main(String args[])
  {
    System.setSecurityManager(new RMISecurityManager());
    try {
      final RemoteTextArea remoteTextArea =
        (RemoteTextArea) Naming.lookup("TextAreaServer");
      Frame f = new Frame("TextAreaClient");
      f.addWindowListener
        (
          new WindowAdapter()
          {
            public void windowClosing(WindowEvent e)
              { System.exit(0); }
          }
        );
      final TextArea localTextArea = new TextArea();
      localTextArea.setText("Enter text to apply here.");
      localTextArea.selectAll();
      f.add("Center",localTextArea);
      Button apply = new Button("Apply to Server");
      apply.addActionListener
        (
          new ActionListener()
          {
            public void actionPerformed(ActionEvent ae)
            {
              try {
                remoteTextArea.setText(localTextArea.
                                      getText());
              } catch (Exception e) {
                e.printStackTrace(System.out);
              }
            }
          }
        );
      f.add("South",apply);
      f.pack();
      f.setVisible(true);
    } catch (Exception e)  {
      e.printStackTrace();
      System.exit(0);
    }
  }
}
```

Figure 11-2
TextAreaClient
and
TextAreaServer

```
final RemoteTextArea remoteTextArea =
        (RemoteTextArea) Naming.lookup("TextAreaServer");
```

In a real-world scenario, you would need to supply a complete URL. Please note that the suffix or server name may contain embedded spaces or perhaps a fully qualified package name to avoid polluting the name space of the RMI registry.

Most of the remaining code has to do with setting up the client for the user so that text can be pumped interactively to the server. Figure 11-2 shows the interaction between the client and server frames immediately after the client user has entered "Hello remote world!" and clicked the "Apply to Server" button. The remote call is actually made to the **ActionListener** attached to the Apply button:

```
remoteTextArea.setText(localTextArea.getText());
```

The contents of the **localTextArea** are simply copied to the **remoteTextArea** via the remote method **setText()**.

Compiling and Running

The three java source code files must be compiled first, of course:

```
javac   RemoteTextArea.java
javac   TextAreaServer.java
javac   TextAreaClient.java
```

Next, the resulting **TextAreaServer.class** bytecode must be compiled with the RMI stub/skeleton compiler:

```
rmic   TextAreaServer
```

Like the java interpreter, **rmic** requires a fully qualified class name. Had our example been placed in the chapter 11 package, the command line would have been:

```
rmic   chapter11.TextAreaServer
```

The RMI compiler generates both the **stub** and **skeleton** classes:

```
TextAreaServer_stub.class
TextAreaServer_skel.class
```

If you would like to see the generated source code, use the following command line:

```
rmic   -keepgenerated   TextAreaServer
```

You are now ready to run this example. You must start the RMI registry before running **TextAreaServer**, which in turn must be started before running **TextAreaClient**. After all, the **TextAreaServer** must be able to bind the server in the registry. Likewise **TextAreaClient** must be able to find the server stub in the registry. The three command lines would be

```
rmiregistry
java TextAreaServer
java TextAreaClient
```

In Unix, you simply run the first two in the background. Under Windows95/NT, you need to open three DOS windows and execute these three commands in their respective windows.

Without UnicastRemoteObject

It is also possible to avoid having to derive your server implementation from **UnicastRemoteObject** or one of its superclasses—that is, **RemoteServer** or **RemoteObject**. This time our example derives directly from **TextArea** itself (see Listing 11-4). The only requirement is that it must at least implement the **Remote** interface, which it does by virtue of implementing the **RemoteTextArea** (refer to Listing 11-1). Please recall that **RemoteTextArea** extends the **Remote** interface.

TextAreaServer2 must now be explicitly exported to the RMI runtime thread with a call to the static **exportObject()** method of the **UnicastRemoteObject** class:

```
UnicastRemoteObject.exportObject(server);
```

Listing 11-4
TextAreaServer2

```java
import java.awt.*;
import java.awt.event.*;
import java.rmi.*;
import java.rmi.server.*;
import java.rmi.registry.*;

public class TextAreaServer2
  extends TextArea
  implements RemoteTextArea
{
  public TextAreaServer2() throws RemoteException
    {}

  public static void main(String args[])
  {
    try  {
      TextAreaServer2 server = new TextAreaServer2();
      UnicastRemoteObject.exportObject(server);
      try  {
        Naming.rebind("rmi://127.0.0.1:1099/
        TextAreaServer",server);
      } catch (Exception e2)  {
        LocateRegistry.createRegistry(1099);
        Naming.rebind("rmi://127.0.0.1:1099/
        TextAreaServer",server);
      }
      Frame f = new Frame("TextAreaServer");
      f.addWindowListener
        (
          new WindowAdapter()
          {
            public void windowClosing(WindowEvent e)
              { System.exit(0); }
          }
        );
      f.add("Center",server);
      f.pack();
      f.setVisible(true);
    } catch (Exception e)  {
      e.printStackTrace();
      System.exit(0);
    }
  }
}
```

If that's all there is to it, why bother extending **UnicastRemoteObject** to begin with? In a moment, we will examine the differences between the two hierarchies to determine what has been lost.

Next, in the try/catch block, the **rebind()** method of **java.rmi.Naming()** is called:

```
Naming.rebind("rmi://127.0.0.1:1099/TextAreaServer",server);
```

Notice this time that we are using a URL that is fully qualified, including a port number. Currently, the default port number for the RMI registry is 1099 and need not be explicitly spelled out as shown. The default port number is defined as the constant **REGISTRY_PORT** in the **java.rmi.registry.Registry** interface. This begs the question: can more than one RMI server be running on a machine at the same time? The answer is yes, provided that each has a unique listening port. You may encounter unusual application requirements where this capability of being able to segregate name spaces by partitioning across registries comes in handy. The default port and registry is usually sufficient, however. If the RMI registry is not running on the first call to **rebind()**, an exception is thrown and caught. The catch block then starts a RMI registry thread using the **java.rmi.Registry.LocateRegistry** class:

```
LocateRegistry.createRegistry(1099);
Naming.rebind("rmi://127.0.0.1:1099/TextAreaServer",server);
```

If the **createRegistry()** method succeeds without throwing an exception, the attempt to **rebind()** is repeated. The remainder of the code is the same as before. This time, however, we do not need to explicitly run an **rmiregistry** background process. Only the **TextAreaServer2** followed by **TextAreaClient** must be run because **TextAreaServer2** automatically starts the RMI registry. The example runs exactly as before but without the benefit of inheriting from **UnicastRemoteObject**. So what exactly has been lost?

Semantics

Figure 11-3 shows the inheritance tree for the prior example, **TextAreaServer**. Find the **TextAreaServer** class at the bottom of this figure. We can cross check Figure 11-3 with Listing 11-2 and verify that **TextAreaServer** does indeed extend **UnicastRemoteObject** while implementing the **RemoteTextArea** interface. The figure further reveals that **TextAreaServer** inherits from **RemoteObject** the overridden methods:

```
equals()
hashCode()
```

igure 11-3
Inheritance tree

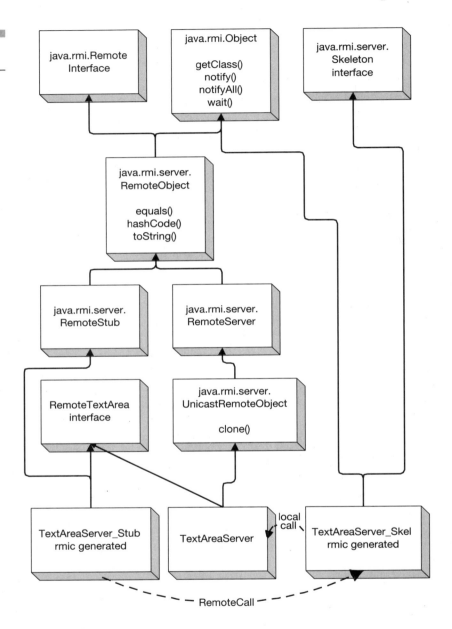

and

```
toString()
```

Notice that the signature of **equals()** as defined in **java.lang.Object** does not allow **RemoteException** to be thrown. In order to compare two remote objects based on content, several remote methods calls would be required, but remote calls must always be allowed to throw at least the **RemoteException**. To work around the problem, the **equals()** method of **RemoteObject** only checks to see whether the remote references are equal —that is, refer to the same global object ID. This is done on the client side without requiring a remote call, thus precluding any possibility of raising a **RemoteException**. Thus the **equals()** method acts like the **==** operator. That is to say that for remote objects, equality is based on identity rather than equivalence of content!

Likewise the **hashCode()** method is overridden so that for all remote references to the same remote object, the **hashCodes** returned are equal. That is, the **hashCode** is derived from the global object ID (resident on the client) rather than resorting to a remote method call or being derived instead from the remote reference object itself. Had **hashCode()** not been overridden, the **hashCode** of two remote object stubs referencing the same remote object would almost never be equal, each having been calculated solely on the reference itself without consideration of the remote objects.

And the **toString()** method includes such items as host name and port number, as well as a remote object identifier.

The only differences that would need to be made to Figure 11-3 to reflect the latter approach taken by **TextAreaServer2** would be to change the three blocks along the bottom of the figure to read **TextAreaServer2_Stub**, **TextAreaServer2**, and **TextAreaServer2_Skel** from left to right. Additionally the line of inheritance, ascending from **TextAreaServer2** up to **UnicastRemoteObject**, would be attached instead to **java.awt.TextArea** (not shown). Thus, with the latter approach, we lose **RemoteObject**'s **equals()**, **hashCode()**, and **toString()**, as well as the automatic call to **exportObject()** found in **UnicastRemoteObject**'s constructor.

Because our **TextAreaClient** does not call **TextAreaServer2_Stub**'s **equals()** or **hashCode()** methods, we're okay. Remember that insertion into **hashtables**, and so forth, causes **hashCode()** to be called. Where in the world did we come up with **TextAreaServer2_Stub**? When **TextAreaClient** retrieves the object reference to **RemoteTextArea**, it is in fact a **TextArea Server2_Stub** when running the latter example (**TextAreaServer_Stub** when running the prior example). That is, if you were to call **getClass()** on the **RemoteTextArea**, it would return the **TextAreaServer2_Stub** metaclass. Therefore, **TextAreaServer2_Stub.equals()** is really **java.lang.Object. equals()**, and we would be checking only for the equality of two object instances if we were to call **equals()**. Therefore, two different remote references to the same remote object would not be recognized as equal in this scenario. However, the latter approach saved us the trouble of redirecting remote calls to **getText()** and **setText()** on to the local **TextArea**.

Figure 11-3 also elucidates some other points we should consider. First, the `clone()` method of `UnicastRemoteObject` takes care of exporting a clone to the RMI runtime thread should your server (that is, the remote object implementation) implement the `Cloneable` interface. However, this type of cloning can be instigated only on the server side itself. The client stub generated by the RMI compiler is declared as final, and unless the remote interface you define extends `java.lang.Cloneable`, the stub may not be cloned. Even so, cloning a client stub only results in the local stub being cloned and not the cloning of the remote object. That is not to say that you could not provide a workaround for remote cloning, but be forewarned and do not blissfully expect more from the Object cloning mechanism than it provides for.

The last point to be gleaned from Figure 11-3 is to consider the semantic shift of certain final methods declared in `java.lang.Object`:

```
getClass(),
notify(),
notifyAll(),
```

and

```
wait().
```

The `getClass()` method returns the stub metaclass on the client side and the implementation metaclass on the server side. By **metaclass**, we mean the `Class` instance of the indicated class. The stub generated by the `rmic` compiler only reflects the remote interfaces implemented by the server and not interfaces local to the server or extensions to base classes implementing remote interfaces.

The `notify()`, `notifyAll()`, and `wait()` methods all have to do with thread synchronization. Please note that synchronizing on a stub protects the stub on the client only and in no way synchronizes the server with regard to other clients.

Generic Remote Wrappers

For every object you want to access remotely via RMI, you need to go through the previously outlined steps: define the remote interface, implement that interface, and compile with `javac`, followed by `rmic`, to generate the stub and skeleton. It would be nice if you didn't have to go through this process every time. You would not if you had a generic remote wrapper class that could effectively export any object. Think of this wrapper as facilitating a form of remote reflections. In other words, you simply use the wrapper to retrieve the metaclass of the underlying remote object to determine which (local) methods are available. You then invoke that method indirectly via the remote wrapper's **invoke()** method, which bridges the platforms. For example, you could export all the AWT components using this mechanism without having to laboriously develop remote versions of each one. We will develop such a wrapper in this section, but before we begin, we must consider the neighborhood that remote objects will be operating in.

Model View Architecture

The model-view architecture is extremely useful for partitioning an application, segregating the underlying data model from various user views. With views being loosely coupled to the model via an established API, both models and views are easier to maintain and modify. The **java.util.Observable** and **java.util.Observer** classes, borrowed from **Smalltalk**, correspond to a model and view, respectively. When the model changes—that is, that which is being observed—the views are updated— that is, those that are observing. Netscape's IFC and Borland JBuilder's JBCL (JavaBean Component Library) are also based on variations of this model-view paradigm.

Now suppose the client view of your distributed application needs to be updated in real time to remain synchronized with the data model running back on the server. After all, if one user modifies the model, the remaining user views should be automatically refreshed. One approach might be for each client to continuously poll the server for changes. It would be far less costly from a network and processing standpoint to receive change notifications from the data model instead.

Listing 11-5 shows the **RemoteListener** and **RemoteModelIntf** interfaces. The view is going to be listening to the model. The view must not only be able to register itself with the model but must also be able to invoke methods on the model. However, the model is only able to invoke the **update()** method of the **RemoteListener** interface. Therefore, the view and the model are both remote objects having remote interfaces.

The **RemoteListener** interface has only one method, **update()**, which takes a **java.util.EventObject** or derivative as an argument. When the model changes, it broadcasts an event to every outstanding **RemoteListener**

Listing 11-5
RemoteListener
and
RemoteModelIntf

```
// file: RemoteListener.java

public interface RemoteListener
   extends java.rmi.Remote
{
   public void update(java.util.EventObject e)
     throws java.rmi.RemoteException;
}


// file: RemoteModelIntf.java

import java.io.*;
import java.rmi.*;

public interface RemoteModelIntf
   extends Remote
{
   void addRemoteListener(RemoteListener rl)
     throws RemoteException;
   void removeRemoteListener(RemoteListener rl)
     throws RemoteException;
   Class getModelClass() throws RemoteException;
   Serializable invoke
     (String methodName, Class[] parameterTypes,
       Serializable[] args) throws RemoteException;
}


// file: LocalListener.java

public interface LocalListener
   extends java.util.EventListener
{
   public void update(java.util.EventObject e);
}
```

via its **update()** method. The interpretation of receiving an **EventObject** update of course has to be defined by the nature of the application. The **RemoteListener** registers an interest in receiving updates by calling the **addRemoteListener()** method of the **RemoteModelIntf** interface. This follows the design pattern of event sources and listeners prescribed for Java-Beans. However, the **RemoteListener** interface is not recognized by the **java.beans.Introspector** class as an event set because it doesn't implement the **java.util.EventListener** interface. Remote interfaces may only extend other Remote interfaces, which precludes extending **java.util.EventListener**. This is quite all right, however, because you wouldn't be connecting remote listeners to local models within a beanbox IDE anyway. The `RemoteModelIntf` interface also defines the `getModelClass()` and `invoke()` methods. The `getModelClass()` method returns the metaclass of the underlying wrapped object that is being exported. Fortunately, the `Class` class is serializable, so it can be returned from a remote method call. The only drawback of `invoke()` is the restriction that the parameters of the underlying method must be serializable, or this mechanism fails. The `LocalListener` interface is used to reroute the call to `RemoteListener update()`, forwarding it to a local object, of which we will see an example shortly.

Listing 11-6 shows the implementation of the `RemoteModelIntf` interface. `RemoteModel` extends `UnicastRemoteObject` and implements the `RemoteModelIntf` interface. The wrapped local object is held internally so that incoming queries via `getModelClass()` may be answered by redirecting those incoming calls to the locally wrapped object. A vector is used to store the currently registered `RemoteListeners`. `RemoteModel` is a JavaBean, so it has the prerequisite default constructor with no parameters. Two additional constructors are also defined, each taking a local object parameter that references the local object that is being "exported." The second constructor allows for a URL to specify the bound name of this `RemoteModel` instance. In the `setOnline()` method, notice that if the RMI registry is not currently running, it is automatically started on the default port. This "online" property is discussed in a moment.

Listing 11-6
RemoteModel

```
import java.io.*;
import java.util.*;
import java.rmi.*;
import java.rmi.server.*;
import java.rmi.registry.*;
import java.lang.reflect.*;
import java.beans.*;

public class RemoteModel
   extends UnicastRemoteObject
   implements RemoteModelIntf
{

   public RemoteModel() throws RemoteException
   {
   }

   public RemoteModel(Serializable model)
      throws RemoteException
```

Continues

Listing 11-6
Continued.

```
{
   setModel(model);
}

public RemoteModel
   (Serializable model, String modelName)
     throws RemoteException,
       java.net.MalformedURLException,
       UnknownHostException
{
   setModel(model);
   setModelName(modelName);
}

public void finalize()
{
   try { setOnline(false); }
   catch (Exception e) {}
}

public final void
   addRemoteListener(RemoteListener rl)
     throws RemoteException
{
   remoteViews.addElement(rl);
}

public final void
   removeRemoteListener(RemoteListener rl)
     throws RemoteException
{
   remoteViews.removeElement(rl);
}

public final Class getModelClass()
   throws RemoteException
{
   return model.getClass();
}

public final Serializable invoke
   (String methodName, Class[] parameterTypes,
    Serializable[] args)
     throws RemoteException
{
   try  {
     Method method =
       model.getClass()
         .getMethod(methodName,parameterTypes);
     return (Serializable)method.invoke(model,args);
   } catch (Exception e)  {
     throw new RemoteException
```

Listing 11-6

```
                        ("RemoteModel::invoke",e);
      }
  }

  public final void broadcast(EventObject e)
  {
    Vector views;
    synchronized (remoteViews)
      { views = (Vector) remoteViews.clone(); }
    for (int i = 0; i < views.size(); i++)
    {
      RemoteListener view =
        (RemoteListener) views.elementAt(i);
      try { view.update(e); }
      catch (Exception t) {
        remoteViews.removeElement(view);
      }
    }
  }

  public final void addPropertyChangeListener
    (PropertyChangeListener l)
  {
    changes.addPropertyChangeListener(l);
  }

  public final void removePropertyChangeListener
    (PropertyChangeListener l)
  {
    changes.removePropertyChangeListener(l);
  }

  public final void setModel(Serializable model)
  {
    try { setOnline(false); }
    catch (Exception e) {}
    changes.firePropertyChange
      ("model",this.model,model);
    if (model == null)
      this.model = NOMODEL;
    else
      this.model = model;
  }

  public final Serializable getModel()
  {
    return model;
  }

  public final void setModelName(String modelName)
    throws RemoteException, UnknownHostException,
```

Continues

Listing 11-6
Continued.

```java
        java.net.MalformedURLException
{
  boolean previouslyOnline = isOnline();
  try { setOnline(false); }
  catch (NotBoundException e1) {}
  if (modelName == null)
    modelName = NONAME;
  changes.firePropertyChange
    ("modelName",this.modelName,modelName);
  this.modelName = modelName;
  if (this.modelName.length() > 0
    && (!Beans.isDesignTime()
    || previouslyOnline))
    try { setOnline(true); }
    catch (NotBoundException e2) {}
}

public final String getModelName()
{
  return modelName;
}

public final void setOnline(boolean newValue)
  throws RemoteException, UnknownHostException,
    NotBoundException,
    java.net.MalformedURLException
{
  if (online != newValue)  {
    if (online)
        Naming.unbind(this.modelName);
    else
      try  {
        Naming.rebind(modelName,this);
      } catch (ConnectException ce)  {
        LocateRegistry.
          createRegistry(Registry.REGISTRY_PORT);
        Naming.rebind(modelName,this);
      };
    changes.firePropertyChange
      (
        "online",
        new Boolean(online),
        new Boolean(!online)
      );
    online = !online;
  }
}

public final boolean isOnline()
{
  return online;
}
```

Listing 11-6

```
public static class NoModel
    implements Serializable
{
    public NoModel() {}
}

public final static NoModel NOMODEL
    = new NoModel();
public final static String NONAME
    = "noname";

private Vector remoteViews = new Vector();
private PropertyChangeSupport changes =
    new PropertyChangeSupport(this);
private Serializable model = NOMODEL;
private String modelName = NONAME;
private boolean online = false;

}
```

The `addRemoteListener()` and `removeRemoteListener()` methods are straightforward at maintaining a vector of current listeners. Likewise, the `getModelClass()` is a simple pass through to **the** `getClass()` method of the underlying wrapped object. Fortunately the `Class` class is serializable —after all, classes can be loaded over the net.

The `invoke()` method looks up the specified method and invokes it locally on the wrapped object. The `getMethod()` method of the `java.lang.Class` class takes the method name as its first parameter, and as its second parameter an array of `Class` instances representing the parameter types of the requested method. The `invoke()` method of the `java.lang.reflect.Method` class takes the local target object as its first parameter and an array of the actual argument objects as its second parameter. It was necessary to define `invoke()` in the `RemoteModelIntf` interface rather than `getModelMethod()` because the `java.lang.reflect.Method` class, unlike the `Class` class, is not serializable. One of the drawbacks with this approach is that the formal parameters of the local method and its return value must be serializable for this scheme to work. Local exceptions, if any, are caught and passed back to the client in a `RemoteException` wrapper.

The `broadcast()` method is used on the server side to notify all current views that a change has occurred on the model. Further information about the nature of the change can be passed via an `EventObject` derivative. The semantics if this mechanism is left up to the application designer. Please note that **EventObject** is serializable. Also notice that the **remoteViews** vector is cloned, acting as a snapshot of the outstanding clients at the precise moment of the broadcast. This cloning prevents a deadlock situation that could arise if the **remoteViews** vector were locked. For example, an update notification received by a view might trigger that view to remove itself from the current views. If this is the case, the call to **removeRemoteListener()** would wait forever because the **broadcast()** method, which triggered the scenario, has the **remoteViews** vector already locked. But **broadcast()** cannot complete until **update()** returns. If any exceptions are thrown by the **update()** method on the client, that view is simply removed from the vector of current views, admittedly a draconian approach.

RemoteModel has three bound properties: **model, modelName**, and **online**. The **model** property holds the local model, whereas the **modelName** property holds the URL of the enclosing wrapper. The **online** property controls binding in the local RMI registry. Please note that being "off-line" simply means that the model is not bound in the registry; however, it is still "exported" to the RMI runtime. When using **RemoteModel** in the beanbox or other JavaBean RAD (rapid application development) tool, you can set these properties at design time. The reason the **model** property takes a **Serializable** parameter is so the configured bean has the option of being saved serially. The **online** property cannot be set to true; however, unless the **RemoteModel_Stub.class** and **RemoteModelIntf.class** are in the CLASSPATH of the IDE (integrated development environment). It is not enough to have them simply zipped into the bean jar. Although the other classes can be loaded from the jar, being referenced from the bean code, these two cannot be because they are not referenced directly. Instead, the RMI runtime fabricates their names via introspection and attempts to load them from a CLASSPATH directory. The class loader of the bean is not visible to the RMI runtime thread. If you absolutely must have a live remote connection at design time, you must copy these two class files to a CLASSPATH directory. Once copied, the **online** property can be set to true at design time.

The rest of the code of Listing 11-6 has to do with supporting the **bound** properties utilizing the **PropertyChangeSupport** class.

Listing 11-7 shows the **RemoteView** class, which implements the **RemoteListener** interface. Remember both the model and the view are remote objects. The model registers remote listeners remotely and allows remote invocation of the local methods of its underlying local object. In contrast, the view receives update notifications remotely from the model.

Listing 11-7
RemoteView

```java
import java.util.*;
import java.rmi.*;
import java.rmi.server.*;
import java.beans.*;

public class RemoteView
   extends UnicastRemoteObject
   implements RemoteListener
{

  public RemoteView() throws RemoteException
    {}

  public RemoteView
    (LocalListener localListener,
      RemoteModelIntf model)
      throws RemoteException
  {
    addLocalListener(localListener);
    setModel(model);
  }

  public RemoteView
    (LocalListener localListener,
      String modelURL)
      throws RemoteException,
        NotBoundException,
        java.net.MalformedURLException
  {
    addLocalListener(localListener);
    setModelURL(modelURL);
  }

  public void finalize()
  {
    try { setOnline(false); }
    catch (Exception e) {}
  }

  public void update(EventObject e)
    throws RemoteException
  {
    Vector views;
    synchronized (localListeners)
      { views = (Vector) localListeners.clone(); }
    for (int i = 0; i < views.size(); i++)
      try {
        ((LocalListener) views.elementAt(i)).update(e);
      } catch (Exception x) {};
  }
```

Continues

Listing 11-7
Continued.

```
public final void addPropertyChangeListener
  (PropertyChangeListener l)
{
  changes.addPropertyChangeListener(l);
}

public final void removePropertyChangeListener
  (PropertyChangeListener l)
{
  changes.removePropertyChangeListener(l);
}

public final void setModel(RemoteModelIntf model)
  throws RemoteException
{
  if (online) {
    changes.firePropertyChange
      ("online",Boolean.TRUE,Boolean.FALSE);
    online = false;
  }
  if (this.model != null)
    try {
      this.model.removeRemoteListener(this);
    } catch (Exception e) {}
  changes.firePropertyChange
    ("model",this.model,model);
  this.model = model;
  if (model != null) {
    model.addRemoteListener(this);
    changes.firePropertyChange
      ("online",Boolean.FALSE,Boolean.TRUE);
    online = true;
  }
}

public final RemoteModelIntf getModel()
{
  return model;
}

public final void setModelURL(String modelURL)
  throws RemoteException, NotBoundException,
    java.net.MalformedURLException,
    UnknownHostException
{
  boolean previouslyOnline = isOnline();
  setOnline(false);
  if (modelURL == null)
    modelURL = NOMODEL;
  changes.firePropertyChange
    ("modelURL",this.modelURL,modelURL);
  this.modelURL = modelURL;
```

Listing 11-7

```
      if (modelURL.length() > 0
        && (!Beans.isDesignTime()
        || previouslyOnline))
        setOnline(true);
    }

    public final String getModelURL()
    {
      return modelURL;
    }

    public final void setOnline(boolean newValue)
      throws RemoteException, NotBoundException,
        java.net.MalformedURLException,
        UnknownHostException
    {
      if (online != newValue)
        if (online)
          setModel(null);
        else  {
          RemoteModelIntf rm;
          for (int i = 1; i < LOOKUP_RETRIES ; i++)
            try  {
              setModel((RemoteModelIntf)
                Naming.lookup(modelURL));
              break;
            } catch (Exception e) {};
          setModel((RemoteModelIntf)
            Naming.lookup(modelURL));
        }
    }

    public final boolean isOnline()
    {
      return online;
    }

    public final void
      addLocalListener(LocalListener localListener)
    {
      localListeners.addElement(localListener);
    }

    public final void
      removeLocalListener(LocalListener localListener)
    {
      localListeners.removeElement(localListener);
    }

    public static final String NOMODEL
      = "rmi://localhost/noname";
```

Continues

Listing 11-7
Continued.

```
public static final int LOOKUP_RETRIES = 4;

private PropertyChangeSupport changes =
   new PropertyChangeSupport(this);
private RemoteModelIntf model = null;
private String modelURL = NOMODEL;
private boolean online = false;
private Vector localListeners = new Vector();

}
```

You can use **RemoteView** several ways. If you extend **RemoteView**, you must override its **update()** method. The overriding **update()** method must not call **super.update()**! If the extended class doesn't introduce a new remote interface (and it shouldn't), there is no need to run the **rmic** compiler. The **RemoteView_Stub** and **Remote_Skel** classes suffice nicely.

The second way to use the **RemoteView** class is by providing a local object that implements the **LocalListener** interface. If the local object you want to wrap doesn't implement the **LocalListener** interface, it is very convenient to use an anonymous inner class that implements the **Local Listener** interface. This inner class functions as the typical protocol adapter. Because **RemoteView** fires genuine JavaBean **localListener** events, you can leave it up to the Bean design tool to create this adapter if you so choose.

The first **RemoteView** constructor (the default) is required because **RemoteView** is a JavaBean. The next two constructors of **RemoteView** take a **localListener** parameter (for convenience) and either a reference to a **RemoteModelIntf** or the URL of the **RemoteModel**. The **update()** method either rebroadcasts the update to local listeners or is overridden by a descendant.

The **RemoteView** bean fires one event—**update()**—and has three bound properties: **model**, **modelURL**, and **online**. Typically, you only configure the **modelURL** and **online** properties at design time. The **model** property is used for establishing a connection given a **RemoteModelIntf** (that is, stub). The **modelURL** property goes to the specified RMI register and fetches the stub, provided the **online** property is true. Notice that the **online** property retries the lookup several times. This is necessary should the connection be broken and a reconnect is later attempted. The retries flush any old connection stub discrepancies.

After compiling all of the classes and interfaces of Listings 11-5 through 11-7, the **rmic** compiler is applied to **RemoteModel** and **RemoteView** to generate the stubs and skeletons for these two classes. We are now done with the **rmic** compiler and can implement a distributed application without again resorting to the **rmic** compiler!

Chat

We shall now implement a chat program using our **RemoteModel** and **RemoteView** beans. This **ChatRoom** bean utilizes the **RemoteModel** bean, and a **ChatRoomVisitor** bean relies on the **RemoteView** bean. Neither the **ChatRoom** nor the **ChatRoomVisitor** need be concerned about RMI issues. These are completely encapsulated in the **RemoteModel** and **RemoteView** beans. The source for **ChatRoom** is shown in Listing 11-8. The chat room moderator needs to view the conversations taking place in the chat room, and thus **ChatRoom** extends Panel. This panel is displayed on the server so that the moderator can chime in. A Panel was chosen instead of a Frame so that the ChatRoom bean could be "contained" in another container if need be. Notice that the **ChatRoom** implements the **Property ChangeListener** interface so that it can listener to what the underlying **RemoteModel** is doing. Because its **subject** and **online** properties are simply re-mappings of the underlying **RemoteModel**'s **modelName** and **online** properties, respectively, these events are transformed to the appropriate names and rebroadcast. Please note the **subject** and **online** properties are also bound; therefore, **ChatRoom** fires property changed events. **ChatRoom** introduces the new property, **moderator**.

Listing 11-8
ChatRoom

```
import java.awt.*;
import java.awt.event.*;
import java.util.*;
import java.rmi.*;
import java.beans.*;

public class ChatRoom extends Panel
  implements PropertyChangeListener
{

  public ChatRoom()
    throws RemoteException
  {
    remoteModel = new RemoteModel();
    remoteModel.setModel(this);
```

Continues

Listing 11-8
Continued.

```java
    remoteModel.addPropertyChangeListener(this);
    addPropertyChangeListener(this);
    setLayout(new BorderLayout());
    add("North",title = new Label());
    setTitle();
    chat = new StringBuffer();
    add("Center",textArea = new TextArea());
    textArea.setEditable(false);
    final TextField textField = new TextField();
    add("South",textField);
    textField.addActionListener
        (
        new ActionListener()
        {
            public void actionPerformed(ActionEvent e)
            {
                appendChat(moderator + ":   " +
                            textField.getText());
                textField.setText("");
            }
        }
        );
    textArea.addFocusListener
        (
        new FocusAdapter()
        {
            public void focusGained(FocusEvent e)
                { textField.requestFocus(); }
        }
        );
}

public ChatRoom
    (String subject, final String moderator)
        throws java.rmi.RemoteException,
        java.net.MalformedURLException,
        java.rmi.UnknownHostException
{
    this();
    setSubject(subject);
    setModerator(moderator);
}

public void dispose()
{
    remoteModel.removePropertyChangeListener(this);
    removePropertyChangeListener(this);
}

public void propertyChange
    (PropertyChangeEvent evt)
{
```

Listing 11-8

```
      if (evt.getSource() == remoteModel)  {
        String pn = evt.getPropertyName();
        if (pn.equals("model"))
          return;
        if (pn.equals("modelName"))
          pn = "subject";
        changes.firePropertyChange
          (pn,evt.getOldValue(),evt.getNewValue());
      }
      else if (evt.getSource() == this)  {
        String pn = evt.getPropertyName();
        if (pn.equals("subject"))
          setTitle((String)evt.getNewValue(),
            getModerator(),isOnline());
        else if (pn.equals("moderator"))
          setTitle(getSubject(),
            (String)evt.getNewValue(),isOnline());
        else if (pn.equals("online"))
          setTitle(getSubject(),getModerator(),
            ((Boolean)evt.getNewValue()).booleanValue());
      }
    }

    public final String getChat()
    {
      return chat.toString();
    }

    public final void appendChat(String text)
    {
      chat.append(text+"\n");
      textArea.setText("");
      textArea.append(chat.toString());
      remoteModel.broadcast(null);
    }

    public final void addPropertyChangeListener
      (PropertyChangeListener l)
    {
      changes.addPropertyChangeListener(l);
    }

    public final void removePropertyChangeListener
      (PropertyChangeListener l)
    {
      changes.removePropertyChangeListener(l);
    }

    public final void setSubject(String subject)
      throws RemoteException, UnknownHostException,
        java.net.MalformedURLException
```

Continues

Listing 11-8
Continued.

```
{
   remoteModel.setModelName(subject);
}

public final String getSubject()
{
   return remoteModel.getModelName();
}

public final void setModerator(String moderator)
{
   if (moderator == null)
     moderator = NONAME;
   changes.firePropertyChange
     ("moderator",this.moderator,moderator);
   this.moderator = moderator;
}

public final String getModerator()
{
   return moderator;
}

public final void setOnline(boolean newValue)
   throws RemoteException, UnknownHostException,
     java.net.MalformedURLException,
     NotBoundException
{
   remoteModel.setOnline(newValue);
}

public final boolean isOnline()
{
   return remoteModel.isOnline();
}

private final void setTitle
   (String subject, String moderator,
    boolean online)
{
   String t = "Chat Room Moderator: "
     + moderator + " @ " + subject;
   if (!online)
     t += " (Off-line)";
   title.setText(t);
}

private final void setTitle()
{
   setTitle(getSubject(),getModerator(),
     isOnline());
}
```

```java
public static final String NONAME = "noname";

private RemoteModel remoteModel;
private StringBuffer chat;
private Label title;
private TextArea textArea;
private PropertyChangeSupport changes =
   new PropertyChangeSupport(this);
String moderator = NONAME;

public static void main(String[] args)
{
   System.setSecurityManager(new RMISecurityManager());
   try  {
     Frame f = new Frame();
     f.addWindowListener
       (
         new WindowAdapter()
         {
            public void windowClosing(WindowEvent e)
              { System.exit(0); }
         }
       );
     f.add("Center",new ChatRoom(args[0],args));
     f.pack();
     f.setVisible(true);
   } catch (Exception e)  {
     e.printStackTrace(System.out);
     System.out.println
       ("usage: java ChatRoom subject moderator");
     System.exit(0);
   }
 }
}
```

Vicki, an administrator who is hosting a chat on nutrition, uses the following command line to invoke the **ChatRoom** server:

```
java  ChatRoom  Nutrition  Vicki
```

Vicki has entered the greeting message, "Welcome to the conference on nutrition!" in the bottom text field. Upon pressing Enter, the text is moved to the conversation text area and prefixed with the name of the speaker. Several visitors have arrived by the time Debra logs in (see Figure 11-4). The command line Debra used to invoke a **ChatRoomVisitor** to join the group was:

```
java  ChatRoomVisitor  Nutrition  Debra
```

As you can see from Figure 11-4, Leif has already joined the conversation as Debra gets ready to send her first message.

Returning to Listing 11-8 we see that the **ChatRoom()** constructor effectively exports itself via its **RemoteModel** instance:

```
remoteModel = new RemoteModel();
remoteModel.setModel(this);
```

With these two lines, the **ChatRoom**'s **getChat()** and **appendChat()** methods are effectively exported and can be readily invoked remotely by a **ChatRoomVisitor**. Thus, **ChatRoom** is remotely accessible without having to go through the typical steps required by RMI. Notice that **append Chat()** calls the **RemoteModel**'s **broadcast()** method.

```
remoteModel.broadcast(null);
```

The **EventObject** parameter isn't used in this example because the **ChatRoomVisitor** calls its own **getChat()** method everytime it receives an update notification. The **getChat()** method calls back to the model's **getChat()** method to refresh the view's conversation area.

Figure 11-4
ChatRoomVisitor
for nutrition

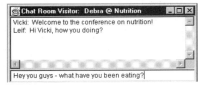

Listing 11-9
ChatRoomVisitor

```
import java.awt.*;
import java.awt.event.*;
import java.util.*;
import java.io.*;
import java.rmi.*;
import java.beans.*;

public class ChatRoomVisitor extends Panel
    implements PropertyChangeListener
{

    public ChatRoomVisitor()
        throws RemoteException
    {
        remoteView = new RemoteView();
```

Listing 11-9

```
remoteView.addLocalListener
  (
    new LocalListener()
    {
      public void update(EventObject e)
        { getChat(); }
    }
  );
remoteView.addPropertyChangeListener(this);
addPropertyChangeListener(this);
setLayout(new BorderLayout());
add("North",title = new Label());
setTitle();
add("Center",textArea = new TextArea());
textArea.setEditable(false);
textField = new TextField();
add("South",textField);
textField.addActionListener
  (
    new ActionListener()
    {
      public void actionPerformed(ActionEvent e)
      {
        try  {
          if (!isOnline())
            try { setOnline(true); }
            catch (Exception e1) {}
          if (!isOnline())
            return;
          remoteView.getModel().invoke(
            "appendChat",
            new Class[] { String.class },
            new Serializable[]
              { visitor + ":  " + textField.getText()
                }
          );
          textField.setText("");
        } catch (Exception e2) {
          try  { setOnline(false); }
          catch (Exception e3) {}
        }
      }
    }
  );
textArea.addFocusListener
  (
    new FocusAdapter()
    {
      public void focusGained(FocusEvent e)
        { textField.requestFocus(); }
    }
```

Continues

Listing 11-9
Continued.

```
    );
}

public ChatRoomVisitor
  (String chatRoomURL, final String visitor)
  throws RemoteException, NotBoundException,
    java.net.MalformedURLException,
    UnknownHostException
{
  this();
  setVisitor(visitor);
  setChatRoomURL(chatRoomURL);
}

public void dispose()
{
  remoteView.removePropertyChangeListener(this);
  removePropertyChangeListener(this);
}

public void propertyChange
  (PropertyChangeEvent evt)
{
  if (evt.getSource() == remoteView)  {
    String pn = evt.getPropertyName();
    if (pn.equals("model"))
      return;
    if (pn.equals("modelURL"))
      pn = "chatRoomURL";
    changes.firePropertyChange
      (pn,evt.getOldValue(),evt.getNewValue());
  }
  else if (evt.getSource() == this)  {
    String pn = evt.getPropertyName();
    if (pn.equals("chatRoomURL"))
      setTitle((String)evt.getNewValue(),
        getVisitor(),isOnline());
    else if (pn.equals("visitor"))
      setTitle(getChatRoomURL(),
        (String)evt.getNewValue(),isOnline());
    else if (pn.equals("online"))  {
      setTitle(getChatRoomURL(),getVisitor(),
        ((Boolean)evt.getNewValue()).booleanValue());
      getChat();
    }
  }
}

public final void addPropertyChangeListener
  (PropertyChangeListener l)
{
  changes.addPropertyChangeListener(l);
```

Listing 11-9

```
  }

  public final void removePropertyChangeListener
    (PropertyChangeListener l)
  {
    changes.removePropertyChangeListener(l);
  }

  public final void setChatRoomURL(String chatRoomURL)
    throws RemoteException, NotBoundException,
      java.net.MalformedURLException,
      UnknownHostException
  {
    remoteView.setModelURL(chatRoomURL);
  }

  public final String getChatRoomURL()
  {
    return remoteView.getModelURL();
  }

  public final void setVisitor(String visitor)
  {
    if (visitor == null)
      visitor = NONAME;
    changes.firePropertyChange
      ("visitor",this.visitor,visitor);
    this.visitor = visitor;
  }

  public final String getVisitor()
  {
    return visitor;
  }

  public final void setOnline(boolean newValue)
    throws RemoteException, NotBoundException,
      java.net.MalformedURLException,
      UnknownHostException
  {
    remoteView.setOnline(newValue);
  }

  public final boolean isOnline()
  {
    return remoteView.isOnline();
  }

  final void getChat()
  {
    try  {
```

Continues

Listing 11-9
Continued.

```java
        textArea.setText("");
        textArea.append((String)
          remoteView.getModel().invoke(
            "getChat",
            new Class[0],
            new Serializable[0]
          )
        );
        textField.requestFocus();
      } catch (Exception t) {}
    }

    private final void setTitle
      (String chatRoomURL, String visitor,
       boolean online)
    {
      String t = "Chat Room Visitor: "
        + visitor + " @ " + chatRoomURL;
      if (!online)
        t += " (Off-line)";
      title.setText(t);
    }

    private final void setTitle()
    {
      setTitle(getChatRoomURL(),getVisitor(),
        isOnline());
    }

    public static final String NONAME = "noname";

    RemoteView remoteView;
    private Label title;
    private TextArea textArea;
    TextField textField;
    private PropertyChangeSupport changes =
      new PropertyChangeSupport(this);
    String visitor = NONAME;

    public static void main(String[] args)
    {
     System.setSecurityManager(new RMISecurityManager());
     try {
        Frame f = new Frame();
        f.addWindowListener
          (
            new WindowAdapter()
            {
                public void windowClosing(WindowEvent e)
                  { System.exit(0); }
            }
          );
```

Listing 11-9

```
        f.add("Center",new ChatRoomVisitor(args[0],args));
        f.pack();
        f.setVisible(true);
    } catch (Exception e)   {
        e.printStackTrace(System.out);
        System.out.println
          ("usage: java ChatRoomVisitor "
           + "chatRoomURL visitorName");
        System.exit(0);
    }
  }
}
```

In the constructor for **ChatRoomVisitor** (Listing 11-9), notice how a **LocalListener** adapter is added to the **RemoteView** because **ChatRoomVisitor** does not implement the **LocalListener** interface. This protocol adapter simply redirects the **update()** call to the **getChat()** method. You can see that the **EventObject** is indeed ignored, having no semantic significance in our design.

```
new LocalListener()
      {
         public void update(EventObject e)
            { getChat(); }
      }
```

Because **ChatRoomVisitor** extends **Panel**, we didn't have the option of extending **RemoteView** itself and overriding the **update()** method.

Like the ChatRoom, the **ChatRoomVisitor** also has a text field at the bottom of the panel that acts as a message input area. The action event, triggered by a carriage return, invokes the **appendChat()** method back on the server.

```
remoteView.model.invoke( "appendChat",
   new Class[] { String.class },  new Serializable[]
      { visitor + ":  " + textField.getText() }  );
```

The call to invoke specifies a method, **appendChat**, which takes one **String** parameter. The actual parameter passed to **appendChat()** is the text of the message input area prefixed with the name of the visitor. Fortunately, **appendChat()**'s one parameter is serializable, so this mechanism works.

The **chatRoomURL** and **online** properties are passed through from the underlying **RemoteView.modelURL** and **online** properties, respectively. The

visitor property is used to identify the person speaking. All three properties are bound.

Chat as an Applet

Listing 11-10 shows the HTML code and corresponding Java code necessary to convert the **ChatRoomVisitor** into a **ChatRoomVisitorApplet**. Figure 11-5 shows what the **ChatRoomVisitorApplet** login panel looks like running in the appletviewer. The user is asked his or her name. Pressing the carriage return in this text field launches a **ChatRoomVisitor** frame similar to that shown in Figure 11-4. The command for invoking the applet via the appletviewer is

```
appletviewer  ChatRoomVisitorApplet.html
```

Notice that the applet html tag passes a **ChatRoomURL** parameter to the **ChatRoomVisitorApplet**. The **getParameter()** method of Applet is used to retrieve the value **rmi://localhost/Nutrition**. Because this applet is meant for logging into the nutrition chat session, the URL points there. And because the applet, as well as the server, are both running on the same machine in our example, the URL also points to the local host. The **ChatRoomVisitorApplet** can be used repeatedly for logging into different chat sessions by simply specifying different URLs in the applet tag. The **ChatRoom** server must be running on the same host as the web server because applet security restricts applet socket connections to the host of the webserver.

Other Remote Paradigms

A method that returns a value is inherently synchronous. The calling program must wait until the value is returned before proceeding. There is no provision for an asynchronously returned value. Because actions in a distributed

Figure 11-5
ChatRoomVisitor
Applet login for
nutrition

**Listing 11-10
ChatRoomVisitor
Applet** (html and
source)

```html
<!- file: ChatRoomVisitorApplet.html ->

<HEAD>
<TITLE>ChatRoomVisitorApplet Demo</TITLE>
</HEAD>
<BODY>
<APPLET code="ChatRoomVisitorApplet.class" width=300
    height=150>
<PARAM name="ChatRoomURL" value="rmi://localhost/
    Nutrition">
</APPLET>
</BODY>
```

```java
// file: ChatRoomVisitorApplet.java

import java.applet.*;
import java.awt.*;
import java.awt.event.*;

public class ChatRoomVisitorApplet extends Applet
{
  public void init()
  {
    setLayout(new GridBagLayout());
    GridBagConstraints c = new GridBagConstraints();
    c.gridwidth = GridBagConstraints.REMAINDER;
    Label l =
      new Label(getParameter("ChatRoomURL")+ "  login:");
    add(l,c);
    final TextField login = new TextField(30);
    add(login,c);
    login.addActionListener
      (
        new ActionListener()
        {
          public void actionPerformed(ActionEvent ae)
          {
            try {
              (new ChatRoomVisitor
                (getParameter("ChatRoomURL"),
                  login.getText())).setVisible(true);
            } catch (Exception e) {
              showStatus("Unable to login");
      e.printStackTrace(System.out);
            }
          }
        }
      );
    login.requestFocus();
    invalidate();
  }
}
```

application occur at unpredictable times, the hapless calling of remote synchronous methods sooner or later proves disastrous for all but the most trivial applications. Why? Because of the overwhelming potential for deadlock.

Imagine one object placing a remote call to a foreign object that happens to be placing a call to the first object at the same time. Oh no, deadly embrace! Sometimes it's not so obvious and the deadly embrace isn't exposed until the application is fielded. After much anxiety and long debugging sessions, you are likely to discover an arcane, cyclic graph of one object waiting on another object, which is waiting on yet another, and so on until the loop is completed and the system hangs. To bring down an entire distributed application is difficult, not to mention embarrassing!

The remote model-view wrapper presented previously got around this problem by implementing an event-driven system. An event delivery system is inherently asynchronous. Event broadcasting is essentially a one-direction affair that greatly reduces the possibility of deadlock. You may recall that the **broadcast()** method first cloned ("took a snapshot of") the outstanding views before updating each one, thus leaving the model unlocked. A view, therefore, could invoke a method back on the model in response to receiving an update from that model. This mechanism is by no means foolproof because the model may cause other objects to lock, and a circuitous deadly embrace eventually is uncovered. You should take these considerations into account when using RMI because remote objects being out of sight are often out of mind from a design perspective.

The folks at JavaSoft have two unofficial research APIs under development that build on top of RMI, namely JSDA (Java Shared Data API) and JavaSpaces. (Actually the JSDA alpha version is based on sockets, but that is likely to change.) Just as RMI can be thought of as a protocol layer on top of sockets, these APIs can be thought of as a distributed data framework protocol layered on top of RMI.

JSDA is meant for developing collaborative, highly interactive, multimedia applications. Its architecture is based on sessions, channels, and subscribers. It also allows for remote change notification, much like the bound properties of JavaBeans.

The JavaSpaces API, on the other hand, presents the notion of a transparent object space that may transcend platforms while being automatically persistent. This combines the notion of a distributed object database with a unified, perpetual platform. However, unlike an object database, query "templates" can be posted before the matching results are! The interested party is subsequently notified via a distributed event model whenever an object matching the query template has arrived in the space. The JavaSpaces API is also formalizing the notion of a distributed transaction within this distributed object space. Thus, the application's designer can be concerned solely with the flow of data and its algorithms and not get bogged down with issues of distributed connections, distributed transactions, forwarding, and persistence.

Both APIs encourage a design to be thought of in terms of data flow rather than terms of an object model. Hence, these APIs foster asynchronous designs which are vitally necessary in a distributed, content-rich environment that are reasonably immune to deadlock. The research conducted on both APIs is publicly available via the Java developers' web site. You are encouraged to learn from and perhaps imitate these design patterns in you own RMI undertakings. Hopefully, these APIs will come to fruition and become a part of the official Java APIs. In any event, studying these APIs is warranted if you are about to undertake a massive distributed design using RMI. Doing so could possibly save you hundreds of hours of logical design time.

In passing, it should be noted that RMI will soon support IIOP (Internet Inter ORB Protocol) and thus be able to "speak" to any CORBA object connected to a IIOP-enabled ORB rather painlessly. Of particular interest is accessing crossware/middleware objects, which would prove to be a real boon to RMI-enabled JavaBean development.

CONCLUSION

A rudimentary understanding of RMI is essential to JavaBean developers because they are often called upon to implement RMI-enabled beans or to at least understand the ramifications of using such beans. This is becoming more and more the norm with the emerging dominance of net-centric applications. With the eventual addition of IIOP transport support, RMI will become ubiquitous within JavaBeans, acting as gateways to crossware and middleware products. Likewise, with the addition of multicast objects, RMI-enabled JavaBeans will be used to conveniently implement industrial-strength application servers. Eventually, Beans that embody the data flow concepts presented in JSDA and JavaSpaces APIs will be used on a daily basis. But most importantly, RMI can be used today to solve demanding distributed application requirements more conveniently than with any other approach. Considering the benefits of n-tier architecture and the productivity gains realized in implementing cross-platform Java to Java solutions, it is easy to see that RMI is not going away—it is just beginning!

 12

JavaBeans and CORBA

As you have seen in the previous chapter, Java, through its RMI specification, and Java Beans promote n-tier solutions. Distributed programming is about taking software problems and breaking them into separate pieces, possibly on separate machines, that accomplish a solution to a problem. While Sun has been busy working on the Java platform, a standards body of which Sun is a part, has been engaged in creating and maintaining a public-distributed object specification. The standards body is known as the Object Management Group (OMG), and their specification is known as The Common Object Request Broker Architecture, or CORBA.

It is no surprise that both the Java Beans and the CORBA technologies capitalize on the interface. The only problem with distributed systems and processes is specifying how the data is moved from one system and set of processes to another. If we thought of one process as a binary image in a system, then the data that system is manipulating and reading is also part of that binary image. In order to be able to move it to a different system for additional computation or processing, one of two things needs to occur. Either the object itself must have certain methods that can be invoked upon it so that the foreign process would "discover" it dynamically, or that object's interface needs to be defined by a public means so that the foreign process has the compatible interface automatically allowing it to interpret data from the sending interface of your client process. The first method outlined coincides with Java Beans, and the second with CORBA. Note that in this chapter we use the same examples provided in Chapter 11 and redo them using the JavaSoft JavaIDL-EA CORBA architecture.

This Chapter Covers

- A summary of CORBA
- Creating CORBA-Based Examples
- When to use CORBA, and when to use RMI

The goal of combining these two technologies is to capitalize on what both offer. As you have read about Java Beans, it has been made increasingly clear that the interface is the same for all the components; therefore, if a developer obtains any Bean, they know that they can call on it, and behavior those calls provide. The dynamic part of the Bean is the data returned. With CORBA, it is different; the interface itself is very dynamic. It is *published* through IDL; then a developer can obtain and/or generate the client-side stub or server-side skeleton for their use.

At the OMG, one standardization effort taking place is known as the *CORBA Component specification*. This is a specification that attempts to create a solution to the problem of exchangable components. In this way, customers can buy components from multiple vendors without having to deal with the vendors' interface creation, and can instead just plug the components into their existing framework.

Over the past few months, Sun Microsystems has been confused as to how to approach the CORBA and Java technologies and how, if at all, they should be blended together. Sun has been a member of the OMG since it began and always has been heavily involved in what CORBA is and where it goes. The first incantation of CORBA from Sun was the project, *Distributed Objects Everywhere (DOE)*. After this proof of concept became a reality, Sun publicized it and created technology camps people could attend and learn more about what distributed objects were and how the objects were going to change the computing world as they knew it. From there Sun's commercial incantation "NEO" was born. In the meantime, Sun had also created and released the Java programming language and specification. It is no surprise that shortly thereafter Sun then released *Java Objects Everywhere (Joe)*, which allowed programmers to build Java objects that interacted with the NEO runtime ORB and services.

After Joe, Sun created the 2.0 release of NEO, which was CORBA 2.0 (and IIOP) compliant. Most recently, Sun has announced that it will abandon NEO and give the technology to leading vendors to integrate into existing operating systems and ORB runtimes. It is Sun's belief that the "network is the computer," and nothing is going to stop the distributed object revolution. It is important that we point out this brief history to illustrate to you where the JavaIDL tool was born and what went into it.

A Summary of CORBA

To understand CORBA, you have to understand the following topics. They are explained in the following sections.

IDL (Interface Definition Language)

The single most important facet of CORBA is the *Interface Definition Language (IDL)* specification. This language looks a lot like C++ and is written like a program using an editor in ASCII. This language has object-oriented properties such as data encapsulation, inheritance, and polymorphism.

With the IDL are the specified mappings to different languages. Right now mappings exist for C, C++, Java, Ada, SmallTalk, and more. You can browse the Java mapping within the docs directory of the JavaIDL package. What you see are all the types defined in IDL and their corresponding types in the language being mapped to. For instance, an IDL string maps to a Java String. There are many more.

IIOP (Internet Inter-ORB Protocol)

Another very important specification within CORBA is its transport layer definition. The *Internet Inter-ORB Protocol (IIOP)* rides on top of the store-and-forward-based Transmission Control Protocol (TCP) and is the default protocol for CORBA transactions. This means that the properties of TCP are maintained in IIOP, namely, reliable, stream-based packet delivery. This shows up in implementation as a port number. Obviously the properties of the Internet Protocol (IP) are also derived, namely, a unique address. IIOP is used through the marshalling and unmarshalling of all CORBA messages. There are seven message types outlined in the *Generic Inter-ORB Protocol (GIOP)* in Table 12-1.

IIOP just maps these seven messages to TCP.

ORB (Object Request Broker)

The *Object Request Broker (ORB)* is the heart of CORBA. This is the proprietary daemon or agent that operates on its own to broker transactions between CORBA components. It almost always runs as its own daemon process on a machine somewhere. When it receives a request for a service or object (usually, a call to the COS Naming Service to look up an object by name) it looks through its interface and implementation repositories for the object, determines where it is, and dispatches the request. In the case of the COS Naming Service call, it looks up an object by string, and locates and return its *Interoperable Object Reference (IOR)*.

Table 12-1

GIOP Message Formats

Message	Type Originator	Value (enum)
Request	Client	0
Reply	Server	1
CancelRequest	Client	2
LocateRequest	Client	3
LocateReply	Server	4
CloseConnection	Server	5
MessageError	Both	6

ORB Services

The ORB services are an important addition to the ORB itself, described above. The services represent all the different facilities necessary to deploy the ORB and create a distributed environment. This is the most expansive part of the CORBA specification(s), and it could easily take another book to explain in detail all the existing services and cover the new ones, so we will try to summarize here. One of the most important services is the lifecycle service. This service enables the ORB to use its interface and implementation repositories to start and stop CORBA-based objects if necessary. The best example of this service is when a client object comes in and requests a service object that is currently not running. The Lifecycle Service enables the ORB to locate the machine and area the object is in, start it, and pass its IOR back to the calling object. Another service is the COS Naming Service outlined previously. This service is responsible for taking an object, when registered and "stringifying" the object to produce a relationship between the desired string of the objects name and the corresponding IOR to the object itself. Other services include transaction, security, event, business application-specific services, and many more.

For further information, you can peruse the OMG website (**www.omg.org**). It has many ongoing specifications and *requests for proposals (RFP's)*. The CORBA 2.0 specification itself, which contains all the sections described previously, can be obtained at **www.omg.org/2.0**. It is also possible to become a member of the OMG for a fee. The fee varies depending on what options you wish to take, what you want to be able to sit in on and vote on, if anything, and the size of company you represent.

Our goal is to create a common distributed channel of functioning objects through the ORB as illustrated in Figure 12-1.

Creating CORBA-Based Examples

For these examples we use the JavaIDL Early Access (EA) Release available from JavaSoft (**www.javasoft.com**). Once you have obtained the release, unpackage it where you plan to install it. It is important to note that if you are using this package with Windows95 or NT, you *must* have already installed Microsoft Visual C++ version 4.0 or higher on your system. It is used by JavaSoft in its simple implementation of the OMG Common Object Service (COS) Naming implementation.

Figure 12-1
An ORB-enabled
distributed database
system

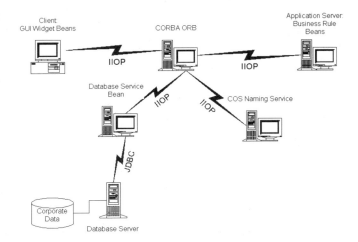

There are many other CORBA architecture implementations to choose from. The most popular are Iona's Orbix and OrbixWeb, and Visigenic's Visibroker. Other commercial implementations include ICL's DAIS ORB, and Chorus Systems CoolOrb. If you are interested in free ORB systems (besides JavaIDL) check out Xerox Parc's Inter-Language Unification (ILU) project. This is not a full CORBA implementation, but it is IDL- and IIOP-compliant and may suit your needs. There is also HORB, which is a free Java implementation of a distributed CORBA-like environment, and is fairly stable. There are more that can be scoured through the web.

First Example: TextArea

As you have seen in the last chapter, with Java it is possible to build distributed applications quickly and easily using the *Remote Method Invocation (RMI)* mechanism. As is shown in this chapter, there is another way to build a distributed application through the use of CORBA. For the first example you re-implement the TextArea example set forth in the last chapter.

The TextArea application is a simple client-server application that exchanges String data from the client to the server via the AWT TextArea widgets. The user types in a string in the client AWT TextArea and selects the *send* button, which then passes the string to the server AWT TextArea where it is repainted and shown. It is important to note that from the onset of this problem you must think differently than in the last chapter. With RMI, you think of the problem as two classes—client and server—where the server resides somewhere on the net and the client on the local machine. You create the classes to handle your interactions and add the methods to them to obtain and post the string data.

With CORBA it is quite different. In the beginning of your thought process, think in terms of the interface only and not even necessarily care if the implementation is in Java or not. You want to think purely of what data types are passing over your communications channel. In the case of this first example, it is simply a string or array of characters. The IDL defines this similarly as a construct of type string. So our interface is defined as shown in Listing 12-1.

IDL allows for comments similar to C++ and Java in that they can either be of type /*...*/ or one-line comments of type //. We chose to just show the title of the file name. Obviously, in more complicated interface definitions, you can comment on the code as you would typically with a programming language.

First, define the module you are defining an interface for. This is similar to how you would think of packages in Java: a collection of methods and interface components for a particular program or task. In this case, the TextArea application example. The server interface in your program consists of two methods: getText() and setText() as you have seen before. That is all there is for this particular example.

Once you have created this interface definition file for your program, use the *stubbing* tool to generate the appropriate stubs and/or skeletons as described previously. For this case, use the tool that comes with the JavaIDL Early Access Release idltojava outlined previously, and execute it as follows:

```
idltojava -fclient -fserver ta.idl
```

This creates in your current directory a subdirectory named after the module in your definition file; in this case TextAreaApp. Within that subdirectory are the generated files: subclasses of various CORBA and Internet Inter-ORB Protocol (IIOP) classes. These are reviewed in more

Listing 12-1
Listing for the Text Area IDL file.

```
// Title: ta.idl
module TextAreaApp{
   interface ta{
      string getText();
      void setText( in string text );
   };
};
```

detail in listing 12-2. It is now time to implement your server and client classes, in this case modifications of the existing files from Chapter 12.

Listing 12-2
TextAreaServer
Java file.

```
import java.awt.*;
import java.awt.event.*;

import TextAreaApp.*;
import org.omg.CosNaming.*;
import org.omg.CosNaming.NamingContextPackage.*;
import org.omg.CORBA.*;

class taServant extends _taImplBase{

  private TextArea textArea;

  public taServant( TextArea ta ){
    this.textArea = ta;
  }

  public String getText(){
    return textArea.getText();
  }
  public void setText( String text ){
    textArea.setText(text);
  }

}

public class TextAreaServer
{
  public static final TextArea textArea = new TextArea();

  public TextAreaServer()
    {}

  public static void main(String args[])
  {
    try  {
      TextAreaServer server = new TextAreaServer();

      ORB orb = ORB.init(args, null);

      taServant TARef = new taServant( textArea );
      orb.connect( TARef );

      org.omg.CORBA.Object objRef =
        orb.resolve_initial_references( "NameService" );
      NamingContext ncRef = NamingContextHelper.narrow(
                            objRef );
```

Listing 12-2

```
NameComponent nc = new NameComponent( "TextArea",
                                       "" );
NameComponent path[] = {nc};
ncRef.rebind(path, TARef);

Frame f = new Frame("TextAreaServer");
f.addWindowListener
  (
     new WindowAdapter()
     {
       public void windowClosing(WindowEvent e)
         { System.exit(0); }
     }
  );
f.add( "Center", textArea );
f.pack();
f.setVisible(true);

java.lang.Object sync = new java.lang.Object();
synchronized (sync) {
  sync.wait();
}

} catch (Exception e)  {
  e.printStackTrace();
  System.exit(0);
}
  }
}
```

The first difference is in what libraries and class files you choose to import into your application. In this instance, you first import your subdirectory of generated stub and skeleton files, then you import three packages from the supplied CORBA libraries of files. First, the **CosNaming** package is included, which provides the implementation of the CORBA Naming Service. As explained previously, the Naming Service is one of the important services provided by the CORBA specification. More particularly, this service provides a "white-pages" naming lookup facility to CORBA applications. Finally, the CORBA package is included which provides the "plumbing" of JavaSoft's CORBA implementation. This includes, but is not limited to IIOP class files, socket and network communication files, and references to a broker, or ORB for requests to be handled by.

Next, create a reference to the **TextAreaApp** servant. The servant is responsible for acting on dispatched requests made through the interface. The two methods **getText()** and **setText()** operate on the server's AWT TextArea, so you must pass it into the constructor of the servant class, so that it can modify the server's AWT TextArea when necessary. The actual methods are implemented in simple fashion. Next, the `TextAreaServer` class is implemented. Note that the AWT TextArea itself used by the server in the application is declared public, final, and static. This is necessary for the servant class to be able to receive dispatched events from the ORB and operate correctly on the server's TextArea. If it is defined without final or static, the compiler complains during compilation.

After the null constructor is declared, the first line of code of interest to you is:

```
ORB orb = ORB.init(args, null);
```

This creates an object that refers to the ORB. This particular `init()` function call sends the command line arguments and a null reference to a set of properties (from `java.util.Property`). Once you have created a reference to the ORB, you must create an object of your servant type to perform the operations requested and then register it with the ORB reference. This is done as follows:

```
taServant TARef = new taServant( textArea );
orb.connect( TARef );
```

Once the reference is created, generate objects and references to manipulate the COS Naming Service. You do so as follows:

```
org.omg.CORBA.Object objRef =
   orb.resolve_initial_references( "NameService" );
NamingContext ncRef = NamingContextHelper.narrow( objRef );
```

After creating the Naming Service references, give the server a name to be recognized by the Naming Service; then bind that to the servant object as follows:

```
NameComponent nc = new NameComponent( "TextArea", "" );
NameComponent path[] = {nc};
ncRef.rebind(path, TARef);
```

Then wait for events from the clients that are to be dispatched on the server as follows:

```
java.lang.Object sync = new java.lang.Object();
     synchronized (sync) {
        sync.wait();
     }
```

The rest of the server side code that implements the AWT widgets and shows them it looks identical as before. On the client side however, you have a slightly different variation. Listing 12-3 is the client side code for this example.

```
import TextAreaApp.*;

import org.omg.CosNaming.*;
import org.omg.CORBA.*;

import java.awt.*;
import java.awt.event.*;

public class TextAreaClient
{
  public static void main( String args[] )
  {
    try {
      ORB orb = ORB.init( args, null );

      org.omg.CORBA.Object objRef =
        orb.resolve_initial_references( "NameService" );
      NamingContext ncRef = NamingContextHelper.narrow(
                             objRef );

      NameComponent nc = new NameComponent( "TextArea",
                                            "" );
      NameComponent path[] = {nc};
      final ta TAref = taHelper.narrow( ncRef.resolve(
                                        path ));

      Frame f = new Frame( "TextAreaClient" );
      f.addWindowListener
        (
          new WindowAdapter()
          {
            public void windowClosing( WindowEvent e )
              { System.exit( 0 ); }
          }
        );
      final TextArea localTextArea = new TextArea();
      localTextArea.setText( "Enter text to apply
                            here." );
      localTextArea.selectAll();
      f.add("Center",localTextArea);
      Button apply = new Button( "Apply to Server" );
      apply.addActionListener
        (
          new ActionListener()
          {
            public void actionPerformed( ActionEvent ae )
            {
              try {
```

Continues

Listing 12-3
Continued.

```
                         TAref.setText( localTextArea.getText() );
                    } catch (Exception e) {
                         e.printStackTrace( System.out );
                    }
                }
            }
        );
        f.add("South",apply);
        f.pack();
        f.setVisible(true);
    } catch (Exception e)  {
        e.printStackTrace();
        System.exit(0);
    }
  }
}
```

As before, import the generated stub and skeleton code, as well as the **CosNaming** and CORBA packages provided. Recall with this code you are implementing the other side of the server already done. Therefore, you can think of the methods in this example as "mirrors" of the server side methods.

First, create a reference to the Naming service object, so you can perform lookups and bindings through it as follows:

```
org.omg.CORBA.Object objRef =
   orb.resolve_initial_references( "NameService" );
NamingContext ncRef = NamingContextHelper.narrow( objRef );
```

You then create an object of type **NameComponent** to refer to your specific object of interest, in this case the **TextArea** server object, illustrated as follows:

```
NameComponent nc = new NameComponent( "TextArea", "" );
NameComponent path[] = {nc};
final ta TAref = taHelper.narrow( ncRef.resolve( path ));
```

Finally, when you are within the event loop and are ready to operate on the remote CORBA object, make a call to its servant method.

```
TAref.setText( localTextArea.getText() );
```

Note, that you could also build operations that perform a **getText()** on the server's servant also, but for the purposes of this example, we chose not to.

Second Example: A Chat Application

In this example, we revisit the Chat application built on RMI in Chapter 12. We will show the new code and only describe the differences in the CORBA implementation. The last example was a good illustration of how CORBA works at a basic level and provided a minimal use case in action. The next example far better shows the differences between the two techniques (RMI and CORBA).

First of all, you need to approach the problem from an entirely different angle. In the RMI example you had the use of the Uniform Resource Locator (URL), the Java RMI Registry service, and most importantly, an end-to-end Java solution. Therefore, you could liberally use Object Serialization to serialize objects back and forth between a Remote Listener and a Remote Model. You could also rely on Java Reflection for run-time dynamic discovery of methods within your Listener or Model (or their underlying classes: ChatRoom and ChatRoomVisitor). With CORBA we *need* to think of solving the problem independent of Java. Recall that the main intent of CORBA is to make the solution become language independent.

CORBA IDL has sequence and octet types. With these you can create dynamic arrays of bytestreams, which, in fact, would really be serialized objects. We choose *not* to do this because if you are using serialization, you are still, in effect, making yourself dependent on Java. So, if you rethink your Chat application and its underlying models and listeners, there is a language-independent type specified in CORBA that is passing between the ChatRoom and its Visitors: strings! Because strings are the only type that needs to pass between components, a good CORBA solution exists.

First think about how you want to define your interface. For the purposes of illustration, we have chosen to implement this CORBA solution as generic and along the same dynamic lines as the last RMI example. There are many ways you could approach this. Recall that the **Remote Model** when updated, would broadcast a signal to all listening clients to update themselves. They then would make a call to the **RemoteModel** for its current discussion text buffer. You might think that you could implement with the broadcast call actually sending the new text buffer within it and the client updating by these means—you would be right! That technique is not as dynamic as your technique, where a lot more information could be sent to the client, and the processing accomplished more on the client side.

Therefore, define your IDL as shown in listing 12-4.

Listing 12-4
The Chat Application
IDL file.

```
// Title: chat.idl

module ChatApp{

    // first a remote interface for the server (RemoteModel)
    interface RM{
        // dynamic method that calls itself by discovery, with
        // string arg
        void callMethod( in string method, in string parm );
        string getChat();
        void addRemoteListener( in string aListener );
        void removeRemoteListener( in string aListener );
    };

    // now for the client (RemoteView)
    interface RV{
        // we just simply want to be able to get it to set its
        // area
        void update();
    };
};
```

There is an overall module called **ChatApp**, that handles the transactions between two types of components. You have two components to define an interface for: a Remote Model, described in the IDL as "RM," and a Remote View, described as "RV."

Within your Remote Model interface, you define four methods. First, define a special method **callMethod**, which later illustrates a limited form of reflection that can be accomplished through CORBA. It takes in two string parameters: a method to invoke, and a string parameter to that method. It is important to note that only methods with one string parameter can be called through this interface method. If you wanted to make it more dynamic, you could change the string parameter to something else, a sequence of strings for example, or maybe even a sequence of octets, but for the purposes of this example we choose not to. Next define the string returnable method **getChat**. This method is responsible for grabbing the most current text buffer from the underlying Remote Model. We then defined **addRemoteListener** and **removeRemoteListener**, which take in string arguments and are used by the underlying Remote Model to track all the different clients that are "listening" to its conversation (i.e. interested in its text buffer).

In the *Remote View (RV)* interface, you have defined only one method, the update method. It is a very simple method, and it is only responsible for directing the underlying View object to request a current text buffer from its model. When you are finished, run:

```
idltojava -fclient -fserver chat.idl
```

This generates the **ChatApp** directory with the associated **stub** servant and skeleton files as before.

The next thing is to build the Remote Model ORB Servant object, and revisit the Remote Model object as in the next listing.

Listing 12-5

The Remote Model and servant Java source code files.

```
import java.io.*;
import java.util.*;
import java.lang.reflect.*;
import java.beans.*;
import ChatApp.*;
import org.omg.CosNaming.*;
import org.omg.CosNaming.NamingContextPackage.*;
import org.omg.CORBA.*;

class RMServant extends _RMImplBase{

  public RMServant( RemoteModel aModel ){
    myModel = aModel;
  }

  public void callMethod( String method, String anArg ){

    String[] args = new String[1];
    args[0] = anArg;

    Class[] parms = new Class[1];
    parms[0] = method.getClass();

    Class c = myModel.getModelClass();

    try{
      Method m = c.getMethod( method, parms );
      m.invoke( (java.lang.Object)myModel.getModel(),
                (java.lang.Object[])args );
    }catch( Exception e ){}
  }

  public String getChat(){
    String[] args = new String[0];
    Class[] parms = new Class[0];
    Class c = myModel.getModelClass();
    String returnString = null;

    try{
      Method m = c.getMethod( "getChat", parms );
      returnString = (String)m.invoke(
                        (java.lang.Object)myModel.getModel(),
```

Continues

Listing 12-5

Continued.

```
                          (java.lang.Object[])args );
    }catch( Exception e ){}

    return returnString;
}

public void addRemoteListener( String aListener ){

    RV rref = null;

    try{
        String[] args = new String[2];
        args[0] = "-ORBInitialPort";
        args[1] = myModel.getORBport();

        ORB orb = ORB.init( args, null );

        org.omg.CORBA.Object objRef =
            orb.resolve_initial_references( "NameService" );
        NamingContext ncRef = NamingContextHelper.narrow(
                        objRef );

        NameComponent nc = new NameComponent( aListener,
                                             "" );

        NameComponent path[] = {nc};
        rref = RVHelper.narrow( ncRef.resolve( path ));
    }
    catch( Exception e ){}

    myModel.addRemoteListener( rref );
}

public void removeRemoteListener( String aListener ){

    RV rref = null;

    try{
        String[] args = new String[2];
        args[0] = "-ORBInitialPort";
        args[1] = myModel.getORBport();

        ORB orb = ORB.init( args, null );

        org.omg.CORBA.Object objRef =
            orb.resolve_initial_references( "NameService" );
        NamingContext ncRef = NamingContextHelper.narrow(
                        objRef );

        NameComponent nc = new NameComponent( aListener,
                                             "" );

        NameComponent path[] = {nc};
        rref = RVHelper.narrow( ncRef.resolve( path ));
```

Listing 12-5

```
      }
      catch( Exception e ){}

      myModel.removeRemoteListener( rref );
   }

   private RemoteModel myModel;
}

public class RemoteModel
   implements RemoteModelIntf
{

   public RemoteModel()
   {
   }

   public RemoteModel(Serializable model)
   {
      setModel(model);
   }

   public RemoteModel
      (Serializable model, String modelName)
   {
      setModel(model);
      setModelName(modelName);
   }

   public void finalize()
   {
      try { setOnline(false); }
      catch (Exception e) {}
   }

   public final void
   addRemoteListener( RV rl )
   {
      remoteViews.addElement(rl);
   }

   public final void
   removeRemoteListener( RV rl )
   {
      remoteViews.removeElement(rl);
   }

   public final Class getModelClass()
   {
      return model.getClass();
   }
```

Continues

Listing 12-5
Continued.

```
public final void broadcast(EventObject e)
{
  Vector views;
  synchronized (remoteViews)
    { views = (Vector) remoteViews.clone(); }
  for (int i = 0; i < views.size(); i++)
  {
    RV view =
      (RV) views.elementAt(i);
    try { view.update(); }
    catch (Exception t) {
      remoteViews.removeElement(view);
    }
  }
}

public final void addPropertyChangeListener
  (PropertyChangeListener l)
{
  changes.addPropertyChangeListener(l);
}

public final void removePropertyChangeListener
  (PropertyChangeListener l)
{
  changes.removePropertyChangeListener(l);
}

public final void setModel(Serializable model)
{
  try { setOnline(false); }
  catch (Exception e) {}
  changes.firePropertyChange
    ("model",this.model,model);
  if (model == null)
    this.model = NOMODEL;
  else
    this.model = model;
}

public final Serializable getModel()
{
  return model;
}

public final void setModelName(String modelName)
{
  boolean previouslyOnline = isOnline();
  try { setOnline(false); }
  catch (Exception e1) {}

  if (modelName == null)
```

Listing 12-5

```
      modelName = NONAME;
    changes.firePropertyChange
      ("modelName",this.modelName,modelName);
    this.modelName = modelName;
    if (this.modelName.length() > 0
      && (!Beans.isDesignTime()
      || previouslyOnline))
      try { setOnline(true); }
      catch (Exception e2) {}
  }

  public final String getModelName()
  {
    return modelName;
  }

  public final void setOnline(boolean newValue)
  {
    if (online != newValue)  {
      try{
        String[] args = new String[2];
        args[0] = "-ORBInitialPort";
        args[1] = this.getORBport();

        ORB orb = ORB.init(args, null);

        RMServant rRef = new RMServant( this );
        orb.connect(rRef);

        org.omg.CORBA.Object objRef =
          orb.resolve_initial_references("NameService");
        NamingContext ncRef =
      NamingContextHelper.narrow(objRef);

        NameComponent nc = new
      NameComponent(this.modelName, "");
        NameComponent path[] = {nc};
        ncRef.rebind(path, rRef);
      }
      catch( Exception e ) {}

      changes.firePropertyChange
        (
          "online",
          new Boolean(online),
          new Boolean(!online)
        );
      online = !online;
    }
  }
}
```

Continues

Listing 12-5
Continued.

```java
public final boolean isOnline()
{
   return online;
}

public static class NoModel
   implements Serializable
{
   public NoModel() {}
}

public final String getORBport()
{
   return ORBport;
}

public void setORBport( String anORBport )
{
   this.ORBport = anORBport;
}

public final static NoModel NOMODEL
   = new NoModel();
public final static String NONAME
   = "noname";

private Vector remoteViews = new Vector();
private PropertyChangeSupport changes =
   new PropertyChangeSupport(this);
private Serializable model = NOMODEL;
private String modelName = NONAME;
private boolean online = false;
private String ORBport = "900";

}
```

The first thing to note is the different packages being imported into this class file. The CORBA packages are being pulled in as well as the generated code from **chat.idl**, **ChatApp.***. As before, the servant class is responsible for implementing the methods defined for its interface in the IDL file. In this case, it extends the RM skeleton, or **impl** file. As you might imagine, it implements **callMethod**, **getChat**, and **addRemoteListener** and **removeRemoteListener**.

As stated before, **callMethod** is somewhat dynamic and relies on reflection. Ultimately it invokes the method sent as the first parameter, sending the string it receives as the single parameter to the invoked method as follows:

```
try{
      Method m = c.getMethod( method, parms );
      m.invoke( (java.lang.Object)myModel.getModel(),
                (java.lang.Object[])args );
      }catch( Exception e ){}
```

The **getChat** method simply invokes the **getChat** method on the underlying model using reflection as follows:

```
try{
      Method m = c.getMethod( "getChat", parms );
      returnString = (String)m.invoke(
                      (java.lang.Object)myModel.getModel(),
                      (java.lang.Object[])args );
      }catch( Exception e ){}
```

The **addRemoteListener** and **removeRemoteListener** methods are very important. They take in a string argument and set up an ORB reference to perform a look up on its naming service as follows:

```
RV rref = null;
```

Note that it is an interface **stub** class object of type **RV**, from our **ChatApp** directory of generated code. In the end, it invokes **addRemoteListener** on its underlying model sending the reference of the successfully looked up object from the COS Naming Service as follows.

```
      myModel.addRemoteListener( rref );
```

This means is that it has turned a string into a live object that can be manipulated. The **removeRemoteListener** operates similarly. The Remote Model is implemented in much the same way as before with appropriate changes to use CORBA instead of RMI. Notice how many fewer exceptions can be thrown (for example, no **RemoteException**, **MalformedURLException**, and the like). It still sets a serializable underlying model, and names it after the conference. This name is also what the ORB COS Naming Service will know this object by as well, the conference name. The **addRemoteListener** and **removeRemoteListener** manipulate the vector as before. The broadcast method is the same, except it now cycles through RV stubs instead of objects of **RemoteListener** interface. For each object, it invokes **update**, which is also defined in the IDL. The Beans-based property listener's stay and operate the same. The first notable change occurs in **setOnline**, where it registers itself as the conference name with the COS Naming Service as follows:

```
NameComponent nc = new NameComponent(this.modelName, "");
      NameComponent path[] = {nc};
      ncRef.rebind(path, rRef);
```

The last change is that the model maintains one more piece of information: the ORB listening port. This is obtained through the `getORBport` access function throughout the code to identify the port on which to contact the COS Naming Service (nameserv). Recall that this is sent in the `-ORBInitialPort` argument to the ORB `init` call. It turns out that there is a `-ORBInitialHost` that enables you to contact a COS Naming Service on another machine, but for this example, we ran everything on one machine.

Next, implement the `Listener`, or `RemoteView` object, and implement its `stub` servant as follows in the next two listings.

Listing 12-6

The Chat Application server-side Java source file.

```java
import ChatApp.*;
import org.omg.CORBA.*;
import java.lang.reflect.*;

class RVServant extends _RVImplBase{

  public RVServant( RemoteView aView ){
    myView = aView;
  }

  public void update() {

    String[] args = new String[0];
    Class[] parms = new Class[0];

    Class c = myView.getView().getClass();

    try{
      Method m = c.getMethod( "getChat", parms );
      m.invoke( (java.lang.Object)myView.getView(),
                (java.lang.Object[])args );
    }catch( Exception e ){}
  }

  private RemoteView myView;
}
```

Listing 12-7

The Remote View Java source code file.

```java
import java.io.*;
import java.util.*;
import java.beans.*;
import java.lang.reflect.*;
import ChatApp.*;
import org.omg.CosNaming.*;
import org.omg.CORBA.*;
```

Listing 12-7

```
public class RemoteView
  implements RemoteListener
{

  public RemoteView()
    {}

  public RemoteView
    (LocalListener localListener,
     RM model)
  {
    addLocalListener(localListener);
    setModel(model);
  }

  public RemoteView
    (LocalListener localListener,
      String modelURL)
  {
    addLocalListener(localListener);
    setModelURL(modelURL,NOMODEL);
  }

  public void finalize()
  {
    try { setOnline(false); }
    catch (Exception e) {}
  }

  public void update(EventObject e)
  {
    Vector views;
    synchronized (localListeners)
      { views = (Vector) localListeners.clone(); }
    for (int i = 0; i < views.size(); i++)
      try {
        ((LocalListener) views.elementAt(i)).update(e);
      } catch (Exception x) {};
  }

  public final void addPropertyChangeListener
    (PropertyChangeListener l)
  {
    changes.addPropertyChangeListener(l);
  }

  public final void removePropertyChangeListener
    (PropertyChangeListener l)
  {
    changes.removePropertyChangeListener(l);
  }
```

Continues

Listing 12-7
Continued.

```java
public final void setModel(RM model)
{
  if (online) {
    changes.firePropertyChange
      ("online",Boolean.TRUE,Boolean.FALSE);
    online = false;
  }
  if (this.model != null)
    try {
    this.getModel().removeRemoteListener(
    this.getMyVisitor() );
    } catch (Exception e) {}
  changes.firePropertyChange
    ("model",this.model,model);
  this.model = model;
  if (model != null) {
    this.getModel().addRemoteListener(
   this.getMyVisitor() );
    changes.firePropertyChange
      ("online",Boolean.FALSE,Boolean.TRUE);
    online = true;
  }
}

public final RM getModel()
{
  return model;
}

public final void setModelURL(String modelURL, String
                                    aVisitor)
{
  boolean previouslyOnline = isOnline();
  setOnline(false);
  if (modelURL == null){
    modelURL = NOMODEL;
    myVisitor = NOMODEL;
  }
  changes.firePropertyChange
    ("modelURL",this.modelURL,modelURL);
  changes.firePropertyChange
    ("myVisitor",this.myVisitor,myVisitor);
  this.modelURL = modelURL;
  this.myVisitor = aVisitor;
  if (modelURL.length() > 0
    && myVisitor.length() > 0
    && (!Beans.isDesignTime()
    || previouslyOnline))
    setOnline(true);
}

public final String getModelURL()
```

Listing 12-7

```
{
   return modelURL;
}

public final String getMyVisitor(){
   return myVisitor;
}

public final void setOnline(boolean newValue)
{
   if (online != newValue)
     if (online){
       setModel(null);
     } else  {
       try{
           // hard code for now
           String[] args = new String[2];
           args[0] = "-ORBInitialPort";
           args[1] = this.getORBport();

           ORB orb = ORB.init(args, null);

           RVServant rRef = new RVServant( this );
           orb.connect(rRef);

           org.omg.CORBA.Object objRef =
              orb.resolve_initial_references("NameService");
           NamingContext ncRef = NamingContextHelper.narrow
                                    (objRef);

           NameComponent nc = new NameComponent(
                             this.myVisitor, "");
           NameComponent path[] = {nc};
           ncRef.rebind(path, rRef);
       }
       catch( Exception e ) {}

       RemoteModelIntf rm;

       RM rref = null;

       try{
           // hard code for now...too complicated otherwise
           String[] args = new String[2];
           args[0] = "-ORBInitialPort";
           args[1] = this.getORBport();

           ORB orb = ORB.init( args, null );

           org.omg.CORBA.Object objRef =
              orb.resolve_initial_references( "NameService"
                                            Continues
```

Listing 12-7
Continued.

```
                                                      );
         NamingContext ncRef = NamingContextHelper.
                                 narrow( objRef );

         NameComponent nc = new NameComponent( modelURL,
                                               "" );

         NameComponent path[] = {nc};
         rref = RMHelper.narrow( ncRef.resolve( path ));
      }
      catch( Exception e ){}

      setModel(rref);
   }

}

public final boolean isOnline()
{
   return online;
}

public final void
   addLocalListener(LocalListener localListener)
{
   localListeners.addElement(localListener);
}

public final void
   removeLocalListener(LocalListener localListener)
{
   localListeners.removeElement(localListener);
}

public final void
   setView( Serializable aView )
{
   if (aView == null)
     this.myView = NOVIEW;
   else
     this.myView = aView;
}

public final Serializable getView()
{
   return myView;
}


public final String getORBport()
{
   return ORBport;
}
```

```
public void setORBport(String anORBport)
{
   this.ORBport = anORBport;
}

public static class NoView
   implements Serializable
{
   public NoView() {}
}

public final static NoView NOVIEW
   = new NoView();

public static final String NOMODEL
   = "noname";

private PropertyChangeSupport changes =
   new PropertyChangeSupport(this);
private RM model = null;
public Serializable myView = NOVIEW;
private String modelURL = NOMODEL;
private String myVisitor = NOMODEL;
private boolean online = false;
private Vector localListeners = new Vector();
private String ORBport = "900";

}
```

First implement the **stub** servant object. It's a very simple object and only defines the **update** method from the IDL by invoking **update** on the underlying Remote View object through reflection as follows:

```
try{
    Method m = c.getMethod( "getChat", parms );
    m.invoke( (java.lang.Object)myView.getView(),
    (java.lang.Object[])args );
   }catch( Exception e ){}
```

Next, move on to implementing the Remote View object itself. First note also that the **Remote View** object now also tracks the private port string to initially call the COS Naming Service. The Remote View is implemented very much as before with the same Beans property and listener operations. In the **setModel** method, the model is now set to an RM interface class as opposed to the **RemoteModelIntf** as before. Then, as mentioned before, the **addRemoteListener** and **removeRemoteListener** methods make calls to the **getMyVisitor** method to obtain the string value of the person chatting, which is also used as the name to register the listener client with the COS Naming Service as follows:

```
this.getModel().removeRemoteListener( this.getMyVisitor()
                                             );
```

and

```
this.getModel().addRemoteListener( this.getMyVisitor() );
```

Instead of just setting the ChatRoom's name, still referred to as **modelURL** so you can compare to the RMI example, the name of the visitor is also set (and tracked) in the Remote View now. Note the difference in the **setOnline** method. It now registers the visitor name (Remote View) with the COS Naming Service, so that lookups can be performed. The following code fragment is where the name is set.

```
NameComponent nc = new NameComponent(this.myVisitor, "");
NameComponent path[] = {nc};
ncRef.rebind(path, rRef);
```

After that in the **setOnline** method, the Remote View must obtain the reference to the Remote Model it wishes to connect to, so it performs a lookup with the COS Naming Service and sets its underlying model reference to the skeleton returned as follows:

```
NameComponent nc = new NameComponent( modelURL, "" );
NameComponent path[] = {nc};
rref = RMHelper.narrow( ncRef.resolve( path ));
```

and then

```
setModel(rref);
```

The ORB Port in both the Remote Model and the Remote View is set to the default (900) as outlined in the JavaIDL documentation. Note that if you wish to bind to this port on a Unix machine, you typically (in Solaris) need to be user **root** to do so successfully. For these examples we used a higher port as you will see during execution.

Lastly, it is time to implement the **ChatRoomVisitor**, which is the object utilizing the **RemoteView** object. Its implementation follows in listing 12-8.

It is implemented much as before with some differences. The first thing to note is that upon a user causing an action to occur on the text field (namely they hit the return key after typing something), the Remote View makes a call on the skeleton of its underlying model.

Listing 12-8
The Chat Room
Visitor client-side Java
source file.

```java
import java.awt.*;
import java.awt.event.*;
import java.util.*;
import java.io.*;
import java.beans.*;

public class ChatRoomVisitor extends Panel
    implements PropertyChangeListener
{

    public ChatRoomVisitor()
    {
        remoteView = new RemoteView();
        remoteView.setView(this);
        remoteView.addLocalListener
            (
                new LocalListener()
                {
                    public void update(EventObject e)
                        { getChat(); }
                }
            );
        remoteView.addPropertyChangeListener(this);
        addPropertyChangeListener(this);
        setLayout(new BorderLayout());
        add("North",title = new Label());
        setTitle();
        add("Center",textArea = new TextArea());
        textArea.setEditable(false);
        textField = new TextField();
        add("South",textField);
        textField.addActionListener
            (
                new ActionListener()
                {
                    public void actionPerformed(ActionEvent e)
                    {
                        try {
                            if (!isOnline())
                                try { setOnline(true); }
                                catch (Exception e1) {}
                            if (!isOnline()){
                                return;
                            }
                            remoteView.getModel().callMethod(
                                "appendChat", visitor + ":  " +
                                textField.getText()
                            );
                            textField.setText("");
                        } catch (Exception e2) {
                            try  { setOnline(false); }
```

Continues

Listing 12-8
Continued.

```
                        catch (Exception e3) {}
                    }
                }
            }
        );
    textArea.addFocusListener
        (
            new FocusAdapter()
            {
                public void focusGained(FocusEvent e)
                    { textField.requestFocus(); }
            }
        );
}

public ChatRoomVisitor
    (String chatRoom, final String visitor, final String
    ORBport)
{
    this();
    setVisitor(visitor);
    remoteView.setORBport(ORBport);
    setChatRoom(chatRoom,visitor);
}

public void dispose()
{
    remoteView.removePropertyChangeListener(this);
    removePropertyChangeListener(this);
}

public void propertyChange
    (PropertyChangeEvent evt)
{
    if (evt.getSource() == remoteView)  {
        String pn = evt.getPropertyName();
        if (pn.equals("model"))
            return;
        if (pn.equals("modelURL"))
            pn = "chatRoom";
        changes.firePropertyChange
            (pn,evt.getOldValue(),evt.getNewValue());
    }
    else if (evt.getSource() == this)  {
        String pn = evt.getPropertyName();
        if (pn.equals("chatRoom"))
            setTitle((String)evt.getNewValue(),
                getVisitor(),isOnline());
        else if (pn.equals("visitor"))
            setTitle(getChatRoom(),
                (String)evt.getNewValue(),isOnline());
        else if (pn.equals("online"))  {
```

Listing 12-8

```
            setTitle(getChatRoom(),getVisitor(),
              ((Boolean)evt.getNewValue()).booleanValue());
            getChat();
          }
        }
      }

      public final void addPropertyChangeListener
        (PropertyChangeListener l)
      {
        changes.addPropertyChangeListener(l);
      }

      public final void removePropertyChangeListener
        (PropertyChangeListener l)
      {
        changes.removePropertyChangeListener(l);
      }

      public final void setChatRoom(String chatRoom, String
                                    aVisitor)
      {
        remoteView.setModelURL(chatRoom,aVisitor);
      }

      public final String getChatRoom()
      {
        return remoteView.getModelURL();
      }

      public final void setVisitor(String visitor)
      {
        if (visitor == null)
          visitor = NONAME;
        changes.firePropertyChange
          ("visitor",this.visitor,visitor);
        this.visitor = visitor;
      }

      public final String getVisitor()
      {
        return visitor;
      }

      public final void setOnline(boolean newValue)
      {
        remoteView.setOnline(newValue);
      }

      public final boolean isOnline()
      {
```

Continues

Listing 12-8
Continued.

```
      return remoteView.isOnline();
  }

  public final void getChat()
  {
    try {
      textArea.setText("");
      textArea.append((String)
remoteView.getModel().getChat() );

      textField.requestFocus();
    } catch (Exception t) {}
  }

  private final void setTitle
    (String chatRoom, String visitor,
     boolean online)
  {
    String t = "Chat Room Visitor: "
      + visitor + " @ " + chatRoom;
    if (!online)
      t += " (Off-line)";
    title.setText(t);
  }

  private final void setTitle()
  {
    setTitle(getChatRoom(),getVisitor(),
      isOnline());
  }

  public static final String NONAME = "noname";

  RemoteView remoteView;
  private Label title;
  private TextArea textArea;
  TextField textField;
  private PropertyChangeSupport changes =
    new PropertyChangeSupport(this);
  String visitor = NONAME;

  public static void main(String[] args)
  {
    try {
      Frame f = new Frame();
      f.addWindowListener
        (
          new WindowAdapter()
          {
            public void windowClosing(WindowEvent e)
              { System.exit(0); }
          }
```

Listing 12-8

```
                  );
        f.add("Center",new
      ChatRoomVisitor(args[0],args[1],args[2]));
        f.pack();
        f.setVisible(true);
    } catch (Exception e)  {
        e.printStackTrace(System.out);
        System.out.println
          ("usage: java ChatRoomVisitor "
          + "chatRoom visitorName ORBport");
        System.exit(0);
    }
  }
}
```

```
remoteView.getModel().callMethod(
    "appendChat", visitor + ":  " + textField.getText()
);
```

The constructor now takes and sets the COS Naming Service initial listening port.

```
public ChatRoomVisitor
     (String chatRoom, final String visitor, final String
     ORBport)
```

The **setChatRoom** method now assigns the visitors name as well. It is used to register the Remote View with the COS Naming Service with:

```
public final void setChatRoom(String chatRoom, String
                                   aVisitor)
{
  remoteView.setModelURL(chatRoom,aVisitor);
}
```

The **getChat** method is invoked on the underlying model skeleton.

```
textArea.append((String)remoteView.getModel().getChat() );
```

The **main()** method now prints that it needs an additional parameter of an ORB port upon failure. That is all there is to it. You compile the code together with a separate compile on the **ChatApp/*.java** files, and you're ready for execution.

First, start the COS Naming Service as before.

```
nameserv -ORBInitialPort 4022
```

Then start the `ChatRoom` as follows:

```
java ChatRoom <conference name> <moderator name> <ORB port>
```

Finally, you start your clients as well.

```
java ChatRoomVisitor <conference name> <visitor name> <ORB
    port>
```

Now you're in business. Try it out!

When to Use CORBA and When to Use RMI

This proves to be a difficult question indeed. For an RMI application, you want to make sure you plan to use and stay 100% Java within your application. As soon as you decide that you want to have the potential to use different languages within your applications, use CORBA. If you decide that you would like to sell or give away various components of your framework to other people and programmers, use CORBA. With that, if they have a set of objects written in C++, and they want to add a web service you have created in Java Beans, they will be able to take your Beans object and register it into their existing framework without difficulty.

It's important to recognize the difference. Java RMI is a wonderful tool if you are only interested in creating an end-to-end Java application. It will be of interest to follow JavaSoft as they merge the RMI and CORBA technologies together with IIOP. If both spoke the same underlying protocol, then there might be a way to run both in tandem within an application. With CORBA, you want to make sure you are thinking correctly. You want to think independent of the language being used, so you, therefore, define the interface in terms of its basic data parts. These parts are found in the IDL definition. You can then publish the IDL for your application and give it away. If everything works properly, another developer could take your IDL, generate stubs and skeletons *with their ORB package*, and then build an object that talks to yours without ever seeing a line of code of that object's implementation. This is still being ironed out in the industry, and as ORB vendors have been catching up to make their ORB's totally CORBA 2.0 compliant, we have seen more convergence in the direction of running different ORB's together and passing requests between both in IIOP. If you are building a straight client/server system with no need for flexibility in the in which the customer just needs a client/server system (most likely on the web), and a *Common Gateway Interface (CGI)* system will suit them just fine. Just try to assimilate how much expandability they might want in the future.

JavaBeans is a Java-dependant architecture as well. So, use them when you wish to use Java. CORBA allows for non-Java Beans that interact with Beans to be developed. This means that you might use the JavaBean implementation of an interface, such as the `RemoteModel` illustrated in this chapter. You could interact with that Bean and reuse it in various Integrated Development Environments (IDE's). Then, someone else develops a client in C++, without being "Beanified." The whole solution will still work because you chose to use CORBA to define the interfaces. Hopefully this gives you some idea of when to use CORBA in your applications, when to use RMI, and when to use neither.

CONCLUSION

In conclusion, it is our hope that you have been exposed enough to CORBA fundamentals and examples in this chapter to provide a good foundation from which to base your programming decisions.

As you can see, there are many directions still to be taken, and CORBA needs a lot of time to grow within the Java platform and API's. We do believe that the IIOP specification portion of CORBA will prove to be quite useful in the next generation of network software products as well. Using CORBA enables any language implementation to be used; using Java-Beans enables Java programs to be exchangeable and plug and playable; and IIOP provides the next layer of transport access control to distributed applications.

There is still a lot of work to be done, so look for a lot more blending, collaboration, and solutions to continue to roll out in the coming years. I hope you enjoyed this book, we have put a lot of time with a lot of peoples' help. If any of the chapters among the lucky 12, helped you in any way, only then will our effort be successful. Happy grinding!

APPENDIX A

JavaBeans 1.0 API Reference

The Java Beans API consists of the **java.beans** package, as well as three classes in the **java.util** package. It is not necessary to use this package to create beans, because any java class is a bean. However, these classes and interfaces enable application developers to create sophisticated beans that are truly portable and reusable.

Package **java.beans**

The **java.beans** package consists of six interfaces. These interfaces provide a framework to bean developers with which describe their beans to tools and other developers. Many of the interfaces, such as **PropertyEditor**, are complex and are only for sophisticated beans. To help with this, several classes in this package implement the interfaces using no-op methods. In any case, these interfaces allow truly customizable beans. The six interfaces are

- **BeanInfo**
- **Customizer**
- **PropertyChangeListener**
- **PropertyEditor**
- **VetoableChangeListener**
- **Visibility**

The package also consists of fifteen classes. They are

- **BeanDescriptor**
- **Beans**
- **EventSetDescriptor**
- **FeatureDescriptor**
- **IndexedPropertyDescriptor**
- **Introspector**
- **MethodDescriptor**
- **ParameterDescriptor**
- **PropertyChangeEvent**

▦ `PropertyChangeSupport`

▦ `PropertyDescriptor`

▦ `PropertyEditorManager`

▦ `PropertyEditorSupport`

▦ `SimpleBeanInfo`

▦ `VetoableChangeSupport`

The classes implement many interfaces that enable bean developers to easily disseminate information about beans. Other classes help manage bound and constrained properties. And other classes allow low-level introspection of classes, as well as the ability to efficiently determine a bean's capabilities. Throughout these classes notice an incredible effort on JavaSoft's part to allow beans to inform, in real time, both application developers and tools about their various characteristics.

There are two exception classes.

▦ `IntrospectionException`

▦ `PropertyVetoException`

Both of these exceptions are important, especially **`PropertyVeto Exception`**. As described later, the `PropertyVetoException` is extremely powerful as it enables constrained properties to exist and allows beans to hold a two-way conversation.

Interface java.beans.BeanInfo

`public interface BeanInfo`   This interface allows a bean developer to provide specific information about a specific bean the **`BeanInfo`** class describes. The **`BeanInfo`** interface is provided so the bean developer can decide which information he or she wants to provide to the application builder or tool. The rest of the information is obtained via automatic analysis from low-level reflection. This interface is usually used through its implementation in the **`SimpleBeanInfo`** class. By overriding the **`SimpleBeanInfo`** classes, the bean developer can decide exactly which properties, events, and methods he or she wishes to describe.

`public final static int ICON_COLOR_16x16`   This is a constant indicating a 16x16 color icon.

`public final static int ICON_COLOR_32x32`   This is a constant indicating a 32x32 color icon.

public final static int ICON_MONO_16x16   This is a constant indicating a 16x16 monochrome icon.

public final static int ICON_MONO_32x32   This is a constant indicating a 32x32 monochrome icon.

public abstract BeanDescriptor getBeanDescriptor()   This returns a **BeanDescriptor** that provides information about the bean's customizer class if it has one. The Bean Descriptor class currently does little more.

public abstract EventSetDescriptor[] getEventSetDescriptors()
Use this method to determine the events that this bean fires.

An array of **EventSetDescriptors** describing the events this bean fires is returned. It returns null if the information should be obtained by automatic inspection.

public abstract int getDefaultEventIndex()   The default event is the event used the most by application builders when using the bean.

An index number of the default event in the array returned by **getEventSetDescriptors** is returned. If there is no default event this method returns **-1**.

public abstract PropertyDescriptor[] getPropertyDescriptors()
Use this method to determine the bean's properties.

An array of **PropertyDescriptors** describing the events this bean fires is returned. It returns null if the information should be obtained by automatic inspection. If an indexed property exists, it is a subclass of the **IndexedPropertyDescriptor** class. Use **instanceof()** to check if this is indeed the case.

public abstract int getDefaultPropertyIndex()   The default property is the property that is updated most commonly by application builders using the bean.

An index number of the default property in the array returned by **getPropertyDescriptors** is returned. If there is no default property, this method returns **-1**.

public abstract MethodDescriptor[] getMethodDescriptors()   Use this method to determine the methods the bean supports. These are the methods accessible to tools and application builders.

An array of **MethodDescriptors** describing the methods supported by the bean is returned. It returns null if the information should be obtained by automatic inspection.

public abstract BeanInfo[] getAdditionalBeanInfo()   This method allows a **BeanInfo** object to return a collection of other **BeanInfo** objects that provide more information about the bean. The **BeanInfo** objects returned are usually **BeanInfo** objects related to parent classes, and allow, in effect, an application builder to step up the bean tree. The current **BeanInfo** takes precedence over the **getAdditionalBeanInfo** objects if there are conflicts between information. Additionally, the closer a **BeanInfo** object is to the current bean, the higher its precedence.

An array of **BeanInfo** objects is returned. If there are no more, it returns null.

public abstract Image getIcon(int iconKind)   This method returns an image object used to represent the bean in tools and application builder environments. Beans are not required in order to provide icons. Though a bean may support all four types of icons (16x16 color, 16x16 mono, and so on) it is recommended that if they only support one, bean developers support 16x16 color.

PARAMETERS iconKind—This is the kind of icon requested. It should be one of the constant values listed previously.

An image object representing the requested icon is returned. If the requested icon does not exist, this method returns null.

Interface java.beans.Customizer

public interface Customizer   This interface allows bean developers to build a custom GUI for customizing each bean. Each customizer should have a null constructor. Because the customizer is not informed of the bean to be customized (it's constructor is null) the constructor does not have access to the bean's properties.

public abstract void setObject(Object bean)   This informs the customizer which bean instance is to be customized. It should be called before the customizer has been added to any parent AWT container.

PARAMETERS bean—This is the object instance to be customized.

public abstract void addPropertyChangeListener(PropertyChange Listener listener)   This method registers a listener for a **Property Change** event. The customizer fires this event whenever it changes the bean in a way that might require the displayed properties to be refreshed.

PARAMETERS **listener**—An   object   to   be   informed   when   a **PropertyChange** event is fired.

public   abstract   void   removePropertyChangeListener(Property ChangeListener   listener)   This method removes a listener for a **PropertyChange** event.

PARAMETERS **listener**—The object to be removed from the list of listeners.

Interface java.beans.PropertyChangeListener

public interface PropertyChangeListener   This interface must be implemented by any object wishing to listen to **PropertyChange** events being fired. When a bean changes a bound property a **PropertyChange** event is fired.

public abstract void propertyChange(PropertyChangeEvent evt) This method is called when a bound property is changed.

PARAMETERS **evt**—A **PropertyChangEvent** object describing the event source and the property that has been changed.

Interface java.beans.PropertyEditor

public interface PropertyEditor   This interface allows an application builder to create a class that supports setting the property value of a given type. The **PropertyEditor** helps make this editing possible in the most intuitive manner. This interface is long and confusing and should be implemented through the **PropertyEditorSupport** class, which implements each method through no-ops. The simplest **PropertyEditors** provide support only for the **getAsText()** and **setAsText()** methods, while more complex **PropertyEditors** provide a GUI through **paintValue()**, or even **getCustomEditor()**. If a **PropertyEditor** does not support a custom editor, it must support the **getAsText()** method, and all **PropertyEditors** must support the **setValue()** method. Because the **PropertyEditor** cannot access the value except through **setValue()**, the constructor should be null.

public abstract void setValue(Object value)   This method is used to to set or update the object that this **PropertyEditor** manages. Primitive types must be wrapped up with their respective **java.lang.*** object type.

PARAMETERS value—The object to be edited. **PropertyEditor** should not modify this object, but should create a new object to hold any modified value.

public abstract Object getValue()   Gets the value of the value **PropertyEditor** is managing.

The property's value is returned. Primitive types are wrapped uPAccording to their respective object types.

public abstract boolean isPaintable()   Informs the user or tool if this **PropertyEditor** has a GUI associated with it.

This returns **true** if the **PropertyEditor** has a valid **paintValue()** method.

public abstract void paintValue(Graphics gfx, Rectangle box) Paints a representation of the value on the screen. The **propertyEditor**'s space is limited to the area described by the parameters. An unused **paintValue** method should be implemented as a silent no-op.

PARAMETERS:
gfx—The graphics object in which to paint.

Box—A rectangle within **gfx** in which the **PropertyEditor** should paint.

public abstract String getJavaInitializationString()   This method can be used to generate Java code to set the property's value. It returns a string fragment of Java code that can be used to initialize the property value.

This returns a string representing Java code to initialize the value.

public abstract String getAsText()   Allows the application builder to simply retrieve the value of a property. Note that not all **Property Editors** support this method.

This returns a string, usable by humans, that is the property value. If the property value cannot be represented as a string, this method returns null.

public abstract void setAsText(String text) throws Illegal ArgumentException Sets the property value by parsing a string. **setAsText()** should be able to parse the string returned by **getAsText()**. If this property cannot be expressed as text then the **IllegalArgument Exception** may be thrown.

PARAMETERS **text**—The String to be parsed.

public abstract String[] getTags() This method can be used to represent enum values. Specifically, if the property must be one of a known set of values then this method returns those values. If a PropertyEditor supports this method then it should support the two xxxAsText() method, using the tags.

This returns the tag values for this property, if they exist. Otherwise this method returns null.

public abstract Component getCustomEditor() A **PropertyEditor** may choose to make available a full custom Component that edits its property value. It is the responsibility of the **PropertyEditor** to hook itself up to its editor Component and report property value changes by firing a **PropertyChange** event.

This returns a **java.awt.Component** that allows an application builder to directly edit the current property value. If this is not supported this method returns null.

public abstract boolean supportsCustomEditor() **true** is returned if the **PropertyEditor** provides a custom editor.

public abstract void addPropertyChangeListener(PropertyChange Listener listener) **PropertyEditors** are required to inform any registered listeners of changes to the value. Thus, when a **PropertyEditor** changes its value, it should fire a **PropertyChangeEvent** to all registered listeners.

PARAMETERS **listener**—A listener to be informed when a **Property ChangeEvent** is fired.

public abstract void removePropertyChangeListener(Property ChangeListener listener)

PARAMETERS `listener`—The listener to be removed.

Interface java.beans.VetoableChangeListener

`public interface VetoableChangeListener` This interface extends EventListener. It must be implemented by any object wishing to listen to `VetoableChange` events being fired. Whenever a bean changes a constrained property, a `VetoableChange` event is fired. A bean must register itself as a `VetoableChangeListener` with a source bean to be informed of constrained property updates.

`public abstract void vetoableChange(PropertyChangeEvent evt) throws PropertyVetoException` This method is called when a constrained property is changed. Each `VetoableChangeListener` must implement this method. If a listener does not agree with a property change, it may throw a `PropertyVetoException`.

PARAMETERS `evt`—A `PropertyChangeEvent` object informing the listener about the event source and the updated property.

Interface java.beans.Visibility

`public interface Visibility` This interface allows the environment to query the bean as to its need for a GUI, as well as for the bean to inform the environment of its GUI needs. When JavaBeans are deployed in embedded applications the host operating system may not have a GUI available. This interface allows beans the ability to determine this information and act accordingly. Most beans will never need this interface; this interface is only for expert developers.

`public abstract boolean needsGui()` Used by the environment to query the bean about its needs.
   `true` is returned if the bean requires a GUI to complete its task.

`public abstract void dontUseGui()` Used by the run-time environment to inform the bean not use the GUI.

`public abstract void okToUseGui()` Used by the run-time environment to inform the bean that it is acceptable to use the GUI.

`public abstract boolean avoidingGui()` Used by the environment to query the bean about its current state.

Because of a call to `dontUseGui()`, `true` is returned if the bean is currently not using the GUI.

Class `java.beans.BeanDescriptor`

`public class BeanDescriptor` The `BeanDescriptor` class can provide information about a bean such as its class or `displayName` (through `FeatureDescriptor`, which it extends). It also keeps track of a bean's customizer class. `BeanDescriptor`, as well as other descriptors, is returned by `BeanInfo` objects to describe beans.

`public BeanDescriptor(Class beanClass)` If a bean doesn't have a customizer, use this constructor.

PARAMETERS `beanClass`—The `Class` object that implements the bean; `sun.beans.Button.class` for example.

`public BeanDescriptor(Class beanClass, Class customizerClass)` If a bean has a customizer, use this constructor.

PARAMETERS:

`beanClass`—The Class object that implements the bean, `sun.beans.Button.class` for example.

`customizerClass`—The Class object that implements the bean's customizer.

`public Class getBeanClass()` The bean's Class object is returned.

`public Class getCustomizerClass()` The Class object of the bean's customizer is returned. If the bean has no customizer, the method returns null.

Class `java.beans.Beans`

`public class Beans` The Beans Class extends Object, provides methods to instantiate beans, determines if objects are beans, and a few other things. Both beans and tools may find this class useful.

public Beans()

`public static Object instantiate(ClassLoader cls,String beanName) throws IOException, ClassNotFoundException` This is used to instantiate a bean. The `beanName` may represent either a serialized object or a class. `Beans.instantiate()` first converts the name to a resource pathname and adds a `.ser` suffix. It tries to read the serialized object from that file. It files it, then attempts to load the `beanName` class and create an instance of it. For example, if you gave the `beanName` of `foo.bar.etc`, `Beans.instantiate()` tries to read a serialized object from `foo/bar/etc.ser`. If it fails it then loads and instantiates `foo.bar.etc`.

PARAMETERS:

`classLoader`—Set this to null if you want to use the default system class loader.

`beanName`—The fully qualified class name of the bean to create.

`public static Object getInstanceOf(Object bean,Class targetType)` This returns some instance of an object from the bean passed in as the first parameter with the type view of `targetType`. The return value may be the object passed in or another. If the specified `targetType` for that bean is not possible then the bean is returned.

PARAMETERS:

`bean`—The object from which you want a view.

`targetType`—The view you want.

`public static boolean isInstanceOf(Object bean,Class targetType)` This is similar to `getInstanceOf()`. It returns true if a bean contains a `targetType` type view.

PARAMETERS:

`bean`—The object from which you want a view.

`targetType`—The view you want.

`true` is returned if the given bean is of the given `targetType`.

`public static boolean isDesignTime()` This indicates whether the bean has been instantiated in a tool for design.

   `true` is returned if the bean is running in a development tool.

`public static boolean isGuiAvailable()`   This indicates whether the bean is an environment that supports an interactive GUI.

`true` is returned if the bean is running in an environment that supports an interactive GUI to provide dialog boxes, buttons, and so on. Usually this returns true in a windows-based environment.

`public static void setDesignTime(boolean isDesignTime) throws SecurityException`   This sets a global flag indicating that the bean is in an application builder environment. Applets are not allowed to set this flag.

PARAMETERS   `isDesignTime`—`true` if the bean is in a development tool.

`public static void setGuiAvailable(boolean isGuiAvailable) throws SecurityException`   Sets a global flag indicating that the bean is in an environment that supports an interactive GUI. Applets are not allowed to set this flag.

PARAMETERS   `isGuiAvailable`—`true` if GUI interaction is possible.

Class `java.beans.EventSetDescriptor`

`public class EventSetDescriptor extends FeatureDescriptor`   This class describes a group of events that a bean fires. Each `EventSet Descriptor` object describes the events for a single listener interface, because a listener interface can have several event target methods.

`public EventSetDescriptor(Class sourceClass,String eventSetName, Class listenerType,StringlistenerMethodName)`   This constructor throws `IntrospectionException` and creates an `EventSetDescriptor` properly only if you are following the JavaBeans conventions for each event `x` of delivering the call to interface `xListener`, having a single argument of type `XEvent`, and registering the `XListener` via `addXListener` at the source component and removing it via the `removeXListener` method.

PARAMETERS:

`sourceClass`—The class that can fire the event.

`eventSetName`—The internal program name of the event.

`listenerType`—Events are delivered to this target interface's class.

`listenerMethodName`—The method called when the event gets delivered to `listenerType`.

`public EventSetDescriptor(Class sourceClass, String eventSetName, Class listenerType, String listenerMethodNames[], String addListenerMethodName, String removeListenerMethodName)` This constructor throws `IntrospectionException` and creates the object based purely on the string names given as parameters.

PARAMETERS:

`sourceClass`—The class that can fire the event.

`eventSetName`—The internal program name of the event.

`listenerType`—The events are delivered to this target interface's class.

`listenerMethodNames`—The methods called when the event gets delivered to `listenerType`.

`addListenerMethodName`—The method name on the event source that is used to register an event listener object.

`removeListenerMethodName`—The method name on the event source that is used to remove an event listener object from the queue of listening objects.

`public EventSetDescriptor(String eventSetName, Class listenerType, Method listenerMethods[], Method addListenerMethod, Method removeListenerMethod)` This constructor throws `Introspection Exception` and creates an `EventSetDescriptor` from scratch.

PARAMETERS:

`eventSetName`—The internal program name of the event.

`listenerType`—The events will be delivered to this target interface's class.

`listenerMethods`—Array of method objects that describes the event handling methods in the listener object.

`addListenerMethodName`—The method name on the event source used to register an event listener object.

`removeListenerMethodName`—The method name on the event source used to remove an event listener object from the listening objects' queue.

`public EventSetDescriptor(String eventSetName, Class listenerType, MethodDescriptor listenerMethodDescriptors[], Method addListenerMethod, Method removeListenerMethod)` This constructor throws `IntrospectionException` and creates an `EventSetDescriptor` from scratch.

PARAMETERS:

`eventSetName`—The internal program name of the event.

`listenerType`—The events are delivered to this target interface's class.

`ListenerMethodDescriptors`—An array of `MethodDescriptor` objects that describes the event handling methods in the listener object.

`addListenerMethodName`—The method name on the event source used to register an event listener object.

`removeListenerMethodName`—The method name on the event source used to remove an event listener object from the listening objects' queue.

`public Class getListenerType()`   The Class object for the target interface invoked when an event is fired is returned.

`public Method[] getListenerMethods()`   Returned are all the Method objects for the methods within the target listener interface that will be invoked when an event is fired.

`public MethodDescriptor[] getListenerMethodDescriptors()`   Returned are all the `MethodDescriptor` objects for the methods within the target listener interface that will be invoked when an event is fired.

`public Method getAddListenerMethod()`   The method signature for the method used to register a listener is returned.

`public Method getRemoveListenerMethod()`   The method signature for the method used to de-register a listener is returned.

`public void setUnicast(boolean unicast)`   This is used to set an event group as unicast.

PARAMETERS `unicast`—`true` if unicast.

`public boolean isUnicast()`   Event sources are generally multicast. `true` is returned if the event group is unicast. The default is `false`.

`public void setInDefaultEventSet(boolean inDefaultEventSet)`   The default is `true`. It allows you to mark an event set as being in the default set.

PARAMETERS `inDefaultEventSet`—`true` if the event set is in the default set.

`public boolean isInDefaultEventSet()` This indicates whether an event set is in the default set. It defaults to **true** if the event set is in the default set.

Class `java.beans.FeatureDescriptor`

`public class FeatureDescriptor` This class is extends Object and is the base class for the `PropertyDescriptor`, `EventSetDescriptor`, `MethodDescriptor`, and `BeanDescriptor` classes. It allows a common set of information to be set and retrieved for each bean and is often used in conjunction with the `BeanInfo` class.

`public String getName()` The internal program name of the feature (whether it's property, event set, or method) is returned. This name is for internal use only.

`public void setName(String name)` Sets the internal name of the feature.

PARAMETERS name—The internal program name of the feature.

`public String getDisplayName()` The localized display name for the feature is returned. If no `displayName` is set, then the same name from `getName()` is returned.

`public void setDisplayName(String displayName)`

PARAMETERS displayName—The localized name for the feature. This name is meant for people to read.

`public boolean isExpert()` If a feature is **expert**, it is intended for expert users, and application builder tools in beginner mode should hide the feature.
   true is returned if the feature is only for experts.

`public void setExpert(boolean expert)` If a feature is **expert** it is intended for expert users, and application builder tools in beginner mode should hide the feature.

PARAMETERS expert—true if the feature is only for experts.

public boolean isHidden()   If a feature is **hidden** it is only to be used by tools and should not be shown to people.

true is returned if the feature is not to be shown to humans.

public void setHidden(boolean hidden)   If a feature is **hidden** it is only to be used by tools and should not be shown to people.

PARAMETERS   **hidden**—**true** if the feature is not to be shown to people.

public String getShortDescription()   This is useful for understanding a feature's use.

A localized, short description of a feature is returned. If not, set it so it defaults to the display name, which if not set, defaults to the internal program name.

public void setShortDescription(String text)   The localized string to describe a feature should not exceed 40 characters in length.

PARAMETERS   **text**—A localized string to describe the feature.

public void setValue(String attributeName, Object value)   An extension mechanism to associate attribute/value pairs for the feature.

PARAMETERS:
attributeName—The locale-independent attribute name.
value—The value.

public Object getValue(String attributeName)   This is an extension mechanism to retrieve an associated attribute and value pair for the feature.

PARAMETERS   **attributeName**—The locale-independent attribute name
The value of the attribute is returned. If the attribute is not defined, null is returned.

public Enumeration attributeNames()   This is used to retrieve all the feature's attributes at one time.

An object of type **java.util.Enumeration** consisting of all the attributes that exist for the feature is returned.

Class `java.beans.IndexedPropertyDescriptor`

public class `IndexedPropertyDescriptor`   This class extends and is a subclass of **`PropertyDescriptor`** and thus functions similarly. However, it enables the added functionality of describing indexed properties, or properties that are arrays and have indexed read and/or indexed write methods. Indexed properties may also provide more traditional non-indexed read and write methods. If they do they must read and write arrays of the same type returned by the indexed read method.

public `IndexedPropertyDescriptor(String propertyName, Class beanClass)`   This constructor throws **`IntrospectionException`** and creates an **`IndexedPropertyDescriptor`** for a property that follows the JavaBeans conventions of having **`getX`** and **`setX`** accessor methods for indexed access, and array access. So it assumes there are two **`getX`** methods and two **`setX`** methods.

PARAMETERS:

`propertyName`—The internal program name of the property.

`beanClass`—The Class object for the target bean.

public `IndexedPropertyDescriptor(String propertyName, Class beanClass, String getterName, String setterName, String indexedGetterName, String indexedSetterName)`   This constructor throws **`IntrospectionException`** and uses the name of the property and a complete set of accessor method names to construct the **`Indexed PropertyDescriptor`**.

PARAMETERS:

`propertyName`—The internal program name of the property.

`beanClass`—The Class object for the target bean.

`getterName`—The method name for reading property values as an array. If the property must be indexed or is write-only this parameter should be null.

`setterName`—The method name for writing property values as an array. If the property must be indexed or is read-only this parameter should be null.

`indexedGetterName`— The method name for reading indexed property values. If the property is write-only this parameter should be null.

`indexedSetterName`—The method name for writing indexed property values. If the property is read-only this parameter should be null.

`public IndexedPropertyDescriptor(String propertyName, Method getter, Method setter, Method indexedGetter, Method indexed Setter)` This constructor throws `IntrospectionException` and takes the program name and four accessor Method objects for both reading and writing.

PARAMETERS:

`propertyName`—The internal program name of the property.

`getter`—The method for reading property values as an array. If the property must be indexed, or is write-only, this parameter should be null.

`setter`—The method for writing property values as an array. If the property must be indexed or is read-only this parameter should be null.

`indexedGetter`—The method for reading indexed property values. If the property is write-only this parameter should be null.

`indexedSetter`—The method for writing indexed property values. If the property is read-only this parameter should be null.

`public Method getIndexedReadMethod()` The Method object containing the method for reading indexed property values is returned. If the property is not indexed or write-only this function will return null.

`public Method getIndexedWriteMethod()` The Method object containing the method for writing indexed property values is returned. If the property is not indexed or read-only this function will return null.

`public Class getIndexedPropertyType()` The Class for the indexed properties type is returned. The Class may describe a primitive such as `boolean`.

Class `java.beans.Introspector`

`public class Introspector` This class extends Object and provides a way for tools or applications to learn about a Java Bean, that is to have a comprehensive understanding of the properties, fired events, and public methods of a bean. The Introspector analyzes the bean's class and super-classes to build a **BeanInfo** object, which describes the target bean. If the bean has an accompanying **BeanInfo** class then this **BeanInfo** object is returned. For a class **X** a corresponding **BeanInfo** class should be entitled **XBeanInfo**. If no **BeanInfo** class is found this way, the **Introspector** class takes the final classname component of the name (**XBeanInfo**) and searches for it in each package in the **BeanInfo** package search path. If not, the **Introspector** class creates a **BeanInfo** object on the fly. If no explicit **BeanInfo** exists **Introspector** uses low-level reflection to examine the bean and the bean class's superclass and construct BeanInfo on the fly. **Introspector** adds to continue analyzing the superclass chain and adding this new information to **BeanInfo**. One more note: All of **Introspector**'s methods are static, so **Introspector** objects never need to be instantiated.

public static BeanInfo getBeanInfo(Class beanClass)   This throws **IntrospectionException**, introspects on a Java bean and merges all **BeanInfo** descriptions of every parent of the bean. Information collected involves properties, public methods, and events.

PARAMETERS **beanClass**—The bean class to be introspected upon.
    A **BeanInfo** object describing **beanClass** and its parents is returned.

public static BeanInfo getBeanInfo(Class beanClass, Class stop-Class)   This throws **IntrospectionException**, introspects on a Java bean and merges **BeanInfo** descriptions of each superclass below a given stop point. Information collected involves properties, public methods, and events.

PARAMETERS:
beanClass—The bean class to be introspected upon.

stopClass—The baseclass at which the analysis stops. Any features in the **stopClass** or its superclasses are not included in the returned **BeanInfo**.

    A **BeanInfo** object is returned.

public static String decapitalize(String name)   This method takes a string and helps it conform to Java name conventions. In Java, the first character of a variable is usually lowercase. In addition, if the first two characters are uppercase the string is left as is. So **JavaBean** becomes **javaBean**, but **URL** remains **URL**.

PARAMETERS `name`—The string to made lowercase.
The lowercase String instance is returned.

`public static String[] getBeanInfoSearchPath()` Returned is the array of package names that are searched in order to find `BeanInfo` classes if there is no accompanying `BeanInfo` class. It defaults to {"sun.beans.infos"}.

`public static void setBeanInfoSearchPath(String path[])` This changes the list of package names used for finding `BeanInfo` classes. It defaults to {"sun.beans.infos"}.

PARAMETERS `path`—Array of package names to be searched on `Introspection`.

Class java.beans.MethodDescriptor

`public class MethodDescriptor` This class extends `FeatureDescriptor` and describes which public methods a Java Bean has available in its interface to other components. The primary use of `MethodDescriptor` objects comes in overriding `BeanInfo.getMethodDescriptors()`.

`public MethodDescriptor(Method method)`

PARAMETERS `method`—A Method object describing the method to be added to the public interface.

`public MethodDescriptor(Method method, ParameterDescriptor parameterDescriptors[])`

PARAMETERS:
`method`—A Method object describing the method to be added to the public interface.
`parameterDescriptors`—Descriptive information for each of the method's parameters.

`public Method getMethod()` This is used to determine the method to which the `MethodDescriptor` applies.
The Method object representing the method is returned.

public ParameterDescriptor[] getParameterDescriptors()   The locale-independent descriptions of the parameters is returned. If the parameter names aren't known the method returns a null array.

Class java.beans.ParameterDescriptor

public class ParameterDescriptor   This class enables bean developers to disseminate additional information about each parameter in a method. It also exends **FeatureDescriptor**. This information augments the low-level type information provided by the **java.lang.reflect. Method** class. This class derives all its functionality from its super class **FeatureDescriptor**.

Class java.beans.PropertyChangeEvent

public class PropertyChangeEvent   This class represents the new event model in AWT 1.1 and is the event model for Java Beans 1.0. It also extends **EventObject**. Whenever a bound or constrained property changes, a PropertyChange Event is delivered to either **property Change()** or **vetoableChange()**. These two methods are the sole methods of the **PropertyChangeListener** and **VetoableChangeListener** interfaces, respectively. **PropertyChangeEvents** contain a number of properties, such as event name, old value, and new value, that allow event handlers to effectively manage the events fired. If either the new or old value is a primitive it must be wrapped using the **java.lang.*** Object type. If the values of the old and new values are not known null values may be provided. An event source may send a null object as the name to signal that an arbitrary set of its properties have changed.

public PropertyChangeEvent(Object source, String propertyName, Object oldValue, Object newValue)   Each time an event is fired a **PropertyChangeEvent** is constructed.

PARAMETERS:

source—The bean that fired the event.

propertyName—The internal program name of the property that was changed.

oldValue—The property's old value.

newValue—The property's new value.

public String getPropertyName() The internal program name of the property that was changed is returned. This may be null if multiple properties have changed.

public Object getNewValue() The property's new value is returned. If the value is a primitive it is wrapped in an equivalent object representation. It may be null if multiple properties have changed.

public Object getOldValue() The property's old value is returned. If the value is a primitive it is wrapped in an equivalent object representation. It may be null if multiple properties have changed.

public void setPropagationId(Object propagationId) If a listener receives an event and then fires its own it must call this method to ensure that the **propagationId** value is passed from the incoming event to the outgoing event.

PARAMETERS **propagationId**—The **propagationId** object for the event.

public Object getPropagationId() The **propagationId** field is primarily being reserved for future use. However, Beans 1.0 requires that a listener that catches a **PropertyChangeEvent** and then proceeds to fire a **PropertyChangEvent** of its own is required to pass on the same **propagationId** value from the incoming event to the outgoing event.

The **propagationId** object associated with a bound/constrained property update is returned.

Class java.beans.PropertyChangeSupport

public class PropertyChangeSupport This class is provided to help beans manage their bound properties. It extends **Object** and implements **Serializable**. Specifically this class can manage the registration and notification of the listeners of various bound properties. To use this class a bean can be subclassed from it, or an instance of this class can exist as a member field of your bean. We recommend the latter option.

public PropertyChangeSupport(Object sourceBean)

PARAMETERS **sourceBean**—The bean for which the **PropertyChangeSupport** class manages bound properties.

public synchronized void addPropertyChangeListener(Property ChangeListener listener) This adds a **PropertyChangeListener** to the list of listeners.

PARAMETERS **listener**—The **PropertyChangeListener** to be added. Usually a this pointer as the object implements the **PropertyChangeListener** interface.

public synchronized void removePropertyChangeListener(Property ChangeListener listener) This removes a **PropertyChangeListener** from the list of listeners.

PARAMETERS **listener**—The **PropertyChangeListener** to be removed

public void firePropertyChange(String propertyName, Object old Value, Object newValue) This fires an event to all registered listeners. If **oldValue** and **newValue** are equal and non-null, no event is fired.

PARAMETERS:

propertyName—The internal program name of the property that was changed.

oldValue—The property's old value. Primitive types must be wrapped as objects.

newValue—The property's new value. Primitive types must be wrapped as objects.

Class java.beans.PropertyDescriptor

public class PropertyDescriptor This class fully describes one property that a bean exports through the **get** and **set** methods. It also extends **FeatureDescriptor**.

public PropertyDescriptor(String propertyName, throws IntrospectionException This constructor assumes that the property follows standard Java conventions and has the **getX** and **setX** accessor methods.

PARAMETERS:

propertyName—The internal program name of the property.

beanClass—The Class object for the bean that has the property. For example **sun.beans.Button.class**.

```
public PropertyDescriptor(String propertyName, Class beanClass,
String getterName, String setterName) throws Introspection
Exception
```

PARAMETERS:

propertyName—The internal program name of the property.

beanClass—The Class object for the bean with the property. For example **sun.beans.Button.class**.

getterName—The String name of the method used for reading the property value. If the property is write-only this parameter should be null.

setterName—The String name of the method used for writing the property value. If the property is read-only this parameter should be null.

```
public PropertyDescriptor(String propertyName, Method getter,
Method setter)
```
This throws **IntrospectionException**.

PARAMETERS:

propertyName—The internal program name of the property.

getter—The method (Method object) used for reading the property value. If the property is write-only this parameter should be null.

setter—The method (Method object) used for writing the property value. If the property is read-only this parameter should be null.

public Class getPropertyType() This is used to determine the property's class.

The type information for the property is returned. The class object may also indicated a primitive type such as **boolean**. The result may be null if the property is an indexed property that doesn't support non-indexed access.

public Method getReadMethod() The Method object that should be used to read the property value—the getter method is returned. If the property can't be read it should return null.

public Method getWriteMethod() The Method object that should be used to write the property value— the setter method is returned. If the property can't be written it should return null.

public boolean isBound() This only updates to bound properties and causes a **PropertyChangeEvent** to be fired when the property is changed. This method determines if the property can expect that sort of behavior.

true is returned if the property is bound.

`public void setBound(boolean bound)` This only updates to bound properties and causes a `PropertyChangeEvent` to be fired when the property is changed. This method allows this sort of behavior to be defined for the property.

PARAMETERS `bound`—`true` if this property is bound.

`public boolean isConstrained()` This only updates to constrained properties and causes a `VetoableChangeEvent` to get fired when the property is changed. This method determines if the property can expect that sort of behavior.

`true` is returned if the property is constrained.

`public void setConstrained(boolean constrained)` This only updates to constrained properties and causes a `VetoableChangeEvent` to be fired when the property is changed. This method allows this sort of behavior to be defined for the property.

PARAMETERS `constrained`—`true` if this property is constrained.

`public void setPropertyEditorClass(Class propertyEditorClass)` `PropertyEditors` usually use the `PropertyEditorManager`, but if you want to associate a certain `PropertyEditor` with a given property use this method

PARAMETERS `propertyEditorClass`—The class for the desired `Property Editor`.

`public Class getPropertyEditorClass()` A `PropertyEditor` class that has been registered for this property with this `PropertyDescriptor` class is returned. Usually the `PropertyEditorManager` is used by `PropertyEditors`, so this method returns null.

Class java.beans.PropertyEditorManager

`public class PropertyEditorManager` This class can be used to both register and find property editors for any given type names. It extends Object. The property editors must support the `java.beans.PropertyEditor` interface to be valid.

To locate an editor for a given type, the `PropertyEditorManager` goes through three steps. First, it has a `registerEditor` method that allows one to specifically link a type to a property editor class. Second, it adds **Editor** to the fully qualified classname and searches for it. Finally it takes the simple classname, appends **Editor** and looks in a search-path of packages. Default **PropertyEditors** are provided for all the primitive types, as well as the classes **java.lang.String**, **java.awt.Color**, and **java.awt.Font**. A final note: all the methods of this class are static, so there is no need to instantiate it.

public PropertyEditorManager()

public static void registerEditor(Class targetType, Class editorClass) This registers an editor class to edit values of a certain type of class.

PARAMETERS:
targetType—The class object of the type to be edited

editorClass—The class object of the editor class. If this is null, any existing definition will be removed.

public static PropertyEditor findEditor(Class targetType) This finds an editor for a given class type.

PARAMETERS **targetType**—The class object for the type to be edited
An editor object that conforms to the **PropertyEditor** interface is returned. A null result means no editor was found.

public static String[] getEditorSearchPath() An array of package names that will be searched in order to find property editors is returned. **Sun.beans.editors** is the default.

public static void setEditorSearchPath(String path[]) Allows one to change the set of package names to be searched for finding property editors.

PARAMETERS **path**—Array of package names.

Class java.beans.PropertyEditorSupport

public class PropertyEditorSupport This class is a skeleton class that provides an implementation of the **PropertyEditor** interface. It extends **Object** and implements **PropertyEditor**. The current implementation of each method uses no-ops, so you can override only those methods that you need to. Please see the **PropertyEditor** interface to see the definition of each method. There are several ways of using the **PropertyEditorSupport** class. If you create a property editor as a direct subclass of the **PropertyEditor Support** class then you simply use the default constructor. However, you can also use an instance of the **PropertyEditorSupport** class in the editor you create and delegate most of the work to this instance. If you do this you should use the second constructor. Also, the **firePropertyChange()** method is called whenever **setValue()** is called.

protected PropertyEditorSupport()   This is a constructor for use by derived **PropertyEditor** classes.

protected PropertyEditorSupport(Object source)   This is the constructor for use when a **PropertyEditor** is delegating to us.

PARAMETERS   source—The source to use for any events fired.

Class java.beans.SimpleBeanInfo

public class SimpleBeanInfo   This class is a skeleton class that provides an implementation of the **BeanInfo** interface. It extends **object** and implements **BeanInfo**. The current implementation of each method uses no-ops, so you can override only those methods you need to. Every method not overriden results in an action being denied to anyone querying the bean to find its properties. Please see the **BeanInfo** interface to see the definition of each method. One item to notice is the method **loadImage()** which makes overriding **getIcon()** much easier.

public SimpleBeanInfo()

public Image loadImage(String resourceName)   This is a simple utility method used in conjunction with **getIcon()** to help load icon images. It takes the name of a resource file associated with the current object's class file and loads an image (usually a GIF) object.

PARAMETERS   resourceName—A pathname relative to the directory holding the class file of the current class.

An image object is returned. If the load failed it returns null.

Class `java.beans.VetoableChangeSupport`

`public class VetoableChangeSupport` This class is a support class for beans that support constrained properties. It extends `Object` and implements `Serializable`. This class, similar to `PropertyChangeSupport`, manages the low-level details of registering listeners of a property as well as informing them when a change takes place. Most importantly, this class also manages the chain reaction that occurs when a listener vetoes a change. You can either use a subclass of this class or you can use an instance of this class as a member of your bean. Be careful not to use the `getter` method of a constrained property because though the value has changed, the `getter` method does not reflect the new value until all listeners have agreed.

`public VetoableChangeSupport(Object sourceBean)` This is a constructor method

PARAMETERS `sourceBean`—The bean for which `VetoableChangeSupport` manages a property.

`public synchronized void addVetoableChangeListener (VetoableChangeListener listener)` This adds a `VetoableListener` to the list of listeners.

PARAMETERS `listener`—The `VetoableChangeListener` to be added to the list.

`public synchronized void removeVetoableChangeListener (VetoableChangeListener listener)` This removes a `VetoableChange Listener` from the list of listeners.

PARAMETERS `listener`—The `VetoableChangeListener` to be removed from the list.

`public void fireVetoableChange(String propertyName, Object old-Value, Object newValue)` This informs all registered listeners of a vetoable property update, and it throws `PropertyVetoException`. If someone vetoes the change this method fires a new event informing all listeners to reregister the old value, and then rethrows the `Property VetoException`. If the old and new event are both equal and non-null then no event is fired.

PARAMETERS:

`propertyName`—The internal program name of the property that has changed.

`oldValue`—The property's old value.

`newValue`—The property's new value.

Class java.beans.IntrospectionException

`public class IntrospectionException` This class represents the exception thrown when an exception happens during the introspection process. Some of the typical reasons for this exception being thrown include not being able to map a string class name to a class object, not being able to resolve a string method name, or specifying a method name that has the wrong type signature for its intended use.

`public IntrospectionException(String mess)`

PARAMETERS `mess`—A message printed when an `Introspection Exception` is thrown.

Class java.beans.PropertyVetoException

`public class PropertyVetoException` This class represents the exception thrown when a proposed change to a property is unacceptable to a listener. The `PropertyChangeEvent` that caused the exception to be thrown is required by the constructor, but this can simply be passed down from `VetoableChangeListener.vetoableChange()`, which must be implemented by each listener in order to veto a property change.

`public PropertyVetoException(String mess, PropertyChangeEvent evt)`

PARAMETERS:

`mess`—A message printed when a `PropertyVetoException` is thrown.

`evt`—A `PropertyChangeEvent` describing the vetoed change.

`public PropertyChangeEvent getPropertyChangeEvent()` This returns the `PropertyChangeEvent` that caused the exception to be thrown.

Partial package java.util

Though the interfaces and classes listed the following sections are not a part of the `java.beans` package, they are heavily used by the JavaBeans model and are a part of the new event model for JDK 1.1.

Interface java.util.EventListener

public interface EventListener   This interface is the prototypical interface from which all event listener interfaces are derived. This interface has no methods and represents merely a way to identify event listeners. Convention states that all derived **EventListener** interfaces specify their event notification methods according to the following method signature:
public void eventNotificationMethodName(EventType e);.

Class java.util.EventObject

public class EventObject   The **Event** class is the abstract root class from which all event state objects shall be derived. Events are constructed with reference to an object source or the object that fired the event.

public EventObject(Object source)   This constructs a prototypical event.

PARAMETERS   source—The object firing the Event.

public Object getSource()   The object firing the Event is returned.

Class java.util.TooManyListenersException

public class TooManyListenersException   This class represents the exception thrown when the application developer desires a unicast special case of a multicast event source. Simply put, this exception allows only one concurrently registered event listener for a given event listener source.

public   TooManyListenersException()   This is a constructor for a **TooManyListenersException** with no descriptive message.

`public TooManyListenersException(String s)` This is the constructor for a `TooManyListenersException` with a descriptive message.

PARAMETERS `s`—The message to describe the exception.

APPENDIX B

The Drag-and-Drop Classes and Interfaces

The DnDConstants Class

The **DnDConstants** class defines the actions that may be associated with a drag-and-drop operation.

The following constants are defined.

- **ACTION_NONE**
- **ACTION_COPY**
- **ACTION_MOVE**
- **ACTION_COPY_OR_MOVE**
- **ACTION_REFERENCE**

The DragSource Class

The **DragSource** class has these methods:

- **public static DragSource getDefaultDragSource();**

  This method returns the default **DragSource** instance, which can be used for the lifetime of the application.

- **public void startDrag(Component c, AWTEvent trigger, int actions, Cursor dragCursor, Image dragImage, Point imageOffset, Transferable transferable, DragSourceListener dsl)**

  throws InvalidDnDOperationException, SecurityException

  This method starts the drag and drop operation. The parameters are:

  c—the component in which the **Drag** trigger occurred

  trigger—the **AWTEvent** that initiated the operation

  actions—the drag *verbs* appropriate

  dragCursor—the initial cursor or null for defaults

`dragImage`—the image to drag or null

`imageOffset`—the image offset origin from the cursor hotspot.

`transferable`—the operation's subject data

`dsl`—the `DragSourceListener` caller must have `AWTPermission` `startDrag` to succeed

■ `public FlavorMap getFlavorMap()`

This method returns a `FlavorMap`

In addition, the following methods are defined (as of now, in beta two, these methods do not exist). They are meant to return the default cursors.

■ `public static Cursor getDefaultCopyDropCursor();`

■ `public static Cursor getDefaultMoveDropCursor();`

■ `public static Cursor getDefaultLinkDropCursor();`

■ `public static Cursor getDefaultCopyNoDropCursor();`

■ `public static Cursor getDefaultMoveNoDropCursor();`

■ `public static Cursor getDefaultLinkNoDropCursor();`

The `DragSourceContext` Class

The `DragSourceContext` class is used to convey information about a particular drag-and-drop operation. A `DragSourceContext` object is created when the `DragSource.startDrag` method is invoked. A single `DragSource` object generates multiple `DragSourceContexts` for each drag-and-drop operation. Thus, it is this class that actually contains all the information relating to a particular operation. It also has the responsibility of managing event notifications. It passes these events on to the `DragSourceListener`.

The methods defined in the class are:

■ `public DragSource getDragSource()`

Returns the `DragSource` that instantiated this `DragSourceContext`

■ `public Component getComponent()`

Returns the component clicked to start the drag operation. This is the same component passed to the `DragSource.startDrag` method.

■ `public AWTEvent getTrigger()`

Returns the event that triggered the drag operation. This is the same event passed to the `DragSource.startDrag` method.

> `public Image getDragImage()`

Returns the drag image, if any, associated with the operation

> `public Point getDragImageOffset()`

Returns the image offset image from the cursor hotspot

> `public int getSourceActions()`

Returns the allowed actions as a combination of action constants from the `DnDConstants` class

> `public void cancelDrag()` throws `InvalidDnDOperationException`

Cancels the drag-and-drop operation.

> `public void setSourceActions(int a)` throws `InvalidDnDOperationException`

Sets the actions to valid for the current operation

> `public int getSourceActions()`

Returns the actions set for the operation.

> `public void setCursor(Cursor c)`

Sets the cursor during the drag operation.

> `public Cursor getCursor()`

Returns the cursor set for the drag operation.

> `public synchronized void addDragSourceListener(DragSourceListener dsl)` throws `TooManyListenersException`

This method adds an `EventListener` for the drag-and-drop events. Usually the sender implements `DragSourceListener`. Only a single `DragSourceListener` can be registered with a `DragSourceContext`. Adding a new listener actually replaces the old listener.

> `public synchronized void removeDragSourceListener(DragSourceListener dsl)`

This method removes a `DragSourceListener`.

There are other methods meant for the interaction between the `DragSourceContext` and its peer, the `DragSourceContextPeer`. These methods redirect the drag-and-drop events from the peer to the `DragSourceListener`. We shall not get into the possibility of implementing a custom drag-and-drop facility, and hence these methods are not covered in this chapter.

The DragSourceListener Interface

The **DragSourceListener** interface is defined for implementing a set of methods for keeping track of the events occuring during the drag-and-drop operation from the Sender's point of view. The methods in the interface are:

- **void dragEnter(DragSourceDragEvent dsde)**

  This method is invoked as the hotspot enters a new drop target. It can be used to retrieve the associated **DragSourceContext** from the **DragSourceDragEvent**.

- **void dragOver(DragSourceDragEvent dsde)**

  This method is invoked as the hotspot moves within a drop site.

- **void dragGestureChanged(DragSourceDragEvent dsde)**

  This method is invoked if and when the state of the input device(s) the user is interacting with in order to perform the drag operation, changes. Typically these input devices are mouse buttons or keyboard modifiers.

- **void dragExit(DragSourceDragEvent dsde)**

  This method is invoked as the hotspot moves out of a drop site.

- **void drop(DragSourceDragEvent dsde)**

  This method is invoked when the user gestures a drop (releasing the mouse button over a drop site).

- **void dragDropEnd(DragSourceDropEvent dsde)**

  This method is invoked when the drag and drop operation ends, usually resulting in the actual **Transferable** object being transferred.

The DragSourceDragEvent Class

The **DragSourceDragEvent** is generated when the hotspot is dragged over the screen. It is delivered from the **DragSourceContext** to the currently registered **DragSourceListener** (Sender) via the **dragEnter**, **dragOver**, **dragGestureChanged** and drop methods of the **DragSourceListener**.

The methods defined in the class, or from its parents are

- **public DragSourceContext getDragSourceContext()**

  Returns the **DragSourceContext** for the operation generating the event.

▓ `public int getTargetActions()`

Returns the actions supported by the component over which the hotspot is currently being dragged.

▓ `public int getGestureModifiers()`

Returns the current state of the input device modifiers, usually the mouse buttons and keyboard modifiers, associated with the user's gesture.

The `DragSourceDropEvent` Class

The `DragSourceDropEvent` is generated when the user gestures a drop over a component on the screen that is a potential Receiver. It is delivered from the `DragSourceContext` to the currently registered `DragSourceListener` (Sender). It is delivered via the drop method of the `DragSourceListener`.

It contains the current state of the operation to enable the Sender to to provide appropriate feedback to the user when the operation completes. Feedback usually means changing the cursor shape by using the `Drag SourceContext.setCursor` method.

The methods defined in the `DragSourceEvent` class, or from its parent are:

▓ `public DragSourceContext getDragSourceContext()`

Returns the `DragSourceContext` for the operation generating the event.

▓ `public boolean isDropSuccessful()`

Returns whether the drop was successfully accepted be the drop site.

Receiver Side Drag-and-Drop Classes and Interfaces

The `DropTarget` class

A `DropTarget` encapsulates all the platform-specific handling of the drag-and-drop protocol from the Receiver's point of view. To enable a Java component to be exposed to the system as a drop site, associate a `DropTarget` with the component. Such a relationship exports the associated component's geometry to the client desktop as being receptive to drag and drop operations when the hotspot location intersects that geometry.

The `DropTarget` can be constructed using one of these constructors.

▪ `public DropTarget(Component c, int actions, DropTargetListener dtl, Insets asins, boolean active)`

Here the component is the one that is to be associated with the `DropTarget`. The actions specify the allowed action types the receiver can accept. The `DropTargetListener` is the one that responds to all the event notifications (the receiver). The insets are in place because of the possibility that the component supports auto-scrolling. The last parameter sets whether this component is ready to accept drops.

▪ `public DropTarget()`

Constructs a `DropTarget`. To use a `DropTarget` so constructed, you need to explicitly associate a component and a `DropTargetListener` by using the `setComponent` and `addDropTargetListener`. The default actions set are `DnDConstants.ACTION_COPY_OR_MOVE` is set to be active.

▪ `public DropTarget(Component c, DropTargetListener dtl)`

Constructs a `DropTarget`. This associates the specified component and `DragSourceListener`. The default actions set are `DnDConstants.ACTION_COPY_OR_MOVE` is set to be active.

▪ `public DropTarget(Component c, int actions, DropTargetListener dtl)`

Constructs a `DropTarget` with the specified component associated and `DropTargetListener` and allowed actions. It is set to be active by default.

▪ `public synchronized void setComponent(Component c) throws IllegalArgumentException`

This sets the association of the `DropTarget` with a component. The same association can be achieved by invoking `component.setDropTarget(droptarget)`, which is a new method introduced in component.

▪ `public synchronized Component getComponent()`

Returns the component associated with the drop target.

▪ `public boolean supportsAutoScrolling()`

Returns if this `DropTarget` and component supports autoscrolling

▓ `public void setAutoscrollInsets(Insets scrollInsets)`

Sets the Autoscrolling insets.

▓ `public Insets getAutoscrollInsets()`

Returns the current autoscrolling insets.

▓ `public synchronized void setDefaultActions(int ops)`

Sets the default acceptable actions for this `DropTarget`

▓ `public synchronized int getDefaultActions()`

Returns the current default actions.

▓ `public synchronized void setActive(boolean isActive)`

Sets whether the `DropTarget` is active, and thus responsive to drops.

▓ `public synchronized boolean isActive()`

Returns the state of the `DropTarget` of being active or responsive to drops.

▓ `public int isDnDTrigger(AWTEvent event)`

Returns whether the specified event is a valid trigger for a drag and drop operation.

▓ `public synchronized void addDropTargetListener` `(DropTargetListener dte)` throws `TooManyListenersException`

Sets or replaces the `DropTargetListener` associated with this `DropTarget`.

▓ `public synchronized void` `removeDropTargetListener(DropTargetListener dte)`

Removes the currently associated `DropTargetListener` with this `DropTarget`.

▓ `public synchronized void dragEnter(DropTargetDragEvent dtde)`

The `DropTarget` intercepts `dragEnter()` notifications before the registered `DropTargetListener` gets them.

▓ `public DropTargetContext getDropTargetContext()`

Returns the `DropTargetContext` associated with this `DropTarget`.

There are other methods in the class that trap the `DropEvents` and redirect it to the `DropTargetListener`, as well as methods to co-ordinate the relationship between the component and the `DropTarget`. These are not necessary for using the drag-and-drop functionality, and hence are left out of the dicussion.

DropTargetContext

A **DropTargetContext** is created whenever the hotspot enters the visible geometry of a component with an associated **DropTarget**. The **DropTarget Context** provides the methods for the receiver to furnish the user with feedback during the drag and drop operation, as well as to carry out the subsequent data transfer.

The methods defined in the **DropTargetContext** class are

- **public DropTarget getDropTarget()**

  Returns the **DropTarget** associated with this context.

- **public Component getComponent()**

  Returns the component associated with this context.

- **public void setTargetActions(int actions)**

  Sets the current actions acceptable to this **DropTarget**.

- **public int getTargetActions()**

  Returns the current actions acceptable to this **DropTarget**.

- **public void dropComplete(boolean success) throws InvalidDnDOperationException**

  Signals that the drop is completed and if it was successful.

- **protected DataFlavor[] getCurrentDataFlavors()**

  Returns the available **data** flavors of the **transferable** object of this operation

- **protected synchronized Transferable getTransferable() throws InvalidDnDOperationException**

  Returns the **Transferable** object of this operation.

The DropTargetListener interface

The **DropTargetListener** interface is defined for implementing a set of methods for keeping track of the events occuring during the drag-and-drop operation from the Receiver's point of view. The methods in the interface are

- **public abstract void dragEnter(DropTargetDragEvent dtde)**

  This method is invoked when the hotspot intersects a visible portion of the **DropTarget**'s associated component. The **DropTargetListener** checks compatibility of the operation actions and the **data** flavors supplied by the **DragSource**.

▨ `public abstract void dragOver(DropTargetDragEvent dtde)`

This method is invoked while the hotspot moves over the `DropTarget`'s associated component.

▨ `public abstract void dragScroll(DropTargetDragEvent dtde)`

This method is invoked when the hotspot has been stationary for a specified period of time and is within the `DropTarget`'s associated component and the scroll insets

▨ `public abstract void dragExit(DropTargetDragEvent dtde)`

This method is invoked when the hotspot moves out of the `DropTarget`'s associated component.

▨ `public abstract void drop(DropTargetDropEvent dtde)`

This method is invoked when the user drops the object into the `DropTarget`'s associated component.

The `DropTargetEvent`, `DropTargetDragEvent` and `DropTargetDropEvent` Classes

The `DropTargetEvent` is the base class for both the `DropTargetDragEvent` and the `DropTargetDropEvent`. It encapsulates the current state of the drag-and-drop operations, such as the current `DropTargetContext`, the cursor location, and the operations supported by the `DragSource`.

The methods are:

▨ `public Point getLocation()`

Returns the current cursor location in component's coordinates.

▨ `public DropTargetContext getDropTargetContext()`

Returns the `DropTargetContext`

▨ `public DataFlavor[] getCurrentDataFlavors()`

Returns current data flavors

▨ `public int getSourceActions()`

Returns source actions.

The `DropTargetDragEvent` class contains no additional methods beyond the base class.

The `DropTargetDropEvent` class is delivered via the `DropTarget Listener.drop()` method It has the following methods beyond those defined by the base class:

▨ `public Transferable getTransferable()`

Returns the `Transferable` associated with the drop

▨ `public void acceptDrop(int dropAction)`

Accept the `Drop` using the specified operation.

▨ `public void rejectDrop()`

Reject the `Drop`.

APPENDIX C

The Runtime Containment Classes and Interfaces

The **BeanContext** Interface

The **BeanContext** interface defines the actions and methods that must be defined by any Bean Context.

The methods are

- **Object instantiateChild(String beanName)**

  This method allows for any process or agent that knows this Bean Context to create one of the children of the context. The **beanName** is a string representation of the child that exists within the context.

- **Object getService(Class serviceClass, BeanContextChild requestor);**

  This method allows for a Bean that is aware of this Bean Context to ask it to return a delegate service object. This allows for Context environment services to be used by a Bean.

- **boolean hasService(Class serviceClass, BeanContextChild requestor);**

  This method allows a Bean that is aware of a Bean Context to ask if it has a specified service. This is quite useful as a test before attempting to get a specific service.

- **public InputStream getResourceAsStream(String name, BeanContextChild requestor);**

  This method allows for a Context to insert environmental logic into the standard **ClassLoader** semantics. A **BeanContextChild** calls this in place of the **ClassLoader**-based method. This method returns the resource as an instance of **InputStream**.

- **public java.net.URL getResource(String name, BeanContextChild requestor);**

  This method allows for a Context to insert environmental logic into the standard **ClassLoader** semantics. A **BeanContextChild** calls this in place of the **ClassLoader**-based method. This method returns the resource as an instance of URL.

▨ **void addPropertyChangeListener (String name,PropertyChangeListener pcl);**

This method allows a Bean Context to register a **PropertyChangeListener** instance.

▨ **void removePropertyChangeListener (String name, PropertyChangeListener pcl);**

This method allows a Bean Context to remove a registered **PropertyChangeListener** instance.

▨ **void removeBeanContextListener (BeanContextListener bcl);**

This method allows a Bean Context to remove a **BeanContextListener** instance.

▨ **void addBeanContextListener(BeanContextListener bcl);**

This method allows a Bean Context to register a **BeanContextListener** instance.

The **BeanContextListener** Interface

The **BeanContextListener** interface defines one method that must further define an **EventListner**.

The method is:

void beanContextChanged(BeanContextEvent bce)

This method states that a Bean Context has been altered in some way. The details of the alteration are found by interrogating the **Bean ContextEvent** instance.

The **BeanContextEvent** Class

The **BeanContextEvent** class extends **EventObject**, is abstract, and has the following methods:

▨ **public BeanContext getBeanContext()**

This method returns an instance of the **BeanContext** that generated the event.

▨ **public synchronized void setPropagatedFrom(BeanContext bc)**

This method allows the event to be modified as to which Bean Context it was propagated from.

▨ `public synchronized BeanContext getPropagatedFrom()`

This method allows the event to be interrogated by the receiving process as to which potential nesting Bean Context it was propagated from. Note that this is independent of what potential Bean Context the process registered its Bean Context Listener within.

▨ `public synchronized boolean isPropagated()`

This method allows a process to interrogate an event instance as to whether it was propagated by a nesting Bean Context.

The `BeanContextMembershipEvent` Class

The `BeanContextMembershipEvent` class extends the `BeanContextEvent` object, is abstract, and has the following methods:

▨ `public boolean isDeltaMember(Object o)`

This method allows an object to be tested as to whether it was a child Bean that was either added to, or removed from the membership list of children in a Bean Context membership.

▨ `public Object[] getDeltas()`

This method returns an instance of all children that have been added to, or removed from a Bean Context's membership list.

▨ `public boolean isChildrenAddedEvent()`

This method allows for this event to be interrogated as to whether it is a child being added to an associated Bean Context.

▨ `public boolean isChildrenRemovedEvent()`

This method allows for this event to be interrogated as to whether it is a child being removed from an associated Bean Context.

The `BeanContextAddedEvent` Class

The `BeanContextAddedEvent` class extends the `BeanContextMember shipEvent` object, and defines the following constructor:

`BeanContextAddedEvent(BeanContext bc, Object[] bccs)`

This constructor takes as parameters the Bean Context that this event is associated with as well as an array of objects representing the children affected by this addition operation.

The `BeanContextRemovedEvent` Class

The `BeanContextRemovedEvent` class extends the `BeanContextMembershipEvent` object and defines the following constructor:

`BeanContextRemovedEvent(BeanContext bc, Object[] bccs)`

This constructor takes as parameters the Bean Context this event is associated with and an array of objects representing the children affected by this removal operation.

The `BeanContextChild` Class

The *BeanContextChild* class extends the BeanContextListener object, and defines the following methods:

▓ `void setBeanContext(BeanContext bc)`

This method allows for a child of a Bean Context, usually another nesting Bean Context or Bean, to set its associated Bean Context that it is contained within.

▓ `BeanContext getBeanContext()`

This method returns the set Bean Context of which this child is a member.

▓ `void addPropertyChangeListener (String name, PropertyChangeListener pcl)`

This method adds a `PropertyChangeListener` to a Bean Context Child. It takes both the actual `PropertyChangeListener` object, and a string by which this child will know it.

▓ `void removePropertyChangeListener (String name, PropertyChangeListener pcl)`

This method removes a **PropertyChangeListener** from a Bean Context Child. It takes both the actual **PropertyChangeListener** object and a string that it was known by to the child.

- **void addVetoableChangeListener (String name, VetoableChangeListener pcl)**

This method adds a **VetoableChangeListener** to a Bean Context Child. It takes both the actual **VetoableChangeListener** object, and a string that it will be known by to this child.

- **void removeVetoableChangeListener (String name, VetoableChangeListener pcl)**

This method removes a **VetoableChangeListener** from a Bean Context Child. It takes both the actual **VetoableChangeListener** object, and a string that it was known by to the child.

APPENDIX D

The Java Activation Framework Classes and Interfaces

The **DataHandler** Class

The **DataHandler** is the main point of interface for access to the JAF. It provides a common access point for all the other sub-classes of the Java Activation Framework. In particular, it has methods to access the **DataSource**, the **DataContentHandler**, the **CommandMap**, and the JavaBean associated with the data it represents.

The **DataHandler** constructors are

▪ **public DataHandler(DataSource ds)**

This constructor creates a **DataHandler** for a specified stream-based **DataSource**.

▪ **public DataHandler(Object obj, String mimeType)**

This constructor creates a **DataHandler** for the specified Java Object and a MIME type.

▪ **public DataHandler(URL url)**

This constructor is useful for creating a **DataHandler** for data from a URL.

The methods in the DataHandler class are

▪ **public DataSource getDataSource() throws IOException**

This method returns the **DataSource** object associated with stream-based data. The documentation provided with the pre-release version indicates that for **DataHandlers** not constructed with a **DataSource**, the **DataHandler** creates one. However, this behavior is not reflected in the implementation.

▪ **public String getName()**

This method returns the name associated with the data object. If this **DataHandler** was created with a **DataSource**, this method invokes **DataSource.getName**. For other **DataHandlers**, it returns null.

■ **public String getContentType()**

This method returns the MIME type of this object. In the event **DataHandler** was constructed with a **DataSource**, it invokes the **DataSource.getContentType**. For **DataHandlers** created from a URL, it can get the content type from the **URLConnection.getContentType** method. For **DataHandlers** created from a Java object, the MIME type is specified during construction. etc.

■ **public InputStream getInputStream()** throws **IOException**

This method returns the **InputStream** associated with the **DataHandler**. In the event **DataHandler** was constructed with a **DataSource**, it invokes the **DataSources getInputStream** method. If the **DataHandler** was created with an object and has a **DataContentHandler** associated with it, a new **InputStream** is created. The associated **DataContentHandler**'s **writeTo** method is used to write into this stream asynchronously in a separate thread. This effectively returns an **InputStream** representing the data.

■ **public void writeTo(OutputStream os)** throws **IOException**

This method writes the data associated with the **DataHandler** to the specified **OutputStream**. In case the **DataHandler** was constructed with a **DataSource**, the data from its **InputStream** is written out to the specified **OutputStream**. In case the **DataHandler** was constructed with an object, this method invokes the **DataContentHandler**'s **writeTo** method.

■ **public OutputStream getOutputStream()** throws **IOException**

This method returns the **OutputStream** associated with the **DataHandler**. This only works for **DataHandlers** constructed using a **DataSource**. For other cases, this method returns null.

■ **public synchronized DataFlavor[] getTransferDataFlavors()**

This method is present to implement the **Transferable** interface of the Uniform Data Transfer Mechanism detailed in Chapter 9. It returns the **DataFlavors** in which the associated data can be presented. In case the **DataHandler** was constructed with a **DataSource**, it returns a **DataFlavor** based on the MIME type of the data. In case the **DataHandler** was constructed with a Java object, and is also associated with a **DataContentHandler**, this method invokes the **DataCotentHandler**'s **getTransferDataFlavors** method.

▦ `public boolean isDataFlavorSupported(DataFlavor flavor)`

This method returns a boolean to indicate whether the specified `DataFlavor` is supported by the associated data. It is also part of the `Transferable` interface and is handled similar to the `getTransferDataFlavors` method described above.

▦ `public Object getTransferData(DataFlavor flavor)` throws `UnsupportedFlavorException, IOException`

This method returns an object representing the data to be transferred in the specified `DataFlavor`. It is also part of the `Transferable` interface and is handled similar to the `getTransferDataFlavors` method described previously.

▦ `public void setCommandMap(CommandMap commandMap)`

This method sets the `CommandMap` that is to be used by the `DataHandler`. If set to null, or not invoked at all, the `DataHandler` uses the default `CommandMap` available from the `CommandMap.getDefaultCommandMap` method.

▦ `public CommandInfo[] getPreferredCommands()`

This method returns a list of `CommandInfo` objects with an entry for every unique command specified in the `CommandMap`. This makes sure that if there is more than one bean associated with a single command, only the "preferred" one is returned. The `CommandMap` does the selection.

▦ `public CommandInfo[] getAllCommands()`

This method returns an array containing all the commands for associated data type. There might be multiple entries for the same command.

▦ `public CommandInfo getCommand(String cmdName)`

This method returns the `CommandInfo` for the specified command. It invokes the `getCommand` method of the associated `CommandMap`.

▦ `public Object getContent()` throws `IOException`

This method returns the object associated with the `DataHandler`. If the `DataHandler` was constructed with a `DataSource`, this method returns the `InputStream` associated with the `DataSource`. If the `DataHandler` is created using a Java Object, the actual object is returned.

▦ `public Object getBean(CommandInfo binfo)`

This method instantiates a new bean associated with the specified command in the `CommandInfo`. If the bean implements the

CommandObject interface, it also invokes the setCommandContext method of CommandObject.

■ **public static synchronized void setDataContentHandler Factory(DataContentHandlerFactory factory)**

This method sets the DataContentHandlerFactory. It is responsible for assigning DataContentHandlers for data objects associated with the DataHandler.

The DataSource Interface

The DataSource interface is an encapsulation of data associated with streams. It also provides data typing for the associated data. It provides access to the input and output streams for the data.

The methods in the interface are

■ **public abstract InputStream getInputStream()** throws **IOException**

This method returns an InputStream representing the data.

■ **public abstract OutputStream getOutputStream()** throws **IOException**

This method returns an OutputStream for writing the data to.

■ **public abstract String getContentType()**

This method returns the MIME type of the data.

■ **public abstract String getName()**

This method returns the name of the data object associated with it. The name assignment is implementation dependant. In the case of file sources, for example, the name might be mapped to the file name.

The CommandMap Class

The CommandMap is an abstract class that maps commands to operations on specific MIME data types. It encapsulates a registry mechanism that does this mapping.

The CommandMap has the following constructors and methods:

■ `public CommandMap()`

This is the default constructor

■ `public static CommandMap getDefaultCommandMap()`

This method returns a reference to the static default `CommandMap`. `CommandMap`, is initially set to the concrete implementation called `MailcapCommandMap`.

■ `public static void setCommandMap(CommandMap commandMap)`

This method sets the default `CommandMap`. Calling this method with a null parameter resets the default to the original `CommandMap` provided by the JAF, viz. `MailcapCommandMap`.

■ `public abstract CommandInfo[] getPreferredCommands(String mimeType)`

This method returns an array of `CommandInfo` objects for a specified MIME type. The `CommandMap` has to make sure there is a unique command bean for each command allowed on the data type.

■ `public abstract CommandInfo[] getAllCommands(String mimeType)`

This method returns an array of all the commands mapped to the specified MIME type. There could be multiple entries for a single command.

■ `public abstract CommandInfo getCommand(String mimeType, String cmdName)`

This method returns the `CommandInfo` for the specified MIME type and corresponding to the specified command name.

The `CommandInfo` Class

The `CommandInfo` class is used to encapsulate the command name or *verb* and the class representing the JavaBean that implements the operation or verb.

The constructors and methods defined are as follows:

■ `public CommandInfo(String verb, String className)`

This constructor constructs a `CommandInfo` object using the specified command name or *verb* and the specified class name of the JavaBean that carries out the command.

- **public String getCommandName()**

  This method returns the name of the command or *verb*.

- **public Object getCommandObject(DataHandler dh, ClassLoader cl)**

  Using the specified class loader, this method intstantiates the JavaBean associated with the command. The **DataHandler** is used in case the JavaBean implements the **CommandObject** interface. In that case, the **setCommandContext** method is also invoked, to which the **DataHandler** is passed as a parameter.

The **DataContentHandler** Interface

The **DataContentHandler** is useful for integrating data sources already existing as Java Objects in memory. In such cases, the **DataContentHandler** is responsible for converting the Java Object into a stream, or vice versa. The **DataContentHandler** also helps the **DataHandler** implement the **Transferable** interface of the Uniform Data Transfer Mechanism.

The methods defined in the interface are as follows:

- **public abstract DataFlavor[] getTransferDataFlavors()**

  This method returns the **DataFlavors** in which the data associated with the **DataContentHandler** can be represented. This method is part of the **Transferable** interface.

- **public abstract Object getTransferData(DataFlavor df, DataSource ds)** throws **UnsupportedFlavorException, IOException**

  This method converts the stream represented by the specified **DataSource** into a Java Object. The returned object is an instance of the class representing the specified **DataFlavor**.

- **public abstract Object getContent(DataSource ds)** throws **IOException**

  This method converts the **InputStream** associated with the specified **DataSource** into a Java Object.

- **public abstract void writeTo(Object obj, String mimeType, OutputStream os)** throws **IOException**

  This method writes the specified Java Object into an **OutputStream** so as to represent the specified MIME type.

The **CommandObject** Interface

The **CommandObject** interface is meant to be implemented by JavaBeans so as to integrate neatly into the JAF. Though this is not compulsory, it is certainly preferred. It allows the JavaBean to access the **DataHandler** associated with the data passed to it.

If the JavaBean does not implement this interface, it needs to be explicitly passed the data on which to operate by using a scheme such as serialization or externalization.

The interface consists of a single method.

```
public abstract void setCommandContext(String
    verb,DataHandler dh)
```

This method passes a reference to the **DataHandler** so it is able to retreive data from the source or write back data to it. It also tells the bean the command name that needs to be operated on. This is useful if the same bean implements more than one command or *verb*.

The **FileDataSource** Class

The **FileDataSource** class is a concrete implementation of the **DataSource** interface. It represents data contained in files. It also provides a mechanism to map file extensions to MIME types using the mime.types file.

The constructors and methods defined in this are as follows:

■ **public FileDataSource(File file)**

This constructor constructs a **FileDataSource** from the specified **File** object.

■ **public FileDataSource(String name)**

This constructor constructs a **FileDataSource** from the specified file name.

■ **public void addMimeTypes(String mime_types)**

This method adds the specified **mime.type** values to the registry.

■ **public abstract InputStream getInputStream()** throws **IOException**

This method returns an **InputStream** representing the file.

- **public abstract OutputStream getOutputStream() throws IOException**

  This method returns an **OutputStream** for writing the data to the file.

- **public abstract String getContentType()**

  This method returns the MIME type of the file.

- **public abstract String getName()**

  This method returns the file name of the associated file.

The **MailcapCommandMap** Class

The **MailcapCommandMap** is a concrete implementation of the abstract **CommandMap** class. It uses the mailcap (RFC 1524) specification to implement a registry so as to map operations to verbs for specified MIME types.

The constructors and methods are as follows:

- **public MailcapCommandMap()**

  This is the default constructor.

- **public MailcapCommandMap(String mailcapFileName)**

  This constructor is used to specify a specific **mailcap** file to be used for the mapping.

- **public void addMailcap(String mail_cap)**

  This method adds a new entry to the associated **mailcap** registry. It overrides any existing mapping for the same command and MIME type

INDEX

ABOUT THE AUTHOR

Reaz Hoque is an author, lecturer and a software developer who works very closely with Netscape Communication Corporation. He contributes web-related articles for online and print magazines around the world. Some of his articles have been seen in *Netscape DevEdge Site*, *ZD Internet Magazine*, *Web Techniques*, *Internet World* and *NetscapeWorld*. His other books include *Practical Javascript Programming* (IDG Books, 1997), *CORBA 3 Developer's Guide* (IDG, 1998), *InfoBus Programming* (Wiley, 1998), and *Programming Web Components* (McGraw-Hill, 1997). Reaz has been seen speaking at various conferences including Netscape, DevCon, Software Development, Web Design, Object Expo and other domestic and international conferences.

About the Contributing Authors

Ashutosh Bijoor is a consultant and runs a software firm specializing in Java-based solutions. He has been involved in developing the Java Compatibility Kit for the 2D graphics API in JDK 1.2. He was the architect of the first major extranet installation in India. He used this extranet for booking advertisements on India's National Television Network.

Trevor Harmon is president of Vocaro Technologies, a development and consulting firm specializing in Java components. His written work includes the book *Web Developer's Guide to Visual J++ and ActiveX*, published by the Coriolis Group, as well as various articles for magazines such as *Visual J++ Informant*, *Windows Developer's Journal*, and Germany's *Java Entwickler Magazine*. Trevor has worked for ProtoView Corporation, Washington University's computer science department, and Jenoptik Systemhaus in Pliezhausen, Germany.

Darren Gibbons is the cofounder of OpenRoad Communications, a Vancouver-based technical Internet development company specializing in Enterprise Java development and Web database integration. He speaks about Java regularly at conferences around the world.

Dave Jarvis is a software architect for more than a decade. His current focus is on object-oriented analysis and design as it relates to Java-related technologies. He works in the telecommunications industry and enjoys the challenge of staying on top of the latest technologies offered by the computer industry.

Gabriel Minton is Chief Technology Officer for Husky Labs, Inc., a Shepherdstown, West Virginia-based software and systems integration company. Gabriel also teaches courses on distributed programming and Java at George Washington University. Gabriel has authored several papers on CORBA and has spoken about Java and ActiveX.

John Small is the president of Rogare Scope, a software consulting company specializing in distributed workflow and data-mining applications written in C/C++, Smalltalk, and Java. His software is in use at such places as NYNEX, Shell Oil, the eastern Canadian Air Traffic Control system, military satellites, nuclear power plants, and automated warehouses throughout the world.

SOFTWARE AND INFORMATION LICENSE